Microsoft® Office

# Word 2003
for **Medical Professionals**

**JENNIFER A. DUFFY**

**CAROL M. CRAM**

D1361109

COURSE TECHNOLOGY
CENGAGE Learning™

Australia • Brazil • Japan • Korea • Mexico • Singapore • Spain • United Kingdom • United States

## COURSE TECHNOLOGY
CENGAGE Learning™

**Microsoft® Office Word 2003 for Medical Professionals**
Jennifer A. Duffy, Carol M. Cram

Managing Editor: Marjorie Hunt

Senior Product Manager: Christina Kling Garrett

Associate Product Manager: Shana Rosenthal

Editorial Assistant: Janine Tangney

Developmental Editor: Pamela Conrad

Production Editor: Summer Hughes

Marketing Manager: Joy Stark

Marketing Coordinator: Melissa Marcoux

QA Manuscript Reviewers: Susan Whalen,
     Alex White, Danielle Shaw, Jeff Schwartz

Text Designer: Joseph Lee, Black Fish Design

Composition House: GEX Publishing Services

Content Consultant: Sally Livingstone

Cover Designer: Abby Scholz

Design Director: Deborah VanRooyen

For product information and technology assistance, contact us at
**Cengage Learning Customer & Sales Support, 1-800-354-9706**
For permission to use material from this text or product, submit all requests online at **cengage.com/permissions**
Further permissions questions can be emailed to
**permissionrequest@cengage.com**

**Trademarks**
Some of the product names and company names used in this book have been used for identification purposes only and may be trademarks or registered trademarks of their respective manufacturers and sellers.

Microsoft and the Office logo are either registered trademarks or trademarks of Microsoft Corporation in the United States and/or other countries. Course Technology is an independent entity from Microsoft Corporation, and not affiliated with Microsoft in any manner.

ISBN-13: 978-1-4188-4320-5

ISBN-10: 1-4188-4320-2

**Course Technology**
25 Thomson Place
Boston, Massachusetts 02210
USA

Cengage Learning is a leading provider of customized learning solutions with office locations around the globe, including Singapore, the United Kingdom, Australia, Mexico, Brazil, and Japan. Locate your local office at:
**international.cengage.com/region**

Cengage Learning products are represented in Canada by Nelson Education, Ltd.

For your lifelong learning solutions, visit **course.cengage.com**

Purchase any of our products at your local college store or at our preferred online store **www.ichapters.com**

Printed in China
6 7 8 9 09

# About This Book

Microsoft Word is the standard word processing product used on millions of computers across this country, and in virtually all medical practices and hospitals. While there are dozens of other books that teach Word, nearly all of them teach skills using a business context. This book is different. It recognizes the specific needs of students who are training to be allied health professionals, and teaches the Word skills most important for their success. What makes this book so unique is that every example features a real-world document related to the medical profession. Students learn skills by creating, editing, and formatting documents that they are likely to encounter in a work setting supporting the front or back office of a medical practice, clinic, or hospital.

As we set out to write this book, our goals were to develop a textbook that:

- meets the needs of students pursuing careers in allied health, medical office administration, medical assisting, or nursing
- provides exercises and examples related to the medical field
- serves as a reference tool
- makes your job as an educator easier, by providing resources above and beyond the textbook to help you teach your course.

Our instructional format is designed to engage the beginning learner by presenting each skill on two facing pages. Step by step instructions are presented on the left page, and screen illustrations are presented on the right. This instructional design combined with high-caliber content provides a comprehensive yet manageable introduction to Microsoft Office Word 2003 for all types of learners, and also makes for a great reference after the course is over.

## About the Authors

*Jennifer A. Duffy* is a freelance writer who lives and works in New Hampshire. She has been writing for Course Technology for seven years, including three editions of Microsoft Word Illustrated for the popular Office series. Jennifer has worked successfully in the business world as a writer, editor, and public relations liaison. She brings her business knowledge, Word expertise, and writing skills to this book.

*Carol M. Cram* is the author of over thirty-five textbooks on computer applications, business communications, and Internet-related subjects. Carol is also a long-time faculty member at Capilano College in North Vancouver, where she is currently the Convenor of the Executive Support and Office Management Program and an instructor of business, communications, and computer-related courses.

## Acknowledgments

Many talented people at Course Technology helped to shape this book — thank you all. I am especially indebted to Pam Conrad for her precision editing, creative ideas, and endless good cheer throughout the many months of writing. I am also grateful to my husband, Fred Eliot, for his patience and support, to Sally Livingstone for inspiring several documents that appear in the book, and to Annika Brown, M.D., for valuable insights into the medical profession and a thick folder of sample documents.
Jennifer A. Duffy

I wish to thank Pam Conrad, who provided so much encouragement, support, and intelligence throughout the editorial process. She is truly beyond compare! I also wish to thank Sally Livingstone, my colleague at Capilano College, for her enthusiastic assistance with this book and my husband, Gregg Simpson, for his ongoing support and encouragement. Finally, I'd like to thank my students at Capilano College in North Vancouver. They are what it's all about.
Carol M. Cram

During the development of this book we interviewed dozens of instructors across the country to better understand their needs and the needs of their students. We thank all of you for your helpful insights and suggestions. We also extend a very special thank you to our reviewers who gave us invaluable feedback as we developed the book and the sample documents it contains: Kennon Brownlee, Remington College; Natasha Freeman-Cauley, MPH, RHIA, DeVry University Online; Deborah Jones, Corporate Director of Curriculum, High-Tech Institute; and Sally Livingstone, Capilano College.

# Preface

Welcome to *Microsoft® Office Word 2003 for Medical Professionals*. Each lesson in this book contains elements pictured to the right.

## Organization

Designed for students in medical assisting, nursing or allied health programs, this text is organized into 9 units covering creating, editing, and formatting text as well as creating tables, merging documents, and building forms. Two appendices cover graphics and collaborating with others in documents. Students will learn to create memos, information sheets, newsletters, forms, reports, and other documents used in a medical setting.

## Assignments

The lessons use Riverwalk Medical Clinic, a fictional outpatient medical facility, as the case study. The assignments on the light purple pages at the end of each unit increase in difficulty. Data Files and case projects use real-world medical examples, and provide a great variety of interesting and relevant industry-specific projects. Assignments include:

- **Concepts Reviews** include multiple choice, matching and screen identification questions.

- **Skills Reviews** provide additional hands-on, step-by-step reinforcement.

- **Independent Challenges** are case projects requiring critical thinking and application of the unit skills. The Independent Challenges increase in difficulty, with the first one in each unit being the easiest (most step-by-step with detailed instructions). Independent Challenges 2 and 3 become increasingly more open-ended, requiring more independent problem solving.

- **E-Quest Independent Challenges** are case projects with a Web focus. E-Quests require the use of the World Wide Web to conduct research to complete the project.

- **Advanced Challenge Exercises** set within the Independent Challenges provide optional steps for more advanced students.

- **Visual Workshops** are practical, self-graded capstone projects that require independent problem solving.

Each 2-page spread focuses on a single skill.

Concise text introduces the basic principles in the lesson and integrates a medical case study.

---

**UNIT C**
**Word 2003**

# Working with Indents

When you **indent** a paragraph, you move its edge in from the left or right margin. You can indent the entire left or right edge of a paragraph, just the first line, or all lines except the first line. The **indent markers** on the horizontal ruler indicate the indent settings for the paragraph in which the insertion point is located. Dragging the indent markers to a new location on the ruler is one way to change the indentation of a paragraph; using the indent buttons on the Formatting toolbar is another. You can also use the Paragraph command on the Format menu to indent paragraphs. Table C-1 describes types of indents and the methods for creating each.  You indent several paragraphs in the information sheet.

**STEPS**

1. **Press [Ctrl][Home], click the** Print Layout View button **on the horizontal scroll bar, click the** Zoom list arrow **on the Standard toolbar, then click** Page Width
   The document is displayed in Print Layout view, making it easier to see the document margins.

2. **Place the insertion point in the italicized paragraph under the title, then click the** Increase Indent button **on the Formatting toolbar**
   The entire paragraph is indented ½" from the left margin, as shown in Figure C-16. The indent marker also moves to the ½" mark on the horizontal ruler. Each time you click the Increase Indent button, the left edge of a paragraph moves another ½" to the right.

   > **QUICK TIP**
   > Press [Tab] at the beginning of a paragraph to indent the first line ½". You can also set a custom indent using the Indents and Spacing tab in the Paragraph dialog box.

3. **Click the** Decrease Indent button **on the Formatting toolbar**
   The left edge of the paragraph moves ½" to the left, and the indent marker moves back to the left margin.

4. **Drag the** First Line Indent marker **to the ¼" mark on the horizontal ruler, as shown in Figure C-17**
   The first line of the paragraph is indented ¼". Dragging the first line indent marker indents only the first line of a paragraph.

   > **TROUBLE**
   > Take care to drag only the First Line Indent marker. If you make a mistake, click the Undo button , then try again.

5. **Scroll to the bottom of page 1, place the insertion point in the** quotation (the last paragraph), **then drag the** Left Indent marker **to the ½" mark on the horizontal ruler**
   When you drag the Left Indent marker, the First Line and Hanging Indent markers move as well. The left edge of the paragraph is indented ½" from the left margin.

6. **Drag the** Right Indent marker **to the 5½" mark on the horizontal ruler**
   The right edge of the paragraph is indented ½" from the right margin, as shown in Figure C-18.

7. **Click the** Save button **on the Standard toolbar**

**TABLE C-1: Types of indents**

| indent type | description | to create |
|---|---|---|
| Left indent | The left edge of a paragraph is moved in from the left margin | Drag the Left Indent marker right to the position where you want the left edge of the paragraph to align, or click the Increase Indent button to indent the paragraph in ½" increments |
| Right indent | The right edge of a paragraph is moved in from the right margin | Drag the Right Indent marker left to the position where you want the right edge of the paragraph to end |
| First-line indent | The first line of a paragraph is indented more than the subsequent lines | Drag the First Line Indent marker right to the position where you want the first line of the paragraph to start |
| Hanging indent | The subsequent lines of a paragraph are indented more than the first line | Drag the Hanging Indent marker right to the position where you want the hanging indent to start |
| Negative indent (or Outdent) | The left edge of a paragraph is moved to the left of the left margin | Drag the Left Indent marker left to the position where you want the negative indent to start |

62 FORMATTING TEXT AND PARAGRAPHS

Tips, as well as trouble-shooting advice, are located right where you need them—next to the steps themselves.

Tables provide quickly accessible summaries of key terms, toolbar buttons, or keyboard alternatives connected with the lesson material. Students can refer easily to this information when working on their own projects at a later time.

Every lesson features large, full-color representations of what the screen should look like as students complete the numbered steps.

Every example is related to the medical profession

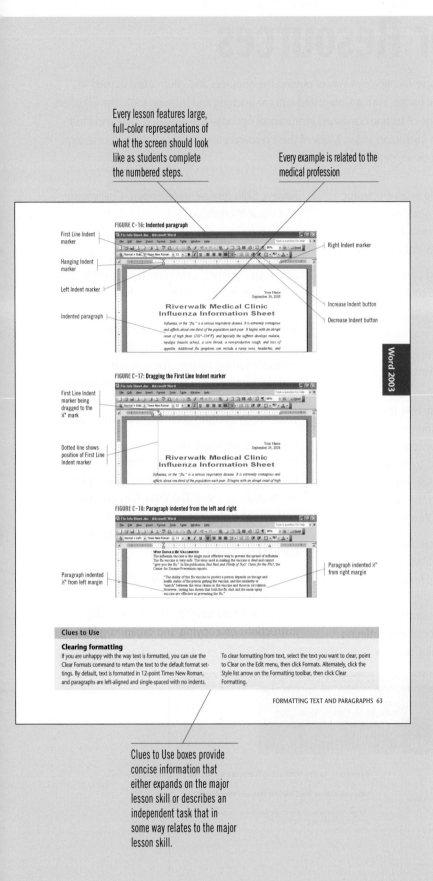

FIGURE C-16: Indented paragraph

First Line Indent marker

Hanging Indent marker

Left Indent marker

Indented paragraph

Right Indent marker

Increase Indent button

Decrease Indent button

FIGURE C-17: Dragging the First Line Indent marker

First Line Indent marker being dragged to the ¼" mark

Dotted line shows position of First Line Indent marker

FIGURE C-18: Paragraph indented from the left and right

Paragraph indented ½" from left margin

Paragraph indented ½" from right margin

**Clues to Use**

**Clearing formatting**

If you are unhappy with the way text is formatted, you can use the Clear Formats command to return the text to the default format settings. By default, text is formatted in 12-point Times New Roman, and paragraphs are left-aligned and single-spaced with no indents.

To clear formatting from text, select the text you want to clear, point to Clear on the Edit menu, then click Formats. Alternately, click the Style list arrow on the Formatting toolbar, then click Clear Formatting.

FORMATTING TEXT AND PARAGRAPHS 63

Clues to Use boxes provide concise information that either expands on the major lesson skill or describes an independent task that in some way relates to the major lesson skill.

# SAM 2003 Assessment & Training

SAM 2003 helps you energize your class exams and training assignments by allowing students to learn and test important computer skills in an active, hands-on environment.

With SAM 2003 Assessment, you create powerful interactive exams on critical applications such as Word, Excel, PowerPoint, Windows, the Internet, and much more. The exams simulate the application environment, allowing your students to demonstrate their knowledge and think through the skills by performing real-world tasks.

Designed to be used with the *Microsoft Office Word 2003 for Medical Professionals*, SAM 2003 Assessment & Training includes built-in page references so students can create study guides that map to this book. Powerful administrative options allow you to schedule exams and assignments, secure your tests, and run reports with almost limitless flexibility.

# Instructor Resources

The Instructor Resources CD is Course Technology's way of putting the resources and information needed to teach and learn effectively into your hands. With an integrated array of teaching and learning tools, the CD offers you and your students a broad range of technology-based instructional options—the highest quality and most cutting-edge resources available to instructors today. Many of these resources are available at www.course.com. The resources available with this book are described below.

- **Instructor's Manual**—Available as an electronic file, the Instructor's Manual is quality-assurance tested and includes unit overviews and detailed lecture topics with teaching tips for each unit.

- **Sample Syllabus**—Prepare and customize your course easily using this sample course outline.

- **PowerPoint Presentations**—Each unit has a corresponding PowerPoint presentation that you can use in a lecture, distribute to your students, or customize to suit your course.

- **Figure Files**—The figures in the text are provided on the Instructor Resources CD to help you illustrate key topics or concepts. You can create traditional overhead transparencies by printing the figure files, or you can create electronic slide shows by using the figures in a presentation program such as PowerPoint.

- **Solutions to Exercises**—The Solutions to Exercises folder contains every file students are asked to create or modify in the lessons and End-of-Unit material. A Help file on the Instructor Resources CD includes information for using the Solution Files. There is also a document outlining the solutions for the End-of-Unit Concepts Review, Skills Review, Independent Challenges, and Visual Workshop.

- **ExamView**—ExamView is a powerful testing software package that allows you to create and administer printed, computer (LAN-based), and Internet exams. ExamView includes hundreds of questions that correspond to the topics covered in this text, enabling students to generate detailed study guides that include page references for further review. The computer-based and Internet testing components allow students to take exams at their computers, and also save you time by grading each exam automatically.

- **Data Files for Students**—To complete most of the units in this book, your students will need Data Files, which you can put on a file server for students to copy. The Data Files are available on the Instructor Resources CD-ROM and in the Review Pack, and can also be downloaded from www.course.com.

  Direct students to use the **Data Files List** located in the Review Pack and on the Instructor Resources CD. This list provides instructions on copying and organizing files.

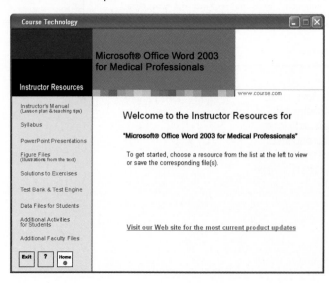

# Brief Contents

# Contents

**UNIT F**      **Merging Word Documents**      **129**

**UNIT G**      **Working with Styles and Templates**      **153**

# Read This Before You Begin

## Software Information and Required Installation

This book was written and tested using Microsoft Office 2003 - Professional Edition (which includes Microsoft Office Word 2003), with a typical installation on Microsoft Windows XP, including installation of the most recent Windows XP Service Pack and with Internet Explorer 6.0 or higher. Some of the exercises in this book assume that your computer is connected to the Internet. If you are not connected to the Internet, see your instructor.

## Tips for Students

### What are Data Files?

To complete many of the units in this book, you need to use Data Files. A Data File contains a partially completed document, so that you don't have to type all the information in the document yourself. Your instructor will either provide you with copies of the Data Files or ask you to make your own copies. Your instructor also can give you instructions on how to organize your files, as well as a complete file listing, or you can find the list and the instructions for organizing your files in the Review Pack. In addition, because Unit A does not have supplied Data Files, you will need to create a Unit A directory at the same level as all of the other unit directories in order to save the files you create in Unit A.

### Why is my screen different from the book?

Your desktop components and some dialog box options might be different if you are using an operating system other than Windows XP.

Depending on your computer hardware and the Display settings on your computer, you may notice the following differences:

- Your screen may look larger or smaller because of your screen resolution (the height and width of your screen).

- Your title bars and dialog boxes may not display file extensions. To display file extensions, click Start on the taskbar, click Control Panel, click Appearance and Themes, then click Folder Options. Click the View tab if necessary, click Hide extensions for known file types to deselect it, then click OK. Your Office dialog boxes and title bars should now display file extensions.

- Depending on your Office settings, your Standard and Formatting toolbars may be displayed on a single row and your menus may display a shortened list of frequently used commands. Office menus and toolbars can modify themselves to your working style by displaying only the most frequently used buttons and menu commands. To view buttons not currently displayed, click a Toolbar Options button ▪ at the right end of either the Standard or Formatting toolbar. To view the full list of menu commands, click the double arrow at the bottom of the menu.

**TOOLBARS ON ONE ROW**

**TOOLBARS ON TWO ROWS**

This book assumes you are displaying toolbars in two rows and displaying full menus. In order to have your toolbars displayed on two rows, showing all buttons, and to have the full menus displayed, you must turn off the personalized menus and toolbars feature. Click Tools on the menu bar, click Customize, select the show Standard and Formatting toolbars on two rows and Always show full menus check boxes on the Options tab, and then click Close.

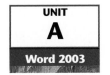

# Getting Started with Word 2003

## OBJECTIVES

| |
|---|
| Understand word processing software |
| Start Word 2003 |
| Explore the Word program window |
| Start a document |
| Save a document |
| Print a document |
| Use the Help system |
| Close a document and exit Word |

If you have a SAM user profile, you may have access to hands-on instruction, practice, and assessment of the skills covered in this unit. Log in to your SAM account and go to your assignments page to see what your instructor has assigned.

Microsoft Office Word 2003 is a word processing program that makes it easy to create a variety of professional-looking documents, from simple letters and memos to newsletters, research papers, Web pages, business cards, resumes, financial reports, and other documents that include multiple pages of text and sophisticated formatting. In this unit, you will explore the editing and formatting features available in Word, learn how to start Word, and create a document. ▰▰▰ You have just been hired at the Riverwalk Medical Clinic, a large outpatient medical facility staffed by family physicians, specialists, nurses, and other allied health professionals. Shortly after reporting to your new position, the office manager, Tony Sanchez, R.N., asks you to familiarize yourself with Word and use it to create a memo to the clinic staff.

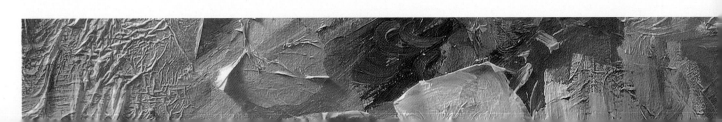

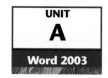

# Understanding Word Processing Software

A **word processing program** is a software program that includes tools for entering, editing, and formatting text and graphics. Microsoft Word is a powerful word processing program that allows you to create and enhance a wide range of documents quickly and easily. Figure A-1 shows the first page of a report created using Word and illustrates some of the Word features you can use to enhance your documents. The electronic files you create using Word are called **documents**. One of the benefits of using Word is that document files can be stored on a disk, making them easy to transport, exchange, and revise. ◼◼◼◼ You need to write a memo to the clinic staff to inform them of an upcoming meeting. Before beginning your memo, you explore the editing and formatting capabilities available in Word.

## DETAILS

### You can use Word to accomplish the following tasks:

- **Type and edit text**

  The Word editing tools make it simple to insert and delete text in a document. You can add text to the middle of an existing paragraph, replace text with other text, undo an editing change, and correct typing, spelling, and grammatical errors with ease.

- **Copy and move text from one location to another**

  Using the more advanced editing features of Word, you can copy or move text from one location and insert it in a different location in a document. You also can copy and move text between documents. Being able to copy and move text means you don't have to retype text that is already entered in a document.

- **Format text and paragraphs with fonts, colors, and other elements**

  The sophisticated formatting tools available in Word allow you to make the text in your documents come alive. You can change the size, style, and color of text, add lines and shading to paragraphs, and enhance lists with bullets and numbers. Formatting text creatively helps you highlight important ideas in your documents.

- **Format and design pages**

  The Word page-formatting features give you power to design attractive newsletters, create powerful resumes, and produce documents such as business cards, CD labels, and books. You can change the paper size and orientation of your documents, add headers and footers to pages, organize text in columns, and control the layout of text and graphics on each page of a document.

- **Enhance documents with tables, charts, diagrams, and graphics**

  Using the powerful graphic tools available in Word, you can spice up your documents with pictures, photographs, lines, shapes, and diagrams. You also can illustrate your documents with tables and charts to help convey your message in a visually interesting way.

- **Create Web pages**

  The Word Web page design tools allow you to create documents that others can read over the Internet or an intranet. You can enhance Web pages with themes and graphics, add hyperlinks, create online forms, and preview Web pages in your Web browser.

- **Use Mail Merge to create form letters and mailing labels**

  The Word Mail Merge feature allows you to easily send personalized form letters to many different people. You can also use Mail Merge to create mailing labels, directories, e-mail messages, and many other types of documents.

Format the size and appearance of text

Insert graphics

Create columns of text

Add bullets to lists

Create tables

Add headers to every page

Align text in paragraphs evenly

Add lines

Create charts

Add page numbers in footers

*Riverwalk Medical Clinic Survey Results, May 2008*

## Riverwalk Medical Clinic Survey Results

In an effort to maintain the high standard of patient care offered at Riverwalk Medical Clinic (RMC), we hired the market research firm Takeshita Consultants, Inc. to create and administer a survey of Riverwalk Medical Clinic patients and local residents. A secondary goal of the survey was to explore the possibility of expanding our facility both in terms of physical size and the range of services offered. Some four thousand patients and local residents completed the survey, which was distributed by mail, in the clinic, and via the Riverwalk Medical Clinic Web site.

### Patient Profile

The typical Riverwalk Medical Clinic patient is an adult resident of Cambridge, Somerville, or Belmont. 52% of all registered patients are female; 12% are under the age of 18. Most registered patients list an RMC physician as their primary care physician.

- 78% have a primary care physician at the clinic.
- 26% use or have used the clinic during drop-in hours.
- 32% have been referred to a specialist on site.
- 23% have visited a physical therapist or massage therapist at the clinic.

### Survey Methods

The survey was distributed by mail to all registered patients and to some 1,000 local residents during January 2008. Throughout February, March, and April 2008, all patients who visited the clinic, including registered patients, walk-in patients, and massage clients, were asked to complete a survey before exiting the building. In addition, the survey was available on the Riverwalk Medical Clinic Web site. Over 4,000 people completed the survey.

| Respondents | Male | Female |
|---|---|---|
| Registered patients | 984 | 1029 |
| Local residents | 437 | 569 |
| Walk-in patients | 229 | 372 |
| Massage clients | 128 | 212 |
| Other | 47 | 73 |
| **Total** | **1825** | **2255** |
| | Grand Total | 4,080 |

### Satisfaction with Clinic Hours

69% of survey respondents were satisfied with the clinic's hours of operation; 31% would like to see the clinic remain open until 9 p.m. on weekdays. 77% of respondents prefer to visit the clinic Monday through Friday; 23% prefer weekend appointments. 45% of respondents saw a need for more appointment availability after 5 p.m. on weekdays.

### Satisfaction with Staff

### Overall Patient Satisfaction

On the whole, the results of the survey were favorable. Patients enjoy the variety of services provided and in particular having a laboratory on site. The reception staff was rated highly as was the location of the clinic. 60% of the respondents were concerned about the wait time to see a doctor during drop-in hours. Patients would also like to see other specialists added to the clinic staff. Respondents strongly supported the addition of a play area for children, as well as additional parking.

1 ▶

## Clues to Use

### Planning a document

Before you create a new document, it's a good idea to spend time planning it. Identify the message you want to convey, the audience for your document, and the elements, such as tables or charts, you want to include. You should also think about the tone and look of your document. Is it a business letter, which should be written in a pleasant, but serious tone and have a formal appearance, or are you creating a flyer that must be colorful, eye-catching, and fun to read?

The purpose and audience for your document determine the appropriate design. Planning the layout and design of a document involves deciding how to organize the text, selecting the fonts to use, identifying the graphics to include, and selecting the formatting elements that will enhance the document's message and appeal. For longer documents, such as newsletters, it can be useful to sketch the layout and design of each page before you begin.

# Starting Word 2003

Before starting Word, you must start Windows by turning on your computer. Once Windows is running, you can start Word or any other application by using the Start button on the Windows taskbar. You can also start Word by clicking the Word icon on the Windows desktop or the Word icon on the Microsoft Office Shortcut bar, if those items are available on your computer. ▓▓▓▓ You use the Start button to start Word so you can familiarize yourself with its features.

## STEPS

1. **Click the Start button** 🔲 **start** **on the Windows taskbar**

   The Start menu opens on the desktop. The left pane of the Start menu includes shortcuts to the most frequently used programs on the computer.

2. **Point to All Programs on the Start menu**

   The All Programs menu opens. The All Programs menu displays the list of programs installed on your computer.

> **TROUBLE**
> If Microsoft Office is not on your All Programs menu, ask your technical support person for assistance.

3. **Point to Microsoft Office**

   A menu listing the Office programs installed on your computer opens, as shown in Figure A-2.

4. **Click Microsoft Office Word 2003 on the Microsoft Office menu**

   The **Word program window** opens and displays a blank document in the document window and the Getting Started task pane, as shown in Figure A-3. The blank document opens in the most recently used view. **Views** are different ways of displaying a document in the document window. Figure A-3 shows a blank document in Print Layout view. The lessons in this unit will use Print Layout view.

5. **Click the Print Layout View button** 🔲 **as shown in Figure A-3**

   If your blank document opened in a different view, the view changes to Print Layout view.

> **TROUBLE**
> If your toolbars are on one row, click the Toolbar Options button at the end of the Formatting toolbar, then click Show Buttons on Two Rows.

6. **Click the Zoom list arrow on the Standard toolbar, as shown in Figure A-3, then click Page Width**

   The blank document fills the document window. Your screen should now match Figure A-3. The blinking vertical line in the upper-left corner of the document window is the **insertion point**. It indicates where text appears as you type.

7. **Move the mouse pointer around in the Word program window**

   The mouse pointer changes shape depending on where it is in the Word program window. In the document window in Print Layout view, the mouse pointer changes to an **I-beam pointer** $\text{I}$ or a **click and type pointer** $\text{I}^{\equiv}$. You use these pointers to move the insertion point in the document or to select text to edit. Table A-1 describes common Word pointers.

8. **Place the mouse pointer over a toolbar button**

   When you place the pointer over a button or some other element of the Word program window, a ScreenTip appears. A **ScreenTip** is a label that identifies the name of the button or feature.

**TABLE A-1: Common Word pointers**

| pointer | use to |
|---|---|
| $\text{I}$ | Move the insertion point in a document or to select text |
| $\text{I}^{\equiv}$ or $\underline{\text{I}}$ | Move the insertion point in a blank area of a document in Print Layout or Web Layout view; automatically applies the paragraph formatting required to position text at that location in the document |
| ⤢ | Click a button, menu command, or other element of the Word program window; appears when you point to elements of the Word program window |
| ⤢ | Select a line or lines of text; appears when you point to the left edge of a line of text in the document window |
| 🖑 | Open a hyperlink; appears when you point to a hyperlink in the task pane or a document |

**FIGURE A-2: Starting Word from the All Programs menu**

Frequently used programs (your list might differ)

Displays menu of programs installed on your computer

Start button

Click to start Word (the order of the programs listed might differ)

**FIGURE A-3: Word program window in Print Layout view**

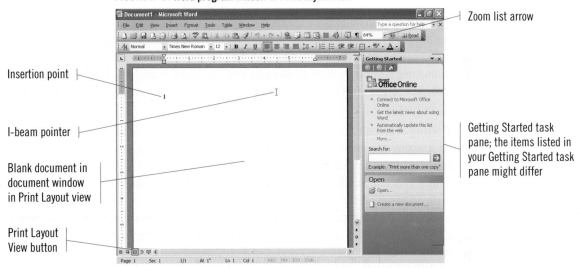

Insertion point

I-beam pointer

Blank document in document window in Print Layout view

Print Layout View button

Zoom list arrow

Getting Started task pane; the items listed in your Getting Started task pane might differ

## Clues to Use

### Using Word document views

Each Word view provides features that are useful for working on different types of documents. The default view, **Print Layout view**, displays a document as it will look on a printed page. Print Layout view is helpful for formatting text and pages, including adjusting document margins, creating columns of text, inserting graphics, and formatting headers and footers. Also useful is **Normal view**, which shows a simplified layout of a document, without margins, headers and footers, or graphics. When you want to quickly type, edit, and format text, it's often easiest to work in Normal view. **Web Layout view** allows you to accurately format Web pages or documents that will be viewed on a computer screen. In Web Layout view, a document appears just as it will when viewed with a Web browser. **Outline view** is useful for editing and formatting longer documents that include multiple headings. Outline view allows you to reorganize text by moving the headings. You switch between these views by clicking the view buttons to the left of the horizontal scroll bar or by using the commands on the View menu.

Two additional views make it easier to read documents on the screen. **Reading Layout view** displays document text so that it is easy to read and annotate. When you are working with highlighting or comments in a document, it's useful to use Reading Layout view. You switch to Reading Layout view by clicking the Read button on the Standard toolbar or the Reading Layout button to the left of the horizontal scroll bar. You return to the previous view by clicking the Close button on the Reading Layout toolbar. **Full Screen view** displays only the document window on screen. You switch to Full Screen view by using the Full Screen command on the View menu; you return to the previous view by pressing [Esc].

Changing views does not affect how the printed document will appear. It simply changes the way you view the document in the document window.

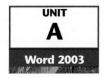

# Exploring the Word Program Window

When you start Word, a blank document appears in the document window and the Getting Started task pane appears. ▄▄▄▄▄ You examine the elements of the Word program window.

### Using Figure A-4 as a guide, find the elements described below in your program window.

- The **title bar** displays the name of the document and the name of the program. Until you give a new document a different name, its temporary name is Document1. The title bar also contains resizing buttons and the program Close button, buttons that are common to all Windows programs.

- The **menu bar** contains the names of the Word menus. Clicking a menu name opens a list of commands. The menu bar also contains the **Type a question for help box** and the Close Window button. You use the Type a question for help box to access the Word Help system.

- The **toolbars** contain buttons for the most commonly used commands. The **Standard toolbar** contains buttons for frequently used operating and editing commands, such as saving a document, printing a document, and cutting, copying, and pasting text. The **Formatting toolbar** contains buttons for commonly used formatting commands, such as changing font type and size, applying bold to text, and changing paragraph alignment. The Clues to Use in this lesson provides more information about working with toolbars and menus in Word.

- The **Getting Started task pane** contains shortcuts for opening a document, for creating new documents, and for accessing information on the Microsoft Web site. The blue words in the Open section of the task pane are **hyperlinks** that provide quick access to existing documents and the New Document task pane. If your computer is connected to the Internet, you can use the Microsoft Office Online section of the task pane to search the Microsoft Web site for information related to Office programs. As you learn more about Word, you will work with other task panes that provide shortcuts to Word formatting, editing, and research features. Clicking a hyperlink in a task pane can be quicker than using menu commands and toolbar buttons to accomplish a task.

- The **document window** displays the current document. You enter text and format your document in the document window.

- The horizontal and vertical rulers appear in the document window in Print Layout view. The **horizontal ruler** displays left and right document margins as well as the tab settings and paragraph indents, if any, for the paragraph in which the insertion point is located. The **vertical ruler** displays the top and bottom document margins.

- The **vertical and horizontal scroll bars** are used to display different parts of the document in the document window. The scroll bars include **scroll boxes** and **scroll arrows**, which you can use to easily move through a document.

- The **view buttons** to the left of the horizontal scroll bar allow you to display the document in Normal, Web Layout, Print Layout, Outline, or Reading Layout view.

- The **status bar** displays the page number and section number of the current page, the total number of pages in the document, and the position of the insertion point in inches, lines, and characters. The status bar also indicates the on/off status of several Word features, including tracking changes, overtype mode, and spelling and grammar checking.

**FIGURE A-4:** Elements of the Word program window

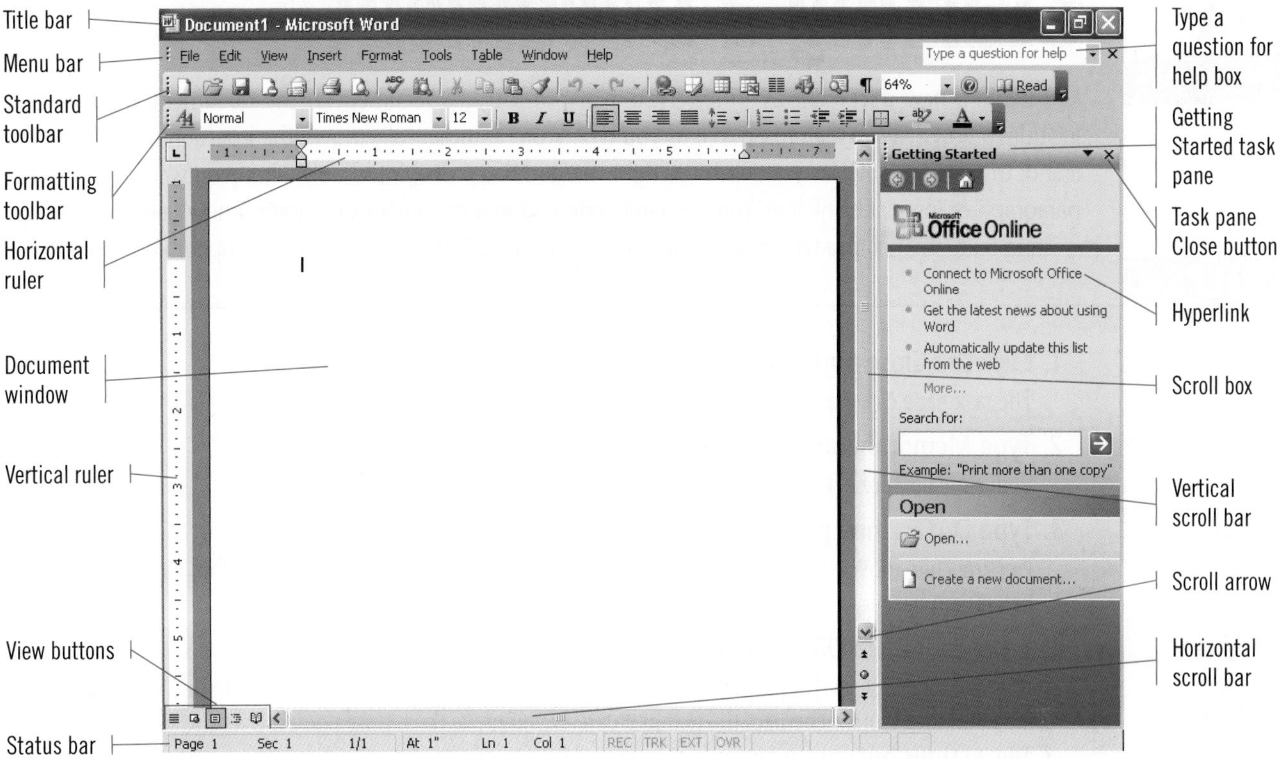

Title bar

Menu bar

Standard toolbar

Formatting toolbar

Horizontal ruler

Document window

Vertical ruler

View buttons

Status bar

Type a question for help box

Getting Started task pane

Task pane Close button

Hyperlink

Scroll box

Vertical scroll bar

Scroll arrow

Horizontal scroll bar

## Clues to Use

### Working with toolbars and menus in Word 2003

The lessons in this book assume you are working with full menus and toolbars visible, which means the Standard and Formatting toolbars appear on two rows and display all the buttons, and the menus display the complete list of menu commands.

You can also set Word to use personalized toolbars and menus that modify themselves to your working style. When you use personalized toolbars, the Standard and Formatting toolbars appear on the same row and display only the most frequently used buttons. To use a button that is not visible on a toolbar, click the Toolbar Options button ⟱ at the end of the toolbar, and then click the button you want on the Toolbar Options list. As you work, Word adds the buttons you use to the visible toolbars, and moves the buttons

you haven't used recently to the Toolbar Options list. Similarly, Word menus adjust to your work habits, so that the commands you use most often appear on shortened menus. You double-click the menu name or click the double arrow at the bottom of a menu to view additional menu commands.

To work with full toolbars and menus visible, you must turn off the personalized toolbars and menus features. To turn off personalized toolbars and menus, double-click Tools on the menu bar, click Customize, click the Options tab, select the Show Standard and Formatting toolbars on two rows and Always show full menus check boxes, then click Close.

# Starting a Document

You begin a new document by simply typing text in a blank document in the document window. Word includes a **word-wrap** feature, so that as you type Word automatically moves the insertion point to the next line of the document when you reach the right margin. You press [Enter] only when you want to start a new paragraph or insert a blank line. You can easily edit text in a document by inserting new text or by deleting existing text.  You type a quick memo to the clinic staff to inform them of an upcoming meeting.

**STEPS**

1. **Click the Close button in the Getting Started task pane**

   The task pane closes and the blank document fills the screen.

2. **Type Memorandum, then press [Enter] four times**

   Each time you press [Enter] the insertion point moves to the start of the next line.

3. **Type DATE:, then press [Tab] twice**

   Pressing [Tab] moves the insertion point several spaces to the right. You can use the [Tab] key to align the text in a memo header or to indent the first line of a paragraph.

4. **Type April 21, 2008, then press [Enter]**

   When you press [Enter], a purple dotted line appears under the date. This dotted underline is a **smart tag**. It indicates that Word recognizes the text as a date. If you move the mouse pointer over the smart tag, a **Smart Tag Actions button** ⓘ appears above the date. Smart tags are one of the many automatic features you will encounter as you type. Table A-2 describes other automatic features available in Word. You can ignore the smart tags in your memo.

5. **Type:**    TO: [Tab][Tab] Clinic Staff [Enter]
       FROM: [Tab] Your Name [Enter]
       RE: [Tab][Tab] Staff Meeting [Enter][Enter]

   Red or green wavy lines may appear under the words you typed. A red wavy line means the word is not in the Word dictionary and might be misspelled. A green wavy line indicates a possible grammar error. You can correct any typing errors you make later.

6. **Type The next clinic staff meeting will be held May 6th at 8 a.m. in the Eliot room on the ground floor., then press [Spacebar]**

   As you type, notice that the insertion point moves automatically to the next line of the document. You also might notice that Word corrects typing errors or makes typographical adjustments as you type. This feature is called **AutoCorrect**. AutoCorrect automatically detects and adjusts typos, certain misspelled words (such as "taht" for "that"), and incorrect capitalization as you type. For example, Word automatically changed "6th" to "6th" in the memo.

7. **Type Heading the agenda will be a discussion of our new community health fair, scheduled for August. Please bring ideas for planning this exciting event to the meeting.**

   When you type the first few characters of "August," the Word AutoComplete feature displays the complete word in a ScreenTip. **AutoComplete** suggests text to insert quickly into your documents. You can ignore AutoComplete for now. Your memo should resemble Figure A-5.

8. **Position the I pointer after new (but before the space) in the second sentence, then click**

   Clicking moves the insertion point after "new."

9. **Press [Backspace] three times, then type upcoming**

   Pressing [Backspace] removes the character before the insertion point.

10. **Move the insertion point before clinic in the first sentence, then press [Delete] seven times to remove the word clinic and the space after it**

    Pressing [Delete] removes the character after the insertion point. Figure A-6 shows the revised memo.

**QUICK TIP**

If you press the wrong key, press [Backspace] to erase the mistake, then try again.

**QUICK TIP**

Smart tags and other automatic feature markers appear on screen but do not print.

**QUICK TIP**

To reverse an AutoCorrect adjustment, immediately click the Undo button ↺ on the Standard toolbar.

**QUICK TIP**

Type just one space after a period at the end of a sentence when typing with a word processor.

**FIGURE A-5:** Memo text in the document window

Blank lines between paragraphs

Purple dotted underline indicates a smart tag

Green wavy underline indicates a possible grammar error (your memo will show your name)

Text wraps to the next line (yours might wrap differently)

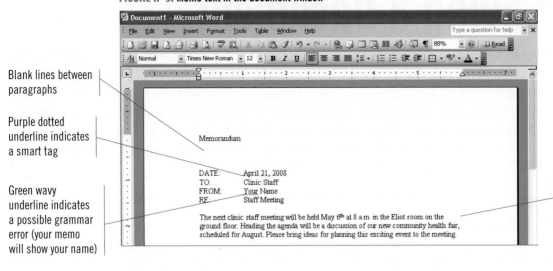

**FIGURE A-6:** Edited memo text

Text inserted in the memo

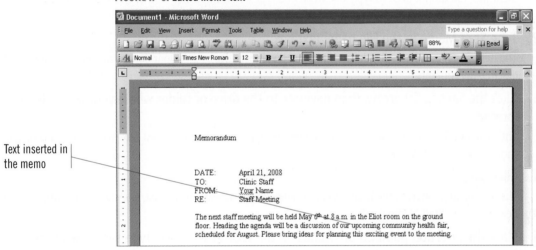

**TABLE A-2:** Automatic features in Word

| feature | what appears | to use |
|---------|--------------|--------|
| AutoComplete | A ScreenTip suggesting text to insert appears | Press [Enter] to insert the text suggested by the ScreenTip; continue typing to reject the suggestion |
| Spelling and Grammar | A red wavy line under a word indicates a possible misspelling; a green wavy line under text indicates a possible grammar error | Right-click red- or green-underlined text to display a shortcut menu of correction options; click a correction to accept it and remove the wavy underline |
| AutoCorrect | A small blue box appears when you place the pointer under text corrected by AutoCorrect; an AutoCorrect Options button ⚡ ▾ appears when you point to the corrected text | Word automatically corrects typos, minor spelling errors, and capital-ization, and adds typographical symbols (such as © and ™) as you type; to reverse an AutoCorrect adjustment, click the AutoCorrect Options button, then click Undo or the option that will undo the action |
| Smart tag | A purple dotted line appears under text Word recognizes as a date, name, address, or place; a Smart Tag Actions button ⓘ appears when you point to a smart tag | Click the Smart Tag Actions button to display a shortcut menu of options (such as adding a name to your address book in Outlook or opening your Outlook calendar); to remove a smart tag, click Remove this Smart Tag on the shortcut menu |

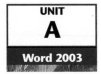
# Saving a Document

To store a document permanently so you can open it and edit it in the future, you must save it as a **file**. When you **save** a document you give it a name, called a **filename**, and indicate the location where you want to store the file. Files can be saved to your computer's internal hard disk, to a floppy disk, or to a variety of other locations. You can save a document using the Save button on the Standard toolbar or the Save command on the File menu. Once you have saved a document for the first time, you should save it again every few minutes and always before printing so that the saved file is updated to reflect your latest changes. You save your memo with the filename Staff Memo.

## STEPS

> **TROUBLE**
> If you don't see the extension .doc on the filename in the Save As dialog box, don't worry. Windows can be set to display or not to display the file extensions.

**1. Click the Save button** ⊟ **on the Standard toolbar**

The first time you save a document, the Save As dialog box opens, as shown in Figure A-7. The default filename, Memorandum, appears in the File name text box. The default filename is based on the first few words of the document. The .doc extension is assigned automatically to all Word documents to distinguish them from files created in other software programs. To save the document with a different filename, type a new filename in the File name text box, and use the Save in list arrow to select where you want to store the document file. You do not need to type .doc when you type a new filename. Table A-3 describes the functions of the buttons in the Save As dialog box.

**2. Type Staff Memo in the File name text box**

The new filename replaces the default filename. It's a good idea to give your documents brief filenames that describe the contents.

> **TROUBLE**
> This book assumes your Data Files for Unit A are stored in a folder titled UnitA. Substitute the correct drive or folder if this is not the case.

**3. Click the Save in list arrow, then navigate to the drive or folder where your Data Files are located**

The drive or folder where your Data Files are located appears in the Save in list box. Your Save As dialog box should resemble Figure A-8.

**4. Click Save**

The document is saved to the location you specified in the Save As dialog box, and the title bar displays the new filename, "Staff Memo.doc."

**5. Place the insertion point before August in the second sentence, type early, then press [Spacebar]**

You can continue to work on a document after you have saved it with a new filename.

**6. Click** ⊟

Your change to the memo is saved. Saving a document after you give it a filename saves the changes you make to the document. You also can click File on the menu bar, and then click Save to save a document.

---

### Clues to Use

#### Recovering lost document files

Sometimes while you are working on a document, Word might freeze, making it impossible to continue working, or you might experience a power failure that shuts down your computer. Should this occur, Word has a built-in recovery feature that allows you to open and save the files that were open at the time of the interruption. When you restart Word after an interruption, the Document Recovery task pane opens on the left side of your screen and lists both the original and the recovered versions of the Word files. If you're not sure which file to open (original or recovered), it's usually better to open the recovered file because it includes your latest changes to the document. You can, however, open and review all the versions of the file that were recovered and select the best one to save. Each file listed in the Document Recovery task pane has a list arrow with options that allow you to open the file, save the file, delete the file, or show repairs made to the file.

**FIGURE A-7:** Save As dialog box

Active folder or drive

Folders and files in the active folder or drive (yours will differ)

Default filename and file extension are selected

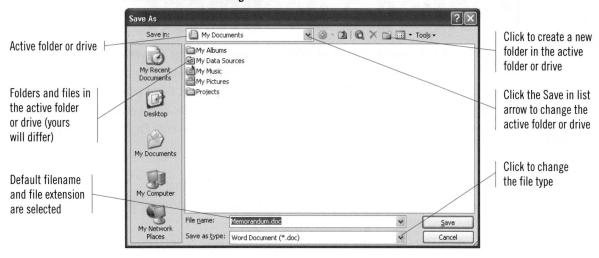

Click to create a new folder in the active folder or drive

Click the Save in list arrow to change the active folder or drive

Click to change the file type

**FIGURE A-8:** File to be saved to the UnitA folder

Location of Data Files (yours might differ)

New filename

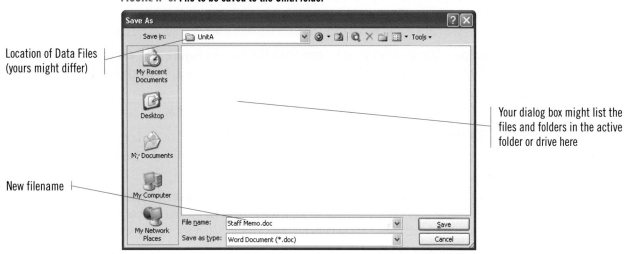

Your dialog box might list the files and folders in the active folder or drive here

**TABLE A-3:** Save As dialog box buttons

| button | use to |
|--------|--------|
| Back | Navigate to the drive or folder previously shown in the Save in list box; click the Back list arrow to navigate to a recently displayed drive or folder |
| Up One Level | Navigate to the next highest level in the folder hierarchy (to the drive or folder that contains the current folder) |
| Search the Web | Connect to the World Wide Web to locate a folder or file |
| Delete | Delete the selected folder or file |
| Create New Folder | Create a new folder in the current folder or drive |
| Views | Change the way folder and file information is shown in the Save As dialog box; click the Views list arrow to open a menu of options |
| Tools | Open a menu of commands related to the selected drive, folder, or file |

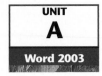
# Printing a Document

Before you print a document, it's a good habit to examine it in **Print Preview** to see what it will look like when printed. When a document is ready to print, you can print it using the Print button on the Standard toolbar or the Print command on the File menu. When you use the Print button, the document prints using the default print settings. If you want to print more than one copy of a document or select other printing options, you must use the Print command. ███████ You display your memo in Print Preview and then print a copy.

## STEPS

1. **Click the Print Preview button 🔍 on the Standard toolbar**

   The document appears in Print Preview. It is useful to examine a document carefully in Print Preview so that you can correct any problems before printing it.

2. **Move the pointer over the memo text until it changes to 🔍 , then click**

   Clicking with the 🔍 pointer magnifies the document in the Print Preview window and changes the pointer to 🔍. The memo appears in the Print Preview window exactly as it will look when printed, as shown in Figure A-9. Clicking with the 🔍 pointer reduces the size of the document in the Print Preview window.

**QUICK TIP**
You can also use the Zoom list arrow on the Print Preview toolbar to change the magnification in the Print Preview window.

3. **Click the Magnifier button 🔍 on the Print Preview toolbar**

   Clicking the Magnifier button turns off the magnification feature and allows you to edit the document in Print Preview. In edit mode, the pointer changes to I. The Magnifier button is a **toggle button**, which means you can use it to switch back and forth between magnification mode and edit mode.

4. **Compare the text on your screen with the text in Figure A-9, examine your memo carefully for typing or spelling errors, correct any mistakes, then click the Close Preview button Close on the Print Preview toolbar**

   Print Preview closes and the memo appears in the document window.

5. **Click the Save button 💾 on the Standard toolbar**

   If you made any changes to the document since you last saved it, the changes are saved.

6. **Click File on the menu bar, then click Print**

   The Print dialog box opens, as shown in Figure A-10. Depending on the printer installed on your computer, your print settings might differ slightly from those in the figure. You can use the Print dialog box to change the current printer, change the number of copies to print, select what pages of a document to print, and modify other printing options.

7. **Click OK**

   The dialog box closes and a copy of the memo prints using the default print settings. You can also click the Print button 🖨 on the Standard toolbar or the Print Preview toolbar to print a document using the default print settings.

FIGURE A-9: Memo in the Print Preview window

Print Preview
toolbar

Magnifier
button

Close Preview
button

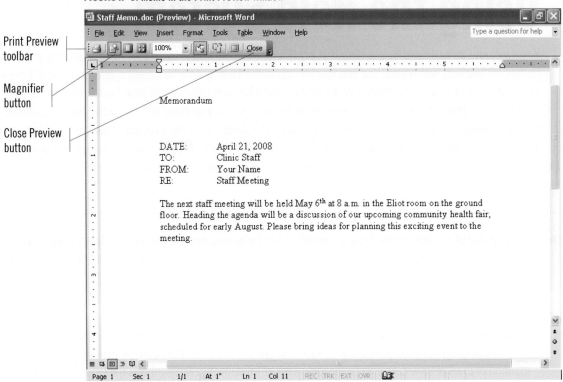

FIGURE A-10: Print dialog box

Default
printer (yours
might differ)

Select the range of
pages to print

Select the special
aspects of the
document to print

Change document
properties for printing,
such as orientation,
page order, and paper
source

Change the number of
copies to print

Change the number of
pages to print on a sheet
of paper

Print using the
current settings

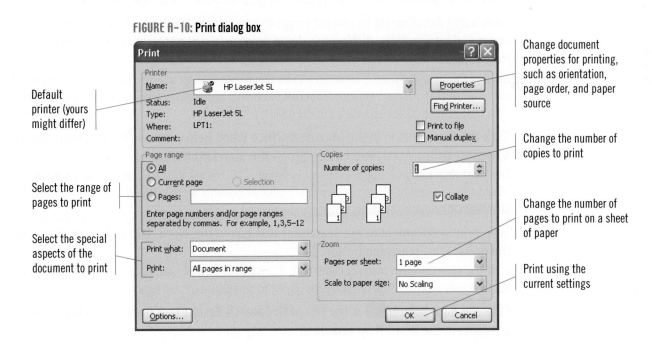

# Using the Help System

Word includes an extensive Help system that provides immediate access to definitions, instructions, and useful tips for working with Word. You can quickly access the Help system by typing a question in the Type a question for help box on the menu bar, by clicking the Microsoft Office Word Help button on the Standard toolbar, or by selecting an option from the Help menu. If you are working with an active Internet connection, your queries to the Help system will also return information from the Microsoft Office Online Web site. Table A-4 describes the many ways to get help while using Word. ▰▰▰▰ You are curious to learn more about typing with AutoCorrect and viewing and printing documents. You search the Word Help system to discover more about these features.

STEPS

TROUBLE
The figures in this lesson reflect an active Internet connection. If you are not connected to the Internet, then connect if possible.

1. **Type AutoCorrect in the Type a question for help box on the menu bar, then press [Enter]**

   The Search Results task pane opens. Help topics related to AutoCorrect are listed in blue in the task pane. Notice that the pointer changes to 👆 when you move it over the blue hyperlink text. If you are working online, it may take a few seconds for information to appear in the task pane.

2. **Click About automatic corrections in the Search Results task pane**

   The Microsoft Office Word Help window opens, as shown in Figure A-11. The Help window displays the "About automatic corrections" Help topic you selected. The colored text in the Help window indicates a link to a definition or to more information about the topic. Like all windows, you can maximize the Help window by clicking the Maximize button on its title bar, or you can resize the window by dragging a top, bottom, or side edge.

TROUBLE
If the hyperlink is not visible in your Help window, click the down scroll arrow until it appears.

3. **Read the information in the Help window, then click the colored text hyperlinks**

   Clicking the link expands the Help topic to display more detailed information. A definition of the word "hyperlink" appears in colored text in the Help window.

4. **Read the definition, then click hyperlinks again to close the definition**

5. **Click Using AutoCorrect to correct errors as you type in the Help window, then read the expanded information, clicking the down scroll arrow as necessary to read the entire Help topic**

   Clicking the up or down scroll arrow allows you to navigate through the Help topic when all the text does not fit in the Help window. You can also **scroll** by clicking the scroll bar above and below the scroll box, or by dragging the scroll box up or down in the scroll bar.

6. **Click the Close button in the Microsoft Office Word Help window title bar, then click the Microsoft Office Word Help button ⊚ on the Standard toolbar**

   The Word Help task pane opens, as shown in Figure A-12. You use this task pane to search for Help topics related to a keyword or phrase, to browse the table of contents for the Help system, or to connect to the Microsoft Office Online Web site, where you can search for more information on a topic.

7. **Type print a document in the Search for text box in the Word Help task pane, then click the green Start searching button ➡**

   After you click the green Start searching button, a list of Help topics related to your query appears in the Search Results task pane. You can also press [Enter] to return a list of Help topics.

8. **Click the Back button ⊛ at the top of the Search Results task pane, then click Table of Contents in the Word Help task pane**

   The table of contents for the Help system appears in the Word Help task pane. To peruse the table of contents, you simply click a category in the list to expand it and see a list of subcategories and Help topics. Categories are listed in black text in the task pane and are preceded by a book icon. Help topics are listed in blue text and are preceded by a question mark icon.

QUICK TIP
Click the Back and Forward buttons on the Word Help window toolbar to navigate between the Help topics you have viewed.

9. **Click Viewing and Navigating Documents, click a blue Help topic, read the information in the Microsoft Office Word Help window, then click the Close button in the Help window**

**FIGURE A-11: Microsoft Office Word Help window**

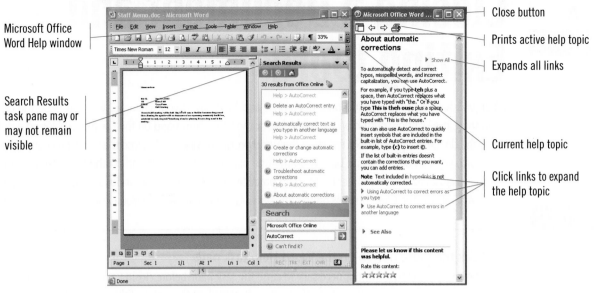

Microsoft Office Word Help window

Search Results task pane may or may not remain visible

Close button

Prints active help topic

Expands all links

Current help topic

Click links to expand the help topic

**FIGURE A-12: Word Help task pane**

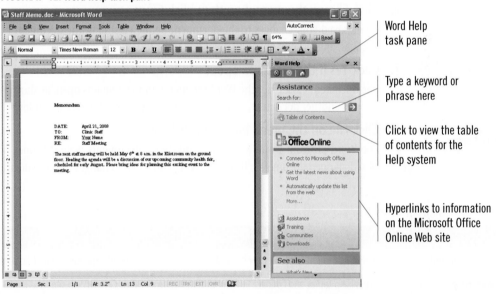

Word Help task pane

Type a keyword or phrase here

Click to view the table of contents for the Help system

Hyperlinks to information on the Microsoft Office Online Web site

**TABLE A-4: Word resources for getting Help**

| resource | function | to use |
|---|---|---|
| Type a question for help box | Provides quick access to the Help system | Type a word or question in the Type a question for help box, then press [Enter] |
| Word Help task pane | Displays the table of contents for the Help system, provides access to a search function, and includes hyperlinks to Help information on the Microsoft Office Online Web site | Press [F1] or click the Microsoft Office Word Help button on the Standard toolbar; in the Word Help task pane, type a word or phrase in the Search for text box to return a list of possible Help topics, click Table of Contents to browse the complete list of Help topics, or click a link to access information on the Microsoft Office Online Web site |
| Microsoft Office Online Web site | Connects to the Microsoft Office Online Web site, where you can search for information on a topic | Click the Microsoft Office Online command on the Help menu, or click a link in the Word Help task pane |
| Office Assistant | Displays tips related to your current task and provides access to the Help system | Click Show the Office Assistant on the Help menu to display the Office Assistant; click Hide the Office Assistant on the Help menu to hide the Office Assistant |

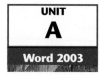

# Closing a Document and Exiting Word

When you have finished working on a document and have saved your changes, you can close the document using the Close Window button on the menu bar or the Close command on the File menu. Closing a document closes the document only, it does not close the Word program window. To close the Word program window and exit Word, you can use the Close button on the title bar or the Exit command on the File menu. Using the Exit command closes all open documents. It's good practice to save and close your documents before exiting Word. Figure A-13 shows the Close buttons on the title bar and menu bar. ▰▰▰▰ You close the memo and exit Word.

**STEPS**

1. **Click the Close button on the Word Help task pane**

   The task pane closes. It is not necessary to close the task pane before closing a file or the program, but it can be helpful to reduce the amount of information displayed on the screen. Table A-5 describes the functions of the Word task panes.

2. **Click File on the menu bar, then click Close**

   If you saved your changes to the document before closing it, the document closes. If you did not save your changes, an alert box opens asking if you want to save the changes.

   **QUICK TIP**
   To create a new blank document, click the New Blank Document button ▢ on the Standard toolbar.

3. **Click Yes if the alert box opens**

   The document closes, but the Word program window remains open, as shown in Figure A-14. You can create or open another document, access Help, or close the Word program window.

4. **Click File on the menu bar, then click Exit**

   The Word program window closes. If any Word documents were still open when you exited Word, Word closed all open documents, first prompting you to save changes to those documents if necessary.

**TABLE A-5: Word task panes**

| task pane | use to |
|---|---|
| Getting Started | Open a document, create a new blank document, or search for information on the Microsoft Office Online Web site |
| Word Help | Access Help topics and connect to Help on the Microsoft Office Online Web site |
| Search Results | View the results of a search for Help topics and perform a new search |
| Clip Art | Search for clip art and insert clip art in a document |
| Research | Search reference books and other sources for information related to a word, such as for synonyms |
| Clipboard | Cut, copy, and paste items within and between documents |
| New Document | Create a new blank document, XML document, Web page, or e-mail message, or create a new document using a template |
| Shared Workspace | Create a Web site (called a document workspace) that allows a group of people to share files, participate in discussions, and work together on a document |
| Document Updates | View information on a document that is available in a document workspace |
| Protect Document | Apply formatting and editing restrictions to a shared document |
| Styles and Formatting | Apply styles to text |
| Reveal Formatting | Display the formatting applied to text |
| Mail Merge | Perform a mail merge |
| XML Structure | Apply XML elements to a Word XML document |

**FIGURE A-13:** Close and Close Window buttons

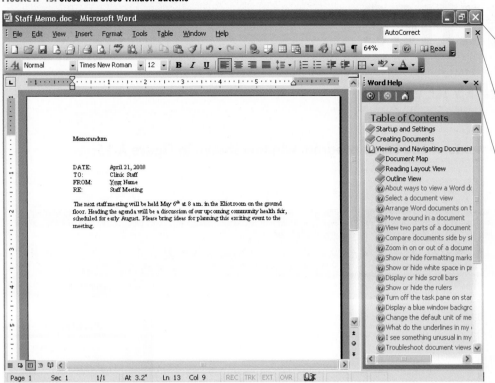

Close button on title bar closes all open documents and exits Word

Close Window button closes the current document

Close button closes the task pane

**FIGURE A-14:** Word program window with no documents open

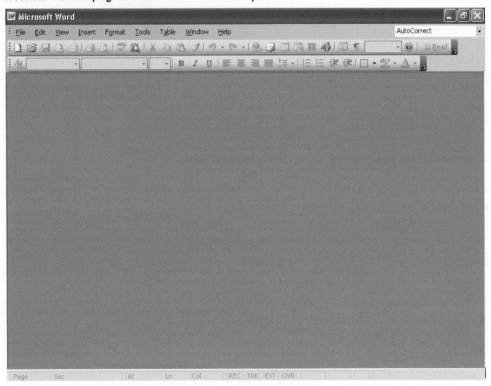

# Practice

## ▼ CONCEPTS REVIEW

**Label the elements of the Word program window shown in Figure A-15.**

FIGURE A-15

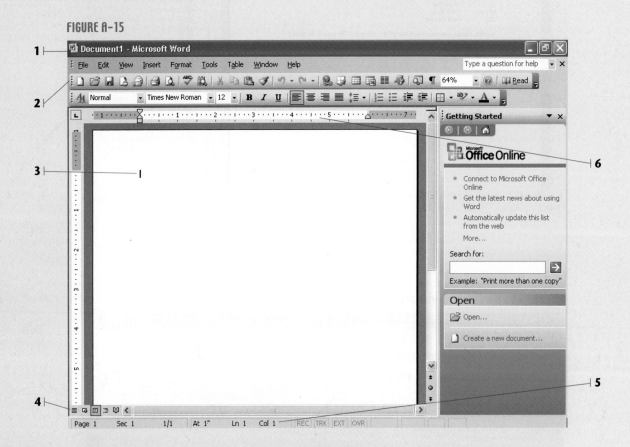

**Match each term with the statement that best describes it.**

7. **Print Preview**          a. Displays the document exactly as it will look when printed

8. **Office Assistant**       b. Displays a simple layout view of a document

9. **Status bar**             c. Fixes certain errors as you type

10. **Menu bar**              d. Displays tips on using Word

11. **AutoComplete**          e. Displays the number of pages in the current document

12. **Horizontal ruler**      f. Provides access to Word commands

13. **AutoCorrect**           g. Suggests text to insert into a document

14. **Normal view**           h. Displays tab settings and paragraph indents

## Select the best answer from the list of choices.

**15. Which of the following does not appear on the status bar?**

  **a.** The Overtype mode status

  **b.** The current line number

  **c.** The current page number

  **d.** The current tab settings

**16. Which task pane opens automatically when you start Word?**

  **a.** Word Help

  **b.** Document Updates

  **c.** New Document

  **d.** Getting Started

**17. Which element of the Word program window shows the settings for the left and right document margins?**

  **a.** Getting Started task pane

  **b.** Horizontal ruler

  **c.** Status bar

  **d.** Formatting toolbar

**18. What is the function of the Exit command on the File menu?**

  **a.** To close all open documents and the Word program window

  **b.** To save changes to and close the current document

  **c.** To close all open programs

  **d.** To close the current document without saving changes

**19. Which view do you use when you want to format headers and footers?**

  **a.** Web Layout view

  **b.** Normal view

  **c.** Print Layout view

  **d.** Outline view

**20. Which of the following is *not* used to access the Help system?**

  **a.** The Research task pane

  **b.** Type a question for help box

  **c.** The Office Assistant

  **d.** Microsoft Office Online

# ▼ SKILLS REVIEW

**1. Start Word 2003.**

  **a.** Start Word.

  **b.** Switch to Print Layout view if your blank document opened in a different view.

  **c.** Change the zoom level to Page Width.

**2. Explore the Word program window.**

  **a.** Identify as many elements of the Word program window as you can without referring to the unit material.

  **b.** Click each menu name on the menu bar and drag the pointer through the menu commands.

  **c.** Point to each button on the Standard and Formatting toolbars and read the ScreenTips.

  **d.** Point to each hyperlink in the Getting Started task pane.

    **e.** Click the view buttons to view the blank document in Normal, Web Layout, Print Layout, Outline, and Reading Layout view, respectively.

    **f.** Click the Close button on the Reading Layout toolbar, then return to Print Layout view.

### 3. Start a document.

    **a.** Close the Getting Started task pane.

    **b.** In a new blank document, type **FAX** at the top of the page, then press [Enter] four times.

    **c.** Type the following, pressing [Tab] as indicated and pressing [Enter] at the end of each line:

        **To:** [Tab] **Dr. Jennifer Lee**

        **From:** [Tab] **Your Name**

        **Date:** [Tab] **Today's date**

        **Re:** [Tab] **New afternoon pick-up time**

        **Pages:** [Tab] **1**

        **Fax:** [Tab] **(212) 555-5359**

    **d.** Press [Enter] again, then type **Effective July 1st, BCH Labs will pick up laboratory specimens at 10:00 a.m. and 4:15 p.m. daily. We trust the addition of the morning pick-up time will improve the efficiency of our service. All abnormal results will continue to be reported to your office by telephone.**

    **e.** Press [Enter] twice, then type **As always, we welcome your comments and suggestions on how we can better serve you.**

    **f.** Insert this sentence at the beginning of the second paragraph: **The lab will continue to be open until 7:00 p.m. for drop-in service.**

    **g.** Using the [Backspace] key, delete **afternoon** in the Re: line, then type **morning**.

    **h.** Using the [Delete] key, delete **4:15** in the first paragraph, then type **3:30**.

### 4. Save a document.

    **a.** Click File on the menu bar, then click Save.

    **b.** Save the document as **Lee Fax** to the drive and folder where your Data Files are located.

    **c.** After your name, type a comma, press [Spacebar], then type **BCH Labs**.

    **d.** Click the Save button to save your changes to the document.

### 5. Print a document.

    **a.** Click the Print Preview button to view the document in Print Preview.

    **b.** Click the word FAX to zoom in on the document, then proofread the fax.

    **c.** Click the Magnifier button to switch to edit mode, then correct any typing errors in your document.

    **d.** Close Print Preview, then save your changes to the document.

    **e.** Print the fax using the default print settings.

### 6. Use the Help system.

    **a.** Click the Microsoft Office Word Help button to open the Word Help task pane.

    **b.** Type **open a document** in the Search text box, then press [Enter].

    **c.** Click the topic Open a file.

    **d.** Read about opening documents in Word by clicking the links to expand the Help topic.

    **e.** Close the Help window, type **viewing documents** in the Type a question for help box, then press [Enter].

    **f.** Click the link Select a document view in the Search Results task pane, then read the Help topic.

    **g.** Close the Help window, then close the Search Results task pane.

### 7. Close a document and exit Word.

    **a.** Close the Lee Fax document, saving your changes if necessary.

    **b.** Exit Word.

# ▼ INDEPENDENT CHALLENGE 1

You are a cardiologist and research investigator in numerous trials pertaining to the study of heart disease. The president of the Allied Cardiology Association, Dr. Emil Gund, has asked you to be the keynote speaker at an upcoming conference on heart disease, to be held at the Ahwahnee Hotel Conference Center in Yosemite National Park. You are pleased about the invitation, and write a letter to Dr. Gund accepting the invitation and confirming the details. Your letter to Dr. Gund should reference the following information:

- The conference will be held May 12–14, 2008, at the Ahwahnee Hotel Conference Center in Yosemite National Park.
- You have been asked to speak for an hour on Saturday, May 13, followed by a half hour for questions.
- Dr. Gund suggested the lecture topic "Hope for the Heart: Advancements in Diagnosis and Treatment."
- Your talk will include a 45-minute slide presentation.
- The Allied Cardiology Association will make your travel arrangements.
- Your preference is to arrive at Fresno-Yosemite Airport on the morning of Friday, May 12 and to depart on Monday, May 15. You would like to rent a car at the airport for the drive to Yosemite National Park.
- You want to fly in and out of the airport closest to your home.

a. Start Word.

b. Save a new blank document as **Gund Letter** to the drive and folder where your Data Files are located.

c. Model your letter to Dr. Gund after the sample business letter shown in Figure A-16. Use the following formatting guidelines: 3 blank lines after the date, 1 blank line after the inside address, 1 blank line after the salutation, 1 blank line after each body paragraph, and 3 blank lines between the closing and your typed name. You do not need to include the sender's address because you plan to print the letter on letterhead.

d. Begin the letter by typing today's date.

e. Type the inside address. Be sure to include Dr. Gund's title and the name of the organization. Make up a street address and zip code.

f. Type a salutation.

g. Using the information listed above, type the body of the letter:

- In the first paragraph, accept the invitation to speak and confirm the important conference details.
- In the second paragraph, confirm your lecture topic and provide any relevant details.
- In the third paragraph, state your travel preferences.
- Type a short final paragraph.

h. Type a closing, then include your name in the signature block.

## Advanced Challenge Exercise

- View the letter in Normal view, then correct your spelling and grammar errors, if any, by right-clicking any red- or green-underlined text, then choosing from the options on the shortcut menu.
- View the letter in Print Layout view, then remove any smart tags.
- View the letter in Reading Layout view, then click the Close button on the Reading Layout toolbar to close Reading Layout view.

i. Proofread your letter, make corrections as needed, then save your changes.

j. Preview the letter, print the letter, close the document, then exit Word.

**FIGURE A-16**

June 12, 2008


Dr. William Hessler
Center for Sports Medicine
Manchester Memorial Hospital
523 Concord Street
Manchester, NH 03258

Dear Dr. Hessler:

Thank you very much for your kind invitation to speak at your conference on sports podiatry, to be held September 16 and 17 at Manchester Memorial Hospital. I am honored to accept your invitation.

I will address my remarks to the topic you suggested, "Put Your Best Foot Forward: Orthotics for Runners." I will plan to speak at 2:30 p.m. on September 16 for forty minutes, with twenty minutes of questions to follow. My talk will include a PowerPoint presentation. I will provide my own laptop and projector system, but would appreciate it if you could arrange for a viewing screen.

My preference is to arrive in Manchester on the morning of September 16, and to depart that evening after 6:00 p.m. It is easiest for me to use New York's LaGuardia Airport. I am grateful that your office will be taking care of my travel arrangements.

I look forward to meeting you in September.

Sincerely,


Alicia Edwards, M.D.

# ▼ INDEPENDENT CHALLENGE 2

Your hospital has recently installed Word 2003 on its computer network. As the computer training manager, it's your responsibility to teach employees how to use the new software productively. Now that they have begun working with Word 2003, several employees have asked you about smart tags. In response to their queries, you decide to write a memo to all employees explaining how to use the smart tag feature. You know that smart tags are designed to help users perform tasks in Word that normally would require opening a different program, such as Microsoft Outlook (a desktop information-management program that includes e-mail, calendar, and address book features). Before writing your memo, you learn more about smart tags by searching the Word Help system.

**a.** Start Word and save a new blank document as **Smart Tags Memo** to the drive and folder where your Data Files are located.

**b.** Type **WORD TRAINING MEMORANDUM** at the top of the document, press [Enter] four times, then type the memo heading information shown in Figure A-17. Make sure to include your name in the From line and the current date in the Date line.

**c.** Press [Enter] twice to place the insertion point where you will begin typing the body of your memo.

**d.** Search the Word Help system for information on working with smart tags.

**e.** Type your memo after completing your research. In your memo, define smart tags, then explain what they look like, how to use smart tags, and how to remove smart tags from a document.

FIGURE A-17

> WORD TRAINING MEMORANDUM
>
>
> To:     All employees
> From:  Your Name, Training Manager
> Date:   Today's date
> Re:      Smart tags in Microsoft Word

## Advanced Challenge Exercise

- Search the Help system for information on how to check for new smart tags developed by Microsoft and third-party vendors.
- Print the information you find.
- Add a short paragraph to your memo explaining how to find new smart tags.

**f.** Save your changes, preview and print the memo, then close the document and exit Word.

# ▼ INDEPENDENT CHALLENGE 3

Yesterday you interviewed for a job as medical office manager at Canyon Medical Associates. You spoke with several people at Canyon Medical Associates, including Samuel Murata, director of human resources, whose business card is shown in Figure A-18. You need to write a follow-up letter to Mr. Murata, thanking him for the interview and expressing your interest in the practice and the position. He also asked you to send him samples of documents you have created, which you will enclose with the letter. You plan to print the letter on your personal letterhead, which includes your name, address, and other contact information.

**a.** Start Word and save a new blank document as **Canyon Medical Letter** to the drive and folder where your Data Files are located.

**b.** Begin the letter by typing today's date.

**c.** Four lines below the date, type the inside address, referring to Figure A-18 for the address information. Be sure to include the recipient's title, company name, and full mailing address in the inside address.

**d.** Two lines below the inside address, type the salutation.

FIGURE A-18

> **Samuel Murata**
>
> Director of Human Resources
>
> **Canyon Medical Associates**
>
> 8472 Claremont Avenue
> Oakland, CA 94618
>
> Phone: 510-555-3299
> Fax: 510-555-7028
> Email: smurata@canyonmed.net

# ▼ INDEPENDENT CHALLENGE 3 (CONTINUED)

 **e.** Two lines below the salutation, type the body of the letter according to the following guidelines:

  • In the first paragraph, thank him for the interview. Then restate your interest in the position and express your desire to work for the practice. Add any specific details you think will enhance the power of your letter.

  • In the second paragraph, note that you are enclosing three samples of your work and explain something about the samples you are enclosing.

  • Type a short final paragraph.

 **f.** Two lines below the last body paragraph, type a closing, then four lines below the closing, type the signature block. Be sure to include your name in the signature block.

 **g.** Two lines below the signature block, type an enclosure notation. (*Hint*: An enclosure notation usually includes the word "Enclosures" or the abbreviation "Enc." followed by the number of enclosures in parentheses.)

 **h.** Save your changes.

 **i.** Preview and print the letter, then close the document and exit Word.

# ▼ INDEPENDENT CHALLENGE 4

The computer keyboard has become as essential an office tool as the pencil. The more adept you become at touch typing—the fastest and most accurate way to type—the more comfortable you will be working with computers and the more saleable your office skills to a potential employer. Understanding ergonomics, the science of designing equipment so that it maximizes productivity by minimizing worker fatigue and discomfort, also can help you remain productive and avoid repetitive stress injuries. The World Wide Web is one source of information on touch typing, and many Web sites include free typing tests and online tutorials to help you practice and improve your typing skills. In this independent challenge, you will take an online typing test to check your typing skills. You will then research the fundamentals of touch typing and investigate some of the ergonomic factors important to becoming a productive keyboard typist.

 **a.** Use your favorite search engine to search the Web for information on typing. Use the keywords **typing** and **typing ergonomics** to conduct your search.

 **b.** Review the Web sites you find. Choose a site that offers a free online typing test, take the test, then print the Web page showing the results of your typing test.

 **c.** Start Word and save a new blank document as **Typing** to the drive and folder where your Data Files are located.

 **d.** Type your name at the top of the document, then press [Enter] twice.

 **e.** Type a brief report on the results of your research. Your report should answer the following questions:

  • What are the URLs of the Web sites you visited to research touch typing and keyboard ergonomics? (*Hint*: A URL is a Web page's address. An example of a URL is www.course.com.)

  • What are some benefits of using the touch typing method?

  • In touch typing, on which keys should the fingers of the left and right hands rest?

  • What ergonomic factors are important to keep in mind while typing?

 **f.** Save your changes to the document, preview and print it, then close the document and exit Word.

# ▼ VISUAL WORKSHOP

Create the letter shown in Figure A-19. Save the document with the name **Insurance Letter** to the drive and folder where your Data Files are stored. Print a copy of the letter for review before it is printed on letterhead, then close the document and exit Word.

FIGURE A-19

Ms. Monica Wilkins
827 Elm Street NE
Albuquerque, NM 87102

Dear Ms. Wilkins:

Thank you for choosing Albuquerque Memorial Healthcare as your healthcare provider.

As a result of your recent visit to our emergency facility, our records show your primary care insurance as Southwest Indemnity (#80053 0331), policy #446 38 9876, and group #732556-22-994. At this time, our records show you do not have a secondary care insurance provider.

If the insurance information in this letter is correct, no action is required on your part.

If the insurance information is incomplete or incorrect, please contact us with more accurate billing information by calling a Financial Counselor at (505) 993-5600.

Once we have billed your insurance, we will send you a statement identifying any patient responsibility.

Sincerely,


Your Name
Patient Business Services
Albuquerque Memorial Healthcare

# Editing Documents

## OBJECTIVES

Open a document

Select text

Cut and paste text

Copy and paste text

Use the Office Clipboard

Find and replace text

Check spelling and grammar

Use the Thesaurus

Use templates and wizards

If you have a SAM user profile, you may have access to hands-on instruction, practice, and assessment of the skills covered in this unit. Log in to your SAM account and go to your assignments page to see what your instructor has assigned.

The sophisticated editing features in Word make it easy to revise and polish your documents. In this unit, you learn how to open an existing file, revise it by replacing, copying, and moving text, and then save the document as a new file. You also learn how to perfect your documents using proofing tools and how to quickly create attractive, professionally designed documents using wizards and templates. You have been asked to create a press release about a new lecture series sponsored by the Riverwalk Medical Clinic. The press release should provide information about the series so that newspapers, radio stations, and other media outlets can announce it to the public. Press releases are often disseminated by fax, so you also need to create a fax coversheet to use when you fax the press release to your list of press contacts.

# Opening a Document

Sometimes the easiest way to create a document is to edit an existing document and save it with a new file-name. To modify a document, you must first **open** it so that it displays in the document window. Word offers several methods for opening documents, described in Table B-1. Once you have opened a file, you can use the Save As command to create a new file that is a copy of the original. You can then edit the new file without making changes to the original. ▰▰▰▰ Rather than write your press release from scratch, you decide to modify a draft press release written by a co-worker. You begin by opening the press release document and saving it with a new filename.

## STEPS

1. **Start Word**

   Word opens and a blank document and the Getting Started task pane appears in the program window, as shown in Figure B-1. The Getting Started task pane contains links for opening existing documents and for creating new documents.

2. **Click the Open or More hyperlink at the bottom of the Getting Started task pane**

   The Open dialog box opens. You use the Open dialog box to locate and select the file you want to open. The Look in list box displays the current drive or folder. You also can use the Open button 📂 on the Standard toolbar or the Open command on the File menu to open the Open dialog box.

3. **Click the Look in list arrow, click the drive containing your Data Files, then double-click the folder containing your Data Files**

   A list of the Data Files for this unit appears in the Open dialog box, as shown in Figure B-2.

4. **Click the filename WMP B-1.doc in the Open dialog box to select it, then click Open**

   The document opens. Notice that the filename WMP B-1.doc appears in the title bar. Once you have opened a file, you can edit it and use the Save or the Save As command to save your changes. You use the **Save** command when you want to save the changes you make to a file, overwriting the file that is stored on a disk. You use the **Save As** command when you want to create a new file with a different filename, leaving the original file intact.

5. **Click File on the menu bar, then click Save As**

   The Save As dialog box opens. By saving a file with a new filename, you create a document that is identical to the original document. The original filename is selected (highlighted) in the File name text box. Any text you type replaces the selected text.

6. **Type Lecture Press Release in the File name text box, then click Save**

   The original file closes and the Lecture Press Release file is displayed in the document window. Notice the new filename in the title bar. You can now make changes to the press release file without affecting the original file.

---

### Clues to Use

#### Managing files and folders

The Open and Save As dialog boxes include powerful tools for navigating, creating, deleting, and renaming files and folders on your computer, a network, or the Web. By selecting a file or folder and clicking the Delete button ✖, you can delete the item and send it to the Recycle Bin. You can also create a new folder for storing files by clicking the Create New Folder button 📁 and typing a name for the folder. The new folder is created in the current folder. To rename a file or folder, simply right-click it in the dialog box, click Rename, type a new name, and then press [Enter].

Using the Save As dialog box, you can create new files that are based on existing files. To create a new file, you can save an existing file with a different filename or save it in a different location on your system. You also can save a file in a different file format so that it can be opened in a different software program. To save a file in a different format, click the Save as type list arrow, then click the type of file you want to create. For example, you can save a Word document (which has a .doc file extension) as a plain text file (.txt), as a Web page file (.htm), or in a variety of other file formats.

**FIGURE B-1:** Getting Started task pane

Open button

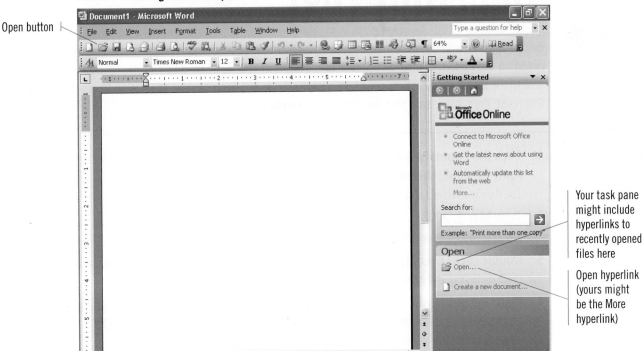

Your task pane might include hyperlinks to recently opened files here

Open hyperlink (yours might be the More hyperlink)

**FIGURE B-2:** Open dialog box

Current drive or folder

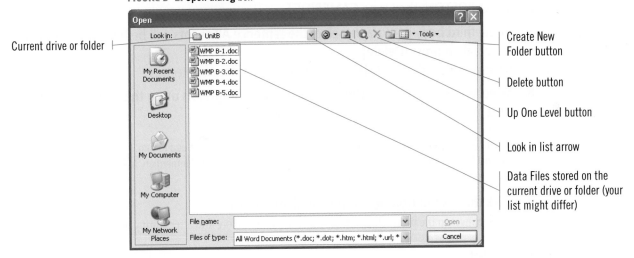

Create New Folder button

Delete button

Up One Level button

Look in list arrow

Data Files stored on the current drive or folder (your list might differ)

**TABLE B-1:** Methods for opening documents

| use | to | if you want to |
|---|---|---|
| The Open button 📂 on the Standard toolbar, the Open command on the File menu, the Open or More hyperlink in the Getting Started task pane, or [Ctrl][O] | Open the Open dialog box | Open an existing file |
| A filename hyperlink in the Getting Started task pane | Open the file in the document window | Open the file; a fast way to open a file that was recently opened on your computer |
| The From existing document hyperlink in the New Document task pane | Open the New from Existing Document dialog box | Create a copy of an existing file; a fast way to open a document you intend to save with a new filename |

# Selecting Text

Before deleting, editing, or formatting text, you must **select** the text. Selecting text involves clicking and dragging the I-beam pointer across text to highlight it. You also can click with the 𝄎 pointer in the blank area to the left of text to select lines or paragraphs. Table B-2 describes the many ways to select text. ▰▰▰▰▰ You revise the press release by selecting text and replacing it with new text.

## STEPS

1. **Click the Zoom list arrow on the Standard toolbar, click Page Width, click before April 14, 2008, then drag the I pointer over the text to select it**

   The date is selected, as shown in Figure B-3.

2. **Type May 1, 2008**

   The text you type replaces the selected text.

3. **Double-click Owen, type your first name, double-click Spade, then type your last name**

   Double-clicking a word selects the entire word.

4. **Place the pointer in the margin to the left of the phone number so that the pointer changes to 𝄎, click to select the phone number, then type (617) 555-1838**

   Clicking to the left of a line of text with the 𝄎 pointer selects the entire line.

5. **Click the down scroll arrow at the bottom of the vertical scroll bar until the headline Dr. Alexander Fogg to Speak... is at the top of your document window**

   The scroll arrows or scroll bars allow you to scroll through a document. You scroll through a document when you want to display different parts of the document in the document window.

6. **Select BOSTON, then type CAMBRIDGE**

7. **In the third body paragraph, select the sentence All events will be held at the St. James Hotel., then press [Delete]**

   Selecting text and pressing [Delete] removes the text from the document.

8. **Select and replace text in the second and last paragraphs using the following table:**

   | select | type |
   | --- | --- |
   | May 12 | June 14 |
   | St. James Hotel in downtown Boston | Riverwalk Medical Clinic auditorium |
   | National Public Radio's Helen DeSaint | Clinic director Carla J. Zimmerman, M.D., |

   The edited press release is shown in Figure B-4.

9. **Click the Save button 🖫 on the Standard toolbar**

   Your changes to the press release are saved. Always save before and after editing text.

**TABLE B-2: Methods for selecting text**

| to select | use the mouse pointer to |
| --- | --- |
| Any amount of text | Drag over the text |
| A word | Double-click the word |
| A line of text | Click with the 𝄎 pointer to the left of the line |
| A sentence | Press and hold [Ctrl], then click the sentence |
| A paragraph | Triple-click the paragraph or double-click with the 𝄎 pointer to the left of the paragraph |
| A large block of text | Click at the beginning of the selection, press and hold [Shift], then click at the end of the selection |
| Multiple nonconsecutive selections | Select the first selection, then press and hold [Ctrl] as you select each additional selection |
| An entire document | Triple-click with the 𝄎 pointer to the left of any text, click Select All on the Edit menu, or press [Ctrl][A] |

**FIGURE B-3:** Date selected in the press release

Selected text

Left document margin

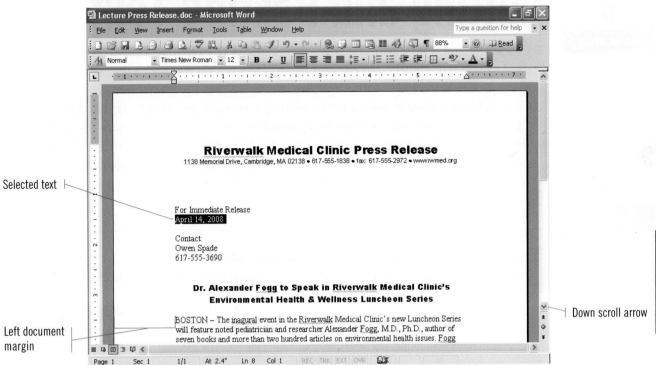

Down scroll arrow

**FIGURE B-4:** Edited press release

Replacement text

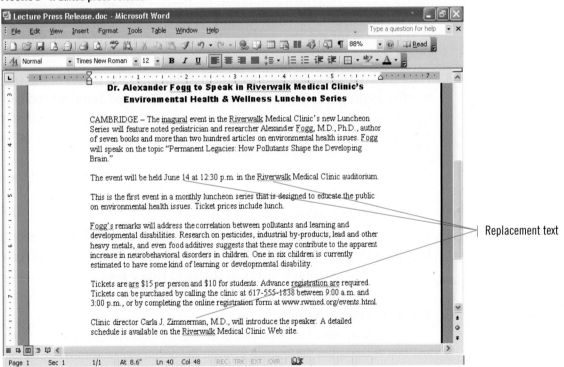

## Clues to Use

### Replacing text in Overtype mode

Normally you must select text before typing to replace the existing characters, but by turning on **Overtype mode** you can type over existing characters without selecting them first. To turn Overtype mode on and off on your computer, double-click OVR in the status bar. On some computers you also can turn Overtype mode on and off by pressing [Insert]. When Overtype mode is on, OVR appears in black in the status bar. When Overtype mode is off, OVR is dimmed.

# Cutting and Pasting Text

The editing features in Word allow you to move text from one location to another in a document. The operation of moving text is often called **cut and paste**. When you cut text from a document, you remove it from the document and add it to the **Clipboard**, a temporary storage area for text and graphics that you cut or copy from a document. You cut text by selecting it and using the Cut command on the Edit menu or the Cut button. To insert the text from the Clipboard into the document, you place the insertion point where you want to insert the text, and then use the Paste command on the Edit menu or the Paste button to paste the text at that location. You also can move text by dragging it to a new location using the mouse. This operation is called **drag and drop**. You reorganize the information in the press release using the cut-and-paste and drag-and-drop methods.

## STEPS

1. **Click the Show/Hide ¶ button ¶ on the Standard toolbar**

   Formatting marks appear in the document window. **Formatting marks** are special characters that appear on your screen and do not print. Common formatting marks include the paragraph symbol (¶), which shows the end of a paragraph—wherever you press [Enter]; the dot symbol (•), which represents a space—wherever you press [Spacebar]; and the arrow symbol (➔), which shows the location of a tab stop—wherever you press [Tab]. Working with formatting marks turned on can help you to select, edit, and format text with precision.

   > **TROUBLE**
   > If the Clipboard task pane opens, close it.

2. **In the fourth paragraph, select lead and other heavy metals, (including the comma and the space after it), then click the Cut button ✂ on the Standard toolbar**

   The text is removed from the document and placed on the Clipboard. Word uses two different clipboards: the **system Clipboard** (the Clipboard), which holds just one item, and the **Office Clipboard**, which holds up to 24 items. The last item you cut or copy is always added to both clipboards. You'll learn more about the Office Clipboard in a later lesson.

3. **Place the insertion point before pesticides (but after the space) in the second line of the fourth paragraph, then click the Paste button ⧉ on the Standard toolbar**

   The text is pasted at the location of the insertion point, as shown in Figure B-5. The Paste Options button ⧉ appears below text when you first paste it in a document. You'll learn more about the Paste Options button in the next lesson. For now, you can ignore it.

4. **Press and hold [Ctrl], click the sentence Ticket prices include lunch. in the third paragraph, then release [Ctrl]**

   The entire sentence is selected.

   > **TROUBLE**
   > If you make a mistake, click the Undo button ↺ on the Standard toolbar, then try again.

5. **Press and hold the mouse button over the selected text until the pointer changes to ▚, then drag the pointer's vertical line to the end of the fifth paragraph (between the period and the paragraph mark), as shown in Figure B-6**

   The pointer's vertical line indicates the location the text will be inserted when you release the mouse button.

6. **Release the mouse button**

   The selected text is moved to the location of the insertion point. It's convenient to move text using the drag-and-drop method when the locations of origin and destination are both visible on the screen. Text is not removed to the Clipboard when you move it using drag-and-drop.

7. **Deselect the text, then click the Save button 🖫 on the Standard toolbar**

   Your changes to the press release are saved.

**FIGURE B-5:** Moved text with Paste Options button

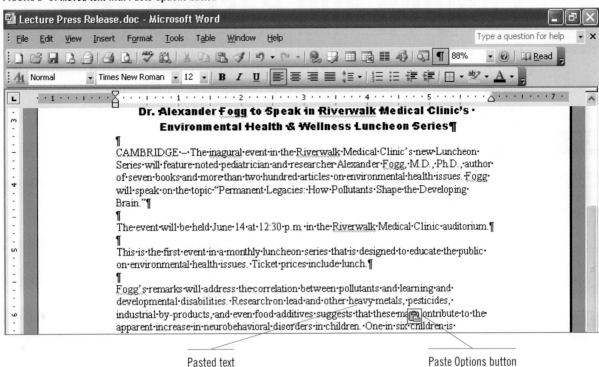

Pasted text          Paste Options button

**FIGURE B-6:** Text being dragged to a new location

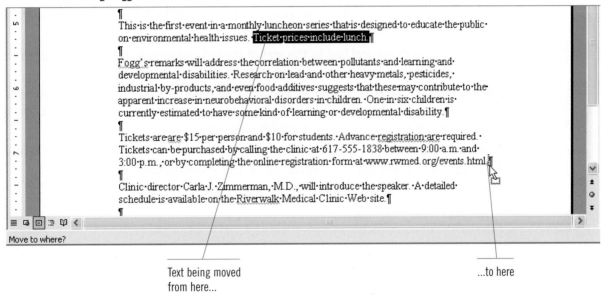

Text being moved                    ...to here
from here...

## Clues to Use

### Using keyboard shortcuts

Instead of using the Cut, Copy, and Paste commands to edit text in Word, you can use the **keyboard shortcuts** [Ctrl][X] to cut text, [Ctrl][C] to copy text, and [Ctrl][V] to paste text. A **shortcut key** is a function key, such as [F1], or a combination of keys, such as [Ctrl][S], that you press to perform a command. For example, pressing [Ctrl][S] saves changes to a document, just as clicking the Save button or using the Save command on the File menu saves a document. Becoming skilled at using keyboard shortcuts can help you to quickly accomplish many of the tasks you perform frequently in Word. If a keyboard shortcut is available for a menu command, then it is listed next to the command on the menu.

# Copying and Pasting Text

Copying and pasting text is similar to cutting and pasting text, except that the text you copy is not removed from the document. Rather, a copy of the text is placed on the Clipboard, leaving the original text in place. You can copy text to the Clipboard using the Copy command on the Edit menu or the Copy button, or you can copy text by pressing [Ctrl] as you drag the selected text from one location to another. ▰▰▰ You continue to edit the press release by copying text from one location to another.

**STEPS**

1. **In the headline, select** Environmental Health & Wellness, **then click the** Copy button 📋 **on the Standard toolbar**

   A copy of the text is placed on the Clipboard, leaving the text you copied in place.

2. **Place the insertion point before** Luncheon **in the first body paragraph, then click the** Paste button 📋 **on the Standard toolbar**

   "Environmental Health & Wellness" is inserted before "Luncheon," as shown in Figure B-7. Notice that the pasted text is formatted differently than the paragraph in which it was inserted.

3. **Click the** Paste Options button 📋, **then click** Match Destination Formatting

   The Paste Options button allows you to change the formatting of pasted text. The formatting of "Environmental Health & Wellness" is changed to match the rest of the paragraph. The options available on the Paste Options menu depend on the format of the text you are pasting and the format of the surrounding text.

4. **Scroll down if necessary so that the last two paragraphs are visible on your screen**

5. **In the fifth paragraph, select** www.rwmed.org, **press and hold** [Ctrl], **then press the mouse button until the pointer changes to** ⏸

6. **Drag the pointer's vertical line to the end of the last paragraph, placing it between** site **and the period, release the mouse button, then release** [Ctrl]

   The text is copied to the last paragraph. Because the formatting of the text you copied is the same as the formatting of the paragraph in which you inserted it, you can ignore the Paste Options button. Text is not copied to the Clipboard when you copy it using the drag-and-drop method.

7. **Place the insertion point before** www.rwmed.org **in the last paragraph, type** at **followed by a space, then click the** Save button 📋 **on the Standard toolbar**

   Compare your document with Figure B-8.

---

### Clues to Use

#### Copying and moving items in a long document

If you want to copy or move items between parts of a long document, it can be useful to split the document window into two panes so that the item you want to copy or move is displayed in one pane, and the destination for the item is displayed in the other pane. To split a window, click the Split command on the Window menu, drag the horizontal split bar that appears to the location you want to split the window, and then click. Once the document window is split into two panes, you can drag the split bar to resize the panes and use the scroll bars in each pane to display different parts of the document. To copy or move an item from one pane to another, you can use the Cut, Copy, and Paste commands, or you can drag the item between the panes. When you are finished editing the document, double-click the split bar to restore the window to a single pane.

**FIGURE B-7:** Text pasted in document

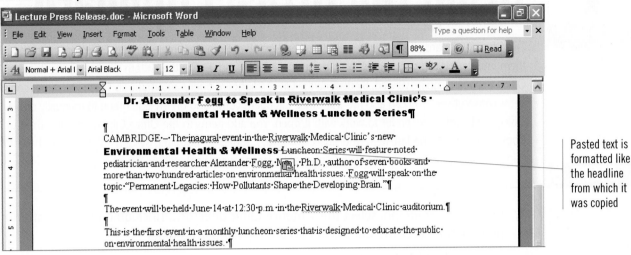

Pasted text is
formatted like
the headline
from which it
was copied

**FIGURE B-8:** Copied text in press release

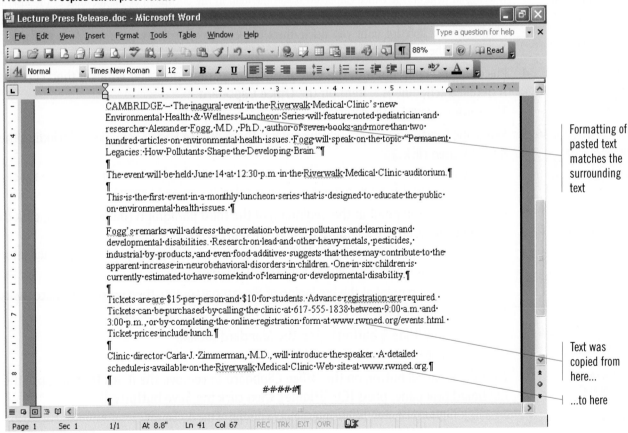

Formatting of
pasted text
matches the
surrounding
text

Text was
copied from
here...

...to here

# Using the Office Clipboard

The Office Clipboard allows you to collect text and graphics from files created in any Office program and insert them into your Word documents. It holds up to 24 items and, unlike the system Clipboard, the items on the Office Clipboard can be viewed. By default, the Office Clipboard opens automatically when you cut or copy two items consecutively. You can also use the Office Clipboard command on the Edit menu to manually display the Office Clipboard if you prefer to work with it open. You add items to the Office Clipboard using the Cut and Copy commands. The last item you collect is always added to both the system Clipboard and the Office Clipboard. ▭▭▭ You use the Office Clipboard to move several sentences in your press release.

## STEPS

**TROUBLE**

If the Office Clipboard does not open, click Office Clipboard on the Edit menu, click the Undo button on the Standard toolbar two times, click Clear All on the Clipboard task pane, then repeat Steps 1 and 2. To restore the default, click Options on the Clipboard task pane, click Show Office Clipboard Automatically to select it, then click outside the menu.

1. **In the last paragraph, select the sentence** Clinic director... **(including the space after the period), then click the** Cut button ✂ **on the Standard toolbar**

   The sentence is cut to the Clipboard.

2. **Select the sentence** A detailed schedule is... **(including the ¶ mark), then click** ✂

   The Office Clipboard opens in the Clipboard task pane, as shown in Figure B-9. It displays the items you cut from the press release. The icon next to each item indicates the items are from a Word document.

3. **Place the insertion point at the end of the second paragraph (after** auditorium. **but before the ¶ mark), then click the** Clinic director... **item on the Office Clipboard**

   Clicking an item on the Office Clipboard pastes the item in the document at the location of the insertion point. Notice that the item remains on the Office Clipboard even after you pasted it. Items remain on the Office Clipboard until you delete them or close all open Office programs. Also, if you add a 25th item to the Office Clipboard, the first item is deleted.

4. **Place the insertion point at the end of the third paragraph (after** issues.**), then click the** A detailed schedule is... **item on the Office Clipboard**

   The sentence is pasted in the document.

**QUICK TIP**

To delete an individual item from the Office Clipboard, click the list arrow next to the item, then click Delete.

5. **Select the fourth paragraph, which contains the sentence** Fogg's remarks... **(including the ¶ mark), then click** ✂

   The paragraph is cut to the Office Clipboard. Notice that the last item collected appears at the top of the Clipboard task pane. The last item collected is also stored on the system Clipboard.

6. **Place the insertion point at the beginning of the third paragraph (before** This...**), click the** Paste button 📋 **on the Standard toolbar, then press** [Enter]

   The "Fogg's remarks..." paragraph is pasted before the "This is the first..." paragraph. You can paste the last item collected using either the Paste command or the Office Clipboard.

7. **Place the insertion point at the beginning of the last paragraph, then press** [Backspace] **twice**

   The ¶ symbols and the blank line between the fourth and fifth paragraphs are deleted.

**QUICK TIP**

Many Word users prefer to work with formatting marks turned on at all times. Experiment for yourself and see which method you prefer.

8. **Click the** Show/Hide ¶ **button** ¶ **on the Standard toolbar**

   Compare your press release with Figure B-10.

9. **Click the** Clear All button **on the Office Clipboard to remove the items from it, close the Clipboard task pane, press** [Ctrl][Home], **then click the** Save button 💾

   Pressing [Ctrl][Home] moves the insertion point to the top of the document.

FIGURE B-9: Office Clipboard in Clipboard task pane

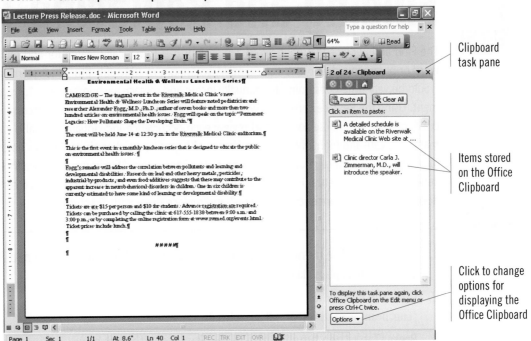

Clipboard task pane

Items stored on the Office Clipboard

Click to change options for displaying the Office Clipboard

FIGURE B-10: Revised press release

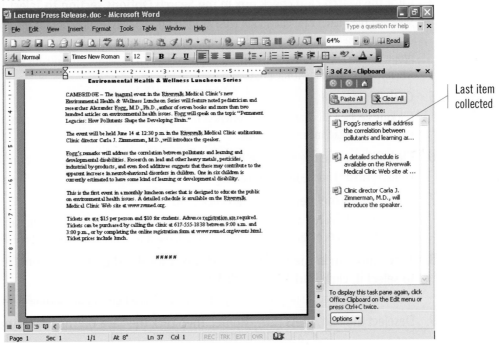

Last item collected

## Clues to Use

### Copying and moving items between documents

The system and Office Clipboards also can be used to copy and move items between Word documents. To copy or cut items from one Word document and paste them into another, first open both documents and the Clipboard task pane in the program window. With multiple documents open, you can copy and move items between documents by copying or cutting the item(s) from one document and then switching to another document and pasting the item(s). To switch between open documents, click the button on the taskbar for the document you want to appear in the document window. You can also display both documents at the same time by clicking the Arrange All command on the Window menu. The Office Clipboard stores all the items collected from all documents, regardless of which document is displayed in the document window. The system Clipboard stores the last item collected from any document.

EDITING DOCUMENTS 35

# Finding and Replacing Text

The Find and Replace feature in Word allows you to automatically search for and replace all instances of a word or phrase in a document. For example, you might need to substitute "surgeon" for "physician," and it would be very time-consuming to manually locate and replace each instance of "physician" in a long document. Using the Replace command you can automatically find and replace all occurrences of specific text at once, or you can choose to find and review each occurrence individually. You also can use the Find command to locate and highlight every occurrence of a specific word or phrase in a document. The clinic director has decided to change the name of the series from "Environmental Health & Wellness Luncheon Series" to "Environmental Health & Wellness Lecture Series." You use the Replace command to search the document for all instances of "Luncheon" and replace them with "Lecture."

## STEPS

1. **Click Edit on the menu bar, click Replace, then click More in the Find and Replace dialog box**
   The Find and Replace dialog box opens, as shown in Figure B-11.

2. **Click the Find what text box, then type Luncheon**
   "Luncheon" is the text that will be replaced.

3. **Press [Tab], then type Lecture in the Replace with text box**
   "Lecture" is the text that will replace "Luncheon."

4. **Click the Match case check box in the Search Options section to select it**
   Selecting the Match case check box tells Word to find only exact matches for the uppercase and lowercase characters you entered in the Find what text box. You want to replace all instances of "Luncheon" in the proper name "Environmental Health & Wellness Luncheon Series." You do not want to replace "luncheon" when it refers to a lunchtime event.

**QUICK TIP**

Click Find Next to find, review, and replace each occurrence individually.

5. **Click Replace All**
   Clicking Replace All changes all occurrences of "Luncheon" to "Lecture" in the press release. A message box reports two replacements were made.

6. **Click OK to close the message box, then click Close to close the Find and Replace dialog box**
   Word replaced "Luncheon" with "Lecture" in two locations, but did not replace "luncheon."

7. **Click Edit on the menu bar, then click Find**
   The Find and Replace dialog box opens with the Find tab displayed. The Find command allows you to quickly locate all instances of text in a document. You can use it to verify that Word did not replace "luncheon."

8. **Type luncheon in the Find what text box, click the Highlight all items found in check box to select it, click Find All, then click Close**
   The Find and Replace dialog box closes and "luncheon" is selected in the document, as shown in Figure B-12.

9. **Deselect the text, press [Ctrl][Home], then click the Save button** 🖫 **on the Standard toolbar**

## Clues to Use

### Inserting text with AutoCorrect

As you type, AutoCorrect automatically corrects many commonly misspelled words. By creating your own AutoCorrect entries, you also can set Word to quickly insert text that you type often, such as your name or contact information, or to correct words you frequently misspell. For example, you could create an AutoCorrect entry so that the name "Tony Sanchez, RN" is automatically inserted whenever you type "ts" followed by a space. To create an AutoCorrect entry, click AutoCorrect Options on the Tools menu. On the AutoCorrect tab in the AutoCorrect dialog box, type the text you want to be automatically corrected in the Replace text box (such as "ts"), type the text you want to be automatically inserted in its place in the With text box (such as "Tony Sanchez, RN"), then click Add. The AutoCorrect entry is added to the list. Note that Word inserts an AutoCorrect entry in a document only when you press [Spacebar] after typing the text you want Word to correct. For example, Word will insert "Tony Sanchez, RN" when you type "ts" followed by a space, but not when you type "tsetse."

**FIGURE B-11:** Find and Replace dialog box

Replace only exact matches of uppercase and lowercase characters

Find only complete words

Use wildcards (*) in a search string

Find words that sound like the Find what text

Find and replace all forms of a word

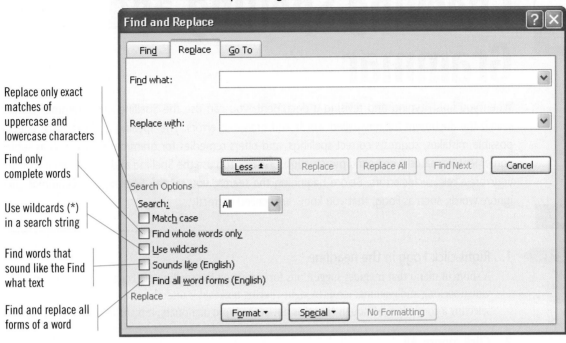

**FIGURE B-12:** Found text highlighted in document

Found text is highlighted

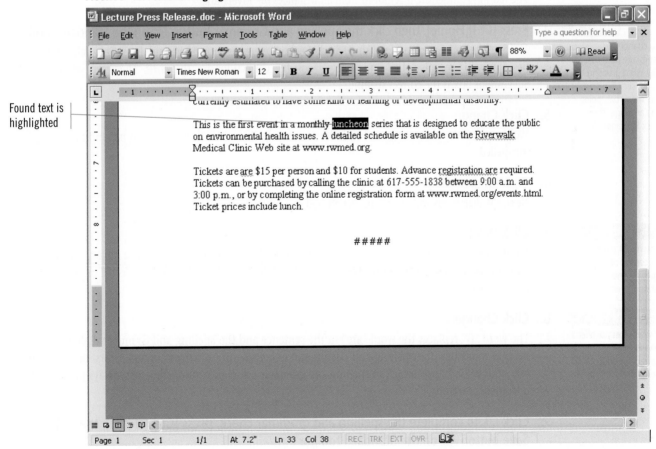

# Checking Spelling and Grammar

When you finish typing and revising a document, you can use the Spelling and Grammar command to search the document for misspelled words and grammar errors. The Spelling and Grammar checker flags possible mistakes, suggests correct spellings, and offers remedies for grammar errors such as subject-verb agreement, repeated words, and punctuation. ▓▓▓▓ You use the Spelling and Grammar checker to search your press release for errors. Before beginning the search, you set the Spelling and Grammar checker to ignore words, such as Fogg, that you know are spelled correctly.

## STEPS

1. **Right-click Fogg in the headline**

   A shortcut menu that includes suggestions for correcting the spelling of "Fogg" opens. You can correct individual spelling and grammar errors by right-clicking text that is underlined with a red or green wavy line and selecting a correction. Although "Fogg" is not in the Word dictionary, it is spelled correctly in the document.

2. **Click Ignore All**

   Clicking Ignore All tells Word not to flag "Fogg" as misspelled.

3. **Right-click Riverwalk at the top of the document, then click Ignore All**

   The red wavy underline is removed from all instances of "Riverwalk."

4. **Press [Ctrl][Home], then click the Spelling and Grammar button ✓ on the Standard toolbar**

   The Spelling and Grammar: English (U.S.) dialog box opens, as shown in Figure B-13. The dialog box identifies "inagural" as misspelled and suggests possible corrections for the error. The word selected in the Suggestions box is the correct spelling.

5. **Click Change**

   Word replaces the misspelled word with the correctly spelled word. Next, the dialog box indicates "Fogg's" is misspelled.

6. **Click Ignore All**

   Next, the dialog box indicates "are" is repeated in a sentence.

7. **Click Delete**

   Word deletes the second occurrence of the repeated word. Next, the dialog box flags a subject-verb agreement error and suggests using "is" instead of "are," as shown in Figure B-14. The phrase selected in the Suggestions box is correct.

8. **Click Change**

   The word "is" replaces the word "are" in the sentence and the Spelling and Grammar dialog box closes. Keep in mind that the Spelling and Grammar checker identifies many common errors, but you cannot rely on it to find and correct all spelling and grammar errors in your documents. Always proofread your documents carefully.

9. **Click OK to complete the spelling and grammar check, press [Ctrl][Home], then click the Save button ⊞ on the Standard toolbar**

**FIGURE B-13:** Spelling and Grammar: English (U.S.) dialog box

Word identified as misspelled

Suggested corrections

Adds the misspelled word and the correction to the AutoCorrect list

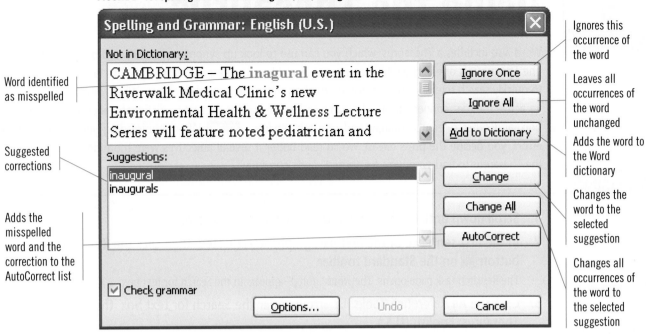

Ignores this occurrence of the word

Leaves all occurrences of the word unchanged

Adds the word to the Word dictionary

Changes the word to the selected suggestion

Changes all occurrences of the word to the selected suggestion

**FIGURE B-14:** Grammar error identified in Spelling and Grammar dialog box

Grammar error identified

Possible corrections

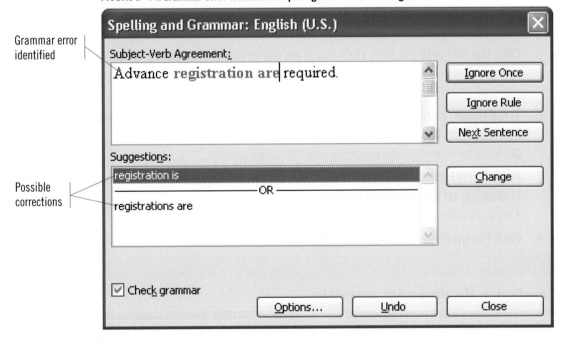

---

## Clues to Use

### Using the Undo, Redo, and Repeat commands

Word remembers the editing and formatting changes you make so that you can easily reverse or repeat them. You can reverse the last action you took by clicking the Undo button on the Standard toolbar, or you can undo a series of actions by clicking the Undo list arrow and selecting the action you want to reverse. When you undo an action using the Undo list arrow, you also undo all the actions above it in the list; that is, all actions that were performed after the action you selected. Similarly, you can keep the changes you just reversed by using the Redo button and the Redo list arrow.

If you want to repeat a change you just made, use the Repeat command on the Edit menu. The name of the Repeat command changes depending on the last action you took. For example, if you just typed "thank you," the name of the command is Repeat Typing. Clicking the Repeat Typing command inserts "thank you" at the location of the insertion point. You also can repeat the last action you took by pressing [F4].

# Using the Thesaurus

Word also includes a Thesaurus, which you can use to look up synonyms for awkward or repetitive words. The Thesaurus is one of the reference sources available in the Research task pane. This task pane allows you to quickly search reference sources for information related to a word or phrase. When you are working with an active Internet connection, the Research task pane provides access to dictionary, encyclopedia, translation, and other reference sources and research services. ▰▰▰▰ After proofreading your document for errors, you decide the press release would read better if several adjectives were more descriptive. You use the Thesaurus to find synonyms for "noted" and "currently".

## STEPS

1. **Scroll down until the headline is displayed at the top of your screen**

2. **In the first sentence of the first paragraph, select noted, then click the Research button 🔍 on the Standard toolbar**

   The Research task pane opens. The word "noted" appears in the Search for text box.

3. **Click the All Reference Books list arrow under the Search for text box, then click Thesaurus: English (U.S.)**

   Possible synonyms for "noted" are listed under the Thesaurus: English (U.S.) heading in the task pane, as shown in Figure B-15.

4. **Point to distinguished in the list of synonyms**

   A box containing an arrow appears around the word.

5. **Click the arrow in the box, click Insert on the menu that appears, then close the Research task pane**

   The word "distinguished" replaces the word "noted" in the press release.

6. **Scroll down, right-click currently in the last sentence of the third paragraph, point to Synonyms on the shortcut menu, then click now**

   The word "now" replaces the word "currently" in the press release.

7. **Press [Ctrl][Home], click the Save button 🖫 on the Standard toolbar, then click the Print button 🖨 on the Standard toolbar**

   A copy of the finished press release prints. Compare your document to Figure B-16.

8. **Click File on the menu bar, then click Close**

## Clues to Use

### Viewing and modifying the document properties

**Document properties** are details about a file that can help you to organize and search your files. The author name, the date the file was created, the title, and keywords that describe the contents of the file are examples of document property information. You can view and modify the properties of an open document by clicking Properties on the File menu to open the Properties dialog box. The General, Statistics, and Contents tabs of the Properties dialog box display information about the file that is automatically created and updated by Word. The General tab shows the file type, location, size, and date and time the file was created and last modified; the Statistics tab displays information about revisions to the document, along with the number of pages, words, lines, paragraphs, and characters in the file; and the Contents tab shows the title of the document.

You can define other document properties using the Summary and Custom tabs of the Properties dialog box. The Summary tab includes identifying information about the document, such as the title, subject, author, and keywords. Some of this information is entered by Word when the document is first saved, but you can modify or add to the summary details by typing new information in the text boxes on the Summary tab. The Custom tab allows you to create new document properties, such as client, project, or date completed. To create a custom property, select a property name in the Name list box on the Custom tab, use the Type list arrow to select the type of data you want for the property, and then type the identifying detail (such as a project name) in the Value text box. When you are finished viewing or modifying the document properties, click OK to close the Properties dialog box.

**FIGURE B-15:** Research task pane

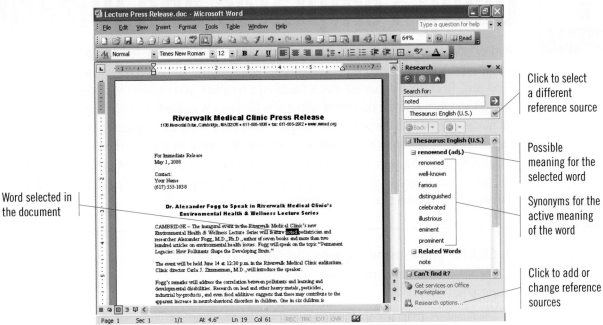

Word selected in
the document

Click to select
a different
reference source

Possible
meaning for the
selected word

Synonyms for the
active meaning
of the word

Click to add or
change reference
sources

**FIGURE B-16:** Completed press release

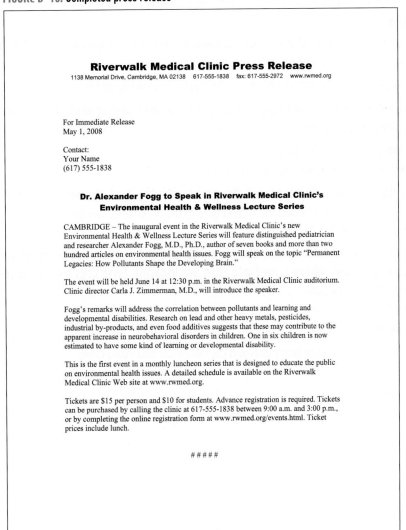

# Using Templates and Wizards

Word includes many templates that you can use to quickly create memos, faxes, letters, reports, brochures, and other professionally designed documents. A **template** is a formatted document that contains place-holder text. To create a document that is based on a template, you replace the placeholder text with your own text and then save the document with a new filename. A **wizard** is an interactive set of dialog boxes that guides you through the process of creating a document. A wizard prompts you to provide information and select formatting options, and then it creates the document for you based on your specifications. You can create a document with a template or wizard using the New command on the File menu. You will fax the press release to your list of press contacts, beginning with the *Boston Globe*. You use a template to create a fax coversheet for the press release.

## STEPS

1. **Click File on the menu bar, then click New**

   The New Document task pane opens.

2. **Click the On my computer hyperlink in the New Document task pane**

   The Templates dialog box opens. The tabs in the dialog box contain icons for the Word templates and wizards.

3. **Click the Letters & Faxes tab, then click the Professional Fax icon**

   A preview of the Professional Fax template appears in the Templates dialog box, as shown in Figure B-17.

   > **QUICK TIP**
   > Double-clicking an icon in the Templates dialog box also opens a new document based on the template.

4. **Click OK**

   The Professional Fax template opens as a new document in the document window. It contains placeholder text, which you can replace with your own information.

5. **Drag to select Company Name Here, type Riverwalk, press [Enter], then type Medical Clinic**

6. **Click the Click here and type return address and phone and fax numbers placeholder**

   Clicking the placeholder selects it. When a placeholder says Click here... you do not need to drag to select it.

7. **Type Tel: (617) 555-1838**

   The text you type replaces the placeholder text.

   > **QUICK TIP**
   > Delete any placeholder text you do not want to replace.

8. **Replace the remaining placeholder text with the text shown in Figure B-18**

   Word automatically inserted the current date in the document. You do not need to replace the current date with the date shown in the figure.

9. **Click File on the menu bar, click Save As, use the Save in list arrow to navigate to the drive or folder where your Data Files are located, type Lecture Fax in the File name text box, then click Save**

   The document is saved with the filename Lecture Fax.

10. **Click the Print button 🖨 on the Standard toolbar, click File on the menu bar, then click Exit**

    A copy of the fax coversheet prints and the document and Word close.

**FIGURE B-17:** Letters & Faxes tab in Templates dialog box

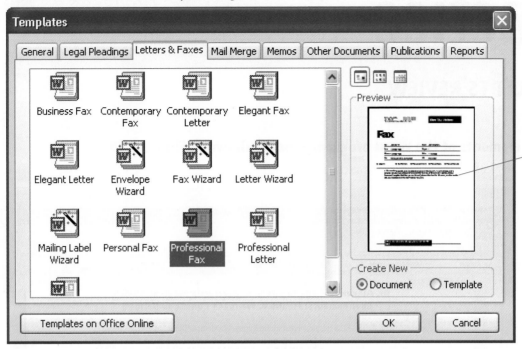

Preview of selected template

**FIGURE B-18:** Completed fax coversheet document

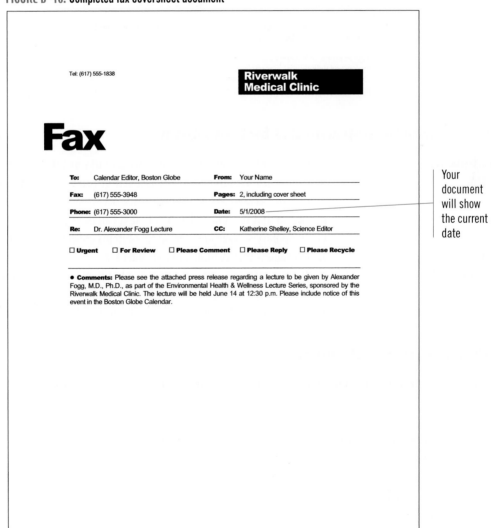

Your document will show the current date

Word 2003

# Practice

## ▼ CONCEPTS REVIEW

**Label the elements of the Word program window shown in Figure B-19.**

FIGURE B-19

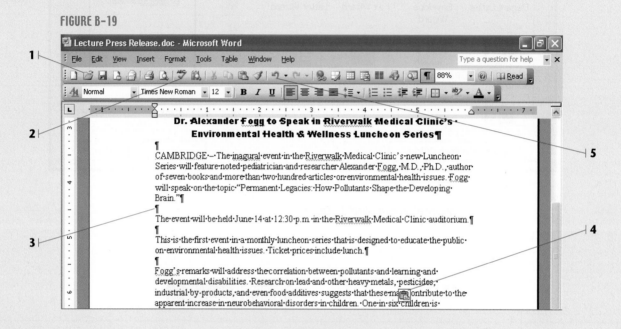

**Match each term with the statement that best describes it.**

6. System Clipboard

7. Show/Hide

8. Select

9. Thesaurus

10. Undo

11. Template

12. Office Clipboard

13. Paste

14. Replace

**a.** Command used to display formatting marks in a document

**b.** Command used to reverse the last action you took in a document

**c.** Command used to locate and replace occurrences of specific text in a document

**d.** Action that must be taken before text can be cut, copied, or deleted

**e.** Temporary storage area for up to 24 items collected from any Office file

**f.** Document that contains placeholder text

**g.** Temporary storage area for only the last item cut or copied from a document

**h.** Feature used to suggest synonyms for words

**i.** Command used to insert text stored on the Clipboard into a document

**Select the best answer from the list of choices.**

15. **What does the symbol ¶ represent when it is displayed in the document window?**

   **a.** A space

   **b.** Hidden text

   **c.** The end of a paragraph

   **d.** A tab stop

16. **Which of the following is *not* used to open an existing document?**

   **a.** Open button on the Standard toolbar

   **b.** Open or More hyperlink in the Getting Started task pane

   **c.** Open command on the File menu

   **d.** Blank document hyperlink in the New Document task pane

**17.** To locate and change all instances of a word in a document, which menu command do you use?

    **a.** Paste                **c.** Find

    **b.** Replace           **d.** Search

**18.** Which of the following statements is *not* true?

    **a.** When you move text by dragging it, a copy of the text you move is stored on the system Clipboard.

    **b.** The last item cut or copied from a document is stored on the system Clipboard.

    **c.** The Office Clipboard can hold more than one item.

    **d.** You can view the contents of the Office Clipboard.

**19.** Which Word feature corrects errors as you type?

    **a.** AutoCorrect         **c.** Undo and Redo

    **b.** Thesaurus           **d.** Spelling and Grammar

**20.** Which command is used to display a document in two panes in the document window?

    **a.** Arrange All          **c.** Split

    **b.** Compare Side by Side with…     **d.** New Window

## ▼ SKILLS REVIEW

**1. Open a document.**

    **a.** Start Word, click the Open button, then open the file WMP B-2.doc from the drive and folder where your Data Files are located.

    **b.** Save the document with the filename **BHF 2008 PR**.

**2. Select text.**

    **a.** Select **Today's Date** and replace it with the current date.

    **b.** Select **Your Name** and **Your Phone Number** and replace them with the relevant information.

    **c.** Scroll down, then select and replace text in the body of the press release using the following table as a guide:

| in paragraph | select | replace with |
|---|---|---|
| 1 | October 13 | **September 22** |
| 1 | eighth | **tenth** |
| 4 | popular folk group Tattoo | **famous children's entertainer Adam Apple** |

    **d.** In the fourth paragraph, delete the sentence **These performances are all free.**

    **e.** Save your changes to the press release.

**3. Cut and paste text.**

    **a.** Display paragraph and other formatting marks in your document if they are not already displayed.

    **b.** Use the Cut and Paste buttons to switch the order of the two sentences in the fourth paragraph (which begins The famous children's entertainer…).

    **c.** Use the drag-and-drop method to switch the order of the second and third paragraphs.

    **d.** Adjust the spacing if necessary so that there is one blank line between paragraphs, then save your changes.

**4. Copy and paste text.**

    **a.** Use the Copy and Paste buttons to copy **BHF 2006** from the headline and paste it before the word **map** in the third paragraph.

    **b.** Change the formatting of the pasted text to match the formatting of the third paragraph, then insert a space between **2006** and **map** if necessary.

    **c.** Use the drag-and-drop method to copy **BHF** from the third paragraph and paste it before the word **stage** in the second sentence of the fourth paragraph, then save your changes.

**5. Use the Office Clipboard.**

  **a.** Use the Office Clipboard command on the Edit menu to open the Clipboard task pane.

  **b.** Scroll so that the first body paragraph is displayed at the top of the document window.

  **c.** Select the fifth paragraph (which begins Health fair maps...) and cut it to the Office Clipboard.

  **d.** Select the third paragraph (which begins Burlington is easily accessible...) and cut it to the Office Clipboard.

  **e.** Use the Office Clipboard to paste the Health fair maps... item as the new fourth paragraph.

  **f.** Use the Office Clipboard to paste the Burlington is easily accessible... item as the new fifth paragraph.

  **g.** Adjust the spacing if necessary so that there is one blank line between each of the six body paragraphs.

  **h.** Turn off the display of formatting marks, clear and close the Office Clipboard, then save your changes.

**6. Find and replace text.**

  **a.** Using the Replace command, replace all instances of **2006** with **2008**.

  **b.** Replace all instances of the abbreviation **st** with **street**, taking care to replace whole words only when you perform the replace. (*Hint*: Click More to expand the Find and Replace dialog box, and then deselect Match case if it is selected.)

  **c.** Use the Find command to find all instances of **st** in the document, and make sure no errors occurred when you replaced st with street. (*Hint*: Deselect the Find whole words only check box.)

  **d.** Save your changes to the press release.

**7. Check Spelling and Grammar and use the Thesaurus.**

  **a.** Move the insertion point to the top of the document, then use the Spelling and Grammar command to search for and correct any spelling and grammar errors in the press release.

  **b.** Use the Thesaurus to replace **famous** in the third paragraph with a different suitable word.

  **c.** Proofread your press release, correct any errors, save your changes, print a copy, then close the document.

**8. Use templates and wizards.**

  **a.** Use the New command to open the New Document task pane.

  **b.** Use the On my computer hyperlink to open the Templates dialog box.

  **c.** Create a new document using the Personal Fax template.

  **d.** Replace the placeholder text in the document using Figure B-20 as a guide. Delete any placeholders that do not apply to your fax. The date in your fax will be the current date.

  **e.** Save the document as **BHF 2008 Fax**, print a copy, close the document, then exit Word.

**FIGURE B-20**

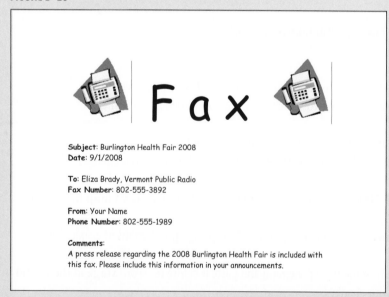

Subject: Burlington Health Fair 2008
Date: 9/1/2008

To: Eliza Brady, Vermont Public Radio
Fax Number: 802-555-3892

From: Your Name
Phone Number: 802-555-1989

Comments:
A press release regarding the 2008 Burlington Health Fair is included with this fax. Please include this information in your announcements.

# ▼ INDEPENDENT CHALLENGE 1

Dr. Callaghan, a physician in your office, is leaving her practice at Rochester General Hospital for a practice at another hospital in Rochester. She asks you to draft a letter to her patients informing them of the move. You'll create a change of address letter for Dr. Callaghan by modifying a letter you wrote for another doctor.

a. Start Word, open the file WMP B-3.doc from the drive and folder where your Data Files are located, then save it as **Change of Address Letter**.

b. Replace the doctor's name and address, the date, the inside address, and the salutation with the text shown in Figure B-21.

c. Use the Replace command to replace all instances of **Saint Mary's** with **Rochester General**.

d. In the second body paragraph, replace the text **1478 Portland Street** with **878 Elmwood Avenue**.

e. Use the Find command to locate the word **superb**, then use the Thesaurus to replace the word with a synonym.

f. Create an AutoCorrect entry that inserts **Strong Memorial Hospital of the University of Rochester** whenever you type **smh**.

g. Select each Highland Hospital, type **smh** followed by a space, then delete the extra space before the period.

h. Move the last sentence of the first body paragraph so that it becomes the first sentence of the third body paragraph.

i. Replace Kate Champlain with Isabella Callaghan in the signature block, then replace the typist's initials yi with your initials.

**FIGURE B-21**

## Isabella Callaghan, M.D.
878 Elmwood Avenue, Rochester, NY 14642; Tel: 585-555-8374

April 14, 2008

Mr. Marshall Ellis
263 Montgomery Street
Rochester, NY 14632

Dear Mr. Ellis,

j. Use the Spelling and Grammar command to check for and correct spelling and grammar errors.

## Advanced Challenge Exercise

■ Open the Properties dialog box, then review the paragraph, line, word, and character count on the Statistics tab.

■ On the Summary tab, change the title to **Isabella Callaghan, M.D.** and add the keywords **address change**.

■ On the Custom tab, add a property named Office with the value **Address Change**, then close the dialog box.

k. Proofread the letter, correct any errors, save your changes, print a copy, close the document, then exit Word.

# ▼ INDEPENDENT CHALLENGE 2

An advertisement for job openings in San Francisco caught your eye and you have decided to apply. The ad, shown in Figure B-22, was printed in last weekend's edition of your local newspaper. You'll use the Letter Wizard to create a cover letter to send with your resume.

**a.** Read the ad shown in Figure B-22 and decide which position to apply for. Choose the position that most closely matches your qualifications.

**b.** Start Word and open the Templates dialog box.

**c.** Double-click Letter Wizard on the Letters & Faxes tab, then select Send one letter in the Letter Wizard dialog box.

**d.** In the Letter Wizard—Step 1 of 4 dialog box, choose to include a date on your letter, select Elegant Letter for the page design, select Modified block for the letter style, include a header and footer with the page design, then click Next.

**e.** In the Letter Wizard—Step 2 of 4 dialog box, enter the recipient's name (Ms. Katherine Winn) and the delivery address, referring to the ad for the address information. Also enter the salutation **Dear Ms. Winn** using the business style, then click Next.

**f.** In the Letter Wizard—Step 3 of 4 dialog box, include a reference line in the letter, enter the appropriate position code (see Figure B-22) in the Reference line text box, then click Next.

**g.** In the Letter Wizard—Step 4 of 4 dialog box, enter your name as the sender, enter your return address, and select an appropriate complimentary closing. Then, because you will be including your resume with the letter, include one enclosure. Click Finish when you are done.

**h.** Save the letter with the filename **Laurel Health Letter** to the drive and folder where your Data Files are located.

**i.** Replace the placeholder text in the body of the letter with three paragraphs that address your qualifications for the job:

- In the first paragraph, specify the job you are applying for, indicate where you saw the position advertised, and briefly state your qualifications and interest in the position.
- In the second paragraph, describe your work experience and skills. Be sure to relate your experience and qualifications to the position requirements listed in the ad.
- In the third paragraph, politely request an interview for the position and provide your phone number and e-mail address.

**j.** When you are finished typing the letter, check it for spelling and grammar errors and correct any mistakes.

**k.** Save your changes to the letter, print a copy, close the document, then exit Word.

**FIGURE B-22**

## *Laurel*Health

### The Neighborhood Health Center

Laurel Comprehensive Community Health Center (LCCHC), offering quality healthcare to the San Francisco community for over thirty years, is seeking candidates for the following positions:

### Registered Nurses
Openings in Adult Medicine and Pediatrics. Must have two years of nursing experience. Current RN license and CPR required. **Position B12C6**

### Laboratory Technician
Perform a variety of routine laboratory tests and procedures. Certification as MLT (ASCP) required, plus two years work experience. **Position C14B5**

### Correspondence Coordinator
Process all correspondence mail in our medical records department. Must have knowledge of HIPAA regulations. Fluency with Microsoft Word required. **Position C13D4**

### Medical Assistant
Maintain patient flow, assist physicians using sterile techniques, and educate patients on health issues. Must enjoy interacting with patients and be proficient with Microsoft Word. MA certification preferred. CPR required. **Position B16F5**

**Positions offer competitive compensation, outstanding benefits, and career growth opportunities.**

*Send resume and cover letter referencing position code to:*

**Katherine Winn**
**Director of Human Resources**
**Laurel Comprehensive Community Health Center**
**3826 Sacramento Street**
**San Francisco, CA 94118**
**Fax to 415-555-2939 or Email to hr@lcchc.com**

# ▼ INDEPENDENT CHALLENGE 3

As director of public affairs education at Hillside Hospital, you drafted a memo to the nursing staff asking them to help you finalize the schedule for the Healthy Living seminar series, which is presented by the nursing staff. Today you'll examine the draft and make revisions before printing it.

   **a.** Start Word and open the file WMP B-4.doc from the drive and folder where your Data Files are located.

   **b.** Open the Save As dialog box, navigate to the drive and folder where your Data Files are located, then use the Create New Folder button to create a new folder called **Memos**.

   **c.** Click the Up One Level button in the dialog box, rename the Memos folder **Healthy Living Memos**, then save the document as **Winter 2009 Memo** in the Healthy Living Memos folder.

   **d.** Replace Your Name with your name in the From line, then scroll down until the first body paragraph is at the top of the screen.

## Advanced Challenge Exercise

   ■ Use the Split command on the Window menu to split the window under the first body paragraph, then scroll until the last paragraph of the memo is displayed in the bottom pane.

   ■ Use the Cut and Paste buttons to move the sentence **If you are planning to lead...** from the first body paragraph to become the first sentence in the last paragraph of the memo.

   ■ Double-click the split bar to restore the window to a single pane.

   **e.** Use the [Delete] key to merge the first two paragraphs into one paragraph.

   **f.** Use the Office Clipboard to reorganize the list of brown bag lunch topics so that the topics are listed in alphabetical order. (*Hint*: Use the Zoom list arrow to enlarge the document as needed.)

   **g.** Use the drag-and-drop method to reorganize the list of Saturday morning lectures so that the lectures are listed in alphabetical order.

   **h.** Use the Spelling and Grammar command to check for and correct spelling and grammar errors. Be sure to read each choice and to make decisions based on the content of the memo.

   **i.** Clear and close the Office Clipboard, save your changes, print a copy, close the document, then exit Word.

# ▼ INDEPENDENT CHALLENGE 4

Reference sources—dictionaries, thesauri, style and grammar guides, and guides to professional etiquette and procedure—are essential for day-to-day use in the workplace. Much of this reference information is available on the World Wide Web. In this independent challenge, you will locate general and medical reference sources on the Web and use some of them to look up definitions of medical terms. Your goal is to familiarize yourself with online reference sources so you can use them later in your work.

   **a.** Start Word, open the file WMP B-5.doc from the drive and folder where your Data Files are located, and save it as **Online Medical References**. This document contains the questions you will answer about the Web reference sources you find. You will type your answers to the questions in the document.

   **b.** Replace the placeholder text at the top of the Online Medical References document with your name and the date.

   **c.** Use your favorite search engine to search the Web for grammar and style guides, dictionaries, and thesauri. Use the keywords **grammar**, **usage**, and **medical dictionary** to conduct your search.

   **d.** Complete the Online Medical References document, then proofread it and correct any mistakes.

   **e.** Save the document, print a copy, close the document, then exit Word.

## ▼ VISUAL WORKSHOP

Using the Professional Letter template, create the letter shown in Figure B-23. Save the document as **Klein Termination Letter**. Check the letter for spelling and grammar errors, then print a copy.

FIGURE B-23

**Your Name, M.D.**

245 Montgomery Street
Syracuse, NY 13218
Phone: 315-555-1728

December 3, 2008

Mr. Martin Klein
44 Burnet Avenue
Syracuse, NY 13219

Dear Mr. Klein:

As a result of a change in our insurance affiliations, I am no longer able to provide medical care to you as your dermatologist. Consequently, you should identify another physician to assume your care. If you have not received a referral to another provider, or if you wish to contact a provider who has not previously cared for you, contact your primary care physician. You may also contact the Onondaga County Medical Society at 315-555-2983.

I will remain available to treat you for a limited time, not to exceed thirty (30) days from the date of this letter. Please try to transfer your care as soon as possible within this period. In the event you have an emergency prior to your transfer of care to another provider, you may contact me through my office.

Copies of your medical record will be sent to the new provider you have selected, upon receipt of your written authorization. A copy of a release form is enclosed for you to complete and return to this office, allowing the record to be transferred.

Sincerely,

Your Name, M.D.

Enc.
Certified Mail, Return Receipt Request
Mailed on December 3, 2008

UNIT
**C**
Word 2003

# Formatting Text and Paragraphs

## OBJECTIVES

| |
|---|
| Format with fonts |
| Change font styles and effects |
| Change line and paragraph spacing |
| Align paragraphs |
| Work with tabs |
| Work with indents |
| Add bullets and numbering |
| Add borders and shading |

If you have a SAM user profile, you may have access to hands-on instruction, practice, and assessment of the skills covered in this unit. Log in to your SAM account and go to your assignments page to see what your instructor has assigned.

Formatting can enhance the appearance of a document, create visual impact, and help illustrate a document's structure. The formatting of a document can also add personality to it and lend it a degree of professionalism. In this unit, you learn how to format text using different fonts and font-formatting options. You also learn how to change the alignment, indentation, and spacing of paragraphs, and how to spruce up documents with borders, shading, bullets, and other paragraph-formatting effects. You have finished drafting the text for an information sheet on the flu to distribute to patients. You now need to format the information sheet so it is attractive and highlights the significant information.

# Formatting with Fonts

Formatting text with different fonts is a quick and powerful way to enhance the appearance of a document. A **font** is a complete set of characters with the same typeface or design. Arial, Times New Roman, Comic Sans, Courier, and Tahoma are some of the more common fonts, but there are hundreds of others, each with a specific design and feel. Another way to alter the impact of text is to increase or decrease its **font size**, which is measured in points. A **point** is 1/72 of an inch. When formatting a document with fonts, it's important to pick fonts and font sizes that augment the document's purpose. You apply fonts and font sizes to text using the Font and Font Size list arrows on the Formatting toolbar. ▨▨▨▨ You change the font and font size of the title and headings in the information sheet, selecting a font that enhances the tone of the document. By formatting the title and headings in a font different from the body text, you help to visually structure the information sheet for readers.

## STEPS

1. **Start Word, open the file** WMP C-1.doc **from the drive and folder where your Data Files are located, then save it as** Flu Info Sheet

   The file opens in Print Layout view.

2. **Click the** Normal View button ▤ **on the horizontal scroll bar, click the** Zoom list arrow **on the Standard toolbar, then click 100% if necessary**

   The document switches to Normal view, a view useful for simple text formatting. The name of the font used in the document, Times New Roman, is displayed in the Font list box on the Formatting toolbar. The font size, 12, appears next to it in the Font Size list box.

3. **Select the title** Riverwalk Medical Clinic Influenza Information Sheet, **then click the** Font list arrow **on the Formatting toolbar**

   The Font list, which shows the fonts available on your computer, opens as shown in Figure C-1. Fonts you have used recently appear above the double line. All the fonts on your computer are listed in alphabetical order below the double line. You can click the font name in either location on the Font list to apply the font to the selected text.

4. **Click** Arial

   The font of the title changes to Arial.

5. **Click the** Font Size list arrow **on the Formatting toolbar, then click 20**

   The font size of the title increases to 20 points.

6. **Click the** Font Color list arrow ▲▾ **on the Formatting toolbar**

   A palette of colors opens.

7. **Click** Plum **on the Font Color palette, as shown in Figure C-2, then deselect the text**

   The color of the title text changes to plum. The active color on the Font Color button also changes to plum.

8. **Scroll down until the heading** Flu Statistics **is at the top of your screen, select** Flu Statistics, **press and hold** [Ctrl], **select the heading** Flu Vaccine, **then release** [Ctrl]

   The Flu Statistics and Flu Vaccine headings are selected. Selecting multiple items allows you to format several items at once.

9. **Click the** Font list arrow, **click** Arial, **click the** Font Size list arrow, **click 14, click the** Font Color button ▲, **then deselect the text**

   The headings are formatted in 14-point Arial with a plum color.

10. **Press** [Ctrl][Home], **then click the** Save button ▥ **on the Standard toolbar**

    Pressing [Ctrl][Home] moves the insertion point to the beginning of the document. Compare your document to Figure C-3.

FIGURE C-1: Font list

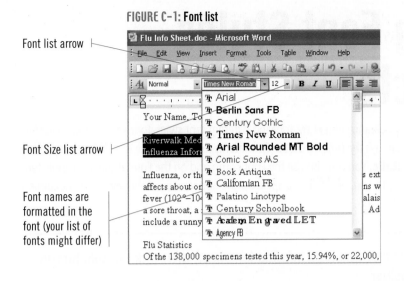

Font list arrow

Font Size list arrow

Font names are formatted in the font (your list of fonts might differ)

FIGURE C-2: Font Color palette

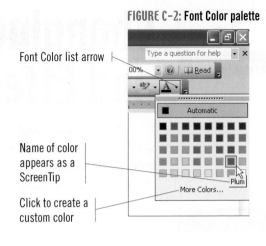

Font Color list arrow

Name of color appears as a ScreenTip

Click to create a custom color

FIGURE C-3: Document formatted with fonts

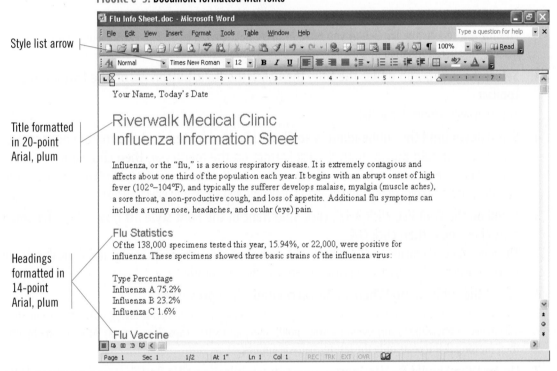

Style list arrow

Title formatted in 20-point Arial, plum

Headings formatted in 14-point Arial, plum

---

## Clues to Use

### Adding a drop cap

A fun way to illustrate a document with fonts is to add a drop cap to a paragraph. A **drop cap** is a large initial capital letter, often used to set off the first paragraph of an article. To create a drop cap, place the insertion point in the paragraph you want to format, and then click Drop Cap on the Format menu to open the Drop Cap dialog box. In the Drop Cap dialog box, shown in Figure C-4, select the position, font, number of lines to drop, and the distance you want the drop cap to be from the paragraph text, and then click OK to create the drop cap. The drop cap is added to the paragraph as a graphic object.

After a drop cap is inserted in a paragraph, you can modify it by selecting it and then changing the settings in the Drop Cap dialog box. For even more interesting effects, try enhancing a drop cap with font color, font styles, or font effects, or try filling the graphic object with shading or adding a border around it. To enhance a drop cap, first select it, and then experiment with the formatting options available in the Font dialog box and in the Borders and Shading dialog box.

FIGURE C-4: Drop Cap dialog box

Word 2003

# Changing Font Styles and Effects

You can dramatically change the appearance of text by applying different font styles, font effects, and character-spacing effects. For example, you can use the buttons on the Formatting toolbar to make text darker by applying **bold**, or to slant text by applying **italic**. You can also use the Font command on the Format menu to apply font effects and character-spacing effects to text. ▰▰▰ You spice up the appearance of the text in the document by applying different font styles and effects.

## STEPS

**QUICK TIP**

Click the Underline button **U** on the Formatting toolbar to underline text.

1. **Select** Riverwalk Medical Clinic Influenza Information Sheet, **then click the** Bold button **B** **on the Formatting toolbar**

   Applying bold makes the characters in the title darker and thicker.

2. **Select** Flu Statistics, **click** **B**, **select** Flu Vaccine, **then press** [F4]

   Pressing [F4] repeats the last action you took, in this case applying bold. The Flu Statistics and Flu Vaccine headings are both formatted in bold.

3. **Select the** paragraph **under the title, then click the** Italic button **I** **on the Formatting toolbar**

   The paragraph is formatted in italic.

4. **Scroll down until the subheading** Who Should Be Vaccinated **is at the top of your screen, select** Who Should Be Vaccinated, **click** Format **on the menu bar, then click** Font

   The Font dialog box opens, as shown in Figure C-5. You can use options on the Font tab to change the font, font style, size, and color of text, and to add an underline and apply font effects to text.

**QUICK TIP**

To hide the selected text, click the Hidden check box on the Font tab. Hidden text is displayed when formatting marks are turned on.

5. **Scroll up the Font list, click** Arial, **click** Bold Italic **in the Font style list box, select the** Small caps check box, **then click** OK

   The subheading is formatted in Arial, bold, italic, and small caps. When you change text to small caps, the lowercase letters are changed to uppercase letters in a smaller font size.

6. **Select the subheading** When To Be Vaccinated, **then press** [F4]

   Because you formatted the previous subheading in one action (using the Font dialog box), the When To Be Vaccinated subheading is formatted in Arial, bold, italic, and small caps. If you apply formats one by one, then pressing [F4] repeats only the last format you applied.

7. **Under Who Should Be Vaccinated, select the publication title** Bed Rest and Plenty of H2O: Cures for the Flu?, **click** **I**, **select** 2 **in the publication title, click** Format **on the menu bar, click** Font, **click the** Subscript check box, **click** OK, **then deselect the text**

   The publication title is formatted in italic and the character 2 is subscript, as shown in Figure C-6.

**QUICK TIP**

To animate the selected text, click the Text Effects tab in the Font dialog box, then select an animation style. The animation appears only when a document is viewed in Word; animation effects do not print.

8. **Press** [Ctrl][Home], **select the** title, **click** Format **on the menu bar, click** Font, **then click the** Character Spacing tab **in the Font dialog box**

   You use the Character Spacing tab to change the scale, or width, of the selected characters, to alter the spacing between characters, or to raise or lower the position of the characters.

9. **Click the** Scale list arrow, **click** 150%, **click** OK, **deselect the text, then click the** Save button **🖫** **on the Standard toolbar**

   Increasing the scale of the characters makes them wider and gives the text a short, squat appearance, as shown in Figure C-7.

**FIGURE C-5:** Font tab in the Font dialog box

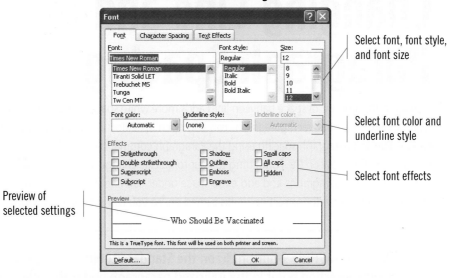

Select font, font style, and font size

Select font color and underline style

Select font effects

Preview of selected settings

**FIGURE C-6:** Font effects applied to text

Subhead formatted in 12-point Arial, bold, italic, and small caps

Publication title formatted in italic

Subscript text

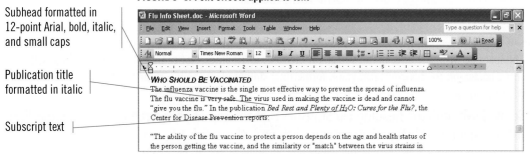

**FIGURE C-7:** Character spacing effect applied to text

Document title formatted in bold with a character scale of 150%

Paragraph formatted in italic

Headings formatted in bold

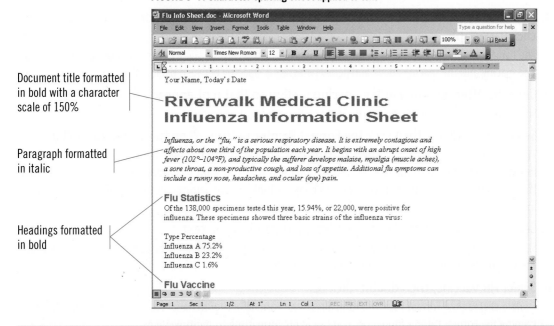

---

## Clues to Use

### Changing the case of letters

The Change Case command on the Format menu allows you to quickly change letters from uppercase to lowercase—and vice versa—saving you the time it takes to retype text you want to change. To change the case of selected text, use the Change Case command to open the Change Case dialog box, then select the case style you want to use. Sentence case capitalizes the first letter of a sentence, title case capitalizes the first letter of each word, and toggle case switches all letters to the opposite case.

# Changing Line and Paragraph Spacing

Increasing the amount of space between lines adds more white space to a document and can make it easier to read. Adding space between paragraphs can also open up a document and improve its appearance. You can change line and paragraph spacing using the Paragraph command on the Format menu. You can also use the Line Spacing list arrow on the Formatting toolbar to quickly change line spacing. ████████ You increase the line spacing of several paragraphs and add extra space under each heading to give the information sheet a more open feel. You work with formatting marks turned on, so you can see the paragraph marks (¶).

1. **Click the Show/Hide ¶ button ¶ on the Standard toolbar to display formatting marks, place the insertion point in the italicized paragraph under the title, then click the Line Spacing list arrow ▯▯ on the Formatting toolbar**
   The Line Spacing list opens. This list includes options for increasing the space between lines.

2. **Click 1.5**
   The space between the lines in the paragraph increases to 1.5 lines. Notice that you do not need to select an entire paragraph to change its paragraph formatting; simply place the insertion point in the paragraph you want to format.

3. **Scroll down until the heading Flu Statistics is at the top of your screen, select the four-line list that begins with Type Percentage, click ▯▯, then click 1.5**
   The line spacing between the selected paragraphs changes to 1.5. To change the paragraph-formatting features of more than one paragraph, you must select the paragraphs.

4. **Place the insertion point in the heading Flu Statistics, click Format on the menu bar, then click Paragraph**
   The Paragraph dialog box opens, as shown in Figure C-8. You can use the Indents and Spacing tab to change line spacing and the spacing above and below paragraphs. Spacing between paragraphs is measured in points.

5. **Click the After up arrow in the Spacing section so that 6 pt appears, then click OK**
   Six points of space are added below the Flu Statistics heading paragraph.

6. **Select Flu Statistics, then click the Format Painter button ✐ on the Standard toolbar**
   The pointer changes to ✐I. The **Format Painter** is a powerful Word feature that allows you to copy all the format settings applied to the selected text to other text that you want to format the same way. The Format Painter is especially useful when you want to copy multiple format settings, but you can also use it to copy individual formats.

7. **Select Flu Vaccine with the ✐I pointer, then deselect the text**
   Six points of space are added below the Flu Vaccine heading paragraph, and the pointer changes back to the I-beam pointer. Compare your document to Figure C-9.

8. **Select Flu Vaccine, then double-click ✐**
   Double-clicking the Format Painter button allows the Format Painter to remain active until you turn it off. By keeping the Format Painter turned on, you can apply formatting to multiple items.

9. **Scroll down, select the headings Other Flu Prevention Measures, Treatment, and Medications with the ✐I pointer, then click ✐ to turn off the Format Painter**
   The headings are formatted in 14-point Arial, bold, plum, with six points of space added below each heading paragraph.

10. **Press [Ctrl][Home], click ¶, then click the Save button 🖫 on the Standard toolbar**

FIGURE C-8: Indents and Spacing tab in the Paragraph dialog box

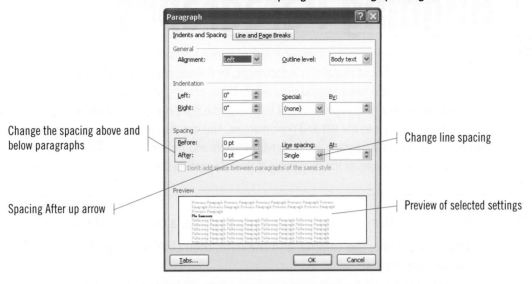

Change the spacing above and below paragraphs

Change line spacing

Spacing After up arrow

Preview of selected settings

FIGURE C-9: Line and paragraph spacing applied to document

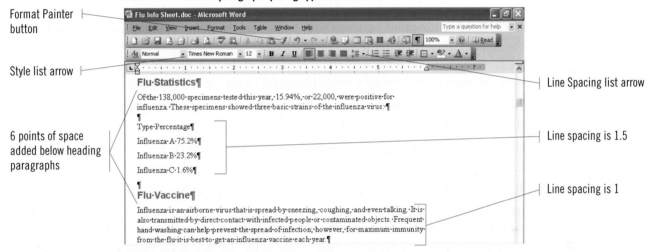

Format Painter button

Style list arrow

Line Spacing list arrow

6 points of space added below heading paragraphs

Line spacing is 1.5

Line spacing is 1

Word 2003

## Clues to Use

### Formatting with styles

You can also apply multiple format settings to text in one step by applying a style. A **style** is a set of formats, such as font, font size, and paragraph alignment, that are named and stored together. Styles can be applied to text, paragraphs, lists, and tables. To work with styles, click the Styles and Formatting button ![44] on the Formatting toolbar to open the Styles and Formatting task pane , as shown in Figure C-10. The task pane displays the list of available styles and the formats you have created for the current document. To view all the styles available in Word, click the Show list arrow at the bottom of the task pane, then click All Styles.

A **character style**, indicated by **a** in the list of styles, includes character format settings, such as font and font size. A **paragraph style**, indicated by **¶** in the list of styles, is a combination of character and paragraph formats, such as font, font size, paragraph alignment, paragraph spacing, indents, and bullets and numbering. A **table style**, indicated by **⊞** in the list of styles, includes format settings for text in tables, as well as for table borders, shading, and alignment. Finally, a **list style**, indicated by **≔** in the list of styles, includes indent and numbering format settings for an outline numbered list.

To apply a style, select the text, paragraph, or table you want to format, then click the style name in the Pick formatting to apply list box. To remove styles from text, select the text, then click Clear Formatting in the Pick formatting to apply list box. You can also apply and remove styles using the Style list arrow on the Formatting toolbar.

FIGURE C-10: Styles and Formatting task pane

# Aligning Paragraphs

Changing paragraph alignment is another way to enhance a document's appearance. Paragraphs are aligned relative to the left and right margins in a document. By default, text is **left-aligned**, which means it is flush with the left margin and has a ragged right edge. Using the alignment buttons on the Formatting toolbar, you can **right-align** a paragraph—make it flush with the right margin—or **center** a paragraph so that it is positioned evenly between the left and right margins. You can also **justify** a paragraph so that both the left and right edges of the paragraph are flush with the left and right margins. You change the alignment of several paragraphs at the beginning of the information sheet to make it more visually interesting.

## STEPS

1. **Replace** Your Name, Today's Date **with your name, a comma, and the date**

2. **Select** your name, **the** comma, **and the** date, **then click the** Align Right button ≡ **on the Formatting toolbar**

   The text is aligned with the right margin. In Normal view, the junction of the white and shaded sections of the horizontal ruler indicates the location of the right margin. The left end of the ruler indicates the left margin.

3. **Place the insertion point between your name and the comma, press** [Delete] **to delete the comma, then press** [Enter]

   The new paragraph containing the date is also right-aligned. Pressing [Enter] in the middle of a paragraph creates a new paragraph with the same text and paragraph formatting as the original paragraph.

4. **Select the** title, **then click the** Center button ≡ **on the Formatting toolbar**

   The two paragraphs that make up the title are centered between the left and right margins.

**QUICK TIP**

Click the Align Left button ≡ on the Formatting toolbar to left-align a paragraph.

5. **Place the insertion point in the** Flu Statistics **heading, then click** ≡

   The Flu Statistics heading is centered.

6. **Place the insertion point in the italicized paragraph under the title, then click the** Justify button ≡

   The paragraph is aligned with both the left and right margins, as shown in Figure C-11. When you justify a paragraph, Word adjusts the spacing between words so that each line in the paragraph is flush with the left and the right margins.

7. **Place the insertion point in** Riverwalk **in the title, click** Format **on the menu bar, then click** Reveal Formatting

   The Reveal Formatting task pane opens in the Word program window, as shown in Figure C-12. The Reveal Formatting task pane shows the formatting applied to the text and paragraph where the insertion point is located. You can use the Reveal Formatting task pane to check or change the formatting of any character, word, paragraph, or other aspect of a document.

8. **Select** Flu Statistics, **then click the** Alignment **hyperlink in the Reveal Formatting task pane**

   The Paragraph dialog box opens with the Indents and Spacing tab displayed. It shows the settings for the selected text.

9. **Click the** Alignment list arrow, **click** Left, **click** OK, **then deselect the text**

   The Flu Statistics heading is left-aligned.

10. **Close the Reveal Formatting task pane, then click the** Save button ≡ **on the Standard toolbar**

**FIGURE C-11:** Modified paragraph alignment

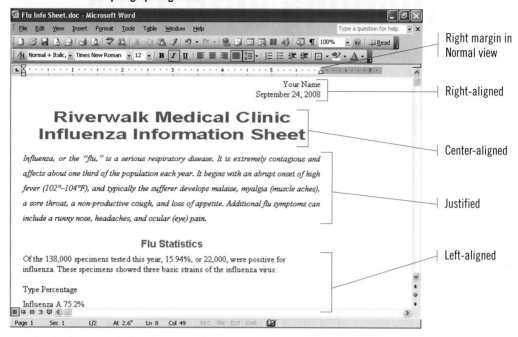

Right margin in Normal view

Right-aligned

Center-aligned

Justified

Left-aligned

**FIGURE C-12:** Reveal Formatting task pane

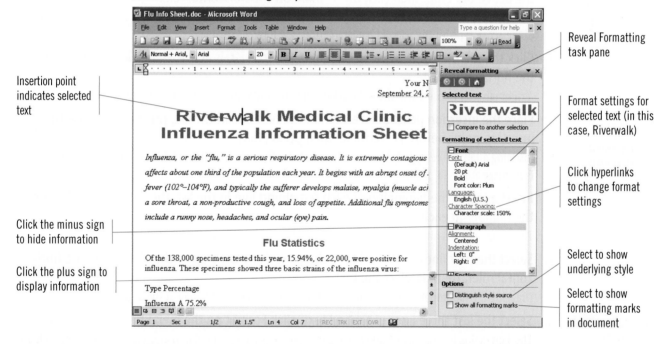

Insertion point indicates selected text

Click the minus sign to hide information

Click the plus sign to display information

Reveal Formatting task pane

Format settings for selected text (in this case, Riverwalk)

Click hyperlinks to change format settings

Select to show underlying style

Select to show formatting marks in document

## Clues to Use

### Comparing formatting

When two words or paragraphs in a document do not look exactly the same but you are not certain of the formatting differences, you can use the Reveal Formatting task pane to compare the two selections to determine the differences. To compare the formatting of two text selections, select the first instance, select the Compare to another selection check box in the Reveal Formatting task pane, and then select the second instance. Differences in formatting between the two selections are listed in the Formatting differences section in the Reveal Formatting task pane. You can then use the

hyperlinks in the Formatting differences section to make changes to the formatting of the second selection. If you want to format the second selection so that it matches the first, you can click the list arrow next to the second selection in the Selected text section, and then click Apply Formatting of Original Selection on the menu that appears. On the same menu, you can also click Select All Text with Similar Formatting to select all the text in the document that is formatted the same, or Clear Formatting to return the formatting of the selected text to the default.

# Working with Tabs

Tabs allow you to align text vertically at a specific location in a document. A **tab stop** is a point on the horizontal ruler that indicates the location at which to align text. By default, tab stops are located every ½" from the left margin, but you can also set custom tab stops. Using tabs, you can align text to the left, right, or center of a tab stop, or you can align text at a decimal point or bar character. You set tabs using the horizontal ruler or the Tabs command on the Format menu. You use tabs to format the statistical information so it is easy to read.

## STEPS

1. **Scroll down until the heading Flu Statistics is at the top of your screen, then select the four-line list beginning with Type Percentage**

   Before you set tab stops for existing text, you must select the paragraphs for which you want to set tabs.

**TROUBLE**

If the horizontal ruler is not visible, click Ruler on the View menu.

2. **Point to the tab indicator 🔲 at the left end of the horizontal ruler**

   The icon that appears in the tab indicator indicates the active type of tab; pointing to the tab indicator displays a ScreenTip with the name of the active tab type. By default, left tab is the active tab type. Clicking the tab indicator scrolls through the types of tabs and indents.

3. **Click the tab indicator to see each of the available tab and indent types, make left tab 🔲 the active tab type, then click the 1" mark on the horizontal ruler**

   A left tab stop is inserted at the 1" mark on the horizontal ruler. Clicking the horizontal ruler inserts a tab stop of the active type for the selected paragraph or paragraphs.

4. **Click the tab indicator twice so the Right Tab icon 🔲 is active, then click the 4½" mark on the horizontal ruler**

   A right tab stop is inserted at the 4½" mark on the horizontal ruler, as shown in Figure C-13.

**QUICK TIP**

Never use the Spacebar to vertically align text; always use tabs or a table.

5. **Place the insertion point before Type in the first line in the list, press [Tab], place the insertion point before Percentage, then press [Tab]**

   Inserting a tab before Type left-aligns the text at the 1" mark. Inserting a tab before Percentage right-aligns Percentage at the 4½" mark.

6. **Insert a tab at the beginning of each remaining line in the list, then insert a tab before the number in each line**

   The paragraphs left-align at the 1" mark. The numbers right-align at the 4½" mark.

7. **Select the four lines of tabbed text, drag the right tab stop to the 5" mark on the horizontal ruler, then deselect the text**

   Dragging the tab stop moves it to a new location. The numbers right-align at the 5" mark.

**QUICK TIP**

Place the insertion point in a paragraph to see the tab stops for that paragraph on the horizontal ruler.

8. **Select the last three lines of tabbed text, click Format on the menu bar, then click Tabs**

   The Tabs dialog box opens, as shown in Figure C-14. You can use the Tabs dialog box to set tab stops, change the position or alignment of existing tab stops, clear tab stops, and apply tab leaders to tabs. **Tab leaders** are lines that appear in front of tabbed text.

9. **Click 5" in the Tab stop position list box, click the 2 option button in the Leader section, click OK, deselect the text, then click the Save button 🔲 on the Standard toolbar**

   A dotted tab leader is added before each 5" tab stop, as shown in Figure C-15.

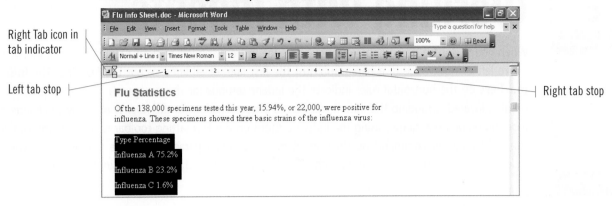

**FIGURE C-13: Left and right tab stops on the horizontal ruler**

Right Tab icon in tab indicator

Left tab stop

Right tab stop

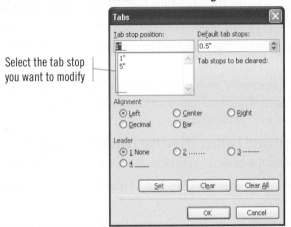

**FIGURE C-14: Tabs dialog box**

Select the tab stop you want to modify

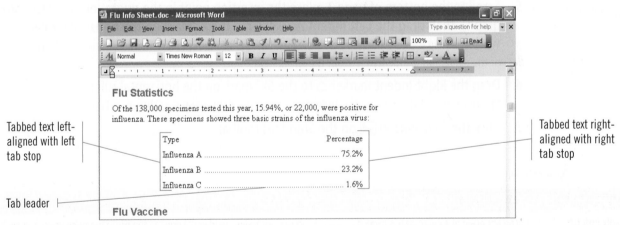

**FIGURE C-15: Tab leaders**

Tabbed text left-aligned with left tab stop

Tabbed text right-aligned with right tab stop

Tab leader

## Clues to Use

### Working with Click and Type

The **Click and Type** feature in Word allows you to automatically apply the paragraph formatting (alignment and indentation) necessary to insert text, graphics, or tables in a blank area of a document in Print Layout or Web Layout view. As you move the pointer around in a blank area of a document, the pointer changes depending on its location. Double-clicking with a click and type pointer in a blank area of a document automatically applies the appropriate alignment and indentation for that location, so that when you begin typing, the text is already formatted. The pointer shape indicates which formatting is applied at each location when you double-click. For example, if you click with the $\underline{\underline{I}}$ pointer, the text you type is center-aligned. Clicking with $I\overline{\overline{\phantom{=}}}$ creates a left tab stop at the location of the insertion point so that the text you type is left-aligned at the tab stop. Clicking with $\overline{\overline{\phantom{=}}}I$ right-aligns the text you type. The $I\overline{\overline{\phantom{=}}}$ pointer creates left-aligned text with a first line indent. The best way to learn how to use Click and Type is to experiment in a blank document.

# Working with Indents

When you **indent** a paragraph, you move its edge in from the left or right margin. You can indent the entire left or right edge of a paragraph, just the first line, or all lines except the first line. The **indent markers** on the horizontal ruler indicate the indent settings for the paragraph in which the insertion point is located. Dragging the indent markers to a new location on the ruler is one way to change the indentation of a paragraph; using the indent buttons on the Formatting toolbar is another. You can also use the Paragraph command on the Format menu to indent paragraphs. Table C-1 describes types of indents and the methods for creating each. ▒▒▒▒ You indent several paragraphs in the information sheet.

## STEPS

1. **Press [Ctrl][Home], click the Print Layout View button ▣ on the horizontal scroll bar, click the Zoom list arrow on the Standard toolbar, then click Page Width**

   The document is displayed in Print Layout view, making it easier to see the document margins.

2. **Place the insertion point in the italicized paragraph under the title, then click the Increase Indent button ▦ on the Formatting toolbar**

   The entire paragraph is indented ½" from the left margin, as shown in Figure C-16. The indent marker △ also moves to the ½" mark on the horizontal ruler. Each time you click the Increase Indent button, the left edge of a paragraph moves another ½" to the right.

3. **Click the Decrease Indent button ▦ on the Formatting toolbar**

   The left edge of the paragraph moves ½" to the left, and the indent marker moves back to the left margin.

4. **Drag the First Line Indent marker ▽ to the ¼" mark on the horizontal ruler, as shown in Figure C-17**

   The first line of the paragraph is indented ¼". Dragging the first line indent marker indents only the first line of a paragraph.

5. **Scroll to the bottom of page 1, place the insertion point in the quotation (the last paragraph), then drag the Left Indent marker ☐ to the ½" mark on the horizontal ruler**

   When you drag the Left Indent marker, the First Line and Hanging Indent markers move as well. The left edge of the paragraph is indented ½" from the left margin.

6. **Drag the Right Indent marker △ to the 5½" mark on the horizontal ruler**

   The right edge of the paragraph is indented ½" from the right margin, as shown in Figure C-18.

7. **Click the Save button ▦ on the Standard toolbar**

**TABLE C-1: Types of indents**

| indent type | description | to create |
|---|---|---|
| Left indent | The left edge of a paragraph is moved in from the left margin | Drag the Left Indent marker ☐ right to the position where you want the left edge of the paragraph to align, or click the Increase Indent button ▦ to indent the paragraph in ½" increments |
| Right indent | The right edge of a paragraph is moved in from the right margin | Drag the Right Indent marker △ left to the position where you want the right edge of the paragraph to end |
| First-line indent | The first line of a paragraph is indented more than the subsequent lines | Drag the First Line Indent marker ▽ right to the position where you want the first line of the paragraph to start |
| Hanging indent | The subsequent lines of a paragraph are indented more than the first line | Drag the Hanging Indent marker △ right to the position where you want the hanging indent to start |
| Negative indent (or Outdent) | The left edge of a paragraph is moved to the left of the left margin | Drag the Left Indent marker ☐ left to the position where you want the negative indent to start |

**FIGURE C-16: Indented paragraph**

First Line Indent marker

Hanging Indent marker

Left Indent marker

Indented paragraph

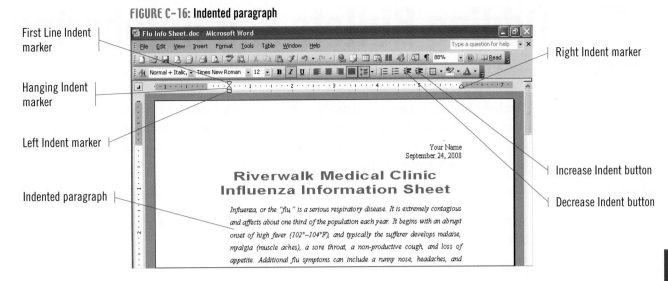

Right Indent marker

Increase Indent button

Decrease Indent button

**FIGURE C-17: Dragging the First Line Indent marker**

First Line Indent marker being dragged to the ¼" mark

Dotted line shows position of First Line Indent marker

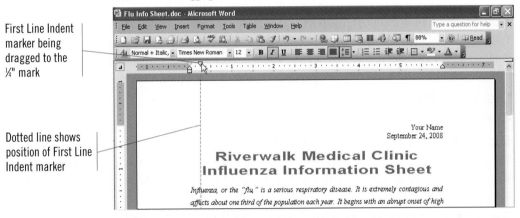

**FIGURE C-18: Paragraph indented from the left and right**

Paragraph indented ½" from left margin

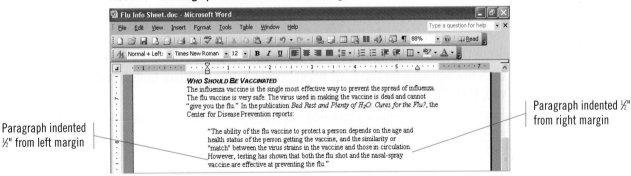

Paragraph indented ½" from right margin

---

### Clues to Use

#### Clearing formatting

If you are unhappy with the way text is formatted, you can use the Clear Formats command to return the text to the default format settings. By default, text is formatted in 12-point Times New Roman, and paragraphs are left-aligned and single-spaced with no indents.

To clear formatting from text, select the text you want to clear, point to Clear on the Edit menu, then click Formats. Alternately, click the Style list arrow on the Formatting toolbar, then click Clear Formatting.

# Adding Bullets and Numbering

Formatting a list with bullets or numbering can help to organize the ideas in a document. A **bullet** is a character, often a small circle, that appears before the items in a list to add emphasis. Formatting a list as a numbered list helps illustrate sequences and priorities. You can quickly format a list with bullets or numbering by using the Bullets and Numbering buttons on the Formatting toolbar. You can also use the Bullets and Numbering command on the Format menu to change or customize bullet and numbering styles. ░░░░ You format the lists in the information sheet with numbers and bullets.

## STEPS

1. **Scroll down until the first paragraph on the second page (There are certain...) is at the top of your screen**

2. **Select the** four-line list **under the paragraph, then click the** Numbering button ▤ **on the Formatting toolbar**
   The paragraphs are formatted as a numbered list.

3. **Place the insertion point after** vaccine. **at the end of the third line, press [Enter], then type** An active neurological disorder.
   Pressing [Enter] in the middle of the numbered list creates a new numbered paragraph and automatically renumbers the remainder of the list. Similarly, if you delete a paragraph from a numbered list, Word automatically renumbers the remaining paragraphs.

4. **Click** 1 **in the list**
   Clicking a number in a list selects all the numbers, as shown in Figure C-19.

5. **Click the** Bold button **B** **on the Formatting toolbar**
   The numbers are all formatted in bold. Notice that the formatting of the items in the list does not change when you change the formatting of the numbers. You can also use this technique to change the formatting of bullets in a bulleted list.

6. **Select the** list of prevention measures **under the Other Flu Prevention Measures heading, scrolling down if necessary, then click the** Bullets button ▤ **on the Formatting toolbar**
   The five paragraphs are formatted as a bulleted list.

7. **With the list still selected, click** Format **on the menu bar, then click** Bullets and Numbering
   The Bullets and Numbering dialog box opens with the Bulleted tab displayed, as shown in Figure C-20. You use this dialog box to apply bullets and numbering to paragraphs, or to change the style of bullets or numbers.

8. **Click the** Square bullets box **or select another style if square bullets are not available to you, click** OK, **then deselect the text**
   The bullet character changes to a small square, as shown in Figure C-21.

9. **Click the** Save button ▤ **on the Standard toolbar**

### Clues to Use

#### Creating outlines

You can create lists with hierarchical structures by applying an outline numbering style to a list. To create an outline, begin by applying an outline numbering style from the Outline Numbered tab in the Bullets and Numbering dialog box, then type your outline, pressing [Enter] after each item. To demote items to a lower level of importance in the outline, place the insertion point in the item, then click the Increase Indent button ▤ on the Formatting toolbar. Each time you indent a paragraph, the item is demoted to a lower level in the outline. Similarly, you can use the Decrease Indent button ▤ to promote an item to a higher level in the outline. You can also create a hierarchical structure in any bulleted or numbered list by using ▤ and ▤ to demote and promote items in the list. To change the outline numbering style applied to a list, select a new style from the Outline Numbered tab in the Bullets and Numbering dialog box.

**FIGURE C-19: Numbered list**

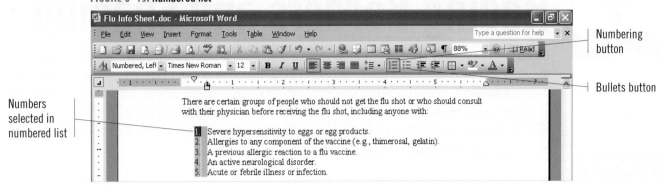

Numbering button

Bullets button

Numbers selected in numbered list

**FIGURE C-20: Bulleted tab in the Bullets and Numbering dialog box**

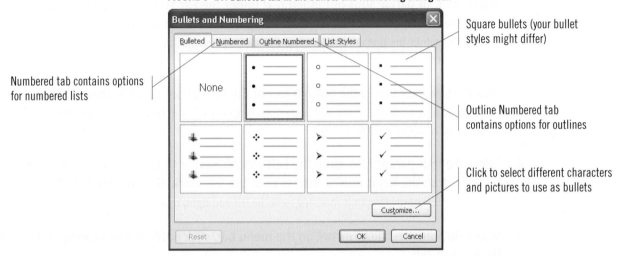

Square bullets (your bullet styles might differ)

Numbered tab contains options for numbered lists

Outline Numbered tab contains options for outlines

Click to select different characters and pictures to use as bullets

**FIGURE C-21: Square bullets applied to list**

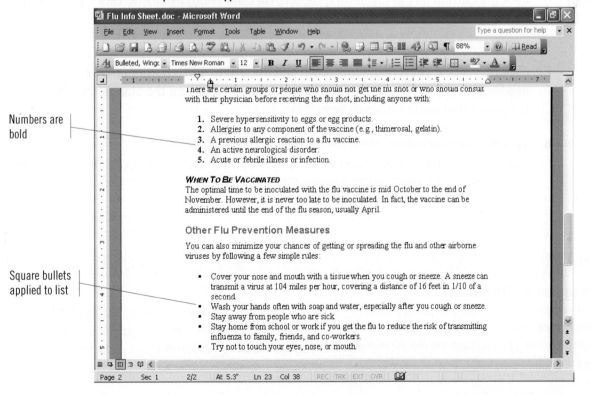

Numbers are bold

Square bullets applied to list

# Adding Borders and Shading

Borders and shading can add color and splash to a document. **Borders** are lines you add above, below, to the side, or around words or a paragraph. You can format borders using different line styles, colors, and widths. **Shading** is a color or pattern you apply behind words or paragraphs to make them stand out on a page. You apply borders and shading using the Borders and Shading command on the Format menu. You enhance the flu statistics table by adding shading to it. You also apply a border under every heading to visually punctuate the sections of the information sheet.

## STEPS

1. **Scroll up until the heading Flu Statistics is at the top of your screen**

2. **Select the four paragraphs of tabbed text under the Flu Statistics heading, click Format on the menu bar, click Borders and Shading, then click the Shading tab**
   The Shading tab in the Borders and Shading dialog box is shown in Figure C-22. You use this tab to apply shading to words and paragraphs.

3. **Click the Lavender box in the bottom row of the Fill section, click OK, then deselect the text**
   Lavender shading is applied to the four paragraphs. Notice that the shading is applied to the entire width of the paragraphs, despite the tab settings.

4. **Select the four paragraphs, drag the Left Indent marker □ to the ¾" mark on the horizontal ruler, drag the Right Indent marker △ to the 5¼" mark, then deselect the text**
   The shading for the paragraphs is indented from the left and right, making it look more attractive.

5. **Select Flu Statistics, click Format on the menu bar, click Borders and Shading, then click the Borders tab**
   The Borders tab is shown in Figure C-23. You use this tab to add boxes and lines to words or paragraphs.

6. **Click the Custom box in the Setting section, click the Width list arrow, click ¾ pt, click the Bottom Border button ▦ in the Preview section, click OK, then deselect the text**
   A ¾-point black border is added below the Flu Statistics paragraph.

7. **Click Flu Vaccine, press [F4], scroll down and use [F4] to add a border under each plum heading, press [Ctrl] [Home], then click the Save button ▦ on the Standard toolbar**
   The completed document is shown in Figure C-24.

8. **Click the Print button ⎙, close the document, then exit Word**
   A copy of the information sheet prints. Depending on your printer, colors might appear differently when you print. If you are using a black-and-white printer, colors will print in shades of gray.

## Clues to Use

### Highlighting text in a document
The Highlight tool allows you to mark and find important text in a document. **Highlighting** is transparent color that is applied to text using the Highlight pointer ⁄. To highlight text, click the Highlight list arrow ▾ on the Formatting toolbar, select a color, then use the I-beam part of the ⁄ pointer to select the text. Click ▾ to turn off the Highlight pointer. To remove highlighting, select the highlighted text, click ▾, then click None. Highlighting prints, but it is used most effectively when a document is viewed on screen.

## FIGURE C-22: Shading tab in the Borders and Shading dialog box

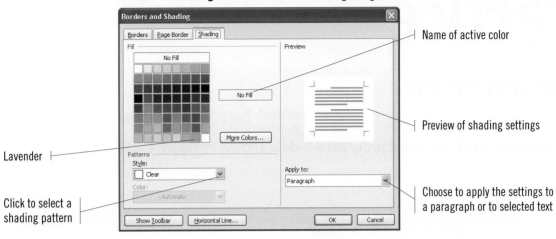

Name of active color

Preview of shading settings

Lavender

Click to select a shading pattern

Choose to apply the settings to a paragraph or to selected text

## FIGURE C-23: Borders tab in the Borders and Shading dialog box

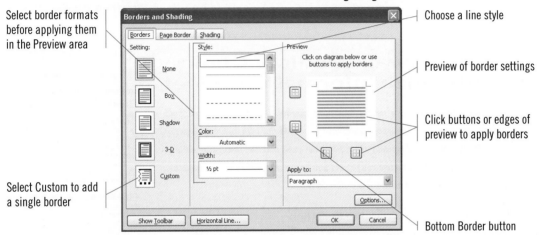

Select border formats before applying them in the Preview area

Choose a line style

Preview of border settings

Click buttons or edges of preview to apply borders

Select Custom to add a single border

Bottom Border button

## FIGURE C-24: Borders and shading applied to the document

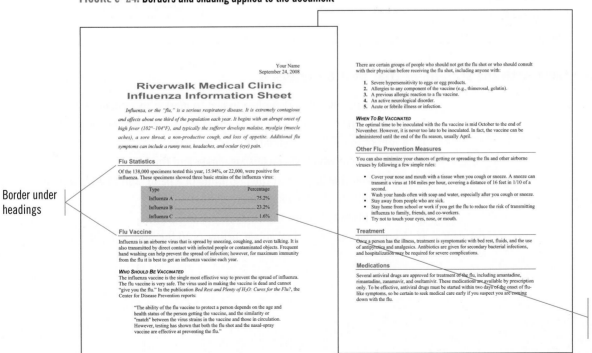

Border under headings

Shading applied to paragraphs

Word 2003

# Practice

## ▼ CONCEPTS REVIEW

**Label each element of the Word program window shown in Figure C-25.**

FIGURE C-25

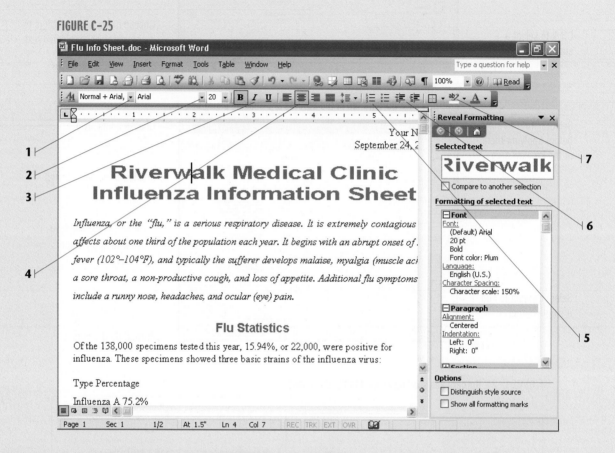

**Match each term with the statement that best describes it.**

8. **Bold**

9. **Shading**

10. **Point**

11. **Style**

12. **Italic**

13. **Highlight**

14. **Bullet**

15. **Border**

a. Transparent color that is applied to text to mark it in a document

b. Color or a pattern that is applied behind text to make it look attractive

c. A unit of measurement equal to ½ of an inch

d. A text style in which characters are darker and thicker

e. A character that appears at the beginning of a paragraph to add emphasis

f. A text style in which characters are slanted

g. A set of format settings

h. A line that can be applied above, below, or to the sides of a paragraph

## Select the best answer from the list of choices.

**16. What is Arial?**
- **a.** A character format
- **b.** A style
- **c.** A font
- **d.** A text effect

**17. What is the most precise way to increase the amount of white space between two paragraphs?**
- **a.** Use the Paragraph command to change the spacing below the first paragraph.
- **b.** Indent the paragraphs.
- **c.** Change the line spacing of the paragraphs.
- **d.** Insert an extra blank line between the paragraphs.

**18. What element of the Word program window can be used to check the tab settings applied to text?**
- **a.** Standard toolbar
- **b.** Formatting toolbar
- **c.** Styles and Formatting task pane
- **d.** Reveal Formatting task pane

**19. Which command would you use to change the scale of characters?**
- **a.** Paragraph
- **b.** Change Case
- **c.** Styles and Formatting
- **d.** Font

**20. Which button is used to align a paragraph with both the left and right margins?**
- **a.**
- **b.**
- **c.**
- **d.**

# ▼ SKILLS REVIEW

**1. Format with fonts.**
- **a.** Start Word, open the file WMP C-2.doc from the drive and folder where your Data Files are located, save it as **Scheduling Guidelines**, then scroll through the document to get a feel for its contents.
- **b.** Press [Ctrl][Home], format the title **Saint Monique Family Health Guidelines for Scheduling and Processing Patients** in 26-point Tahoma. Choose a different font if Tahoma is not available to you.
- **c.** Change the font color of the title to Teal.
- **d.** Place the insertion point in the first body paragraph under the title, then add a two-line drop cap to the paragraph using the Dropped position.
- **e.** Format each of the following headings in 14-point Tahoma with the Teal font color: **Our policy, Five-step approach... Determining the time... Processing new patients**.
- **f.** Press [Ctrl][Home], then save your changes to the document.

**2. Change font styles and effects.**
- **a.** Apply bold to the document title and to each heading in the document.
- **b.** Show formatting marks, then format the paragraph under the Our policy heading in italic.
- **c.** Format **Appointment Time**, the first line in the six-line list under the Determining the time... heading, in bold, small caps, with a Teal font color.
- **d.** Change the font color of the next five lines under Appointment Time to Teal.
- **e.** Scroll to the top of the document, change the character scale of **Saint Monique Family Health** to 80%, then save your changes.

**3. Change line and paragraph spacing.**

**a.** Change the line spacing of the three-line list under the first body paragraph to 1.5 lines.

**b.** Add 12 points of space before the Guidelines for Scheduling... line in the title.

**c.** Add 12 points of space after each heading in the document (but not the title).

**d.** Add 6 points of space after each paragraph in the list under the Five-step approach... heading.

**e.** Add 6 points of space after each paragraph under the Processing new patients heading.

**f.** Press [Ctrl][Home], then save your changes to the document.

**4. Align paragraphs.**

**a.** Press [Ctrl][A] to select the entire document, then justify all the paragraphs.

**b.** Center the three-line title.

**c.** Press [Ctrl][End], type your name, press [Enter], type the current date, then right-align your name and the date.

**d.** Save your changes to the document.

**5. Work with tabs.**

**a.** Scroll up and select the six-line list of appointment time information under the Determining the time... heading.

**b.** Set left tab stops at the 1¾" mark and the 4" mark.

**c.** Insert a tab at the beginning of each line in the list.

**d.** In the first line, insert a tab before Time. In the second line, insert a tab before 45. In the remaining lines, insert a tab before each number.

**e.** Select all the lines, then drag the second tab stop to the 3½" mark on the horizontal ruler.

**f.** Select the last five lines, then insert dotted line tab leaders before the 3.5" tab stop.

**g.** Press [Ctrl][Home], then save your changes to the document.

**6. Work with indents.**

**a.** Indent the paragraph under the Our policy heading ½" from the left and ½" from the right.

**b.** Indent the first line of each of the three body paragraphs under the Determining the time... heading ½".

**c.** Press [Ctrl][Home], then save your changes to the document.

**7. Add bullets and numbering.**

**a.** Apply bullets to the three-line list under the first body paragraph.

**b.** Change the bullet style to small black circles (or choose another bullet style if small black circles are not available to you).

**c.** Change the font color of the bullets to Teal.

**d.** Scroll down until the Five-step approach... heading is at the top of your screen.

**e.** Format the five-paragraph list under the Five-step approach...heading as a numbered list.

**f.** Format the numbers in 11-point Tahoma bold, then change the font color to Teal.

**g.** Scroll down until the Processing new patients heading is near the top of your screen, then format the paragraphs under the heading as a bulleted list using check marks as the bullet style. If checkmarks are not available, click Reset or choose another bullet style.

**h.** Change the font color of the bullets to Teal if necessary, press [Ctrl][Home], then save your changes to the document.

**8. Add borders and shading.**

**a.** Change the font color of **Saint Monique Family Health Guidelines for Scheduling and Processing Patients** to Light Yellow, apply Teal shading to the paragraphs, then change the font color of **Saint Monique Family Health** to White.

**b.** Add a 1-point Teal border below the Our policy heading.

**c.** Use the Format Painter to copy the formatting of the Our policy heading to the other headings in the document.

**d.** Under the Determining the time... heading, select the six lines of tabbed text, which are formatted in Teal.

**e.** Apply Light Yellow shading to the paragraphs, then add a 1-point Teal box border around the paragraphs.

**f.** Indent the shading and border around the paragraphs 1½" from the left and 1½" from the right.

**g.** Press [Ctrl][Home], save your changes to the document, view the document in Print Preview, then print a copy. The formatted document is shown in Figure C-26.

**h.** Close the file and exit Word.

FIGURE C-26

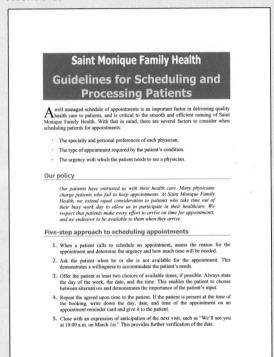
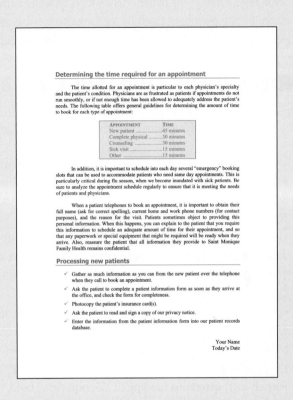

# ▼ INDEPENDENT CHALLENGE 1

You work for Metropolitan Eye Associates. Your boss has given you the text for a Notice of Patient Rights and Responsibilities and asked you to format it on letterhead. It's important that the Notice have a clean, striking design, and reflect the practice's professionalism.

**a.** Start Word, open the file WMP C-3.doc from the drive and folder where your Data Files are located, save it as **Patient Rights**, then read the document to get a feel for its contents. Figure C-27 shows how you will format the letterhead.

FIGURE C-27

**Metropolitan Eye Associates**

Karl Rattan, M.D.   Margaret Canton, M.D.   Elise McDonald, M.D.   Edward Kaplan, M.D.

1900 East Prairie SE, Suite 108  |  Grand Rapids, MI 49503  |  tel: 616-555-2921  |  fax: 616-555-2231

**b.** In the first paragraph, format **Metropolitan Eye Associate** in 28-point Arial Black, then change the character scale to 90%. (*Hint*: Select a similar font if Arial Black is not available to you.)

**c.** Format the second line in 10-point Arial, bold, format the third line in 9-point Arial, then center the three-line letterhead.

**d.** Change the paragraph spacing of the second line to add 3 points of space below, then add a 1-point black border above the third line.

**e.** Format the title **Patient Rights and Responsibilities** in 16-point Arial Black, then center the title.

**f.** Format the following headings (including the colons) in 12-point Arial Black: **Your Rights as a Patient**, **Your Responsibilities as a Patient**, **Advance Directives**, **Financial Concerns**, **Income Guidelines**, and **Acknowledgement of Receipt...**

**g.** Format the lists under **Your Rights as a Patient** and **Your Responsibilities as a Patient** as bulleted lists, using a bullet style of your choice.

## ▼ INDEPENDENT CHALLENGE 1 (CONTINUED)

**h.** Apply bold italic to Living Wills and Durable Powers of Attorney for Healthcare under the Advance Directives heading.

**i.** Center the heading Income Guidelines, select the 9-line list under the heading, then set left tab stops at the 1½", 2½", and 3½" mark. With the list selected, set a right tab stop at the 5¾" mark, insert tabs before every line in the list, then insert tabs before every $.

**j.** Select Family Size No Charge Reduced Rate, then apply an underline.

**k.** Type your name as the patient name, then type the current date.

**l.** Examine the document carefully for formatting errors and make any necessary adjustments.

**m.** Save and print the document, then close the file and exit Word.

## ▼ INDEPENDENT CHALLENGE 2

Your employer, Learn and Be Healthy, is a nonprofit organization devoted to educating the public on health issues. Your boss has written the text for a flyer about Peripheral Artery Disease, and asks you to format it so that it is eye catching and attractive.

**a.** Open the file WMP C-4.doc from the drive and folder where your Data Files are located, save it as **PAD Flyer**, then read the document. Figure C-28 shows how you will format the first several paragraphs of the flyer.

**b.** Select the entire document and format it in 10-point Arial Narrow.

**c.** Center the first line, **LEARN AND BE HEALTHY**, and apply indigo shading to the paragraph. Format the text in 18-point Arial Black, with a white font color. Expand the character spacing by 5 points.

**d.** Format the second line, **Peripheral Artery Disease**, in 48-point Arial Narrow, bold, and change the character scale to 90%. Center the line, then add 12 points of space before the paragraph.

FIGURE C-28

**LEARN AND BE HEALTHY**

**Peripheral Artery Disease**

What is peripheral artery disease?
Peripheral artery disease (PAD) is a circulation disorder that is caused by fatty buildups (atherosclerosis) in the inner walls of arteries. These fatty buildups block normal blood flow. PAD is a type of peripheral vascular disease (PVD), which refers to diseases of blood vessels outside the heart and brain.

**e.** Format each **question** heading in 12-point Arial, bold, with an indigo font color. Add a single line ½-point border under each heading.

**f.** Format each subheading (**PAD may require... and Lifestyle changes...**) in 10-point Arial, bold. Add 3 points of spacing before each paragraph.

**g.** Indent each body paragraph and subheading ¼", except for the last two lines in the document.

**h.** Format the three lines under the PAD may require... subheading as a bulleted list. Use a bullet symbol of your choice and format the bullets in the indigo color.

**i.** Format the six lines under the Lifestyle changes...subheading as a bulleted list. Use the Format Painter to copy the indigo bullet style you just created to the six-line list.

**j.** Format the **For more information...** heading in 14-point Arial, bold, with an indigo font color, then center the heading.

**k.** Format the last line in 11-point Arial Narrow, and center the line. In the contact information, replace Your Name with your name, then apply bold to your name.

### Advanced Challenge Exercise

■ At the top of the page, change the font color of **Peripheral Artery Disease** to 80% gray and add a shadow effect.

■ Add an emboss effect to each question heading.

■ Add a 3-point dotted black border above the **For more information...** heading.

**l.** Examine the document carefully for formatting errors and make any necessary adjustments.

**m.** Save and print the flyer, then close the file and exit Word.

## ▼ INDEPENDENT CHALLENGE 3

One of your responsibilities as patient care coordinator at Upper Valley Healthcare is to facilitate patient-staff interactions to achieve excellent care for patients at the facility. You have drafted a memo to Upper Valley Healthcare staff to outline several ways they can encourage patients to be involved in their own healthcare. You need to format the memo so it is professional looking and easy to read.

**a.** Start Word, open the file WMP C-5.doc from the drive and folder where your Data Files are located, then save it as **Upper Valley Memo**.

**b.** Select the heading **Upper Valley Healthcare Memorandum**, then apply the paragraph style Heading 1 to it. (*Hint*: Open the Styles and Formatting task pane, click the Show list arrow, click Available styles if necessary, then click Heading 1.)

**c.** In the memo header, replace Today's Date and Your Name with the current date and your name.

**d.** Select the four-line memo header, set a left tab stop at the ¾" mark, then insert tabs before the date, the recipient's name, your name, and the subject of the memo.

**e.** Double-space the four lines in the memo header, then apply the character style Strong to **Date:**, **To:**, **From:**, and **Re:**.

**f.** Apply a 1½-point double line border below the blank line under the memo header. (*Hint*: Turn on formatting marks, select the paragraph symbol below the memo header, then apply a border below it.)

**g.** Apply the paragraph style Heading 3 to the headings **Encourage questions**, **Offer an interpreter**, **Identify yourself**, and **Ensure medication safety**.

**h.** Under the Offer an interpreter heading, format the words **Interpreters' hours** and **Languages** in bold italic.

**i.** Add 6 points of space before the Interpreters' hours and Languages paragraphs.

### Advanced Challenge Exercise

■ Use the **Change Case** command to change the case of the headings formatted with the Heading 3 style in the body of the memo to uppercase.

■ Center the heading **Upper Valley Healthcare Memorandum**, change the font size to 22, then apply an outline effect.

■ In the Interpreters' hours paragraph, apply yellow highlighting to the times.

**j.** On the second page of the document, format the list under the **Ensure medication safety** heading as an outline. Figure C-29 shows the hierarchical structure of the outline. (*Hint*: Format the list as an outline numbered list, then use the Increase Indent and Decrease Indent buttons to change the level of importance of each item.)

**k.** Change the outline numbering style to the bullet numbering style shown in Figure C-29, if necessary.

**l.** Save and print the document, then close the file and exit Word.

**FIGURE C-29**

> ❖ Information patients need to share with healthcare providers
> > ➢ Details about *everything* they take
> > > ▪ Prescription medications
> > > ▪ Non-prescription medications
> > > > • Aspirin
> > > > • Antacids
> > > > • Laxatives
> > > > • Cough medicines
> > > > • Etc.
> > > ▪ Vitamins
> > > ▪ Herbs or other supplements
> > > > • St. John's Wort
> > > > • Ginko biloba
> > > > • Etc.
> > ➢ Information about allergic reactions to medications
> > > ▪ Rashes
> > > ▪ Difficulty breathing
> > > ▪ Etc.
> > ➢ Details of illnesses or medical conditions
> > > ▪ High blood pressure
> > > ▪ Glaucoma
> > > ▪ Diabetes
> > > ▪ Thyroid disease
> > > ▪ Etc.
> ❖ Information healthcare providers need to share with patients
> > ➢ What each prescribed medication is and what it is for
> > > ▪ Name of medication
> > > ▪ Purpose of medication
> > > ▪ Dosage
> > > ▪ Side effects
> > > ▪ Drug interactions
> > ➢ Written directions for the dosage and purpose
> > > ▪ "Take once a day for high blood pressure"

## ▼ INDEPENDENT CHALLENGE 4

The fonts you choose for a document can have a major effect on the document's tone. Not all fonts are appropriate for use in a medical document, and some fonts, especially those with a definite theme, are appropriate only for specific purposes. The World Wide Web includes hundreds of Web sites devoted to fonts and text design. Some Web sites sell fonts, others allow you to download fonts for free and install them on your computer. In this Independent Challenge, you will research Web sites related to fonts and find examples of fonts you can use in your work.

**a.** Start Word, open the file WMP C-6.doc from the drive and folder where your Data Files are located, and save it as **Font Research**. This document contains the questions you will answer about the fonts you find.

**b.** Use your favorite search engine to search the Web for Web sites related to fonts. Use the keyword font to conduct your search.

**c.** Explore the fonts available for downloading. As you examine the fonts, notice that fonts fall into two general categories: serif fonts, which have a small stroke, called a serif, at the ends of each character, and sans serif fonts, which do not have a serif. Times New Roman is an example of a serif font and Arial is an example of a sans serif font.

**d.** Replace Your Name and Today's Date with the current date and your name, type your answers in the Font Research document, save it, print a copy, then close the file and exit Word.

Using the file WMP C-7.doc found in the drive and folder where your Data Files are located, create the flyer shown in Figure C-30. (*Hints*: Use Berlin Sans FB or a similar font, such as Eras Demi ITC or Tahoma. Use paragraph spacing to adjust the spacing between paragraphs so that all the text fits on one page.) Save the menu as **Simple Steps**, then print a copy.

FIGURE C-30

# Simple Steps

## 10 Week Adult Weight Management and Exercise Program

This series will help you find a balanced approach to healthy eating and consistent activity. The program includes group exercise, behavioral nutrition classes, and individual counseling.

### Free information session
### Wednesday, April 20th, 6 p.m.
The Wellness Center at Mountain Community Hospital

## Call: 555-3374

**Program participants receive:**
- A free fitness assessment
- An individualized fitness plan
- A pedometer

| Register by: | **April 27th** |
|---|---|
| Classes begin: | **May 4th** |
| Space is limited: | **Call today!** |

*Fee for the program is $259. The cost may be reimbursed by insurance. For more information, contact Your Name.*

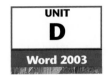

UNIT
**D**
Word 2003

# Creating and Formatting Tables

## OBJECTIVES

| |
|---|
| Insert a table |
| Insert and delete rows and columns |
| Modify table rows and columns |
| Sort table data |
| Split and merge cells |
| Perform calculations in tables |
| Use Table AutoFormat |
| Create a custom format for a table |

If you have a SAM user profile, you may have access to hands-on instruction, practice, and assessment of the skills covered in this unit. Log in to your SAM account and go to your assignments page to see what your instructor has assigned.

Tables are commonly used to display information for quick reference and analysis. In this unit, you learn how to create and modify a table in Word, how to sort table data and perform calculations, and how to format a table with borders and shading. You also learn how to use a table to structure the layout of a page. You are preparing a summary budget for an advertising campaign aimed at the greater Cambridge market. The goal of the ad campaign is to educate the community about the services provided by the Riverwalk Medical Clinic, and to attract new patients. You decide to format the budget information as a table so that it is easy to read and analyze.

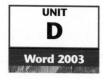

# Inserting a Table

A **table** is a grid made up of rows and columns of cells that you can fill with text and graphics. A **cell** is the box formed by the intersection of a column and a row. The lines that divide the columns and rows and help you see the grid-like structure of a table are called **borders**. You can create a table in a document by using the Insert Table button on the Standard toolbar or the Insert command on the Table menu. Once you have created a table, you can add text and graphics to it. You begin by inserting a blank table into the document and then adding text to it.

**STEPS**

1. **Start Word, close the** Getting Started task pane, **click the** Print Layout View button 🖻 **on the horizontal scroll bar if it is not already selected, click the** Zoom list arrow **on the Standard toolbar, then click** Page Width

   A blank document appears in Print Layout view.

2. **Click the** Insert Table button 🎬 **on the Standard toolbar**

   A grid opens below the button. You move the pointer across this grid to select the number of columns and rows you want the table to contain. If you want to create a table with more than five columns or more than four rows, then expand the grid by dragging the lower-right corner.

3. **Point to the** second box **in the fourth row to select 4x2 Table, then click**

   A table with two columns and four rows is inserted in the document, as shown in Figure D-1. Black borders surround the table cells. The insertion point is in the first cell in the first row.

4. **Type** Location, **then press** [Tab]

   Pressing [Tab] moves the insertion point to the next cell in the row.

5. **Type** Cost, **press** [Tab], **then type** Boston Globe

   Pressing [Tab] at the end of a row moves the insertion point to the first cell in the next row.

6. **Press** [Tab], **type** 5,075, **press** [Tab], **then type the following text in the table, pressing** [Tab] **to move from cell to cell**

   | | |
   |---|---|
   | Switchboard.com | 1,080 |
   | Cambridge River Fest | 450 |

7. **Press** [Tab]

   Pressing [Tab] at the end of the last cell of a table creates a new row at the bottom of the table, as shown in Figure D-2. The insertion point is located in the first cell in the new row.

**TROUBLE**

If you pressed [Tab] after the last row, click the Undo button 🔄 on the Standard toolbar to remove the new blank row.

8. **Type the following, pressing** [Tab] **to move from cell to cell and to create new rows**

   | | |
   |---|---|
   | Boston Herald | 1,760 |
   | MyPages.com | 480 |
   | Mass mailing | 1,560 |
   | Cambridge Chronicle | 1,840 |

9. **Click the** Save button 🖫 **on the Standard toolbar, then save the document with the filename** Clinic Ad Budget **to the drive and folder where your Data Files are located**

   The table is shown in Figure D-3.

**FIGURE D-1: Blank table**

Column

Table move handle

Insertion point

Row

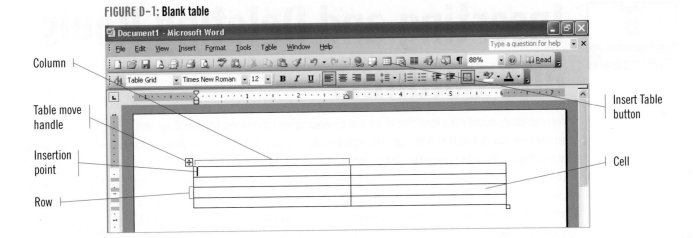

Insert Table button

Cell

**FIGURE D-2: New row in table**

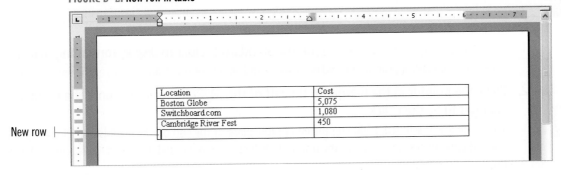

| Location | Cost |
|---|---|
| Boston Globe | 5,075 |
| Switchboard.com | 1,080 |
| Cambridge River Fest | 450 |

New row

**FIGURE D-3: Text in the table**

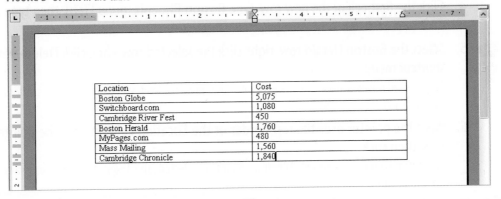

| Location | Cost |
|---|---|
| Boston Globe | 5,075 |
| Switchboard.com | 1,080 |
| Cambridge River Fest | 450 |
| Boston Herald | 1,760 |
| MyPages.com | 480 |
| Mass Mailing | 1,560 |
| Cambridge Chronicle | 1,840 |

### Clues to Use

### Converting text to a table and a table to text

Another way to create a table is to convert text that is separated by a tab, a comma, or another separator character into a table. For example, if you want to create a two-column table of last and first names, you could type the names as a list with a comma separating the last and first name in each line, and then convert the text to a table. The separator character—a comma in this example—indicates where you want to divide the table into columns, and a paragraph mark indicates where you want to begin a new row. To convert tabbed or comma-delimited text to a table, select the text, point to

Convert on the Table menu, and then click Text to Table. In the Convert Text to Table dialog box, select from the options for structuring and formatting the table, and then click OK to create the table. You can also select the text and then click the Insert Table button on the Standard toolbar to convert the text to a table.

Conversely, you can convert a table to text that is separated by tabs, commas, or some other character by selecting the table, pointing to Convert on the Table menu, and then clicking Table to Text.

# Inserting and Deleting Rows and Columns

You can easily modify the structure of a table by adding and removing rows and columns. First, you must select an existing row or column in the table to indicate where you want to insert or delete information. You can select any element of a table using the Select command on the Table menu, but it is often easier to select rows and columns using the mouse: click in the margin to the left of a row to select the row; click the top border of a column to select the column. Alternatively, you can drag across a row or down a column to select it. To insert rows and columns, use the Insert command on the Table menu or the Insert Rows and Insert Columns buttons on the Standard toolbar. To delete rows and columns, use the Delete command on the Table menu. You add a new row to the table and delete an unnecessary row. You also add new columns to the table to provide more detailed information.

**STEPS**

1. **Click the Show/Hide ¶ button ¶ on the Standard toolbar to display formatting marks**
   An end of cell mark appears at the end of each cell and an end of row mark appears at the end of each row.

2. **Place the pointer in the margin to the left of the MyPages.com row until the pointer changes to ⌐, then click**
   The entire row is selected, including the end of row mark. If the end of row mark is not selected, you have selected only the text in a row, not the row itself. When a row is selected, the Insert Table button changes to the Insert Rows button.

3. **Click the Insert Rows button ⊞ on the Standard toolbar**
   A new row is inserted above the MyPages.com row, as shown in Figure D-4.

4. **Click the first cell of the new row, type Boston Phoenix, press [Tab], then type 2,580**
   Clicking in a cell moves the insertion point to that cell.

5. **Select the Boston Herald row, right-click the selected row, then click Delete Rows on the shortcut menu**
   The selected row is deleted. If you select a row and press [Delete], you delete only the contents of the row, not the row itself.

6. **Place the pointer over the top border of the Location column until the pointer changes to ↓, then click**
   The entire column is selected. When a column is selected, the Insert Table button changes to the Insert Columns button.

7. **Click the Insert Columns button ⊞ on the Standard toolbar, then type Type**
   A new column is inserted to the left of the Location column, as shown in Figure D-5.

8. **Click in the Location column, click Table on the menu bar, point to Insert, click Columns to the Right, then type Details in the first cell of the new column**
   A new column is added to the right of the Location column. You can also use the Insert command to add columns to the left of the active column or to insert rows above or below the active row.

9. **Press [↓] to move the insertion point to the next cell in the Details column, enter the text shown in Figure D-6 in each cell in the Details and Type columns, click ¶ to turn off the display of formatting marks, then save your changes**
   You can use the arrow keys to move the insertion point from cell to cell. Notice that text wraps to the next line in the cell as you type. Compare your table to Figure D-6.

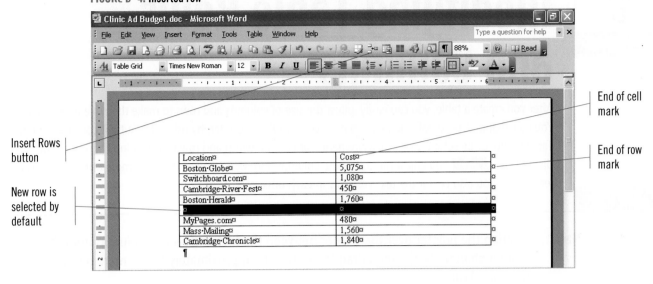

Insert Rows button

End of cell mark

End of row mark

New row is selected by default

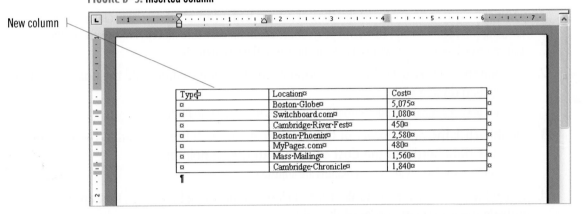

New column

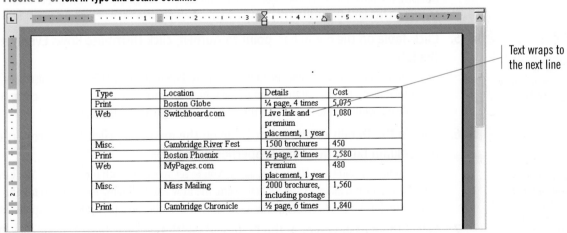

Text wraps to the next line

| Type | Location | Details | Cost |
|------|----------|---------|------|
| Print | Boston Globe | ¼ page, 4 times | 5,075 |
| Web | Switchboard.com | Live link and premium placement, 1 year | 1,080 |
| Misc. | Cambridge River Fest | 1500 brochures | 450 |
| Print | Boston Phoenix | ½ page, 2 times | 2,580 |
| Web | MyPages.com | Premium placement, 1 year | 480 |
| Misc. | Mass Mailing | 2000 brochures, including postage | 1,560 |
| Print | Cambridge Chronicle | ½ page, 6 times | 1,840 |

## Clues to Use

### Copying and moving rows and columns

You can copy and move rows and columns within a table in the same manner you copy and move text. Select the row or column you want to move, then use the Copy or Cut button to place the selection on the Clipboard. Place the insertion point in the location you want to insert the row or column, then click the Paste button to paste the selection. Rows are inserted above the row containing the insertion point; columns are inserted to the left of the column containing the insertion point. You can also copy or move columns and rows by selecting them and using the ☒ to drag them to a new location in the table.

Word 2003

# Modifying Table Rows and Columns

After you create a table, you can easily adjust the size of columns and rows to make the table easier to read. You can change the size of columns and rows by dragging a border, by using the AutoFit command on the Table menu, or by setting exact measurements for column width and row height using the Table Properties dialog box. ▓▓▓▒▒▒ You adjust the size of the columns and rows to make the table more attractive and easier to read. You also center the text vertically in each table cell.

**STEPS**

1. **Position the pointer over the border between the first and second columns until the pointer changes to ╫, then drag the border to approximately the ½" mark on the horizontal ruler**

    The dotted line that appears as you drag represents the border. Dragging the column border changes the width of the first and second columns: the first column is narrower and the second column is wider. When dragging a border to change the width of an entire column, make sure no cells are selected in the column. You can also drag a row border to change the height of the row above it.

2. **Position the pointer over the right border of the Location column until the pointer changes to ╫, then double-click**

    Double-clicking a column border automatically resizes the column to fit the text.

3. **Double-click the right border of the Details column with the ╫ pointer, then double-click the right border of the Cost column with the ╫ pointer**

    The widths of the Details and Cost columns are adjusted.

4. **Move the pointer over the table, then click the table move handle ⊞ that appears outside the upper-left corner of the table**

    Clicking the table move handle selects the entire table. You can also use the Select command on the Table menu to select an entire table.

5. **Click Table on the menu bar, point to AutoFit, click Distribute Rows Evenly, then deselect the table**

    All the rows in the table become the same height, as shown in Figure D-7. You can also use the commands on the AutoFit menu to make all the columns the same width, to make the width of the columns fit the text, and to adjust the width of the columns so the table is justified between the margins.

6. **Click in the Details column, click Table on the menu bar, click Table Properties, then click the Column tab in the Table Properties dialog box**

    The Column tab, shown in Figure D-8, allows you to set an exact width for columns. You can specify an exact height for rows and an exact size for cells using the Row and Cell tabs. You can also use the Table tab to set a precise size for the table, to change the alignment of the table on a page, and to wrap text around a table.

7. **Select the measurement in the Preferred width text box, type 3, then click OK**

    The width of the Details column changes to 3".

8. **Click ⊞ to select the table, click Table on the menu bar, click Table Properties, click the Cell tab, click the Center box in the Vertical alignment section, click OK, deselect the table, then save your changes**

    The text is centered vertically in each table cell, as shown in Figure D-9.

**FIGURE D-7:** Resized columns and rows

Table move handle: click to select the table; drag to move the table

Rows are all the same height

Table resize handle; drag to change the size of all the rows and columns

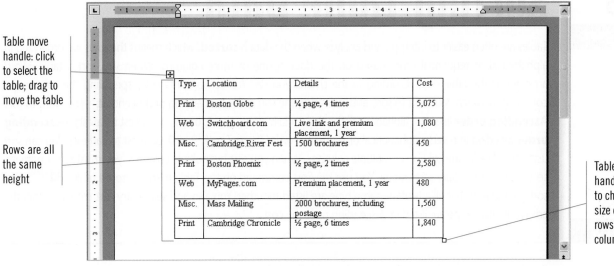

| Type | Location | Details | Cost |
|------|----------|---------|------|
| Print | Boston Globe | ¼ page, 4 times | 5,075 |
| Web | Switchboard.com | Live link and premium placement, 1 year | 1,080 |
| Misc. | Cambridge River Fest | 1500 brochures | 450 |
| Print | Boston Phoenix | ½ page, 2 times | 2,580 |
| Web | MyPages.com | Premium placement, 1 year | 480 |
| Misc. | Mass Mailing | 2000 brochures, including postage | 1,560 |
| Print | Cambridge Chronicle | ½ page, 6 times | 1,840 |

**FIGURE D-8:** Table Properties dialog box

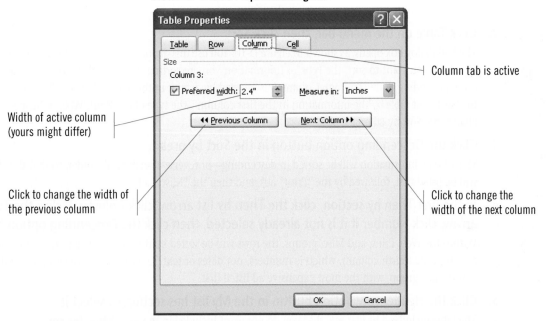

Column tab is active

Width of active column (yours might differ)

Click to change the width of the previous column

Click to change the width of the next column

**FIGURE D-9:** Text centered vertically in cells

Column is widened

Text is centered vertically in the cell

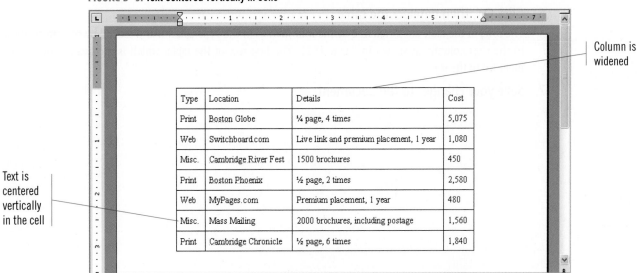

| Type | Location | Details | Cost |
|------|----------|---------|------|
| Print | Boston Globe | ¼ page, 4 times | 5,075 |
| Web | Switchboard.com | Live link and premium placement, 1 year | 1,080 |
| Misc. | Cambridge River Fest | 1500 brochures | 450 |
| Print | Boston Phoenix | ½ page, 2 times | 2,580 |
| Web | MyPages.com | Premium placement, 1 year | 480 |
| Misc. | Mass Mailing | 2000 brochures, including postage | 1,560 |
| Print | Cambridge Chronicle | ½ page, 6 times | 1,840 |

# Sorting Table Data

Tables are often easier to interpret and analyze when the data is **sorted**, which means the rows are organized in alphabetical or sequential order based on the data in one or more columns. When you sort a table, Word arranges all the table data according to the criteria you set. You set sort criteria by specifying the column (or columns) by which you want to sort, and indicating the sort order—ascending or descending—you want to use. **Ascending order** lists data alphabetically or sequentially (from A to Z, 0 to 9, or earliest to latest). **Descending order** lists data in reverse alphabetical or sequential order (from Z to A, 9 to 0, or latest to earliest). You can sort using the data in one column or multiple columns. When you sort by multiple columns, you must select primary, secondary, and tertiary sort criteria. You use the Sort command on the Table menu to sort a table. You sort the table so that all ads of the same type are listed together. You also add secondary sort criteria so that the ads within each type are listed in descending order by cost.

## STEPS

### QUICK TIP
To quickly sort a table by a single column, click in the column, then click the Sort Ascending ![A↓] or Sort Descending button ![Z↓A] on the Tables and Borders toolbar. When you use these buttons, Word does not include the header row in the sort.

1. **Place the insertion point anywhere in the table**

   To sort an entire table, you simply need to place the insertion point anywhere in the table. If you want to sort specific rows only, then you must select the rows you want to sort.

2. **Click Table on the menu bar, then click Sort**

   The Sort dialog box opens, as shown in Figure D-10. You use this dialog box to specify the column or columns by which you want to sort, the type of information you are sorting (text, numbers, or dates), and the sort order (ascending or descending). Column 1 is selected by default in the Sort by list box. Because you want to first sort your table by the information in the first column—the type of ad (Print, Web, or Misc.)—you don't change the Sort by criteria.

3. **Click the Descending option button in the Sort by area**

   The ad type information will be sorted in descending—or reverse alphabetical—order, so that the "Web" ads will be listed first, followed by the "Print" ads, and then the "Misc." ads.

4. **In the first Then by section, click the Then by list arrow, click Column 4, click the Type list arrow, click Number if it is not already selected, then click the Descending option button**

   Within the Web, Print, and Misc. groups, the rows will be sorted by the cost of the ad—the information contained in the fourth column, which is numbers, not dates or text. The rows will appear in descending order within each group, with the most expensive ad listed first.

5. **Click the Header row option button in the My list has section to select it**

   The table includes a header row that you do not want included in the sort. A **header row** is the first row of a table that contains the column headings.

6. **Click OK, then deselect the table**

   The rows in the table are sorted first by the information in the Type column and second by the information in the Cost column, as shown in Figure D-11. The first row of the table, which is the header row, is not included in the sort.

7. **Save your changes to the document**

FIGURE D-10: Sort dialog box

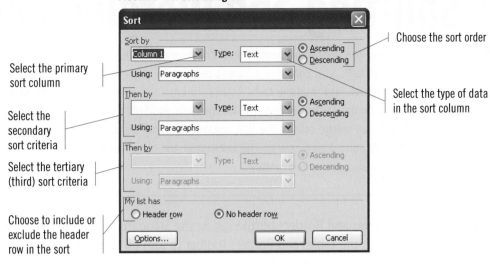

Select the primary sort column

Select the secondary sort criteria

Select the tertiary (third) sort criteria

Choose to include or exclude the header row in the sort

Choose the sort order

Select the type of data in the sort column

FIGURE D-11: Sorted table

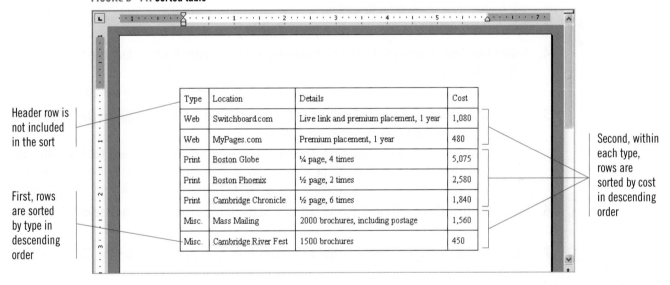

Header row is not included in the sort

First, rows are sorted by type in descending order

Second, within each type, rows are sorted by cost in descending order

| Type | Location | Details | Cost |
|------|----------|---------|------|
| Web | Switchboard.com | Live link and premium placement, 1 year | 1,080 |
| Web | MyPages.com | Premium placement, 1 year | 480 |
| Print | Boston Globe | ¼ page, 4 times | 5,075 |
| Print | Boston Phoenix | ½ page, 2 times | 2,580 |
| Print | Cambridge Chronicle | ½ page, 6 times | 1,840 |
| Misc. | Mass Mailing | 2000 brochures, including postage | 1,560 |
| Misc. | Cambridge River Fest | 1500 brochures | 450 |

## Clues to Use

### Sorting lists and paragraphs

In addition to sorting table data, you can use the Sort command on the Table menu to sort lists and paragraphs. For example, you might want to sort a list of names alphabetically. To sort lists and paragraphs, select the items you want included in the sort, click Table on the menu bar, and then click Sort. In the Sort Text dialog box, use the Sort by list arrow to select the sort by criteria (paragraphs or fields), use the Type list arrow to select the type of data (text, numbers, or dates), and then click the Ascending or Descending option button to choose a sort order.

When sorting text information in a document, the term "fields" refers to text or numbers that are separated by a character, such as a tab or a comma. For example, if the names you want to sort are listed in "Last name, First name" order, then last name and first name are each considered a field. You can choose to sort the list in alphabetical order by last name or by first name. Use the Options button in the Sort Text dialog box to specify the character that separates the fields in your lists or paragraphs. You can also use the Sort Text dialog box to specify other sort options.

# Splitting and Merging Cells

A convenient way to change the format and structure of a table is to merge and split the table cells. When you **merge** cells, you combine adjacent cells into a single larger cell. When you **split** a cell, you divide an existing cell into multiple cells. You can merge and split cells using the Merge Cells and Split Cells commands on the Table menu, or the Merge Cells and Split Cells buttons on the Tables and Borders toolbar. ▓▓▓ You merge cells in the first column to create a single cell for each ad type—Web, Print, and Misc. You also add a new row to the bottom of the table, and split the cells in the row to create three new rows with a different structure.

## STEPS

**TROUBLE**

To move the Tables and Borders toolbar, click its title bar and drag it to a new location.

1. **Click the Tables and Borders button ▦ on the Standard toolbar, then click the Draw Table button ▦ on the Tables and Borders toolbar to turn off the Draw pointer ⸓ if necessary**

   The Tables and Borders toolbar, which includes buttons for formatting and working with tables, opens. See Table D-1.

2. **Select the two Web cells in the first column of the table, click the Merge Cells button ▦ on the Tables and Borders toolbar, then deselect the text**

   The two Web cells merge to become a single cell. When you merge cells, Word converts the text in each cell into a separate paragraph in the merged cell.

3. **Select the first Web in the cell, then press [Delete]**

4. **Select the three Print cells in the first column, click ▦, type Print, select the two Misc. cells, click ▦, then type Misc.**

   The three Print cells merge to become one cell, and the two Misc. cells merge to become one cell.

5. **Click the Cambridge River Fest cell, click the Insert Table list arrow ▦▾ on the Tables and Borders toolbar, then click Insert Rows Below**

   A row is added to the bottom of the table. The Insert Table button on the Tables and Borders toolbar also changes to the Insert Rows Below button. The active buttons on the Tables and Borders toolbar reflect the most recently used commands. You can see a menu of related commands by clicking the list arrow next to a button.

6. **Select the first three cells in the new last row of the table, click ▦, then deselect the cell**

   The three cells in the row merge to become a single cell.

**QUICK TIP**

To split a table in two, click the row you want to be the first row in the second table, click Table on the menu bar, then click Split Table.

7. **Click the first cell in the last row, then click the Split Cells button ▦ on the Tables and Borders toolbar**

   The Split Cells dialog box opens, as shown in Figure D-12. You use this dialog box to split the selected cell or cells into a specific number of columns and rows.

8. **Type 1 in the Number of columns text box, press [Tab], type 3 in the Number of rows text box, click OK, then deselect the cells**

   The single cell is divided into three rows of equal height. When you split a cell into multiple rows and/or columns, the width of the original column does not change. If the cell you split contains text, all the text appears in the upper-left cell.

9. **Click the last cell in the Cost column, click ▦, repeat Step 8, then save your changes**

   The cell is split into three rows, as shown in Figure D-13. The last three rows of the table now have only two columns.

FIGURE D-12: Split Cells dialog box

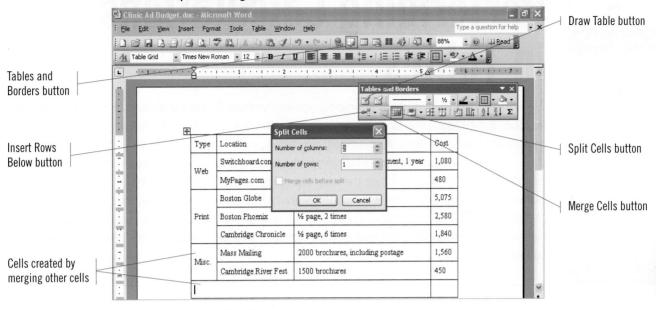

Tables and Borders button

Insert Rows Below button

Cells created by merging other cells

Draw Table button

Split Cells button

Merge Cells button

FIGURE D-13: Cells split into three rows

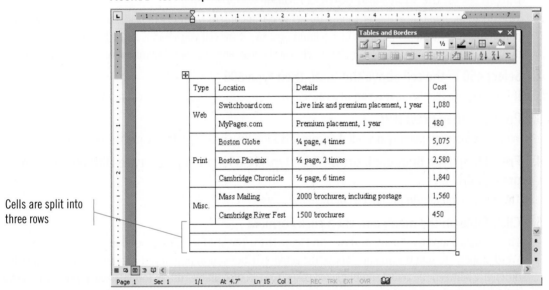

Cells are split into three rows

TABLE D-1: Buttons on the Tables and Borders toolbar

| button | use to | button | use to |
|---|---|---|---|
| | Draw a table or cells | | Divide a cell into multiple cells |
| | Remove a border between cells | | Change the alignment of text in cells |
| | Change border line style | | Make rows the same height |
| ½ | Change the thickness of borders | | Make columns the same width |
| | Change the border color | | Format the table with a Table AutoFormat table style |
| | Add or remove individual borders | | Change the orientation of text |
| | Change the shading color of cells | | Sort rows in ascending order |
| | Insert rows, columns, cells, or a table, and AutoFit columns | | Sort rows in descending order |
| | Combine the selected cells into a single cell | Σ | Calculate the sum of values above or to the left of the active cell |

Word 2003

CREATING AND FORMATTING TABLES 85

# Performing Calculations in Tables

If your table includes numerical information, you can perform simple calculations in the table. The Word AutoSum feature allows you to quickly total the numbers in a column or row. In addition, you can use the Formula command to perform other standard calculations, such as averages. When you calculate data in a table using formulas, you use cell references to refer to the cells in the table. Each cell has a unique **cell reference** composed of a letter and a number; the letter represents its column and the number represents its row. For example, the cell in the third row of the fourth column is cell D3. Figure D-14 shows the cell references in a simple table. ▧▧▧ You use AutoSum to calculate the total cost of the Clinic ad campaign. You also add information about the budgeted cost and create a formula to calculate the difference between the actual and budgeted costs.

## STEPS

1. **Click the first blank cell in column 1, type Total Cost, press [Tab], then click the AutoSum button Σ on the Tables and Borders toolbar**

   Word totals the numbers in the cells above the active cell and inserts the sum as a field. You can use the AutoSum button to quickly total the numbers in a column or a row. If the cell you select is at the bottom of a column of numbers, AutoSum totals the column. If the cell is at the right end of a row of numbers, AutoSum totals the row.

2. **Select 450 in the cell above the total, then type 600**

   If you change a number that is part of a calculation, you must recalculate the field result.

3. **Press [↓], then press [F9]**

   When the insertion point is in a cell that contains a formula, pressing [F9] updates the field result.

4. **Press [Tab], type Budgeted, press [Tab], type 12,850, press [Tab], type Difference, then press [Tab]**

   The insertion point is in the last cell of the table.

5. **Click Table on the menu bar, then click Formula**

   The Formula dialog box opens, as shown in Figure D-15. The SUM formula appears in the Formula text box. Word proposes to sum the numbers above the active cell, but you want to insert a formula that calculates the difference between the actual and budgeted costs. You can type simple custom formulas using a plus sign (+) for addition, a minus sign (-) for subtraction, an asterisk (*) for multiplication, and a slash (/) for division.

6. **Select =SUM(ABOVE) in the Formula text box, then type =B9-B10**

   You must type an equal sign (=) to indicate that the text following it is a formula. You want to subtract the budgeted cost in the second column of row 10 from the actual cost in the second column of row 9; therefore, you type a formula to subtract the value in cell B10 from the value in cell B9.

7. **Click OK, then save your changes**

   The difference appears in the cell, as shown in Figure D-16.

FIGURE D-14: Cell references in a table

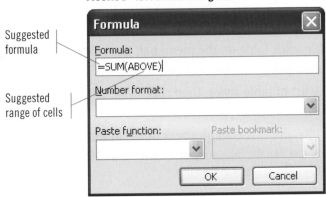

FIGURE D-15: Formula dialog box

Suggested formula

Suggested range of cells

FIGURE D-16: Difference calculated in table

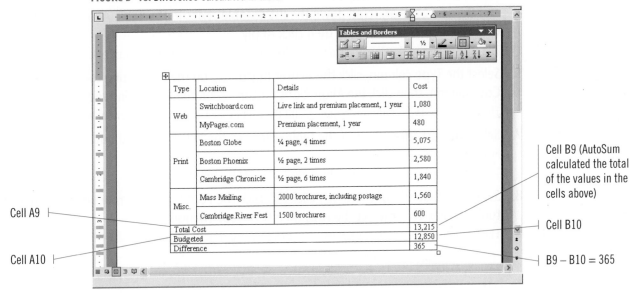

Cell A9

Cell A10

Cell B9 (AutoSum calculated the total of the values in the cells above)

Cell B10

B9 − B10 = 365

## Clues to Use

### Working with formulas

In addition to the SUM function, Word includes formulas for averaging, counting, and rounding data, to name a few. To use a Word formula, click the Paste function list arrow in the Formula dialog box, select a function, and then insert the cell references of the cells you want included in the calculation in parentheses after the name of the function. When entering formulas, you must separate cell references by a comma. For example, if you want to average the values

in cells A1, B3, and C4, enter the formula =AVERAGE(A1,B3,C4). You must also separate cell ranges by a colon. For example, to total the values in cells A1 through A9, enter the formula =SUM(A1:A9). To display the result of a calculation in a particular number format, such as a decimal percentage (0.00%), click the Number format list arrow in the Formula dialog box and select a number format. Word inserts the result of a calculation as a field in the selected cell.

# Using Table AutoFormat

Adding shading and other design elements to a table can help give it a polished appearance and make the data easier to read. The Word Table AutoFormat feature allows you to quickly apply a table style to a table. Table styles include borders, shading, fonts, alignment, colors, and other formatting effects. You can apply a table style to a table using the Table AutoFormat command on the Table menu or the Table AutoFormat button on the Tables and Borders toolbar. ▰▰▰▰▰ You want to enhance the appearance of the table with shading, borders, and other formats. You use the Table AutoFormat feature to quickly apply a table style to the table.

## STEPS

1.  **Click in the table, click Table on the menu bar, then click Table AutoFormat**
    The Table AutoFormat dialog box opens, as shown in Figure D-17.

2.  **Scroll down the list of table styles, then click Table List 7**
    A preview of the Table List 7 style appears in the Preview area.

3.  **Clear the Last row and Last column check boxes in the Apply special formats to section**
    The Preview area shows that the formatting of the last row and column of the table now match the formatting of the other rows and columns in the table.

> **QUICK TIP**
> Use the Reveal Formatting task pane to view the format settings applied to tables and cells.

4.  **Click Apply**
    The Table List 7 style is applied to the table, as shown in Figure D-18. Because of the structure of the table, this style neither enhances the table nor helps make the data more readable.

5.  **With the insertion point in the table, click the Table AutoFormat button 🖼 on the Tables and Borders toolbar, scroll down the list of table styles in the Table AutoFormat dialog box, click Table Professional, then click Apply**
    The Table Professional style is applied to the table. This style works with the structure of the table.

> **TROUBLE**
> When you select the Type column, the first column in the last three rows is also selected.

6.  **Select the Type column, click the Center button ≡ on the Formatting toolbar, select the Cost column, then click the Align Right button ≡ on the Formatting toolbar**
    The data in the Type column is centered, and the data in the Cost column is right-aligned.

7.  **Select the last three rows of the table, click ≡, then click the Bold button B on the Formatting toolbar**
    The text in the last three rows is right-aligned and bold is applied.

8.  **Select the first row of the table, click ≡, click the Font Size list arrow on the Formatting toolbar, click 16, deselect the row, then save your changes**
    The text in the header row is centered and enlarged, as shown in Figure D-19.

---

### Clues to Use

#### Using tables to lay out a page

Tables are often used to display information for quick reference and analysis, but you can also use tables to structure the layout of a page. You can insert any kind of information in the cell of a table—including graphics, bulleted lists, charts, and other tables (called **nested tables**). For example, you might use a table to lay out a resume, a newsletter, or a Web page. When you use a table to lay out a page, you generally remove the table borders to hide the table structure from the reader. After you remove borders, it can be helpful to display the table gridlines onscreen while you work. **Gridlines** are light gray lines that show the boundaries of cells, but do not print. If your document will be viewed online—for example, if you are planning to e-mail your resume to potential employers—you should turn off the display of gridlines before you distribute the document so that it looks the same online as it looks when printed. To turn gridlines off or on, click the Hide Gridlines or Show Gridlines command on the Table menu.

FIGURE D-17: Table AutoFormat dialog box

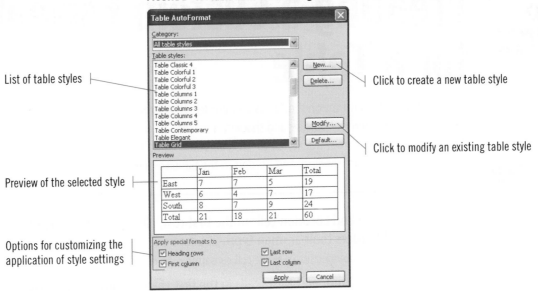

List of table styles

Preview of the selected style

Options for customizing the application of style settings

Click to create a new table style

Click to modify an existing table style

FIGURE D-18: Table List 7 style applied to table

The shading applied to the merged cells is confusing

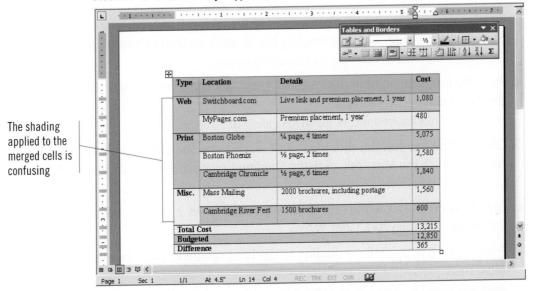

FIGURE D-19: Table Professional style applied to table

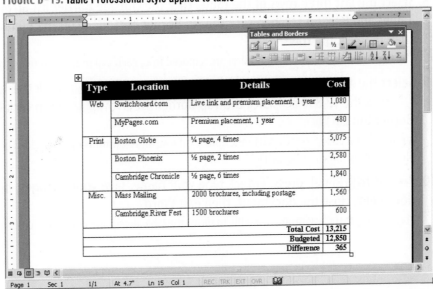

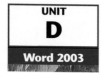

# Creating a Custom Format for a Table

You can also use the buttons on the Tables and Borders toolbar to create your own table designs. For example, you can add or remove borders and shading, vary the line style, thickness, and color of borders, change the orientation of text from horizontal to vertical, and change the alignment of text in cells. You adjust the text direction, shading, and borders in the table to make it easier to understand at a glance.

## STEPS

1. **Select the Type and Location cells in the first row, click the Merge Cells button on the Tables and Borders toolbar, then type Ad Location**

   The two cells are combined into a single cell containing the text "Ad Location."

2. **Select the Web, Print, and Misc. cells in the first column, click the Change Text Direction button on the Tables and Borders toolbar twice, then deselect the cells**

   The text is rotated 270 degrees.

3. **Position the pointer over the right border of the Web cell until the pointer changes to ↔, then drag the border to approximately the ¼" mark on the horizontal ruler**

   The width of the column containing the vertical text narrows.

4. **Place the insertion point in the Web cell, then click the Shading Color list arrow on the Tables and Borders toolbar**

   The Shading Color palette opens, as shown in Figure D-20.

5. **Click Gold on the palette, click the Print cell, click the Shading Color list arrow, click Pink, click the Misc. cell, click the Shading Color list arrow, then click Aqua**

   Shading is applied to each cell.

6. **Drag to select the six white cells in the Web rows (rows 2 and 3), click the Shading Color list arrow, then click Light Yellow**

7. **Repeat Step 6 to apply Rose shading to the Print rows and Light Turquoise shading to the Misc. rows**

   Shading is applied to all the cells in rows 1–8.

8. **Select the last three rows of the table, click the Outside Border list arrow on the Tables and Borders toolbar, click the No Border button on the menu that appears, then deselect the rows**

   The top, bottom, left, and right borders are removed from each cell in the selected rows.

9. **Select the Total Cost row, click the No Border list arrow, click the Top Border button, click the 12,850 cell, click the Top Border list arrow, then click the Bottom Border button**

   A top border is added to each cell in the Total Cost row, and a bottom border is added below 12,850. The completed table is shown in Figure D-21.

10. **Press [Ctrl][Home], press [Enter], type your name, save your changes, print a copy of the document, close the document, then exit Word**

    Press [Enter] at the beginning of a table to move the table down one line in a document.

**FIGURE D-20:** Shading Color palette

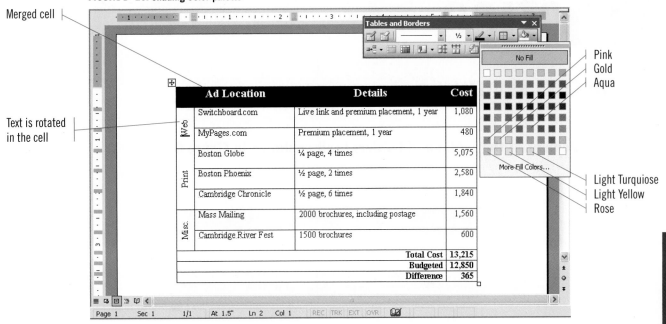

Merged cell

Text is rotated
in the cell

Pink
Gold
Aqua

Light Turquiose
Light Yellow
Rose

**FIGURE D-21:** Completed table

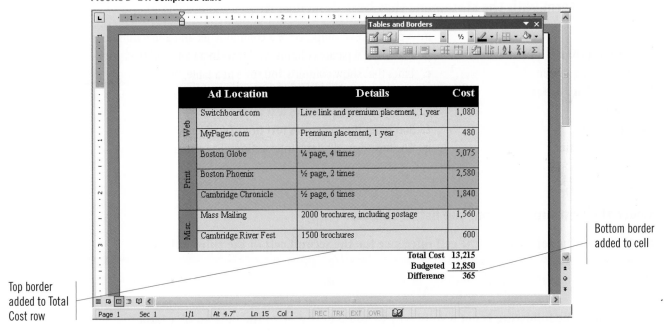

Bottom border
added to cell

Top border
added to Total
Cost row

## Clues to Use

### Drawing a table

The Word Draw Table feature allows you to draw table cells exactly where you want them. To draw a table, click the Draw Table button on the Tables and Borders toolbar to turn on the Draw pointer , and then click and drag to draw a cell. Using the same method, you can draw borders within the cell to create columns and rows, or draw additional cells attached to the first cell. Click the Draw Table button to turn off the draw feature.

If you want to remove a border from a table, click the Eraser button on the Tables and Borders toolbar to activate the Eraser pointer , and then click the border you want to remove. Click the Eraser button to turn off the erase feature. You can use the Draw pointer and the Eraser pointer to change the structure of any table, not just the tables you draw from scratch.

# Practice

## ▼ CONCEPTS REVIEW

**Label each element of the Tables and Borders toolbar shown in Figure D-22.**

FIGURE D-22

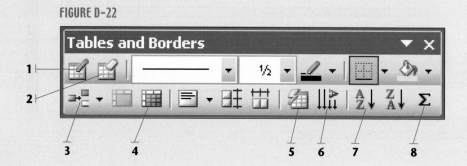

**Match each term with the statement that best describes it.**

9. Cell
10. Nested table
11. Ascending order
12. Descending order
13. Borders
14. Gridlines
15. Cell reference

a. A cell address composed of a column letter and a row number
b. Lines that separate columns and rows in a table and that print
c. Lines that show columns and rows in a table, but do not print
d. An object inserted in a table cell
e. Sort order that organizes text from A to Z
f. Sort order that organizes text from Z to A
g. The box formed by the intersection of a column and a row

**Select the best answer from the list of choices.**

16. **Which of the following is the cell reference for the second cell in the third column?**
   a. C2
   b. 2C
   c. 3B
   d. B3

17. **Which of the following is *not* a valid way to add a new row to the bottom of a table?**
   a. Click in the bottom row, then click the Insert Rows Below button on the Tables and Borders toolbar
   b. Click in the bottom row, point to Insert on the Table menu, then click Rows Below
   c. Place the insertion point in the last cell of the last row, then press [Tab]
   d. Click in the bottom row, then click the Insert Rows button on the Standard toolbar

18. **Which button do you use to change the orientation of text in a cell?**
   a. ▣
   b. ▥
   c. ▦
   d. ▧

**19. Which of the following is *not* a correct formula for adding the values in cells A1, A2, and A3?**

    **a.** =SUM(A1:A3)

    **b.** =SUM(A1, A2, A3)

    **c.** =SUM(A1~A3)

    **d.** =A1+A2+A3

**20. What happens when you double-click a column border?**

    **a.** A new column is added to the left.

    **b.** The column width is adjusted to fit the text.

    **c.** The columns in the table are distributed evenly.

    **d.** A new column is added to the right.

# ▼ SKILLS REVIEW

**1. Insert a table.**

    **a.** Start Word, close the Getting Started task pane, then save the new blank document as **Flu Mortality** to the drive and folder where your Data Files are located.

    **b.** Type your name, press [Enter] twice, type **Influenza Mortality in Selected Major Cities**, then press [Enter].

    **c.** Insert a table that contains four columns and four rows.

    **d.** Type the text shown in Figure D-23, pressing [Tab] to add rows as necessary.

    **e.** Save your changes.

**FIGURE D-23**

| City | >=65 | 25-64 | <25 |
|------|------|-------|-----|
| Boston | 272 | 115 | 8 |
| San Francisco | 129 | 68 | 3 |
| New York | 523 | 198 | 27 |
| Chicago | 217 | 143 | 17 |
| Seattle | 186 | 98 | 9 |
| Denver | 138 | 57 | 6 |

**2. Insert and delete rows and columns.**

    **a.** Insert a row above the New York row, then type the following text in the new row:

    **Dallas   315   112   13**

    **b.** Delete the Boston row.

    **c.** Insert a column to the right of the <25 column, type **Date Reported** in the header row, then enter a June 2008 date in each cell in the column using the format MM/DD/YY (for example, 06/27/08).

    **d.** Move the Date Reported column to the right of the City column, then save your changes.

**3. Modify table rows and columns.**

    **a.** Double-click the border between the first and second columns to resize the columns.

    **b.** Drag the border between the second and third columns to the 2¼" mark on the horizontal ruler.

    **c.** Double-click the right border of the >=65, 25–64, and <25 columns.

    **d.** Select the >=65, 25–64, and <25 columns, then distribute the columns evenly.

    **e.** Select rows 2–7, use the Table Properties dialog box to set the row height to exactly .3", then save your changes.

**4. Sort table data.**

    **a.** Sort the table data in descending order by the information in the >=65 column.

    **b.** Sort the table data in ascending order by date reported.

    **c.** Sort the table data by city name in alphabetical order, then save your changes.

**5. Split and merge cells.**

   **a.** Insert a row above the header row.

   **b.** Merge the first cell in the new row with the City cell.

   **c.** Merge the second cell in the new row with the Date Reported cell.

   **d.** Merge the three remaining blank cells in the first row into a single cell, then type **Mortality by Age** in the merged cell.

   **e.** Add a new row to the bottom of the table.

   **f.** Merge the first two cells in the new row, then type **Average Mortality by Age** in the merged cell.

   **g.** Select the first seven cells in the first column (from City to Seattle), open the Split Cells dialog box, clear the Merge cells before split check box, then split the cells into two columns.

   **h.** Type **State** as the heading for the new column, then enter the following text in the remaining cells in the column: **IL, TX, CO, NY, CA, WA.**

   **i.** Double-click the right border of the first column to resize the column, double-click the right border of the 25–64 column, select all the cells in rows 2–8 in the last three columns, distribute the columns evenly, then save your changes.

**6. Perform calculations in tables.**

   **a.** Place the insertion point in the last cell in the >=65 column, then open the Formula dialog box.

   **b.** Delete the text in the Formula text box, type **=average(above)**, then click OK.

   **c.** Repeat Step b to insert the average return in the last cell in the 25–64 and <25 columns.

   **d.** Change the value of the >=65 mortality rate for Denver to **182**.

   **e.** Use [F9] to recalculate the average for the number of cases reported for the >=65 category, then save your changes.

**7. Using Table AutoFormat.**

   **a.** Open the Table AutoFormat dialog box, select an appropriate table style for the table, then apply the style to the table. Was the style you chose effective?

   **b.** Using Table AutoFormat, apply the Table List 3 style to the table.

   **c.** Change the font of all the text in the table to 10-point Arial. (*Hint*: Select the entire table.)

   **d.** Apply bold to the >=65, 24–65, and <25 column headings, and to the bottom row of the table.

   **e.** Center the table between the margins, center the table title **Influenza Mortality in Selected Major Cities**, format the title in 14-point Arial, apply bold, then save your changes.

**8. Create a custom format for a table.**

   **a.** Select the entire table, then use the Align Center button on the Tables and Borders toolbar to center the text in every cell vertically and horizontally.

   **b.** Right-align the numbers in columns 4–6.

   **c.** Left-align the city names and state abbreviations in columns 1 and 2.

   **d.** Right-align the text in the bottom row. Make sure the text in the header row is still centered.

   **e.** Select all the cells in the header row, including the >=65, 25–64, and <25 column headings, change the shading color to indigo, then change the font color to white.

   **f.** Apply rose shading to the cells containing the city names and state abbreviations.

   **g.** Apply pale blue, light yellow, and lavender shading to the cells containing the >=65, 25–64, and <25 data, respectively. Do not apply shading to the bottom row of the table.

   **h.** Remove all the borders in the table.

   **i.** Add a ½-point white bottom border to the Mortality by Age cell. (*Hint*: Use the Tables and Borders toolbar.)

   **j.** Add a 2¼-point black border around the outside of the table. Also add a top border to the last row of the table.

   **k.** Examine the table, make any necessary adjustments, then save your changes.

   **l.** Preview the table in Print Preview, print a copy, close the file, then exit Word.

# ▼ INDEPENDENT CHALLENGE 1

You are the office manager for a dental office. In preparation for a meeting about next year's budget, you create a table showing quarterly expenditures for the fiscal year 2008.

**a.** Start Word, then save the new blank document as **2008 Expenditures** to the drive and folder where your Data Files are located.

**b.** Type the table heading **Quarterly Expenditures, Fiscal Year 2008** at the top of the document, then press [Enter] twice.

**c.** Insert a table with five columns and four rows, then enter the data shown in Figure D-24 into the table, adding rows as necessary.

**d.** Resize the columns to fit the text.

**e.** Sort the table rows in alphabetical order by Item.

FIGURE D-24

| Item | Q1 | Q2 | Q3 | Q4 |
|------|----|----|----|----|
| Disposables | 1283 | 1627 | 1374 | 1723 |
| Orthodontics | 920 | 847 | 862 | 798 |
| Anesthetics | 1023 | 948 | 926 | 897 |
| Instruments | 834 | 812 | 912 | 1029 |
| Finishing and Polishing | 463 | 394 | 472 | 289 |
| Pins and Posts | 730 | 695 | 463 | 586 |

**f.** Add a new row to the bottom of the table, type **Total** in the first cell, then enter a formula in each remaining cell in the new row to calculate the sum of the cells above it.

**g.** Add a new column at the right end of the table, type **Total** in the first cell, then enter a formula in each remaining cell in the new column to calculate the sum of the cells to the left of it. (*Hint*: Make sure the formula you insert in each cell sums the cells to the left, not the cells above.)

**h.** Using Table AutoFormat, apply a table style to the table. Select a style that enhances the information contained in the table.

**i.** Center the text in the header row, left-align the remaining text in the first column, then right-align the numerical data in the table.

**j.** Enhance the table with fonts, font colors, shading, and borders to make the table attractive and easy to read at a glance.

**k.** Increase the font size of the table heading to 18 points, then center the table heading and the table on the page.

**l.** Press [Ctrl][End], press [Enter], type your name, save your changes, print the table, close the file, then exit Word.

# ▼ INDEPENDENT CHALLENGE 2

You are a medical assistant in a busy family practice office. One of your responsibilities at your office is to create a list of scheduled appointments for the day. You find it easiest to format this information as a table.

**a.** Start Word, open the file WMP D-1.doc, then save it as **June 12 Appointments** to the drive and folder where your Data Files are located.

**b.** Format the heading in 18-point Arial, apply bold, then center the heading.

**c.** Turn on formatting marks, select the tabbed text in the document, then convert the text to a 6-column table. (*Hint*: Select the separate text at tabs option.)

**d.** Autofit the contents of the table.

**e.** Add a row above the first row in the table, then enter the following column headings in the new header row: **Last Name, First Name, DOB, Phone, Physician, Time**.

**f.** Format the table text in 10-point Arial.

**g.** Apply an appropriate Table AutoFormat style to the table. Apply bold to the header row if necessary.

**h.** Adjust the column widths so that the table is attractive and readable.

**i.** Make the height of each row at least .25".

**j.** Center Left align the text in each cell in the table, including the column headings.

**k.** Center Right align the text in each cell in the DOB, Phone, and Time columns.

**l.** Center the column headings, then center the entire table on the page.

**m.** Sort the table by last name and then by first name in alphabetical order. (*Hint*: Use the Sort dialog box.)

# ▼ INDEPENDENT CHALLENGE 2 (CONTINUED)

**Advanced Challenge Exercise**

- Sort the entire table by physician.
- Change the font color of the Boxer rows to red, change the font color of the Dixon rows to blue, then change the font color of the Wilson rows to green.
- Sort the table by Time and then by Physician, in ascending order.
- Move the Time column to become the first column in the table, then adjust the column width to fit the text.
- Move the rows for the appointments from 9:00 to 12:30 to the beginning of the table.

**n.** Enhance the table with borders, shading, fonts, and other formats if necessary, to make it attractive and readable. Adjust the table as necessary so it fits on one page.

**o.** Type your name at the bottom of the document, save your changes, print a copy of the table, close the document, then exit Word.

# ▼ INDEPENDENT CHALLENGE 3

You work in a pediatrician's office. Your boss has given you data on appropriate ibuprofen and acetaminophen doses for children, and has asked you to format the information for parents. You'll use tables to lay out the information so it is easily understandable.

**a.** Start Word, open the file WMP D-2.doc from the drive and folder where your Data Files are located, then save it as **Dosages**. Read the document to get a feel for its contents.

**b.** Merge the cells in the first row of the table, then merge the cells in the Acetaminophen Doses row.

**c.** Insert a new row under the first row. Type **One dose lasts 6-8 hours** in the new cell.

**d.** Insert a new row under the Acetaminophen Doses row. Type **One dose lasts 4-6 hours** in the new row.

**e.** Change all the text in the table to 10-point Arial, then center all the text vertically and horizontally in the cells.

**f.** Make the height of each row at least .25".

**g.** Select the third row of the table, copy it, then paste the row below the One dose lasts 4-6 hours row.

**h.** Split the table above the Acetaminophen Doses row, then press [Enter] twice.

**i.** Refer to Figure D-25 as you format the Ibuprofen table.

**j.** Format the header row in 14-point Arial, bold, then remove all the borders.

**k.** Format the second row in 12-point Arial, then remove all the borders.

FIGURE D-25

## Ibuprofen Doses (Brand names Motrin or Advil)
### One dose lasts 6-8 hours

| Weight | Infants' concentrated drops 50 mg/1.25 ml | Children's suspension 100 mg/5 ml | Children's chewable tablets 50 mg | Children's chewable tablets 100 mg | Junior caplets 100 mg |
|---|---|---|---|---|---|
|  | Dropperful | Teaspoon | Tablet | Tablet | Caplet |
| Under 6 months | Consult your doctor | | | | |
| 12-16 lbs. | 1 dropperful | | | | |
| 17-21 lbs. | 1 1/2 droppersful | | | | |
| 22-32 lbs. | | 1 teaspoon | | | |
| 33-43 lbs. | | 1 1/2 teaspoons | 3 tablets | | |
| 44-54 lbs. | | 2 teaspoons | 4 tablets | 2 tablets | 2 caplets |
| 55-65 lbs. | | 2 1/2 teaspoons | 5 tablets | 2 1/2 tablets | 2 1/2 caplets |
| 66-95 lbs. | | 3 teaspoons | 6 tablets | 3 tablets | 3 caplets |

**l.** In each column, merge the cells in rows 3 and 4. Remove the left border from the first cell in the new row 3. In the remianing cells in the row, apply bold to the text, apply red shading to the cells, then add a top border.

**m.** Apply bold to the text in the fourth row, then apply gold shading to the cells.

**n.** Apply red shading to the cells in column 1, rows 5–12.

**o.** In the fifth row, merge the cells in columns 2–6, then apply bold to the text in the merged cell.

**p.** In columns 2–5, merge all adjoining blank cells, fill the blank cells with light yellow, then remove the borders between the light yellow cells. (*Hint*: You might need to reapply borders to some adjacent cells after you remove the borders from the light yellow cells.)

**q.** Repeat steps j–p to format the Acetaminophen table.

**Advanced Challenge Exercise**

■ In both tables, change the font color of the third row to white, then change the font color of the cells in column 1, rows 5–12 to white.

■ In the Acetaminophen table, change the shading color of the red cells to teal.

■ In the Acetaminophen table, change the shading color of the light yellow cells to light green.

**r.** Examine the document for errors, then make any necessary adjustments.

**s.** Press [Ctrl][End], press [Enter], type your name, save your changes to the document, preview it, print a copy, close the file, then exit Word.

▼ **INDEPENDENT CHALLENGE 4**

A well-written and well-formatted resume gives you an advantage in getting a job interview. In a winning resume, the content and format support your career objective and effectively present your background and qualifications. One simple way to create a resume is to lay out the page using a table. In this independent challenge, you research guidelines for writing and formatting resumes. You then create your own resume using a table for its layout.

**a.** Use your favorite search engine to search the Web for information on writing and formatting resumes. Use the keywords **resume templates**.

**b.** Print helpful advice on writing and formatting resumes from at least two Web sites.

**c.** Think about the information you want to include in your resume. The resume header should include your name, address, telephone number, and e-mail address. The body of the resume should include your career objective and information on your education, work experience, and skills. You might want to add additional information.

**d.** Sketch a layout for your resume using a table as the underlying grid. Include the table rows and columns in your sketch.

**e.** Start Word, open a new blank document, then save it as **My Resume** to the drive and folder where your Data Files are located.

**f.** Set appropriate margins, then insert a table to serve as the underlying grid for your resume. Split and merge cells and adjust the size of the table columns as necessary.

**g.** Type your resume in the table cells. Take care to use a professional tone and keep your language to the point.

**h.** Format your resume with fonts, bullets, and other formatting features. Adjust the spacing between sections by resizing the table columns and rows.

**i.** When you are satisfied with the content and format of your resume, remove the borders from the table, then hide the gridlines if they are visible. (*Hint*: To help visually separate the sections of your resume, you might want to add some of the borders you removed.)

**j.** Check your resume for spelling and grammar errors.

**k.** Save your changes, preview your resume, print a copy, close the file, then exit Word.

Create the calendar shown in Figure D-26 using a table to lay out the entire page. (*Hint*: The font is Century Gothic.) Type your name in the last table cell, save the calendar with the filename **April 2008** to the drive and folder where your Data Files are located, then print a copy.

FIGURE D-26

## Warner Community Hospital
# Community Education Calendar

# April 2008

| Sunday | Monday | Tuesday | Wednesday | Thursday | Friday | Saturday |
|---|---|---|---|---|---|---|
| | | *1* <br> Diabetes Mgmt. Education 1:30 p.m. | *2* | *3* | *4* <br> Yoga 9:00 a.m. | *5* <br> Women's AA 9:00 a.m. <br><br> AA 8:00 p.m. |
| *6* <br> OA 6:30 p.m. | *7* | *8* <br> Diabetes Mgmt. Education 1:30 p.m. | *9* | *10* <br> Nursing Mother's Support Group 10:00 a.m. | *11* <br> Yoga 9:00 a.m. | *12* <br> Women's AA 9:00 a.m. <br><br> AA 8:00 p.m. |
| *13* <br> OA 6:30 p.m. | *14* <br> Cancer Support Group 7:00 p.m. | *15* <br> Diabetes Mgmt. Education 1:30 p.m. | *16* | *17* | *18* <br> Yoga 9:00 a.m. | *19* <br> Women's AA 9:00 a.m. <br><br> AA 8:00 p.m. |
| *20* <br> OA 6:30 p.m. | *21* | *22* <br> Diabetes Mgmt. Education 1:30 p.m. | *23* <br> Stroke Support Group 1:30 p.m. | *24* <br> Nursing Mother's Support Group 10:00 a.m. | *25* <br> Yoga 9:00 a.m. | *26* <br> Women's AA 9:00 a.m. <br><br> AA 8:00 p.m. |
| *27* <br> OA 6:30 p.m. | *28* <br> Cancer Support Group 7:00 p.m. | *29* <br> Diabetes Mgmt. Education 1:30 p.m. | *30* | | | Your Name |

### All groups meet in Conference Room 1.
### For more information, call 555-3939

# Formatting Documents

## OBJECTIVES

| |
|---|
| Set document margins |
| Divide a document into sections |
| Insert page breaks |
| Insert page numbers |
| Add headers and footers |
| Edit headers and footers |
| Format columns |
| Insert a table |
| Insert WordArt |
| Insert clip art |

If you have a SAM user profile, you may have access to hands-on instruction, practice, and assessment of the skills covered in this unit. Log in to your SAM account and go to your assignments page to see what your instructor has assigned.

The page-formatting features of Word allow you to creatively lay out and design the pages of your documents. In this unit, you learn how to change the document margins, determine page orientation, add page numbers, and insert headers and footers. You also learn how to format text in columns and how to illustrate your documents with tables, clip art, and WordArt. ▰▰▰ You have prepared and formatted the text for the Riverwalk Medical Clinic's Healthy Kids newsletter. You are now ready to lay out and design the newsletter pages. You plan to organize the articles in columns and to illustrate the newsletter with a table, clip art, and WordArt.

# Setting Document Margins

Changing a document's margins is one way to change the appearance of a document and control the amount of text that fits on a page. The **margins** of a document are the blank areas between the edge of the text and the edge of the page. When you create a document in Word, the default margins are 1" at the top and bottom of the page, and 1.25" on the left and right sides of the page. You can adjust the size of a document's margins using the Page Setup command on the File menu, or using the rulers. ▚▚▞▞▞ The newsletter should be a four-page document when finished. You begin formatting the newsletter pages by reducing the size of the document margins so that more text fits on each page.

## STEPS

1. **Start Word, open the file** WMP E-1.doc **from the drive and folder where your Data Files are located, then save it as** Healthy Kids

   The newsletter opens in Print Layout view.

2. **Scroll through the newsletter to get a feel for its contents, then press** [Ctrl][Home]

   The newsletter is currently six pages long. Notice the status bar indicates the page where the insertion point is located and the total number of pages in the document.

3. **Click** File **on the menu bar, click** Page Setup, **then click the** Margins tab **in the Page Setup dialog box if it is not already selected**

   The Margins tab in the Page Setup dialog box is shown in Figure E-1. You can use the Margins tab to change the top, bottom, left, or right document margins, to change the orientation of the pages from portrait to land-scape, and to alter other page layout settings. **Portrait orientation** means a page is taller than it is wide; **landscape orientation** means a page is wider than it is tall. This newsletter uses portrait orientation.

QUICK TIP

The minimum allow-able margin settings depend on your printer and the size of the paper you are using. Word displays a warning message if you set margins that are too narrow for your printer.

4. **Click the** Top down arrow **three times until 0.7" appears, then click the** Bottom down arrow **until 0.7" appears**

   The top and bottom margins of the newsletter will be .7". Notice that the margins in the Preview section of the dialog box change as you adjust the margin settings.

5. **Press** [Tab], **type** .7 **in the Left text box, press** [Tab], **then type** .7 **in the Right text box**

   The left and right margins of the newsletter will also be .7". You can change the margin settings by using the arrows or by typing a value in the appropriate text box.

6. **Click** OK

   The document margins change to .7", as shown in Figure E-2. At the intersection of the white and shaded areas on the horizontal and vertical rulers is a bar that indicates the location of the margin. You can also change a document's margins by dragging the bar to a new location. Notice the status bar now indicates the document is five pages long. Reducing the size of the margins increased the amount of text that fits on each page.

QUICK TIP

Use the Reveal For-matting task pane to quickly check the margin, orientation, paper size, and other page layout settings for a document.

7. **Click the** Zoom list arrow **on the Standard toolbar, then click** Two Pages

   The first two pages of the document appear in the document window.

8. **Scroll down to view all five pages of the newsletter, press** [Ctrl][Home], **click the** Zoom list arrow, **click** Page Width, **then click the** Save button 🖫 **on the Standard toolbar to save the document**

FIGURE E-1: Margins tab in Page Setup dialog box

Default margin settings

Set gutter margin

Select page orientation

Select part of document to apply settings to

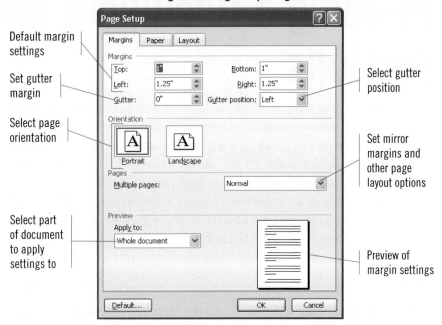

Select gutter position

Set mirror margins and other page layout options

Preview of margin settings

FIGURE E-2: Newsletter with smaller margins

Ruler shows location of left margin

Ruler shows location of top margin

Document margins are narrower than the original default margins

Document is now five pages long

Page 1 is the active page

Zoom list arrow

Ruler shows location of right margin

## Clues to Use

### Changing orientation, margin settings, and paper size

By default, the documents you create in Word use an 8½" × 11" paper size in portrait orientation with the default margin settings. You can adjust these settings in the Page Setup dialog box to create documents that are a different size, shape, or layout. On the Margins tab, change the orientation of the pages by selecting Portrait or Landscape. To change the layout of multiple pages, use the Multiple pages list arrow to create pages that use mirror margins, that include two pages per sheet of paper, or that are formatted like a folded booklet. **Mirror margins** are used in documents with facing pages, such as a magazine, where the margins on the left page of the document are a mirror image of the margins on the right page. Documents with mirror margins have inside and outside margins, rather than right and left margins. Another type of margin is a gutter margin, which is used in bound documents, such as books. A **gutter** adds extra space to the left, top, or inside margin to allow for the binding. Add a gutter to a document by adjusting the setting in the Gutter text box on the Margins tab. If you want to change the size of the paper used in a document, use the Paper tab in the Page Setup dialog box. Use the Paper size list arrow to select a standard paper size, or enter custom measurements in the Width and Height text boxes.

# Dividing a Document into Sections

Dividing a document into sections allows you to format each section of the document with different page layout settings. A **section** is a portion of a document that is separated from the rest of the document by section breaks. **Section breaks** are formatting marks that you insert in a document to show the end of a section. After you have divided a document into sections, you can format each section with different column, margin, page orientation, header and footer, and other page layout settings. By default, a document is formatted as a single section, but you can divide a document into as many sections as you like. ▰▰▰ You want to format the body of the newsletter in two columns, but leave the masthead and the headline "Reading to Your Child..." as a single column. You insert a section break before the headline "A Letter from the Director" to divide the document into two sections, and then change the number of columns in the second section to two.

## STEPS

1. **Click the** Show/Hide ¶ button ¶ **on the Standard toolbar to display formatting marks if they are not visible**

   Turning on formatting marks allows you to see the section breaks you insert in a document.

**QUICK TIP**

When you insert a section break at the beginning of a paragraph, Word inserts the break at the end of the previous paragraph. A section break stores the formatting information for the preceding section.

2. **Place the insertion point before the headline** A Letter from the Director, **click** Insert **on the menu bar, then click** Break

   The Break dialog box opens, as shown in Figure E-3. You use this dialog box to insert different types of section breaks. Table E-1 describes the different types of section breaks.

3. **Click the** Continuous option button, **then click** OK

   Word inserts a continuous section break, shown as a dotted double line, above the headline. A continuous section break begins a new section of the document on the same page. The document now has two sections. Notice that the status bar indicates that the insertion point is in section 2.

4. **With the insertion point in section 2, click the** Columns button ▦ **on the Standard toolbar**

   A grid showing four columns opens. You use the grid to select the number of columns you want to create.

5. **Point to the** second column **on the grid, then click**

   Section 2 is formatted in two columns, as shown in Figure E-4. The text in section 1 remains formatted in a single column. Notice the status bar now indicates the document is four pages long. Formatting text in columns is another way to increase the amount of text that fits on a page.

6. **Click the** Zoom list arrow **on the Standard toolbar, click** Two Pages, **then scroll down to examine all four pages of the document**

   The text in section 2—all the text below the continuous section break—is formatted in two columns. Text in columns flows automatically from the bottom of one column to the top of the next column.

7. **Press** [Ctrl][Home], **click the** Zoom list arrow, **click** Page Width, **then save the document**

**TABLE E-1: Types of section breaks**

| section | function |
|---|---|
| Next page | Begins a new section and moves the text following the break to the top of the next page |
| Continuous | Begins a new section on the same page |
| Even page | Begins a new section and moves the text following the break to the top of the next even-numbered page |
| Odd page | Begins a new section and moves the text following the break to the top of the next odd-numbered page |

**FIGURE E-3:** Break dialog box

**FIGURE E-4:** Continuous section break and columns

Text in section 1 is formatted in one column

Text in section 2 is formatted in two columns

Section 2 is the active section

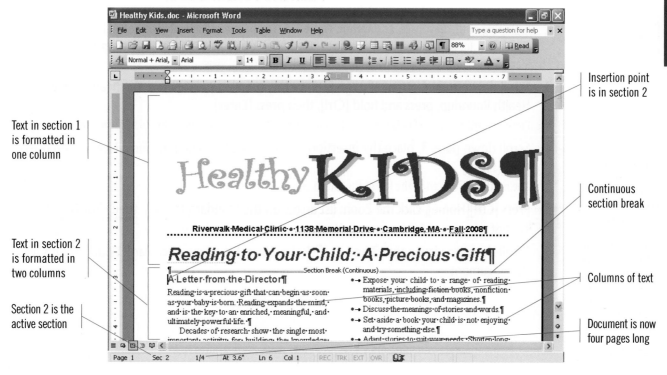

Insertion point is in section 2

Continuous section break

Columns of text

Document is now four pages long

## Clues to Use

### Changing page layout settings for a section

Dividing a document into sections allows you to vary the layout of a document. In addition to applying different column settings to sections, you can apply different margins, page orientation, paper size, vertical alignment, header and footer, page numbering, and other page layout settings. For example, if you are formatting a report that includes a table with many columns, you might want to change the table's page orientation to landscape so that it is easier to read. To do this, you would insert a section break before and after the table to create a section that contains only the table. Then you would use the Margins tab in the Page Setup dialog box to change the page orientation of the section that contains the table to landscape.

To change the page layout settings for an individual section, place the insertion point in the section, open the Page Setup (or Columns) dialog box, select the options you want to change, click the Apply to list arrow, click This section, then click OK. When you select This section in the Apply to list box, the settings are applied to the current section only. If you select Whole document in the Apply to list box, the settings are applied to all the sections in the document.

# Inserting Page Breaks

As you type text in a document, Word automatically inserts an **automatic page break** (also called a soft page break) when you reach the bottom of a page, allowing you to continue typing on the next page. You can also force text onto the next page of a document by using the Break command to insert a **manual page break** (also called a hard page break). █████ You insert manual page breaks where you know you want to begin each new page of the newsletter.

## STEPS

1. **Scroll down to the bottom of page 1, place the insertion point before the headline** 13 **Tips..., click** Insert **on the menu bar, then click** Break

   The Break dialog box opens. You also use this dialog box to insert page, column, and text-wrapping breaks. Table E-2 describes these types of breaks.

2. **Make sure the** Page break option button **is selected, then click** OK

   Word inserts a manual page break before "13 Tips" and moves all the text following the page break to the beginning of the next page, as shown in Figure E-5. The page break appears as a dotted line in Print Layout view when formatting marks are displayed. Page break marks are visible on the screen but do not print. Manual and automatic page breaks are always visible in Normal view.

3. **Scroll down to the bottom of page 2, place the insertion point before the headline** Kids Health Roundup, **press and hold** [Ctrl], **then press** [Enter]

   Pressing [Ctrl][Enter] is a fast way to insert a manual page break. The headline is forced to the top of the third page.

4. **Scroll down page 3, place the insertion point before the headline** Clinic News, **then press** [Ctrl][Enter]

   The headline is forced to the top of the fourth page.

5. **Press** [Ctrl][Home], **click the** Zoom list arrow **on the Standard toolbar, then click** Two Pages

   The first two pages of the document are displayed, as shown in Figure E-6.

6. **Scroll down to view pages 3 and 4, click the** Zoom list arrow, **click** Page Width, **then save the document**

---

### Clues to Use

#### Vertically aligning text on a page

By default, text is vertically aligned with the top margin of a page, but you can change the vertical alignment of text so that it is centered between the top and bottom margins, justified between the top and bottom margins, or aligned with the bottom margin of the page. You vertically align text on a page only when the text does not fill the page; for example, if you are creating a flyer or a title page for a report. To change the vertical alignment of text in a section (or a document), place the insertion point in the section you want to align, open the Page Setup dialog box, use the Vertical alignment list arrow on the Layout tab to select the alignment you want (top, center, justified, or bottom), use the Apply to list arrow to select the part of the document you want to align, then click OK.

**FIGURE E-5:** Manual page break in document

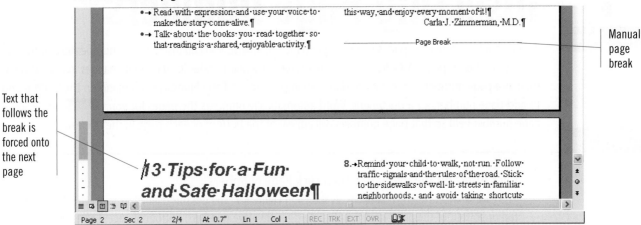

Text that follows the break is forced onto the next page

Manual page break

**FIGURE E-6:** Pages 1 and 2

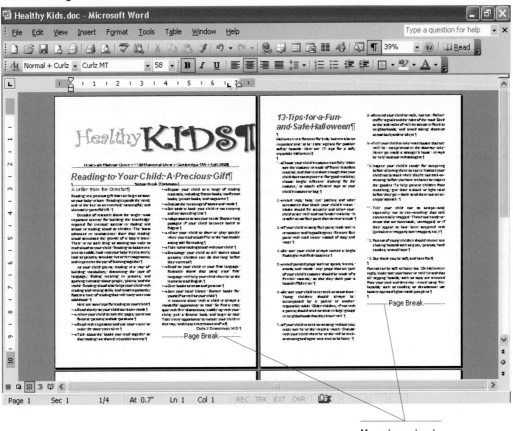

Manual page breaks

**TABLE E-2:** Types of breaks

| break | function |
| --- | --- |
| Page break | Forces the text following the break to begin at the top of the next page |
| Column break | Forces the text following the break to begin at the top of the next column |
| Text wrapping break | Forces the text following the break to begin at the beginning of the next line |

# Inserting Page Numbers

If you want to number the pages of a multiple-page document, you can insert a page number field at the top or bottom of each page. A **field** is a code that serves as a placeholder for data that changes in a document, such as a page number or the current date. When you use the Page Numbers command on the Insert menu to add page numbers to a document, Word automatically numbers the pages for you. ▰▰▰ You insert a page number field so that page numbers will appear at the bottom of each page in the document.

## STEPS

1. **Click Insert on the menu bar, then click Page Numbers**

   The Page Numbers dialog box opens, as shown in Figure E-7. You use this dialog box to specify the position—top or bottom of the page—and the alignment for the page numbers. Bottom of page (Footer) is the default position.

**QUICK TIP**

You can also align page numbers with the left, right, inside, or outside margins of a document.

2. **Click the Alignment list arrow, then click Center**

   The page numbers will be centered between the left and right margins at the bottom of each page.

3. **Click OK, then scroll to the bottom of the first page**

   The page number 1 appears in gray at the bottom of the first page, as shown in Figure E-8. The number is gray, or dimmed, because it is located in the Footer area. When the document is printed, the page numbers appear as normal text. You will learn more about headers and footers in the next lesson.

4. **Click the Print Preview button** 🄰 **on the Standard toolbar, then click the One Page button** 🄰 **on the Print Preview toolbar if necessary**

   The first page of the newsletter appears in Print Preview. Notice the page number.

5. **Click the page number with the** 🔍 **pointer to zoom in on the page**

   The page number is centered at the bottom of the page, as shown in Figure E-9.

6. **Scroll down the document to see the page number at the bottom of each page**

   Word automatically numbered each page of the newsletter.

**QUICK TIP**

To display more than six pages of a document in Print Preview, drag to expand the Multiple Pages grid.

7. **Click the Multiple Pages button** 🄳 **on the Print Preview toolbar, point to the second box in the bottom row on the grid to select 2 × 2 pages, then click**

   All four pages of the newsletter appear in the Print Preview window.

8. **Click Close on the Print Preview toolbar, press [Ctrl][Home], then save the document**

### Clues to Use

#### Inserting the date and time

Using the Date and Time command on the Insert menu, you can insert the current date or the current time into a document, either as a field or as static text. Word uses the clock on your computer to compute the current date and time. To insert the current date or time at the location of the insertion point, click Date and Time on the Insert menu, then select the date or time format you want to use from the list of available formats in the Date and Time dialog box. If you want to insert the date or time as a field that is updated automatically each time you open or print the document, select the Update automatically check box, then click OK. If you want the current date or time to remain in the document as static text, deselect the Update automatically check box, and then click OK.

Set location for
page number
(header or footer)

Set alignment of
page number

Clear to hide the
page number on
the first page

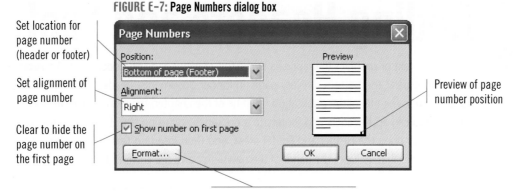

Preview of page
number position

Click to change numbering format

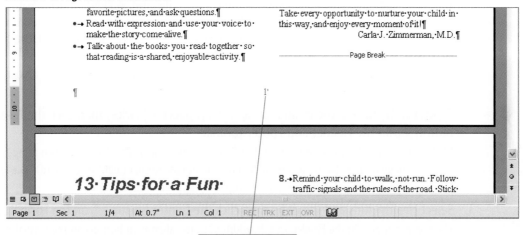

Page number is dimmed

One Page
button

Magnifier
button

Multiple
Pages
button

Page
number
in Print
Preview

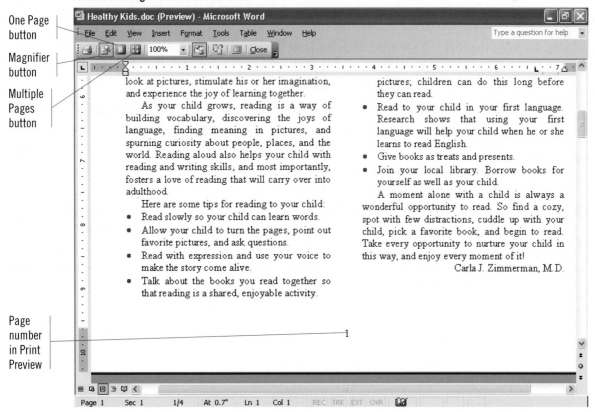

Word 2003

# Adding Headers and Footers

A **header** is text or graphics that appears at the top of every page of a document. A **footer** is text or graphics that appears at the bottom of every page. In longer documents, headers and footers often contain information such as the title of the publication, the title of the chapter, the name of the author, the date, or a page number. You can add headers and footers to a document by using the Header and Footer command on the View menu to open the Header and Footer areas, and then inserting text and graphics in them. ████ You create a header that includes the name of the newsletter and the current date.

## STEPS

1. **Click View on the menu bar, then click Header and Footer**

   The Header and Footer areas open and the document text is dimmed, as shown in Figure E-10. When the document text is dimmed, it cannot be edited. The Header and Footer toolbar also opens. It includes buttons for inserting standard text into headers and footers and for navigating between headers and footers. See Table E-3. The Header and Footer areas of a document are independent of the document itself and must be formatted separately. For example, if you select all the text in a document and then change the font, the header and footer font does not change.

   **QUICK TIP**

   You can change the date format by right-clicking the field, clicking Edit Field on the shortcut menu, then selecting a new date format in the Field properties list in the Field dialog box.

2. **Type Healthy Kids in the Header area, press [Spacebar] twice, then click the Insert Date button ▦ on the Header and Footer toolbar**

   Clicking the Insert Date button inserts a date field into the header. The date is inserted using the default date format (usually month/date/year, although your default date format might be different). The words "Healthy Kids" and the current date will appear at the top of every page in the document.

3. **Select Healthy Kids and the date, then click the Center button ▤ on the Formatting toolbar**

   The text is centered in the Header area. In addition to the alignment buttons on the Formatting toolbar, you can use tabs to align text in the Header and Footer areas. Notice the tab stops shown on the ruler. The tab stops are the default tab stops for the Header and Footer areas and are based on the default margin settings. If you change the margins in a document, you can adjust the tab stops in the Header or Footer area to align with the new margin settings.

   **QUICK TIP**

   Unless you set different headers and footers for different sections, the information you insert in any Header or Footer area appears on every page in the document.

4. **With the text still selected, click the Font list arrow on the Formatting toolbar, click Arial, click the Bold button ▣, then click in the Header area to deselect the text**

   The header text is formatted in 12-point Arial bold.

5. **Click the Switch Between Header and Footer button ▦ on the Header and Footer toolbar**

   The insertion point moves to the Footer area, where a page number field is centered in the Footer area.

6. **Double-click the page number to select the field, click the Font list arrow, click Arial, click ▣, then click in the Footer area to deselect the field**

   The page number is formatted in 12-point Arial bold.

   **QUICK TIP**

   To change the distance between the header and footer and the edge of the page, change the From edge settings on the Layout tab in the Page Setup dialog box.

7. **Click Close on the Header and Footer toolbar, save the document, then scroll down until the bottom of page 1 and the top of page 2 appear in the document window**

   The Header and Footer areas close and the header and footer text is dimmed, as shown in Figure E-11. The header text—"Healthy Kids" and the current date—appear at the top of every page in the document, and a page number appears at the bottom of every page.

**FIGURE E-10: Header area**

Header area is open

Tab stops for the header are set for the default document margins

Header and Footer toolbar (yours may open in a different location)

Document text is dimmed

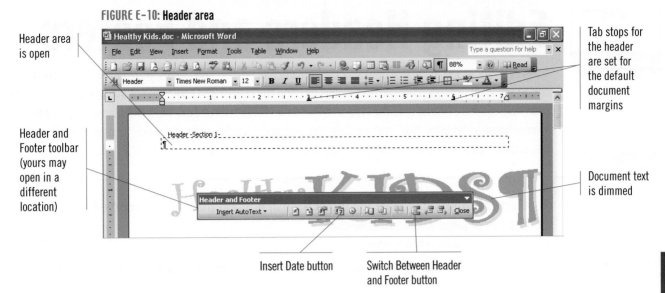

Insert Date button

Switch Between Header and Footer button

**FIGURE E-11: Header and footer in document**

Page number appears in the footer area on every page

Header text appears centered in the header area on every page (your date will differ)

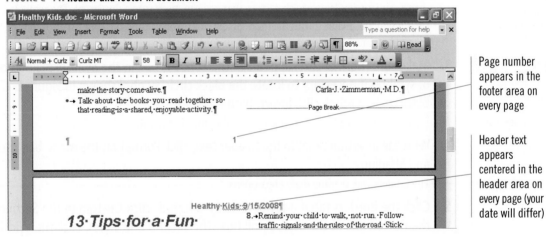

**TABLE E-3: Buttons on the Header and Footer toolbar**

| button | function |
| --- | --- |
| Insert AutoText ▾ | Inserts an AutoText entry, such as a field for the filename, or the author's name |
| Insert Page Number | Inserts a field for the page number so that the pages are numbered automatically |
| Insert Number of Pages | Inserts a field for the total number of pages in the document |
| Format Page Number | Opens the Page Number Format dialog box; use to change the numbering format or to begin automatic page numbering with a specific number |
| Insert Date | Inserts a field for the current date |
| Insert Time | Inserts a field for the current time |
| Page Setup | Opens the Page Setup dialog box |
| Show/Hide Document Text | Hides and displays the document text |
| Link to Previous | Switches the link between headers and footers in adjoining sections on and off; use to make headers and footers in adjoining sections the same or different |
| Switch Between Header and Footer | Moves the insertion point between the Header and Footer areas |
| Show Previous | Moves the insertion point to the header or footer in the previous section |
| Show Next | Moves the insertion point to the header or footer in the next section |

# Editing Headers and Footers

To change header and footer text or to alter the formatting of headers and footers, you must first open the Header and Footer areas. You open headers and footers by using the Header and Footer command on the View menu or by double-clicking a header or footer in Print Layout view. ▆▆▆▆ You modify the header by adding a small circle symbol between "Healthy Kids" and the date. You also add a border under the header text to set it off from the rest of the page. Finally, you remove the header and footer text from the first page of the document.

## STEPS

1. **Place the insertion point at the top of page 2, position the pointer over the header text at the top of page 2, then double-click**

   The Header and Footer areas open.

2. **Place the insertion point between the two spaces after Kids, click Insert on the menu bar, then click Symbol**

   The Symbol dialog box opens and is similar to Figure E-12. **Symbols** are special characters, such as graphics, shapes, and foreign language characters, that you can insert into a document. The symbols shown in Figure E-12 are the symbols included with the (normal text) font. You can use the Font list arrow on the Symbols tab to view the symbols included with each font on your computer.

3. **Make sure (normal text) appears in the Font list box in the Symbol dialog box, scroll the list of symbols if necessary to locate the black circle symbol shown in Figure E-12, select the black circle symbol, click Insert, then click Close**

   A circle symbol is added at the location of the insertion point.

4. **With the insertion point in the header text, click Format on the menu bar, then click Borders and Shading**

   The Borders and Shading dialog box opens.

5. **Click the Borders tab if it is not already selected, click Custom in the Setting section, click the dotted line in the Style scroll box (the second line style), click the Width list arrow, click 2¼ pt, click the Bottom border button in the Preview section, make sure Paragraph is selected in the Apply to list box, click OK, click Close on the Header and Footer toolbar, then scroll as needed to see the top of page 2**

   A dotted line border is added below the header text, as shown in Figure E-13.

6. **Press [Ctrl][Home] to move the insertion point to the beginning of the document**

   The newsletter already includes the name of the document at the top of the first page, making the header information redundant. You can modify headers and footers so that the header and footer text does not appear on the first page of a document or a section.

7. **Click File on the menu bar, click Page Setup, then click the Layout tab**

   The Layout tab of the Page Setup dialog box includes options for creating a different header and footer for the first page of a document or a section, and for creating different headers and footers for odd- and even-numbered pages. For example, in a document with facing pages, such as a magazine, you might want the publication title to appear in the left-page header, and the publication date to appear in the right-page header.

8. **Click the Different first page check box to select it, click the Apply to list arrow, click Whole document, then click OK**

   The header and footer text is removed from the Header and Footer areas on the first page.

9. **Scroll to see the header and footer on pages 2, 3, and 4, then save the document**

FIGURE E-12: Symbol dialog box

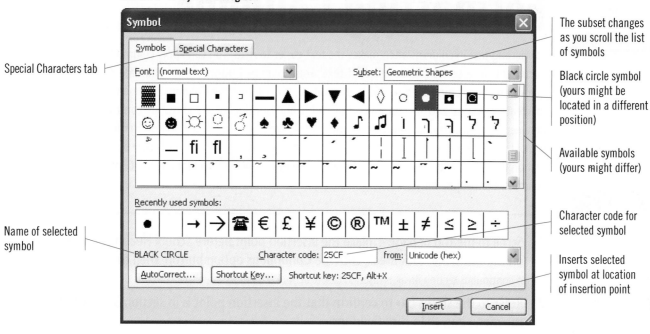

Special Characters tab

The subset changes as you scroll the list of symbols

Black circle symbol (yours might be located in a different position)

Available symbols (yours might differ)

Character code for selected symbol

Name of selected symbol

Inserts selected symbol at location of insertion point

FIGURE E-13: Symbol and border added to header

Dotted line border added to header

Symbol inserted in header

## Clues to Use

### Inserting and creating AutoText entries

Word includes several built-in AutoText entries, including salutations and closings for letters, as well as information for headers and footers. To insert a built-in AutoText entry at the location of the insertion point, point to AutoText on the Insert menu, point to a category on the AutoText menu, then click the AutoText entry you want to insert. You can also use the Insert AutoText button on the Header and Footer toolbar to insert an AutoText entry from the Header/Footer category into a header or footer.

The Word AutoText feature also allows you to store text and graphics that you use frequently so you can easily insert them in a

document. To create a custom AutoText entry, enter the text or graphic you want to store—such as a hospital name or logo—in a document, select it, point to AutoText on the Insert menu, then click New. In the Create AutoText dialog box, type a name for your AutoText entry, then click OK. The text or graphic is saved as a custom AutoText entry. To insert a custom AutoText entry in a document, point to AutoText on the Insert menu, click AutoText, select the entry name on the AutoText tab in the AutoCorrect dialog box, click Insert, then click OK.

# Formatting Columns

Formatting text in columns often makes the text easier to read. You can apply column formatting to a whole document, to a section, or to selected text. The Columns button on the Standard toolbar allows you to quickly create columns of equal width. In addition, you can use the Columns command on the Format menu to create columns and to customize the width and spacing of columns. To control the way text flows between columns, you can insert a **column break**, which forces the text following the break to move to the top of the next column. You can also balance columns of unequal length on a page by inserting a continuous section break at the end of the last column on the page. ▟▟▟▟ You format the Clinic News page in three columns, then adjust the flow of text.

## STEPS

1. **Scroll to the top of page 4, place the insertion point before** School Health Forms, **click** Insert **on the menu bar, click** Break, **click the** Continuous **option button, then click** OK

   A continuous section break is inserted before School. The newsletter now contains three sections.

**QUICK TIP**

To change the width and spacing of existing columns, you can use the Columns dialog box or drag the column markers on the horizontal ruler.

2. **Refer to the status bar to confirm that the insertion point is in section 3, click** Format **on the menu bar, then click** Columns

   The Columns dialog box opens, as shown in Figure E-14.

3. **Select** Three **in the Presets section, click the** Spacing down arrow **twice until 0.3" appears, select the** Line between **check box, then click** OK

   All the text in section 3 is formatted in three columns of equal width with a line between the columns, as shown in Figure E-15.

**QUICK TIP**

To create a banner headline that spans the width of a page, select the headline text, click the Columns button, then click 1 Column.

4. **Click the** Zoom list arrow **on the Standard toolbar, then click** Whole Page

   Notice that the third column of text is much shorter than the first two columns. Page 4 would look better if the three columns were balanced—each the same length.

5. **Place the insertion point at the end of the third column, click** Insert **on the menu bar, click** Break, **click the** Continuous **option button, then click** OK

   The columns in section 3 adjust to become roughly the same length.

6. **Scroll up to page 3**

   The two columns on page 3 are also uneven. You want the article about Teaching Kids Firearm Safety to appear at the top of the second column.

**QUICK TIP**

If a section contains a column break, you cannot balance the columns by inserting a continuous section break.

7. **Click the** Zoom list arrow, **click** Page Width, **scroll down page 3, place the insertion point before the headline** Teaching Kids..., **click** Insert **on the menu bar, click** Break, **click the** Column break **option button, then click** OK

   The text following the column break is forced to the top of the next column.

8. **Click the** Zoom list arrow, **click** Two Pages, **then save the document**

   The columns on pages 3 and 4 are formatted as shown in Figure E-16.

## Clues to Use

### Hyphenating text in a document

Hyphenating text in a document is another way to control the flow of text in columns. Hyphens are small dashes that break words that fall at the end of a line. Hyphenation diminishes the gaps between words in justified text and reduces ragged right edges in left-aligned text. If a document has narrow columns, hyphenating the text can help give the pages a cleaner look. To hyphenate a document automatically, point to Language on the Tools menu, click Hyphenation, select the Automatically hyphenate document check box in the Hyphenation dialog box, then click OK. You can also use the Hyphenation dialog box to change the hyphenation zone—the distance between the margin and the end of the last word in the line. A smaller hyphenation zone results in a greater number of hyphenated words and a cleaner look to columns of text.

## FIGURE E-14: Columns dialog box

Select a preset format for columns

Change the number of columns

Select to add a line between columns

Set custom width and spacing for columns

Preview of current settings

Select to create columns of equal width

Select part of document to apply format to

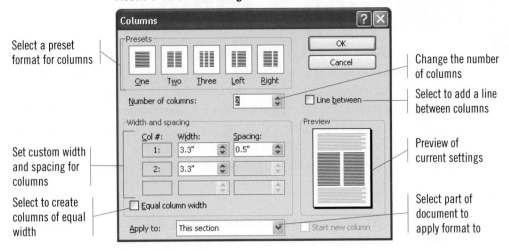

## FIGURE E-15: Text formatted in three columns

Text in section 3 is formatted in three columns

Column markers show the width and spacing of columns

Section break is at end of section 2

Line added between columns

## FIGURE E-16: Columns on pages 3 and 4 of the newsletter

Text following column break is forced to top of next column

Column break

Continuous section break

Columns in section are balanced

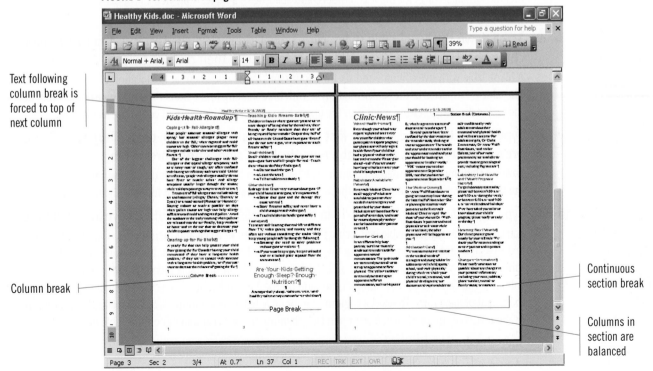

# Inserting a Table

Adding a table to a document is a useful way to illustrate information that is intended for quick reference and analysis. A **table** is a grid of columns and rows of cells that you can fill with text and graphics. A **cell** is the box formed by the intersection of a column and a row. The lines that divide the columns and rows of a table and help you see the grid-like structure of the table are called **borders**. A simple way to insert a table into a document is to use the Insert command on the Table menu. This command allows you to determine the dimensions and format of a table before it is inserted. ▰▰▰▰ You add a table showing the average sleep, calcium, iron, and calorie requirements for children to the bottom of page 3.

## STEPS

1. **Click the Zoom list arrow on the Standard toolbar, click Page Width, then scroll down page 3 until the headline Are Your Kids... is at the top of your screen**

   The bottom of page three is displayed.

2. **Place the insertion point before the headline Are Your Kids..., click Insert on the menu bar, click Break, click the Continuous option button, then click OK**

   A continuous section break is inserted before the headline Are Your Kids.... The document now includes four sections, with the headline Are Your Kids... in the third section.

3. **Click the Columns button 🔳 on the Standard toolbar, point to the first column on the grid, then click**

   Section 3 is formatted as a single column.

4. **Place the insertion point before the paragraph mark below the heading Average daily..., click Table on the menu bar, point to Insert, then click Table**

   The Insert Table Dialog box opens, as shown in Figure E-17. You use this dialog box to create a blank table with a set number of columns and rows, and to choose an option for sizing the width of the columns in the table.

### QUICK TIP
To apply a different table style to a table after it is created, place the insertion point in the table, click Table Auto-Format on the Table menu, and then modify the selections in the Table Auto-Format dialog box.

5. **Verify 5 is in the Number of columns text box, press [Tab], type 6 in the Number of rows text box, make sure the Fixed column width option button is selected, then click AutoFormat**

   The Table AutoFormat dialog box opens. You use this dialog box to apply a table style to the table. Table styles include format settings for the text, borders, and shading in a table. A preview of the selected style appears in the Preview section of the dialog box.

6. **Scroll down the list of table styles, click Table Grid 8, clear the Last row and Last column check boxes in the Apply special formats to section, then click OK twice**

   A blank table with five columns and six rows is inserted in the document at the location of the insertion point. The table is formatted in the Table Grid 8 style, with blue shading in the header row and blue borders that define the table cells. The insertion point is in the upper-left cell of the table, the first cell in the header row.

7. **Type Age in the first cell in the first row, press [Tab], type Sleep, press [Tab], type Calcium, press [Tab], type Iron, press [Tab], type Healthy Calories, then press [Tab]**

   Pressing [Tab] moves the insertion point to the next cell in the row. At the end of a row, pressing [Tab] moves the insertion point to the first cell in the next row. You can also click in a cell to move the insertion point to it.

### TROUBLE
If you pressed [Tab] after the last row, click the Undo button 🔄 on the Standard toolbar to remove the blank row.

8. **Type the text shown in Figure E-18 in the table cells, pressing [Tab] to move from cell to cell**

   You can edit the text in a table by placing the insertion point in a cell and then typing. You can also select the text in a table and then format it using the buttons on the Formatting toolbar. If you want to modify the structure of a table, you can use the Insert and Delete commands on the Table menu to add and remove rows and columns. You can also use the AutoFit command on the Table menu to change the width of table columns and the height of table rows. To select a column, row, or table before performing an action, place the insertion point in the row, column, or table you want to select, then use the Select command on the Table menu.

9. **Save the document**

**FIGURE E-17:** Insert Table dialog box

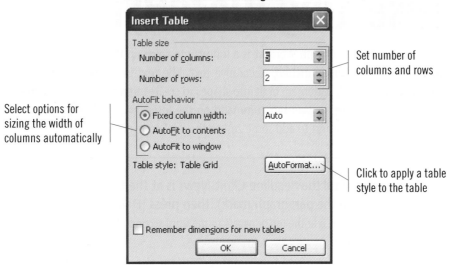

Set number of columns and rows

Select options for sizing the width of columns automatically

Click to apply a table style to the table

**FIGURE E-18:** Completed table

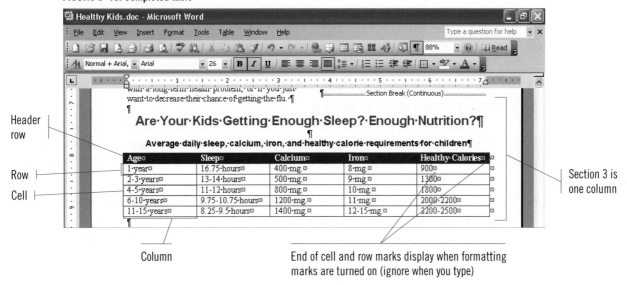

Header row

Row

Cell

Section 3 is one column

Column

End of cell and row marks display when formatting marks are turned on (ignore when you type)

## Clues to Use

### Moving around in a long document

Rather than scrolling to move to a different place in a long document, you can use the Browse by Object feature, the Go To command, or the Document Map to quickly move the insertion point to a specific location. Browse by Object allows you to browse to the next or previous page, section, line, table, graphic, or other item of the same type in a document. To do this, first click the Select Browse Object button below the vertical scroll bar to open a palette of object types. On this palette, click the button for the type of item by which you want to browse, then click the Next or Previous buttons to scroll through the items of that type in the document.

To move a specific page, section, or other item in a document,

you can click the Go To command on the Edit menu. On the Go To tab in the Find and Replace dialog box, select the type of item in the Go to what list box, type the item number in the text box, then click Go To to move the insertion point to the item.

If your document is formatted with heading styles, you can also use the Document Map to navigate a document. The Document Map is a separate pane in the document window that displays a list of headings in the document. You click a heading in the Document Map to move the insertion point to that heading in the document. To open and close the Document Map, click Document Map on the View menu or click the Document Map button on the Standard toolbar.

# Inserting WordArt

Illustrating a document with WordArt is a fun way to spice up the layout of a page. **WordArt** is an object that contains specially formatted, decorative text. The text in a WordArt object can be skewed, rotated, stretched, shadowed, patterned, or fit into shapes to create interesting effects. To insert a WordArt object into a document, you use the WordArt command on the Insert menu. ▄▄▄▄ You decide to format the Clinic News headline as WordArt to add some zest to the final page of the newsletter.

## STEPS

1. **Scroll down until the headline** Clinic News **is at the top of your screen, select** Clinic News **(not including the paragraph mark), then press** [Delete]
   The insertion point is at the top of page 4 in the third section of the document. The third section is formatted as a single column.

2. **Click** Insert **on the menu bar, point to** Picture, **then click** WordArt
   The WordArt Gallery dialog box opens, as shown in Figure E-19. You use the WordArt Gallery to select a style for the WordArt object.

3. **Click the** fourth style in the third row, **then click** OK
   The Edit WordArt Text dialog box opens. You type the text you want to format as WordArt in this dialog box. You can also use the Edit WordArt Text dialog box to change the font and font size of the WordArt text.

4. **Type** Clinic News, **then click** OK
   The WordArt object appears at the location of the insertion point. The object is an **inline graphic**, or part of the line of text in which it was inserted.

5. **Click the** WordArt object **to select it**
   The black squares that appear on the corners and sides of the object are the **sizing handles**. Sizing handles appear when a graphic object is selected. You can drag a sizing handle to change the size of the object. The WordArt toolbar also appears when a WordArt object is selected. You use the buttons on the WordArt toolbar to edit and modify the format of WordArt objects.

6. **Position the pointer over the** lower-right sizing handle, **when the pointer changes to** ↘ **drag down and to the right to make the object about 1½" tall and 6" wide**
   Refer to the vertical and horizontal rulers for guidance as you drag the sizing handle to resize the object. When you release the mouse button, the WordArt object is enlarged, as shown in Figure E-20.

7. **Click the** Center button ☰ **on the Formatting toolbar**
   The WordArt object is centered between the margins.

8. **Click the** WordArt Shape button ◮ **on the WordArt toolbar, then click the** Wave 1 shape **(the fifth shape in the third row)**
   The shape of the WordArt text changes.

9. **Click outside the WordArt object to deselect it, click the** Zoom list arrow **on the Standard toolbar, click** Two Pages, **then save the document**
   The completed pages 3 and 4 are displayed, as shown in Figure E-21.

**FIGURE E-19:** WordArt Gallery dialog box

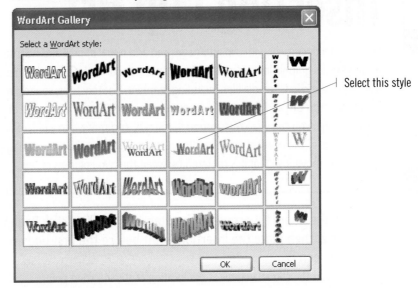

Select this style

**FIGURE E-20:** Resized WordArt object

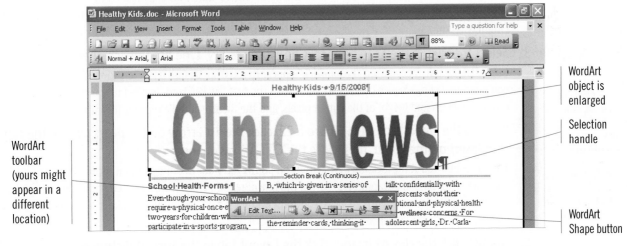

WordArt object is enlarged

Selection handle

WordArt toolbar (yours might appear in a different location)

WordArt Shape button

**FIGURE E-21:** Completed pages 3 and 4

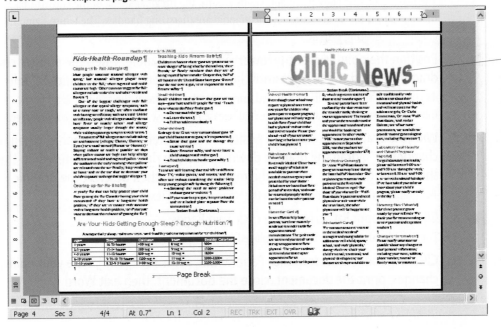

WordArt centered with the Wave 1 shape applied

# Inserting Clip Art

Illustrating a document with clip art images can add visual appeal and help communicate your ideas. **Clip art** is a collection of graphic images you can insert into a document. Clip art images are stored in the **Clip Organizer**, a library of the **clips**—media files, including graphics, photographs, sounds, movies, and animations—that come with Word. You can add a clip to a document using the Clip Art command on the Insert menu. After you insert a clip art image, you can wrap text around it, resize it, and move it to a different location. ▰▰▰▰ You illustrate the second page of the newsletter with a clip art image. After you insert the image, you wrap text around it, enlarge it, and then move it so that it is centered between the two columns of text.

## STEPS

1. **Click the Zoom list arrow on the Standard toolbar, click Page Width, scroll to the top of page 2, then place the insertion point before the first body paragraph, which begins Halloween is...**

   You insert the clip art graphic at the location of the insertion point.

2. **Click Insert on the menu bar, point to Picture, then click Clip Art**

   The Clip Art task pane opens. You can use this task pane to search for clips related to a keyword. If you are working with an active Internet connection, your search results will include clip art from the Microsoft Office Online Web site.

**TROUBLE**

Make sure All media file types shows in the Results should be list box. If not, click the Results should be list arrow, then click the All media types check box. Select a different clip if the clip shown in Figure E-22 is not available to you.

3. **Select the text in the Search for text box if necessary, type broomstick, then click Go**

   Clips that include the keyword "broomstick" appear in the Clip Art task pane, as shown in Figure E-22. When you point to a clip, a ScreenTip appears and shows the first few keywords applied to the clip (listed alphabetically), the width and height of the clip in pixels, and the file size and file type for the clip.

4. **Point to the clip called out in Figure E-22, click the list arrow that appears next to the clip, click Insert on the menu, then close the Clip Art task pane**

   The clip is inserted at the location of the insertion point. You want to center the graphic on the page. Until you apply text wrapping to a graphic, it is part of the line of text in which it was inserted (an **inline graphic**). To move a graphic independently of text, you must wrap the text around it to make it a **floating graphic**, which can be moved anywhere on a page.

5. **Double-click the clip art image, click the Layout tab in the Format Picture dialog box, click Tight, then click OK**

   The text in the first body paragraph wraps around the irregular shape of the clip art image. The white circles that appear on the square edges of the graphic are the sizing handles. The white sizing handles indicate the graphic is a floating graphic.

**QUICK TIP**

To verify the size of a graphic or to set precise measurements, double-click the graphic to open the Format Picture dialog box, then adjust the Height and Width settings on the Size tab.

6. **Position the pointer over the lower-right sizing handle, when the pointer changes to ↘ drag down and to the right until the graphic is about 2½" wide and 2¾" tall**

   As you drag a sizing handle, the dotted lines show the outline of the graphic. Refer to the dotted lines and the rulers as you resize the graphic. When you release the mouse button, the image is enlarged.

7. **With the graphic still selected, position the pointer over the graphic, when the pointer changes to ✛ drag the graphic down and to the right so it is centered on the page, as shown in Figure E-23, release the mouse button, then deselect the graphic**

   The graphic is now centered between the two columns of text.

**TROUBLE**

If page 3 is a blank page or contains text continued from page 2, reduce the size of the graphic on page 2.

8. **Click the Zoom list arrow, then click Two Pages**

   The completed pages 1 and 2 are displayed, as shown in Figure E-24.

9. **Click the Zoom list arrow, click Page Width, press [Ctrl][End], type your name, save your changes, print the document, close the document, then exit Word**

**FIGURE E-22:** Clip Art task pane

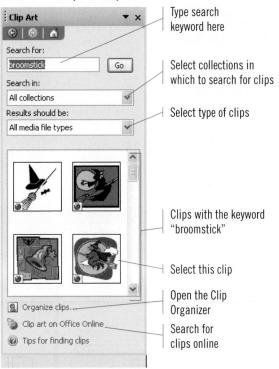

Type search keyword here

Select collections in which to search for clips

Select type of clips

Clips with the keyword "broomstick"

Select this clip

Open the Clip Organizer

Search for clips online

**FIGURE E-23:** Graphic being moved to a new location

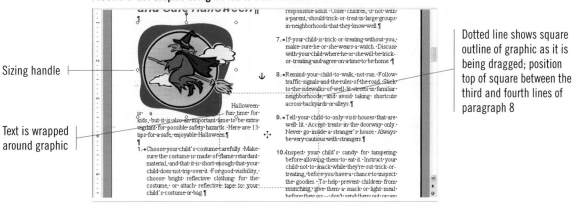

Sizing handle

Text is wrapped around graphic

Dotted line shows square outline of graphic as it is being dragged; position top of square between the third and fourth lines of paragraph 8

**FIGURE E-24:** Completed pages 1 and 2 of newsletter

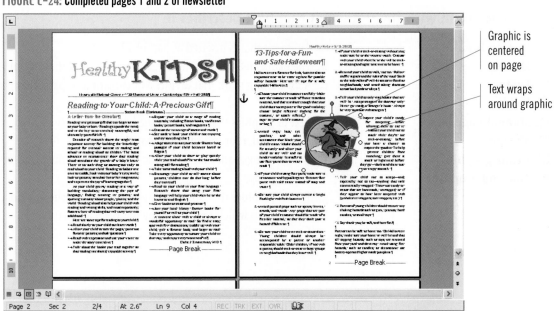

Graphic is centered on page

Text wraps around graphic

# Practice

## ▼ CONCEPTS REVIEW

**Label each element shown in Figure E-25.**

FIGURE E-25

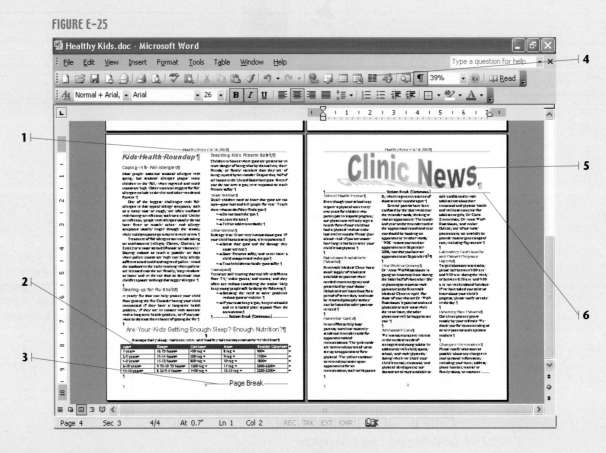

**Match each term with the statement that best describes it.**

7. **Section break**

8. **Header**

9. **Footer**

10. **Field**

11. **Manual page break**

12. **Margin**

13. **Inline graphic**

14. **Floating graphic**

a. An image that is inserted as part of a line of text

b. The blank area between the edge of the text and the edge of the page

c. A formatting mark that divides a document into parts that can be formatted differently

d. Text or graphics that appear at the bottom of every page in a document

e. A placeholder for information that changes

f. A formatting mark that forces the text following the mark to begin at the top of the next page

g. Text or graphics that appear at the top of every page in a document

h. An image to which text wrapping has been applied

**Select the best answer from the list of choices.**

**15.** Pressing [Ctrl][Enter] does which of the following?

 **a.** Inserts a continuous section break

 **b.** Inserts an automatic page break

 **c.** Moves the insertion point to the beginning of the document

 **d.** Inserts a manual page break

**16.** Which of the following do documents with mirror margins always have?

 **a.** Different first page headers and footers

 **b.** Gutters

 **c.** Landscape orientation

 **d.** Inside and outside margins

**17.** Which button is used to insert a field into a header or footer?

 **a.** 🖼️ **c.** 🖼️

 **b.** 🖼️ **d.** 🖼️

**18.** Which type of break do you insert if you want to force text to begin on the next page?

 **a.** Manual page break **c.** Continuous section break

 **b.** Text wrapping break **d.** Automatic page break

**19.** Which type of break do you insert if you want to balance the columns in a section?

 **a.** Automatic page break **c.** Column break

 **b.** Continuous section break **d.** Text wrapping break

**20.** What must you do to change an inline graphic to a floating graphic?

 **a.** Anchor the graphic **c.** Move the graphic

 **b.** Apply text wrapping to the graphic **d.** Resize the graphic

# ▼ SKILLS REVIEW

**1. Set document margins.**

 **a.** Start Word, open the file WMP E-2.doc from the drive and folder where your Data Files are located, then save it as **Springfield Fitness**.

 **b.** Change the top and bottom margins to 1.2" and the left and right margins to 1".

 **c.** Save your changes to the document.

**2. Divide a document into sections.**

 **a.** Hide the white space in the document by moving the pointer to the top of a page, then clicking the Hide White Space pointer that appears.

 **b.** Scroll down, then insert a continuous section break before the **Facilities** heading.

 **c.** Format the text in section 2 in two columns, then save your changes to the document.

**3. Insert page breaks.**

 **a.** Insert a manual page break before the heading **Welcome to the Springfield Fitness Center!**.

 **b.** Scroll down and insert a manual page break before the heading **Services**.

 **c.** Scroll down and insert a manual page break before the heading **Membership**.

 **d.** Show the white space in the document by moving the pointer over the thick black line that separates the pages, then clicking the Show White Space pointer that appears.

 **e.** Press [Ctrl][Home], then save your changes to the document.

**4. Insert page numbers.**

 **a.** Insert page numbers in the document. Center the page numbers at the bottom of the page.

 **b.** View the page numbers on each page in Print Preview, close Print Preview, then save your changes to the document.

**5. Add headers and footers.**

  **a.** Open the Header and Footer areas.

  **b.** Type your name in the Header area, press [Tab] twice, then use the Insert Date button on the Header and Footer toolbar to insert the current date.

  **c.** On the horizontal ruler, drag the right tab stop from the 6" mark to the 6½" mark so that the date aligns with the right margin of the document.

  **d.** Move the insertion point to the Footer area.

  **e.** Double-click the page number to select it, then format the page number in bold italic.

  **f.** Close headers and footers, preview the header and footer on each page in Print Preview, close Print Preview, then save your changes to the document.

**6. Edit headers and footers.**

  **a.** Open headers and footers, then apply italic to the text in the header.

  **b.** Move the insertion point to the Footer area, double-click the page number to select it, then press [Delete].

  **c.** Click the Align Right button on the Formatting toolbar.

  **d.** Use the Symbol command on the Insert menu to open the Symbol dialog box.

  **e.** Insert a black, right-pointing triangle symbol (character code: 25BA), then close the Symbol dialog box. (*Note*: Select a different symbol if 25BA is not available to you.)

  **f.** Use the Insert Page Number button on the Header and Footer toolbar to insert a page number.

  **g.** Use the Page Setup button on the Header and Footer toolbar to open the Page Setup dialog box.

  **h.** Use the Layout tab to create a different header and footer for the first page of the document.

  **i.** Scroll to the beginning of the document, type your name in the First Page Header area, then apply italic to your name.

  **j.** Close headers and footers, preview the header and footer on each page in Print Preview, close Print Preview, then save your changes to the document.

**7. Format columns.**

  **a.** On page 2, select **Facilities** and the paragraph mark below it, use the Columns button to format the selected text as one column, then center **Facilities** on the page.

  **b.** Balance the columns on page 2 by inserting a continuous section break at the bottom of the second column.

  **c.** On page 3, select **Services** and the paragraph mark below it, format the selected text as one column, then center the text.

  **d.** Balance the columns on page 3.

  **e.** On page 4, select **Membership** and the paragraph mark below it, format the selected text as one column, then center the text.

  **f.** Insert a column break before the **Membership Cards** heading, press [Ctrl][Home], then save your changes to the document.

**8. Insert a table.**

  **a.** Click the Document Map button on the Standard toolbar to open the Document Map.

  **b.** In the Document Map, click the heading Membership Rates, then close the Document Map. (*Hint*: The Document Map button is a toggle button.)

  **c.** Select the word Table at the end of the Membership Rates section, press [Delete], then open the Insert Table dialog box.

  **d.** Create a table with two columns and five rows, open the Table AutoFormat dialog box, then apply the Table Classic 2 style to the table, clearing the Last row check box. Close the dialog boxes.

  **e.** Press [Tab] to leave the first cell in the header row blank, then type **Rate**.

  **f.** Press [Tab], then type the following text in the table, pressing [Tab] to move from cell to cell.

| | |
|---|---|
| **Enrollment/Individual** | $100 |
| **Enrollment/Couple** | $150 |
| **Monthly membership/Individual** | $35 |
| **Monthly membership/Couple** | $60 |

**g.** With the insertion point in the table, right-click the table, point to AutoFit on the shortcut menu, then click AutoFit to Contents.

**h.** With the insertion point in the table, right-click again, point to AutoFit, then click AutoFit to Window.

**i.** Save your changes to the document.

**9. Insert WordArt.**

**a.** Scroll to page 3, place the insertion point before the **Personal Training** heading, then insert a WordArt object.

**b.** Select any horizontal WordArt style, type **Get Fit!**, then click OK.

**c.** Click the WordArt object to select it, click the Text Wrapping button on the WordArt toolbar, then apply the Tight text-wrapping style to the object so that it is a floating object.

**d.** Move the object so that it is centered below the text at the bottom of the page (below the page break mark).

**e.** Adjust the size and position of the object so that the page looks attractive. (*Hint*: The sizing handles on floating objects are white circles.)

**f.** Apply a different WordArt shape to the object, preview the page, adjust the size and position of the WordArt object if necessary, then save your changes to the document.

**10. Insert clip art.**

**a.** On page 1, place the insertion point in the second blank paragraph below **A Rehabilitation and Exercise Facility**. (*Hint*: Place the insertion point to the left of the paragraph mark.)

**b.** Open the Clip Art task pane. Search for clips related to the keyword **fitness**.

**c.** Insert the clip shown in Figure E-26. (*Note*: An active Internet connection is needed to select the clip shown in the figure. Select a different clip if this one is not available to you. If you are working offline, you might need to search using a keyword such as sports.)

**d.** Select the graphic, then drag the lower-right sizing handle down and to the right so that the graphic is about 3" wide and 3" tall. Size the graphic so that all the text and the manual page break fit on page 1. (*Hint*: The sizing handles on inline graphics are black squares.)

**e.** Save your changes to the document. Preview the document, print a copy, then close the document and exit Word.

FIGURE E-26

*Your Name*

# The Springfield Fitness Center

## A Rehabilitation and Exercise Facility

## Member Services

### *Hours of Operation*

**Monday – Friday:**
6:00 a.m. to 10:00 p.m.

**Saturday:**
7:00 a.m. to 10:00 p.m.

**Sunday:**
1:00 p.m. to 5:00 p.m.

# ▼ INDEPENDENT CHALLENGE 1

You are the director of the Muscular Therapy Center, which offers a variety of massage services to customers. You have begun work on the text for a brochure advertising your business and are ready to lay out the pages and prepare the final copy. The brochure will be printed on both sides of an 8½" × 11" sheet of paper, and folded in thirds.

**a.** Start Word, open the file WMP E-3.doc from the drive and folder where your Data Files are located, then save it as **Massage Brochure**. Read the document to get a feel for its contents.

**b.** Change the page orientation to landscape, and change all four margins to .6".

**c.** Format the document in three columns of equal width.

**d.** Insert a manual page break before the heading **Welcome to the Muscular Therapy Center**.

**e.** On page 1, insert column breaks before the heading **Menu of Massage Services** and the subheading **Shiatsu Massage**.

**f.** On page 1, insert a continuous section break at the end of the third column to create separate sections on pages one and two.

**g.** Add lines between the columns on the first page.

**h.** Create a different header and footer for the first page. Type **A variety of choices to meet your needs** in the First Page Footer area.

**i.** Center the text in the footer area, format it in 20-point Comic Sans MS, all caps, with a violet font color, then close headers and footers.

**j.** On page 2, insert a column break before Your Name. Press [Enter] as many times as necessary to move the contact information to the bottom of the second column. Be sure all six lines of the contact information are in column 2 and do not flow to the next column.

**k.** Replace Your Name with your name, then center the contact information in the column.

**l.** Insert a column break at the bottom of the second column. Then, type the text shown in Figure E-27 in the third column. Refer to the figure as you follow the instructions for formatting the text in the third column.

**m.** Format Therapeutic Massage at the Muscular Therapy Center in Comic Sans MS, bold, with a violet font color. Format **Therapeutic Massage** as 32-point text, **at the** as 14-point text, and **Muscular Therapy Center** as 22-point text.

**n.** Format the remaining text in 12-point Comic Sans MS, with a violet font color. Center the text in the third column if it is not already centered.

**o.** Insert the clip art graphic shown in Figure E-27 or another appropriate clip art graphic. Do not wrap text around the graphic.

**p.** Resize the graphic and add and remove blank paragraphs in the third column of your brochure so that the spacing between elements roughly matches the spacing shown in Figure E-27.

### Advanced Challenge Exercise

■ Format Therapeutic Massage as a WordArt object using a WordArt style and shape of your choice.

■ Format Muscular Therapy Center as a WordArt object using a WordArt style and shape of your choice.

■ Adjust the size, position, and spacing of the WordArt objects, clip art graphic, and text in the third column so that the brochure is attractive and eye-catching.

**q.** Save your changes, preview the brochure in Print Preview, then print a copy. If possible, print the two pages of the brochure back to back so that the brochure can be folded in thirds.

**r.** Close the document and exit Word.

**FIGURE E-27**

# Therapeutic Massage

at the
## Muscular Therapy Center

*The Skill of Massage*
*The Art of Healing*

# ▼ INDEPENDENT CHALLENGE 2

You work in the Parking and Shuttle Service Office at Hudson State University Hospital. You have written the text for an informational flyer about parking regulations on the hospital campus and now you need to format the flyer so it is attractive and readable.

**a.** Start Word, open the file WMP E-4.doc from the drive and folder where your Data Files are located, then save it as **Hospital Parking FAQ**. Read the document to get a feel for its contents.

**b.** Change all four margins to .7".

**c.** Insert a continuous section break before **1. May I drive a car to work at the hospital?** (*Hint:* Place the insertion point before May.)

**d.** Scroll down and insert a next page section break before **Sample Parking Permit**.

**e.** Format the section 2 text in three columns of equal width with .3" of space between the columns.

**f.** Hyphenate the document using the automatic hyphenation feature. (*Hint:* If the Hyphenation feature is not installed on your computer, skip this step.)

**g.** Add a 3-point dotted-line bottom border to the blank paragraph under Hudson State University Hospital (HSUH). (*Hint:* Place the insertion point before the paragraph mark under Hudson State University Hospital (HSUH), then apply a bottom border to the paragraph.)

**h.** Add your name to the header. Right-align your name, and format it in 10-point Arial.

**i.** Add the following text to the footer, inserting symbols between words as indicated: **Parking and Shuttle Service Office • Hudson State University Hospital • 942-555-2227.**

**j.** Format the footer text in 9-point Arial Black and center it in the footer. Use a different font if Arial Black is not available to you. If necessary, adjust the font and font size so that the entire address fits on one line.

**k.** Apply a 3-point dotted-line border above the footer text. Make sure to apply the border to the paragraph.

**l.** Balance the columns in section 2.

**m.** Add the clip art graphic shown in Figure E-28 (or another appropriate clip art graphic) to the upper-right corner of the document, above the border. Make sure the graphic does not obscure the border. (*Hint:* Apply text wrapping to the graphic before positioning it.)

FIGURE E-28

**Frequently Asked Questions**

**Parking & Shuttle Service Office**

Hudson State University Hospital (HSUH)

**n.** Place the insertion point on page 2 (which is section 4). Change the left and right margins in section 4 to 1". Also change the page orientation of section 4 to landscape.

**o.** Change the vertical alignment of section 4 to center.

**p.** Save your changes, preview the flyer in Print Preview, then print a copy. If possible, print the two pages of the flyer back to back.

**q.** Close the document and exit Word.

# ▼ INDEPENDENT CHALLENGE 3

A book publisher would like to publish an article you wrote on the health effects of stormwater pollution as a chapter in a forth-coming book called *Environmental Health Issues for the New Millennium*. The publisher has requested that you format your article like a book chapter before submitting it for publication, and has provided you with a style sheet.

**a.** Start Word, open the file WMP E-5.doc from the drive and folder where your Data Files are located, then save it as **Chapter 4**.

**b.** Change the font of the entire document to 11-point Book Antiqua. If this font is not available to you, select a different font suitable for the pages of a book. Change the alignment to justified.

**c.** Change the paper size to 6" × 9".

**d.** Create mirror margins. (*Hint*: Use the Multiple pages list arrow on the Margins tab.) Change the top and bottom margins to .8", change the inside margin to .4", change the outside margin to .6", and create a .3" gutter to allow room for the book's binding.

**e.** Change the Zoom level to Two Pages, then apply the setting to create different headers and footers for odd- and even-numbered pages.

**f.** Change the Zoom level to Page Width. In the odd-page header, type **Chapter 4**, insert a symbol of your choice, then type **The Health Effects of Stormwater Pollution**.

**g.** Format the header text in 9-point Book Antiqua italic, then right-align the text.

**h.** In the even-page header, type your name, insert a symbol of your choice, then insert a date field. (*Hint*: Scroll down or use the Show Next button to move the insertion point to the even-page header.)

**i.** Change the format of the date to include just the month and the year. (*Hint*: Right-click the date field, then click Edit Field.)

**j.** Format the header text in 9-point Book Antiqua italic. The even-page header should be left-aligned.

**k.** Insert a left-aligned page number field in the even-page footer area, and a right-aligned page number field in the odd-page footer area. Format the page numbers in 10-point Book Antiqua.

**l.** Format the page numbers so that the first page of your chapter, which is Chapter 4 in the book, begins on page 65. (*Hint*: Select a page number field, then use the Format Page Number button.)

**m.** Go to the beginning of the document, press [Enter] 10 times, type **Chapter 4: The Health Effects of Stormwater Pollution**, press [Enter] twice, type your name, then press [Enter] twice.

**n.** Format the chapter title in 16-point Century Gothic bold, format your name in 14-point Century Gothic using small caps, then left-align the title text and your name. If Century Gothic is not available to you, select a different sans serif font.

## Advanced Challenge Exercise

■ Use the Browse by Object feature to move the insertion point to page 4 in the document, scroll down, place the insertion point at the end of the paragraph above the Potential health effects... heading, press [Enter] twice, type **Table 1: Total annual pollutant loads per year in the Fairy Creek Catchment**, format the text as bold, then press [Enter] twice.

■ Insert a table with four columns and four rows that is formatted in the Table Professional style.

■ Type the text shown in Figure E-29 in the table. Do not be concerned when the text wraps to the next line in a cell.

■ Make sure the text in the header row is bold, then remove any bold formatting from the text in the remaining rows.

■ Place the insertion point in the table, point to AutoFit on the Table menu, click Distribute Rows Evenly, point to AutoFit on the Table menu a second time, then click AutoFit to Contents.

**o.** Save your changes, preview the chapter in Print Preview, print the first four pages of the chapter, then close the document and exit Word.

**FIGURE E-29**

| Area | Nitrogen | Phosphorus | Suspended solids |
|------|----------|------------|------------------|
| Fairy Creek | 9.3 tonnes | 1.2 tonnes | 756.4 tonnes |
| Durras Arm | 6.2 tonnes | .9 tonnes | 348.2 tonnes |
| Cabbage Tree Creek | 9.8 tonnes | 2.3 tonnes | 485.7 tonnes |

# ▼ INDEPENDENT CHALLENGE 4

One of the most common opportunities to use the page layout features of Word is when formatting a research paper. The format recommended by the *Publication Manual of the American Psychological Association*, a style guide that includes information on preparing, writing, and formatting research papers, is the standard format used by many programs for medical professionals. In this independent challenge, you will research the APA (American Psychological Association) guidelines for formatting a research paper and use the guidelines you find to prepare the first few pages of a sample research report.

a. Use your favorite search engine to search the Web for information on the APA guidelines for formatting a research report. Use the keywords **APA style** and **research paper format** to conduct your search.

b. Look for information on the proper formatting for the following aspects of a research paper: paper size, margins, line spacing, paragraph indentation, page numbers, short title, title page, abstract, first page of the body of the report, and references. Print the information you find.

c. Start Word, open the file WMP E-6.doc from the drive and folder where your Data Files are located, then save it as **APA Research Paper**. Using the information you learned, format this document as a research report.

d. Adjust the margins, set the line spacing, and add a short title and page numbers to the document header in the format recommended by the APA. Use **Diabetes Advancements** as the short title of the sample report.

e. Create a title page for the sample report. Use **Advances in the Treatment of Type 1 Diabetes** as the title for your sample report, use your name as the author name, and make up information about your affiliation (for example, your school or class), if necessary. You do not need to include a running head. Make sure to format the title page exactly as the APA style dictates.

f. Format the remaining text as the abstract, body, and references of the research report.

g. Save the document to the drive and folder where your Data Files are located, print a copy, close the document, then exit Word.

Use the file WMP E-7.doc, found on the drive and folder where your Data Files are located, to create the article shown in Figure E-30. (*Hint*: Change all four margins to .6". To locate the tick clip art image, search using the keyword **tick**, and be sure the Everywhere check box in the Search in list box in the Clip Art task pane has a check mark. Select a different clip if the clip shown in the figure is not available to you.) Save the document with the filename **Lyme Disease**, then print a copy.

FIGURE E-30

## TRAVELER'S HEALTH WATCH

# On the Lookout for Lyme Disease

*By Your Name*

Lyme disease, an inflammatory disease transmitted by the bite of a deer tick, has become a serious public health risk in certain areas of the United States and Canada. Campers, hikers, fishermen, outdoor enthusiasts, and other travelers or residents in endemic areas who have frequent or prolonged exposure to tick habitats are at increased risk for Lyme disease.

### How ticks spread the disease

The bacterium that causes Lyme disease is spread by the bite of infected *Ixodes* ticks. Ticks can attach to any part of the human body, but are most often found in hairy areas such as the scalp, groin, and armpit. In most cases the tick must be attached for at least 48 hours before the bacteria can be transmitted. During the spring and summer months, when people dress lightly and spend more time outdoors, the young (nymphal) ticks are most often responsible for spreading the disease. These ticks are tiny (about the size of the head of a pin) and rarely noticed, making it difficult for people to find and remove an infected tick.

### Tick habitat and geographic distribution

The risk of exposure to infected ticks in greatest in woods and in thick brush or long grass, but ticks can also be carried by animals into lawns and gardens and into houses by pets. In the United States, most infections occur in the:
- Northeast, from Maryland to Massachusetts.
- North central states, mostly in Wisconsin and Minnesota.
- West coast, particularly California.

*Allotrombium argenteocinctum*

### Symptoms and signs

Early Lyme disease is characterized initially by *erythema migrans*, the bull's eye rash that often occurs on the skin around a tick bite. The rash usually appears within three days to one month after being bitten. Other flulike symptoms of early Lyme disease include fatigue, headache, chills and fever, muscle and joint pain, and swollen lymph nodes. If left untreated, Lyme disease can result in chronic arthritis and nerve and heart dysfunction.

### Treatment and prognosis

Lyme disease can usually be cured by antibiotics if treatment begins in the early stages of infection. Most people who are treated in the later stages also respond well to antibiotics, although some may have persistent or recurring symptoms.

### Protection from tick bites

Here are some precautions to decrease the chances of being bitten by a tick:
- Avoid tick-infested areas, particularly in May, June, and July.
- Wear light-colored clothing, including long pants, socks, and long-sleeved shirts.
- Tuck pant legs into socks or boots and shirt into pants so ticks cannot crawl under clothing.
- Spray insect repellent containing a 20-30% concentration of DEET on clothes and exposed skin other than the face.
- Walk in the center of trails to avoid contact with overgrown brush and grass.
- Wash and dry clothing at a high temperature, inspect body surfaces carefully, and remove attached ticks with tweezers. ■

# Merging Word Documents

**OBJECTIVES**

| |
|---|
| Understand mail merge |
| Create a main document |
| Design a data source |
| Enter and edit records |
| Add merge fields |
| Merge data |
| Create labels |
| Sort and filter records |

If you have a SAM user profile, you may have access to hands-on instruction, practice, and assessment of the skills covered in this unit. Log in to your SAM account and go to your assignments page to see what your instructor has assigned.

A mail merge operation combines a standard document, such as a form letter, with customized data, such as a set of names and addresses, to create a set of personalized documents. You can perform a mail merge to create documents used in mass mailings, such as letters and labels. You also can use mail merge to create documents that include customized information, such as business cards. In this unit, you learn how to use the Mail Merge task pane to set up and perform a mail merge. You need to send a letter to patients who recently had a routine mammogram screening, informing them that their mammogram showed no evidence of cancer. You also need to send a reminder card to patients who need to schedule an appointment for a routine mammogram. You use mail merge to create a personalized form letter about the mammogram results and mailing labels for the reminder cards.

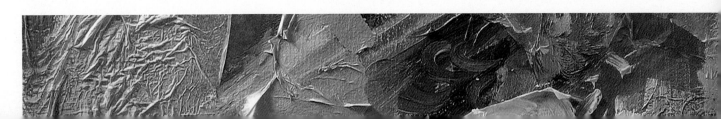

# Understanding Mail Merge

When you perform a mail merge, you merge a standard Word document with a file that contains customized information for many individuals or items. The standard document is called the **main document**. The file with the unique data for individual people or items is called the **data source**. Merging the main document with a data source results in a merged document that contains customized versions of the main document, as shown in Figure F-1. The Mail Merge task pane steps you through setting up and performing a mail merge. ⬛⬛⬛ You use the Mail Merge task pane to create your form letters and mailing labels. Before beginning, you explore the steps involved in performing a mail merge.

**DETAILS**

- **Create the main document**

    The main document contains the text—often called **boilerplate text**—that appears in every version of the merged document. The main document also includes the merge fields, which indicate where the customized information is inserted when you perform the merge. You insert the merge fields in the main document after you have created or selected the data source. You use the Mail Merge task pane to create a main document using either the current document, a template, or an existing document.

- **Create a data source or select an existing data source**

    The data source is a file that contains the unique information for each individual or item. It provides the information that varies in every version of the merged document. A data source is composed of data fields and data records. A **data field** is a category of information, such as last name, first name, street address, city, or postal code. A **data record** is a complete set of related information for an individual or an item, such as one person's name and address. It is easiest to think of a data source file as a table: the header row contains the names of the data fields (the **field names**), and each row in the table is an individual data record. You can use the Mail Merge task pane to create a new data source, or you can merge a main document with an existing data source, such as a data source created in Word, an Outlook contact list, or an Access database.

- **Identify the fields to include in the data source and enter the records**

    When you create a new data source, you must first identify the fields to include. It's important to think of and include all the fields before you begin to enter data. For example, if you are creating a data source that includes addresses, you might need to include fields for a person's middle name, title, department name, or country, even though every address in the data source does not include that information. Once you have identified the fields and set up your data source, you are ready to enter the data for each record.

- **Add merge fields to the main document**

    A **merge field** is a placeholder that you insert in the main document to indicate where the data from each record should be inserted when you perform the merge. For example, in the location you want to insert a zip code, you insert a zip code merge field. The merge fields in a main document must correspond with the field names in the associated data source. Merge fields must be inserted, not typed, in the main document. The Mail Merge task pane provides access to the dialog boxes you use to insert merge fields.

- **Merge the data from the data source into the main document**

    Once you have established your data source and inserted the merge fields in the main document, you are ready to perform the merge. You can merge to a new file, which contains a customized version of the main document for each record in the data source, or you can merge directly to a printer, fax, or e-mail message.

Data source document

| Exam Date | Title | First Name | Last Name | Address Line 1 | City | State | Zip Code | Country |
|-----------|-------|------------|-----------|----------------|------|-------|----------|---------|
| 5/2/08 | Ms. | Linda | Barker | 62 Cloud St. | Somerville | MA | 02144 | US |
| 5/3/08 | Ms. | Claudia | Cruz | 23 Plum St. | Boston | MA | 02483 | US |
| 4/30/08 | Ms. | Joan | Yatco | 456 Elm St. | Arlington | MA | 02474 | US |
| 5/2/08 | Ms. | Anne | Butler | 48 East Ave. | Vancouver | BC | V6F 1AH | CANADA |
| 5/1/08 | Ms. | Laura | Silver | 56 Pearl St. | Cambridge | MA | 02139 | US |

Field name

Data record

Word 2003

Main document

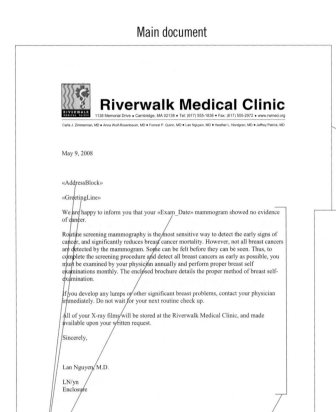

Merged document

Merge fields

Boilerplate text

Customized information

# Creating a Main Document

The first step in performing a mail merge is to create the main document—the file that contains the boiler-plate text. You can create a main document from scratch, save an existing document as a main document, or use a mail merge template to create a main document. The Mail Merge task pane walks you through the process of selecting the type of main document to create. ▰▰▰▰ You use an existing form letter for your main document. You begin by opening the Mail Merge task pane.

## STEPS

1. **Start Word, click** Tools **on the menu bar, point to** Letters and Mailings, **then click** Mail Merge

   The Mail Merge task pane opens, as shown in Figure F-2, and displays information for the first step in the mail merge process: selecting the type of merge document to create.

2. **Make sure the** Letters option button **is selected, then click** Next: Starting document **to continue with the next step**

   The task pane displays the options for the second step: selecting the main document. You can use the current document, start with a mail merge template, or use an existing file.

3. **Select the** Start from existing document option button, **make sure** More files **is selected in the Start from existing list box, then click** Open

   The Open dialog box opens.

4. **Use the** Look in list arrow **to navigate to the drive and folder where your Data Files are located, select the file** WMP F-1.doc, **then click** Open

   The letter that opens contains the boilerplate text for the main document. Notice the filename in the title bar is Document1. When you create a main document that is based on an existing document, Word gives the main document a default temporary filename.

5. **Click the** Save button 🖫 **on the Standard toolbar, then save the main document with the filename** Mammogram Results Letter Main **to the drive and folder where your Data Files are located**

   It's a good idea to include "main" in the filename so that you can easily recognize the file as a main document.

6. **Click the** Zoom list arrow **on the Standard toolbar, click** Text Width, **scroll down, select** Lan Nguyen, **type your name, press** [Ctrl][Home], **then save your changes**

   The edited main document is shown in Figure F-3.

7. **Click** Next: Select recipients **to continue with the next step**

   You continue with Step 3 of 6 in the next lesson.

---

**Clues to Use**

### Using a mail merge template

If you are creating a letter, fax, or directory, you can use a mail merge template to start your main document. Each template includes boiler-plate text, which you can customize, and merge fields, which you can match to the field names in your data source. To create a main document that is based on a mail merge template, click the Start from a template option button in the Step 2 of 6 Mail Merge task pane, then click Select template. In the Select Template dialog box, select a template on the Mail Merge tab, then click OK to create the document. Once you have created the main document, you can customize it with your own information: edit the boilerplate text, change the document format, or add, remove, or modify the merge fields. Before performing the merge, make sure to match the names of the address merge fields used in the template with the field names used in your data source. To match the field names, click the Match Fields button 🖳 on the Mail Merge toolbar, and then use the list arrows in the Match Fields dialog box to select the field name in your data source that corresponds to each address field component in the main document.

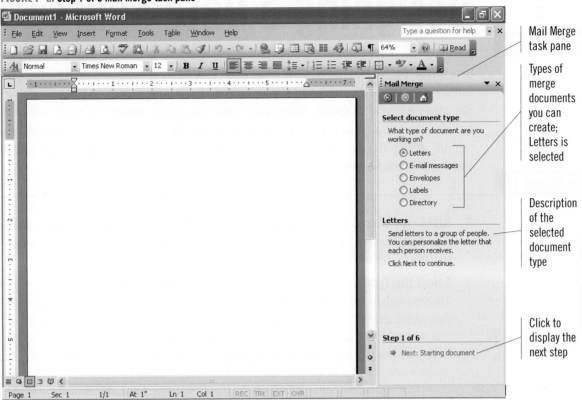

Mail Merge task pane

Types of merge documents you can create; Letters is selected

Description of the selected document type

Click to display the next step

Word 2003

FIGURE F-3: Main document with Step 2 of 6 Mail Merge task pane

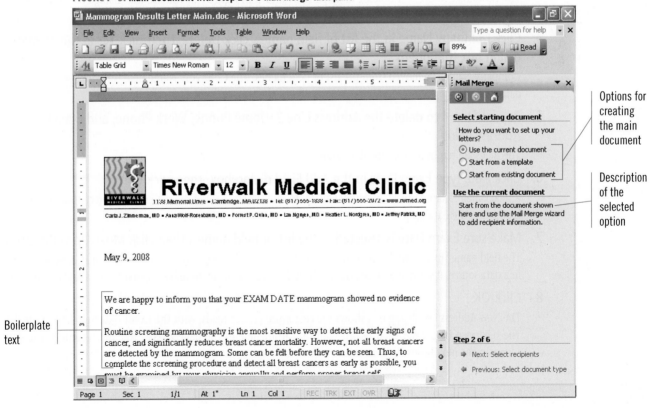

Boilerplate text

Options for creating the main document

Description of the selected option

# Designing a Data Source

After you have identified the main document, the next step in the mail merge process is to identify the data source, the file that contains the information that differs in each version of the merge document. You can use an existing data source that already contains the records you want to include in your merge, or you can create a new data source. When you create a new data source you must determine the fields to include—the categories of information, such as a first name, last name, city, or zip code—and then add the records. You create a new data source that includes fields for the name, address, and exam date for each recent mammogram patient.

## STEPS

1. **Make sure Step 3 of 6 is displayed at the bottom of the Mail Merge task pane**

   Step 3 of 6 involves selecting a data source to use for the merge. You can use an existing data source, a list of contacts created in Microsoft Outlook, or a new data source.

2. **Select the Type a new list option button, then click Create**

   The New Address List dialog box opens, as shown in Figure F-4. You use this dialog box both to design your data source and to enter records. The Enter Address information section of the dialog box includes fields that are commonly used in form letters, but you can customize your data source by adding and removing fields from this list. A data source can be merged with more than one main document, so it's important to design a data source to be flexible. The more fields you include in a data source, the more flexible it is. For example, if you include separate fields for a person's title, first name, middle name, and last name, you can use the same data source to create an envelope addressed to "Mr. John Montgomery Smith" and a form letter addressed to "Dear John."

3. **Click Customize**

   The Customize Address List dialog box opens, as shown in Figure F-5. You use this dialog box to add, delete, rename, and reorder the fields in the data source.

4. **Click Company Name in the list of field names, click Delete, then click Yes in the warning dialog box that opens**

   Company Name is removed from the list of field names. The Company Name field is no longer a part of the data source.

5. **Repeat Step 4 to delete the Address Line 2, Home Phone, Work Phone, and E-mail Address fields**

   The fields are removed from the data source.

6. **Click Add, type Exam Date in the Add Field dialog box, then click OK**

   A field called "Exam Date," which you will use to indicate the date of the patient's most recent mammogram, is added to the data source.

7. **Make sure Exam Date is selected in the list of field names, then click Move Up eight times**

   The field name "Exam Date" is moved to the top of the list. Although the order of field names does not matter in a data source, it's convenient to arrange the field names logically to make it easier to enter and edit records.

8. **Click OK**

   The New Address List dialog box shows the customized list of fields, with the Exam Date field first in the list. The next step is to enter each record you want to include in the data source. You add records to the data source in the next lesson.

FIGURE F-4: New Address List dialog box

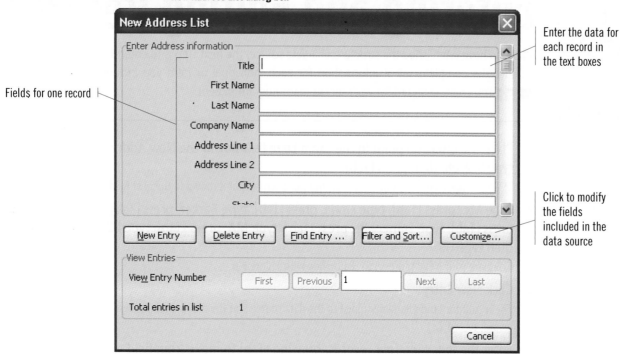

Fields for one record

Enter the data for each record in the text boxes

Click to modify the fields included in the data source

FIGURE F-5: Customize Address List dialog box

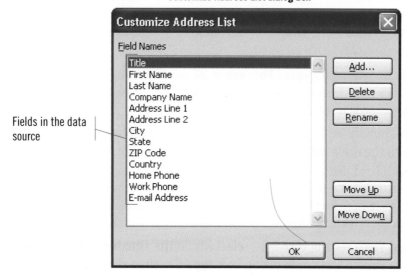

Fields in the data source

## Clues to Use

### Merging with an Outlook data source

If you maintain lists of contacts in Microsoft Outlook, you can use one of your Outlook contact lists as a data source for a merge. To merge with an Outlook data source, click the Select from Outlook contacts option button in the Step 3 of 6 Mail Merge task pane, then click Choose Contacts Folder to open the Select Contact List Folder dialog box. In this dialog box, select the contact list you want to use as the data source, and then click OK. All the contacts included in the selected folder appear in the Mail Merge Recipients dialog box. Here you can refine the list of recipients to include in the merge by sorting and filtering the records. When you are satisfied, click OK in the Mail Merge Recipients dialog box.

# Entering and Editing Records

After you have established the structure of a data source, the next step is to enter the records. Each record includes the complete set of information for each individual or item you include in the data source. ▒▒▒ You create a record for each recent mammogram patient.

1. **Place the insertion point in the Exam Date text box in the New Address List dialog box, type 5/2/08, then press [Tab]**

   "5/2/08" appears in the Exam Date field and the insertion point moves to the next field in the list, the Title field.

2. **Type Ms., press [Tab], type Linda, press [Tab], type Barker, press [Tab], type 62 Cloud St., press [Tab], type Somerville, press [Tab], type MA, press [Tab], type 02144, press [Tab], then type US**

   Compare your New Address List dialog box with Figure F-6.

3. **Click New Entry**

   The record for Linda Barker is added to the data source and the dialog box displays empty fields for the next record, record 2.

4. **Enter the following four records, pressing [Tab] to move from field to field, and clicking New Entry at the end of each record except the last:**

   | Exam Date | Title | First Name | Last Name | Address Line 1 | City | State | ZIP Code | Country |
   |---|---|---|---|---|---|---|---|---|
   | 5/3/08 | Ms. | Claudia | Cruz | 23 Plum St. | Boston | MA | 02483 | US |
   | 4/30/08 | Ms. | Joan | Yatco | 456 Elm St. | Arlington | MA | 02474 | US |
   | 5/2/08 | Ms. | Anne | Butler | 48 East Ave. | Vancouver | BC | V6F 1AH | CANADA |
   | 5/1/08 | Ms. | Laura | Silver | 56 Pearl St. | Cambridge | MA | 02139 | US |

5. **Click Close**

   The Save Address List dialog box opens. Data sources are saved by default in the My Data Sources folder so that you can easily locate them to use in other merge operations. Data sources you create in Word are saved in Microsoft Office Address Lists (*.mdb) format.

6. **Type New Mammogram Patient Data in the File name text box, use the Save in list arrow to navigate to the drive and folder where your Data Files are located, then click Save**

   The data source is saved, and the Mail Merge Recipients dialog box opens, as shown in Figure F-7. The dialog box shows the records in the data source in table format. You can use the dialog box to edit, sort, and filter records, and to select the recipients to include in the mail merge. You will learn more about sorting and filtering in a later lesson. The check marks in the first column indicate the records that will be included in the merge.

7. **Click the Joan Yatco record, click Edit, select Ms. in the Title text box in the New Mammogram Patient Data.mdb dialog box, type Dr., then click Close**

   The data in the Title field for Joan Yatco changes from "Ms." to "Dr." and the New Mammogram Patient Data.mdb dialog box closes.

8. **Click OK in the Mail Merge Recipients dialog box**

   The dialog box closes. The file type and filename of the data source attached to the main document now appear under Use an existing list in the Mail Merge task pane, as shown in Figure F-8. The Mail Merge toolbar also appears in the program window when you close the data source. You learn more about the Mail Merge toolbar in later lessons.

**FIGURE F-6: Record in New Address List dialog box**

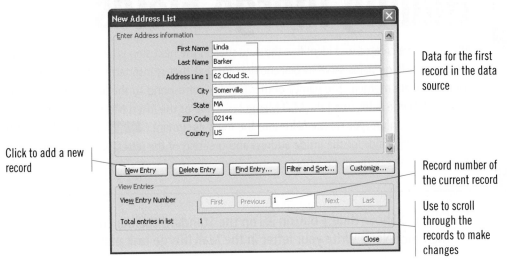

Click to add a new record

Data for the first record in the data source

Record number of the current record

Use to scroll through the records to make changes

**FIGURE F-7: Mail Merge Recipients dialog box**

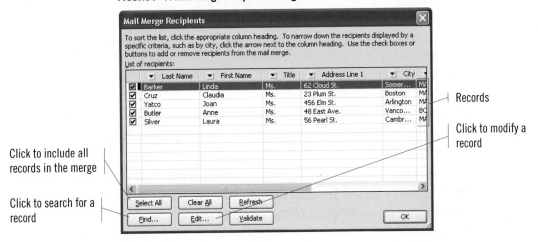

Click to include all records in the merge

Click to search for a record

Records

Click to modify a record

**FIGURE F-8: Data source attached to the main document**

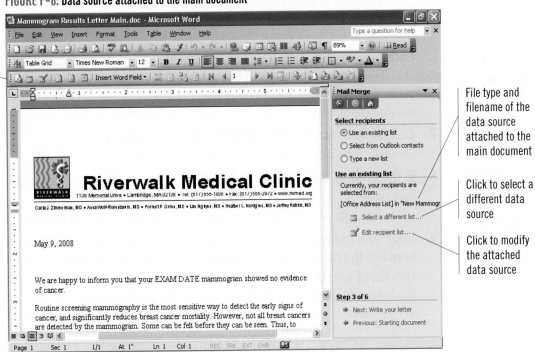

Mail Merge toolbar (yours might open in a different location)

File type and filename of the data source attached to the main document

Click to select a different data source

Click to modify the attached data source

# Adding Merge Fields

After you have created and identified the data source, the next step is to insert the merge fields in the main document. Merge fields serve as placeholders for text that is inserted when the main document and the data source are merged. The names of merge fields correspond to the field names in the data source. You can insert merge fields using the Mail Merge task pane or the Insert Merge Field button on the Mail Merge toolbar. You cannot type merge fields into the main document. ▰▰▰ You use the Mail Merge task pane to insert merge fields for the inside address and greeting of the letter. You also insert a merge field for the exam date in the body of the letter.

## STEPS

1. **Click the** Show/Hide ¶ button **¶** **on the Standard toolbar to display formatting marks, then click** Next: Write your letter **in the Mail Merge task pane**

   The Mail Merge task pane shows the options for Step 4 of 6, writing the letter and inserting the merge fields in the main document. Because your form letter is already written, you are ready to add the merge fields to it.

   > **QUICK TIP**
   > You can also click the Insert Address Block button 🔲 on the Mail Merge toolbar to insert an address block.

2. **Place the insertion point in the blank line above the first body paragraph, then click** Address block **in the Mail Merge task pane**

   The Insert Address Block dialog box opens, as shown in Figure F-9. You use this dialog box to specify the fields you want to include in an address block. In this merge, the address block is the inside address of the form letter. An address block automatically includes fields for the street, city, state, and postal code, but you can select the format for the recipient's name and indicate whether to include a company name or country in the address.

3. **Scroll the list of formats for a recipient's name to get a feel for the kinds of formats you can use, then click** Mr. Joshua Randall Jr. **if it is not already selected**

   The selected format uses the recipient's title, first name, and last name.

4. **Make sure the** Only include the country/region if different than: option button **is selected, select** United States **in the text box, type** US**, then deselect the** Format address according to the destination country/region check box

   You need to include the country in the address block only if the country is different from the United States, so you indicate that all entries in the Country field except "US" should be included in the printed address.

   > **QUICK TIP**
   > You cannot simply type chevrons around a field name. You must insert merge fields using the Mail Merge task pane or the buttons on the Mail Merge toolbar.

5. **Click** OK**, then press** [Enter] **twice**

   The merge field AddressBlock is added to the main document. Chevrons (<< and >>) surround a merge field to distinguish it from the boilerplate text.

6. **Click** Greeting line **in the Mail Merge task pane**

   The Greeting Line dialog box opens. You want to use the format "Dear Mr. Randall:" (the recipient's title and last name, followed by a colon) for a greeting. The default format uses a comma, so you have to change the comma to a colon.

7. **Click the** , list arrow**, click** :**, click** OK**, then press** [Enter]

   The merge field GreetingLine is added to the main document.

   > **QUICK TIP**
   > You can also click the Insert Merge Fields button 🔲 on the Mail Merge toolbar to insert a merge field.

8. **In the body of the letter select** EXAM DATE**, then click** More items **in the Mail Merge task pane**

   The Insert Merge Field dialog box opens and displays the list of field names included in the data source.

9. **Make sure** Exam Date **is selected, click** Insert**, click** Close**, press** [Spacebar] **to add a space between the merge field and mammogram if there is no space, save your changes, then click** ¶ **to turn off the display of formatting marks**

   The merge field Exam Date is inserted in the main document, as shown in Figure F-10. You must type spaces and punctuation between merge fields if you want spaces and punctuation to appear between the data in the merged documents. You preview the merged data and perform the merge in the next lesson.

**FIGURE F-9: Insert Address Block dialog box**

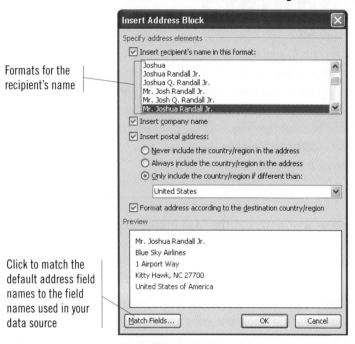

Formats for the recipient's name

Click to match the default address field names to the field names used in your data source

**FIGURE F-10: Merge fields in the main document**

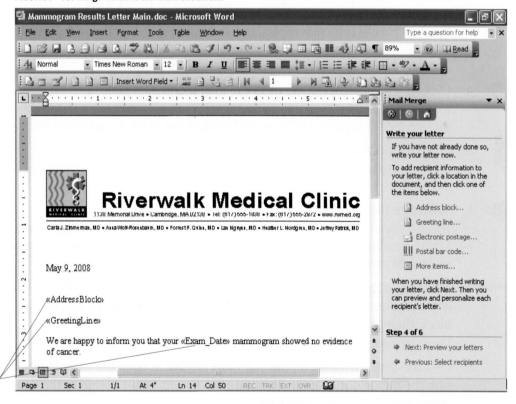

Merge fields

## Clues to Use

### Matching fields

The merge fields you insert in a main document must correspond with the field names in the associated data source. If you are using the Address Block merge field, you must make sure that the default address field names correspond with the field names used in your data source. If the default address field names do not match the field names in your data source, click Match Fields in the Insert Address Block dialog box, then use the list arrows in the Match Fields dialog box to select the field name in the data source that corresponds to each default address field name.

# Merging Data

After you have added records to your data source and inserted merge fields in the main document, you are ready to perform the merge. Before merging, it's a good idea to preview the merged data to make sure the printed documents will appear as you want them to. You can preview the merge using the task pane or the View Merged Data button on the Mail Merge toolbar. When you merge the main document with the data source, you must choose between merging to a new file or directly to a printer. Before merging the form letter with the data source, you preview the merge to make sure the data appears in the letter as you intended. You then merge the two files to a new document.

## STEPS

**QUICK TIP**

To adjust the main document, click the View Merged Data button on the Mail Merge toolbar, then make any necessary changes. Click again to preview the merged data.

1. **Click Next: Preview your letters in the Mail Merge task pane**

   The data from the first record in the data source appears in place of the merge fields in the main document, as shown in Figure F-11. Always check the preview document to make sure the merge fields, punctuation, page breaks, and spacing all appear as you intend before you perform the merge.

2. **Click the Next Recipient button >> in the Mail Merge task pane**

   The data from the second record in the data source appears in place of the merge fields.

3. **Click the Go to Record text box on the Mail Merge toolbar, press [Backspace], type 4, then press [Enter]**

   The data for the fourth record appears in the document window. The non-US country name, in this case Canada, is included in the address block, just as you specified. You can also use the First Record ◄|, Previous Record ◄, Next Record ►, and Last Record |► buttons on the Mail Merge toolbar to preview the merged data. Table F-1 describes other buttons on the Mail Merge toolbar.

**QUICK TIP**

If your data source contains many records, you can merge directly to a printer to avoid creating a large file.

4. **Click Next: Complete the merge in the Mail Merge task pane**

   The options for Step 6 of 6 appear in the Mail Merge task pane. Merging to a new file creates a document with one letter for each record in the data source. This allows you to edit the individual letters.

5. **Click Edit individual letters to merge the data to a new document**

   The Merge to New Document dialog box opens. You can use this dialog box to specify the records to include in the merge.

**QUICK TIP**

To restore a main document to a regular Word document, click the Main document setup button on the Mail Merge toolbar, then click Normal Word document. Restoring a main document removes the associated data source from it.

6. **Make sure the All option button is selected, then click OK**

   The main document and the data source are merged to a new document called Letters1, which contains a customized form letter for each record in the data source. You can now further personalize the letters without affecting the main document or the data source.

7. **Click the Zoom list arrow on the Standard toolbar, click Page Width, scroll to the fourth letter (addressed to Ms. Anne Butler), place the insertion point before V6F in the address block, then press [Enter]**

   The postal code is now consistent with the proper format for a Canadian address.

8. **Click the Save button on the Standard toolbar to open the Save As dialog box, then save the merge document as Mammogram Results Letter Merge to the drive and folder where your Data Files are located**

   You might decide not to save a merged file if your data source is large. After you have created the main document and the data source, you can create the letters by performing the merge again.

9. **Click File on the menu bar, click Print, click the Current page option button in the Page range section of the Print dialog box, click OK, then close all open Word files, saving changes if prompted**

   The letter to Anne Butler prints.

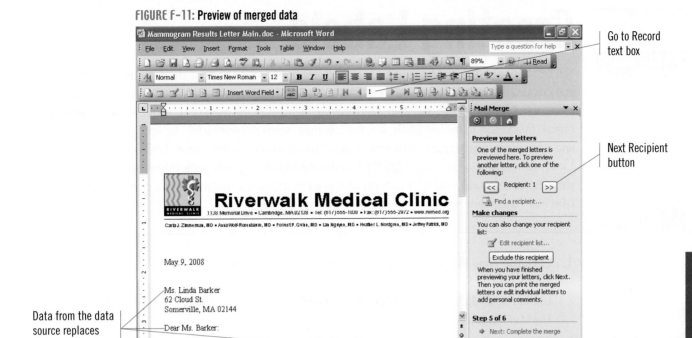

Go to Record text box

Next Recipient button

Data from the data source replaces the merge fields

TABLE F-1: Buttons on the Mail Merge toolbar

| button | use to | button | use to |
|---|---|---|---|
|  | Change the main document to a different type, or convert it to a normal Word document |  | Highlight the merge fields in the main document |
|  | Select an existing data source |  | Match address fields with the field names used in the data source |
|  | Edit, sort, or filter the associated data source |  | Search for a record in the merged documents |
|  | Insert an Address Block merge field |  | Check for errors in the merged documents |
|  | Insert a Greeting Line merge field |  | Merge the data to a new document and display it on-screen |
|  | Insert a merge field from the data source |  | Print the merged documents without first reviewing them on-screen |
|  | Switch between viewing the main document with merge fields and with merged data |  |  |

# Creating Labels

You can also use the Mail Merge task pane to create mailing labels or print envelopes for a mailing. When you create labels or envelopes, you must select a standard label or envelope size to use as the main document, select a data source, and then insert the merge fields in the main document before performing the merge. In addition to mailing labels, you can use mail merge to create labels for floppy disks, CDs, videos, and other items, and to create documents that are based on standard or custom label sizes, such as business cards, nametags, and postcards. ▰▰▰▰ You use the Mail Merge task pane to create mailing labels for a reminder card you will send to all patients who need to schedule a routine mammogram. You create a new label main document and attach an existing data source.

## STEPS

1. **Click the** New Blank Document button ▢ **on the Standard toolbar, click the** Zoom list arrow **on the Standard toolbar, click** Page Width, **click** Tools **on the menu bar, point to** Letters and Mailings, **then click** Mail Merge

   The Mail Merge task pane opens.

> **TROUBLE**
> If your dialog box does not show Avery standard, click the Label products list arrow, then click Avery standard.

2. **Click the** Labels option button **in the Mail Merge task pane, click** Next: Starting document **to move to Step 2 of 6, make sure the** Change document layout option button **is selected, then click** Label options

   The Label Options dialog box opens, as shown in Figure F-12. You use this dialog box to select a label size for your labels and to specify the type of printer you plan to use. The default brand name Avery standard appears in the Label products list box. You can use the Label products list arrow to select other label products or a custom label. The many standard types of Avery labels for mailings, file folders, floppy disks, postcards, and other types of labels are listed in the Product number list box. The type, height, width, and paper size for the selected product are displayed in the Label information section.

> **TROUBLE**
> If your gridlines are not visible, click Table on the menu bar, then click Show Gridlines.

3. **Scroll down the Product number list, click** 5161 – Address, **then click** OK

   A table with gridlines appears in the main document, as shown in Figure F-13. Each table cell is the size of a label for the label product you selected.

4. **Save the label main document with the filename** Mammogram Reminder Labels Main **to the drive and folder where your Data Files are located**

   Next you need to select a data source for the labels.

5. **Click** Next: Select recipients **to move to Step 3 of 6, make sure the** Use an existing list option button **is selected, then click** Browse

   The Select Data Source dialog box opens.

6. **Use the** Look in list arrow **to navigate to the drive and folder where your Data Files are located, then open the file** WMP F-2.mdb

   The Mail Merge Recipients dialog box opens and displays all the records in the data source. In the next lesson, you sort and filter the records before performing the mail merge.

**FIGURE F-12: Label Options dialog box**

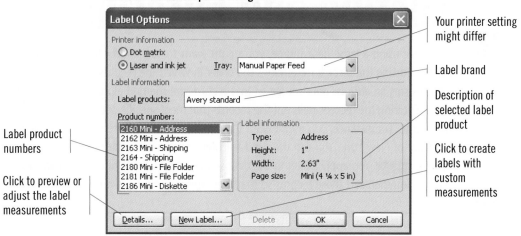

Label product numbers

Click to preview or adjust the label measurements

Your printer setting might differ

Label brand

Description of selected label product

Click to create labels with custom measurements

**FIGURE F-13: Label main document**

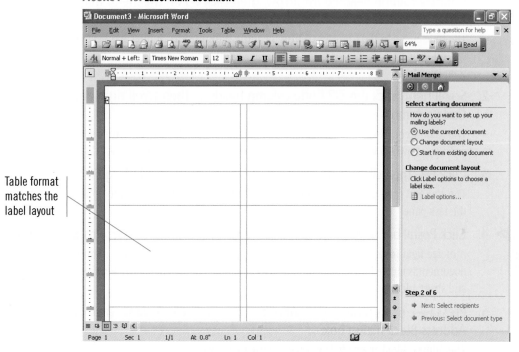

Table format matches the label layout

## Clues to Use

### Printing individual envelopes and labels

The Mail Merge task pane enables you to easily print envelopes and labels for mass mailings, but you can also quickly format and print individual envelopes and labels using the Envelopes and Labels dialog box. To open the Envelopes and Labels dialog box, point to Letters and Mailings on the Tools menu, then click Envelopes and Labels. On the Envelopes tab, shown in Figure F-14, type the recipient's address in the Delivery address box and the return address in the Return address box. Click Options to open the Envelope Options dialog box, which you can use to select the envelope size, add a postal bar code, change the font and font size of the delivery and return addresses, and change the printing options. When you are ready to print the envelope, click Print in the Envelopes and Labels dialog box. The procedure for printing an individual label is similar to printing an individual envelope: enter the recipient's address on the Labels tab, click Options to select a label product number, click OK, then click Print.

**FIGURE F-14: Envelopes and Labels dialog box**

Word 2003

# Sorting and Filtering Records

If you are using a large data source, you might want to sort and/or filter the records before performing a merge. Sorting the records determines the order in which the records are merged. For example, you might want to sort an address data source so that records are merged alphabetically by last name or in zip code order. Filtering the records pulls out the records that meet specific criteria and includes only those records in the merge. For instance, you might want to filter a data source to send a mailing only to people who live in the state of New York. You can use the Mail Merge Recipients dialog box both to sort and to filter a data source.  You apply a filter to the data source so that only United States addresses are included in the merge. You then sort those records so that they merge in zip code order.

## STEPS

1. **In the Mail Merge Recipients dialog box, scroll right to display the Country field, click the Country column heading list arrow, then click US on the menu that opens**

   A filter is applied to the data source so that only the records with "US" in the Country field will be merged. The blue arrow in the Country column heading indicates that a filter has been applied to the column. You can filter a data source by as many criteria as you like. To remove a filter, click a column heading list arrow, then click "All."

2. **Scroll right, click the ZIP Code column heading, then scroll right again to see the ZIP Code column**

   The Mail Merge Recipients dialog box now displays only the records with a US address sorted in zip code order, as shown in Figure F-15. If you want to reverse the sort order, you can click a column heading again.

3. **Click OK, then click Next: Arrange your labels in the Mail Merge task pane**

   The sort and filter criteria you set are saved for the current merge, and the options for Step 4 of 6 appear in the task pane.

4. **Click Postal bar code in the task pane, then click OK in the Insert Postal Bar Code dialog box**

   A merge field for a U.S. postal bar code is inserted in the first label in the main document. When the main document is merged with the data source, a customized postal bar code determined by the recipient's zip code and street address will appear on every label.

5. **Press [→], press [Enter], click Address block in the task pane, then click OK in the Insert Address Block dialog box**

   The Address Block merge field is added to the first label.

6. **Point to the down arrow at the bottom of the task pane to scroll down if necessary, then click Update all labels in the task pane**

   The merge fields are copied from the first label to every label in the main document.

7. **Click Next: Preview your labels in the task pane**

   A preview of the merged label data appears in the main document. Only U.S. addresses are included, and the labels are organized in zip code order.

8. **Click Next: Complete the merge in the task pane, click Edit individual labels, then click OK in the Merge to New Document dialog box**

   The merged labels document is shown in Figure F-16.

9. **Replace Ms. Julia Packer with your name in the first label, save the document with the file-name US Mammogram Reminder Labels Zip Code Merge to the drive and folder where your Data Files are located, print the labels, save and close all open files, then exit Word**

**FIGURE F-15:** US records sorted in zip code order

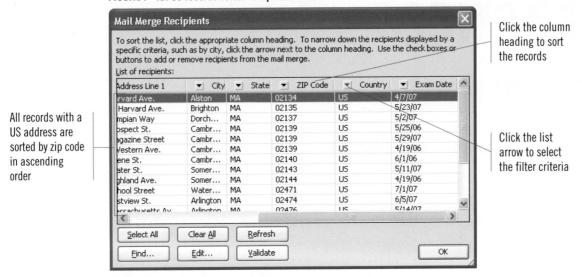

Click the column heading to sort the records

All records with a US address are sorted by zip code in ascending order

Click the list arrow to select the filter criteria

**FIGURE F-16:** Merged labels

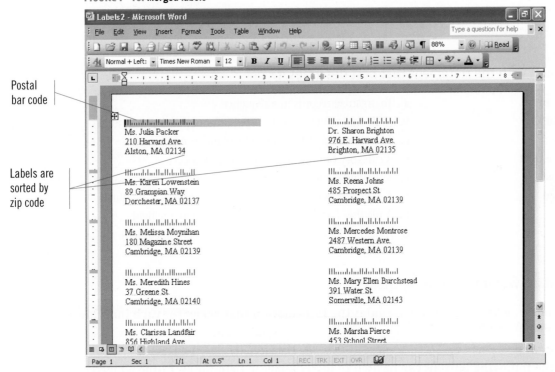

Postal bar code

Labels are sorted by zip code

## Clues to Use

### Inserting individual merge fields

You can insert an individual merge field by selecting the field name in the Insert Merge Field dialog box, clicking Insert, and then clicking Close. You can also insert several merge fields at once by clicking a field name in the Insert Merge Field dialog box, clicking Insert, clicking another field name, clicking Insert, and so on. When you have finished inserting the merge fields, click Close. You can then add spaces, punctuation, and lines between the merge fields you inserted in the main document.

You must include proper punctuation, spacing, and blank lines between the merge fields in a main document if you want punctuation, spaces, and blank lines to appear between the data in the merge documents. For example, to create an address line with a city, state, and zip code, you insert the City merge field, type a comma and a space, insert the State merge field, type a space, and then insert the Zip Code merge field: <<City>>, <<State>> <<Zip Code>>.

# Practice

## ▼ CONCEPTS REVIEW

Label each toolbar button shown in Figure F-17.

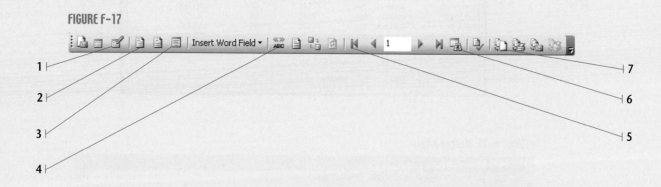

FIGURE F-17

Match each term with the statement that best describes it.

**8. Main document**             **a.** To organize records in a sequence

**9. Merge field**             **b.** A file that contains customized information for each item or individual

**10. Data field**             **c.** To pull out records that meet certain criteria

**11. Boilerplate text**             **d.** A category of information in a data source

**12. Data source**             **e.** The standard text that appears in every version of a merged document

**13. Data record**             **f.** A complete set of information for one item or individual

**14. Filter**             **g.** A file that contains boilerplate text and merge fields

**15. Sort**             **h.** A placeholder for merged data in the main document

Select the best answer from the list of choices.

**16. In a mail merge, which type of file contains the information that varies for each individual or item?**

  **a.** Data source           **c.** Label document

  **b.** Main document        **d.** Data record

**17. Which of the following buttons can be used to insert a merge field for an inside address?**

  **a.**                 **c.**

  **b.**                 **d.**

**18. Which of the following buttons can be used to preview the merged data in the main document?**

  **a.**                 **c.**

  **b.**                 **d.**

**19. To change the font of merged data, which element should you format?**

  **a.** Data record           **c.** Field name

  **b.** Merge field            **d.** Boilerplate text

**20. Which of the following is included in a data source?**

  **a.** Records             **c.** Labels

  **b.** Boilerplate text        **d.** Merge fields

# ▼ SKILLS REVIEW

## 1. Create a main document.

**a.** Start Word, then open the Mail Merge task pane.

**b.** Use the Mail Merge task pane to create a letter main document, click Next, then select the current (blank) document.

**c.** At the top of the blank document, press [Enter] four times, type today's date, press [Enter] five times, then type **We are writing to confirm your choice of a Primary Care Physician in STATE.**

**d.** Press [Enter] twice, then type **According to our records, you selected PCP as your Primary Care Physician.**

**e.** Press [Enter] twice, then type **It's important that you contact your Primary Care Physician to coordinate all your medical care. If you need to see a specialist, your Primary Care Physician will refer you to one who is affiliated with his or her hospital or medical group. If the physician listed above is not the one you selected, please call Member Services right away at 1-800-555-1328.**

**f.** Press [Enter] twice, type **Sincerely**, press [Enter] four times, type your name, press [Enter], then type **Member Services.**

**g.** Save the main document as **PCP Letter Main** to the drive and folder where your Data Files are located.

## 2. Design a data source.

**a.** Click Next, select the Type a new list option button in the Step 3 of 6 Mail Merge task pane, then click Create.

**b.** Click Customize in the New Address List dialog box, then remove these fields from the data source: Company Name, Address Line 2, Country, Home Phone, Work Phone, and E-mail Address.

**c.** Add an **ID** field and a **PCP** field to the data source. Be sure these fields follow the ZIP Code field.

**d.** Rename the Address Line 1 field **Street**, then click OK to close the Customize Address List dialog box.

## 3. Enter and edit records.

**a.** Add the following records to the data source:

| Title | First Name | Last Name | Street | City | State | Zip Code | ID | PCP |
|-------|-----------|-----------|--------|------|-------|----------|-----|-----|
| Mr. | John | Conlin | 34 Mill St. | Exeter | NH | 03833 | MT3948 | Susan Trifilo, M.D. |
| Mr. | Bill | Webster | 289 Sugar Hill Rd. | Franconia | NH | 03632 | CZ2846 | Richard Pattavina, M.D. |
| Ms. | Susan | Janak | 742 Main St. | Derby | VT | 04634 | MT1928 | Edwin Marsh, M.D. |
| Mr. | Derek | Gray | 987 Ocean Rd. | Portsmouth | NH | 03828 | CF8725 | Rebecca Keller, M.D. |
| Ms. | Rita | Murphy | 73 Bay Rd. | Durham | NH | 03814 | MK2991 | Anna Doherty, M.D. |
| Ms. | Amy | Hunt | 67 Apple St. | Northfield | MA | 01360 | CG8231 | Bruce Dewey, M.D. |
| Ms. | Eliza | Perkins | 287 Mountain Rd. | Dublin | NH | 03436 | MT1878 | Luisa Giaimo, M.D. |

**b.** Save the data source as **Subscriber Data** to the drive and folder where your Data Files are located.

**c.** Change the PCP for record 2 (Bill Webster) to **Blake Swan, M.D.**

**d.** Click OK to close the Mail Merge Recipients dialog box.

## 4. Add merge fields.

**a.** Click Next, then in the blank line above the first body paragraph, insert an Address Block merge field.

**b.** In the Insert Address Block dialog box, click Match Fields.

**c.** Click the list arrow next to Address 1 in the Match Fields dialog box, click Street, then click OK.

**d.** In the Insert Address Block dialog box, select the Never include the country/region in the address option button, then click OK.

**e.** Press [Enter] twice, type **Member ID:**, then insert the ID merge field.

**f.** Press [Enter] twice, insert a Greeting Line merge field using the default greeting line format, then press [Enter].

**g.** In the first body paragraph, replace STATE with the State merge field and PCP with the PCP merge field. (*Note*: Make sure to insert a space before or after each merge field as needed.)

**h.** Save your changes to the main document.

5. **Merge data.**

   a. Click Next to preview the merged data, then scroll through each letter.

   b. Click the View Merged Data button on the Mail Merge toolbar, place the insertion point before "If the physician" in the third sentence of the third body paragraph, then press [Enter] twice to create a new paragraph.

   c. Combine the first and second body paragraphs into a single paragraph.

   d. Make any other necessary adjustments to the letter, save your changes, then click the View Merged Data button to return to the preview of the document.

   e. Click Next, click Edit individual letters, then merge all the records to a new file.

   f. Save the merged document as **PCP Letter Merge** to the drive and folder where your Data Files are located, print a copy of the first letter, then save and close all open files.

6. **Create labels.**

   a. Open a new blank document, then open the Mail Merge task pane.

   b. Create a label main document, click Next, then select the Change document layout option button if necessary, in the Step 2 of 6 Mail Merge task pane.

   c. Open the Label Options dialog box, select Avery standard 5162 – Address labels, then click OK.

   d. Save the label main document as **Subscriber Labels Main** to the drive and folder where your Data Files are located, then click Next.

   e. Select the Use an existing list option button, click Browse, then open the Subscriber Data.mdb file you created.

7. **Sort and filter records.**

   a. Filter the records so that only the records with NH in the State field are included in the merge.

   b. Sort the records in ascending order by zip code, then click OK.

   c. If the Mail Merge toolbar is not open, point to Toolbars on the View menu, then click Mail Merge.

   d. Click Next, insert a Postal bar code merge field using the default settings, press [→], then press [Enter].

   e. Insert an Address Block merge field using the default settings, click the View Merged Data button on the Mail Merge toolbar, then notice that the street address is missing.

   f. Click the View Merged Data button again, click the Address Block merge field in the upper-left table cell to select it if necessary, then click Address block in the Mail Merge task pane.

   g. Click Match Fields in the Insert Address Block dialog box to open the Match Fields dialog box.

   h. Click the list arrow next to Address 1, click Street, click OK, then click OK again.

   i. Click the View Merged Data button to preview the merged data, and notice that the address block now includes the street address.

   j. Click Update all labels in the Mail Merge task pane, then click Next to move to Step 5.

   k. Examine the merged data for errors, then click Next to move to Step 6.

   l. Click Edit individual labels, merge all the records, then save the merged file as **NH Subscriber Labels Merge** to the drive and folder where your Data Files are located.

   m. In the first label, change Ms. Eliza Perkins to your name, save the document, then print it.

   n. Save and close all open Word files, then exit Word.

# ▼ INDEPENDENT CHALLENGE 1

You work for Rocky Mountain Eye Care. Your office has designed a maintenance program for gas permeable (GP) contact lenses, and you want to send a letter introducing the program to all patients who wear GP lenses. You'll use Mail Merge to create the letter. If you are performing the ACE steps and are able to print envelopes on your printer, you will also use Word to print an envelope for one letter.

**a.** Start Word, then use the Mail Merge task pane to create a letter main document using the file WMP F-3.doc, found on the drive and folder where your Data Files are located.

**b.** Replace Your Name with your name in the signature block, then save the main document as **GP Letter Main** to the drive and folder where your Data Files are located.

**c.** Use the file WMP F-4.mdb, found on the drive and folder where your Data Files are located, as the data source.

**d.** Sort the data source by last name, then filter the data so that only records with GP as the lens are included in the merge.

**e.** Insert an Address Block and a Greeting Line merge field in the main document, preview the merged letters, then make any necessary adjustments.

**f.** Merge all the records to a new document, then save it as **GP Letter Merge** to the drive and folder where your Data Files are located.

**g.** Print the first letter.

### Advanced Challenge Exercise

- If you can print envelopes, select the inside address in the first merge letter, click Tools on the menu bar, point to Letters and Mailings, then click Envelopes and Labels.
- On the Envelopes tab, verify that no check mark appears in the check box next to Omit, type your name in the Return address text box, type **Rocky Mountain Eye Care**, **60 Crandall Street**, **Boulder, CO 80306** (pressing [Enter] as needed to create a proper address). Click Options, make sure the Envelope size is set to Size 10, then change the font of the Delivery address and the Return address to 12-point Times New Roman.
- On the Printing Options tab, select the appropriate Feed method for your printer, then click OK.
- Click Print, then click No to save the return address as the default.

**h.** Close all open Word files, saving changes, and then exit Word.

# ▼ INDEPENDENT CHALLENGE 2

One of your responsibilities at Northwest Family Health, a growing family health clinic, is to create business cards for the staff. You use mail merge to create the cards so that you can easily produce standard business cards for future employees.

**a.** Start Word, then use the Mail Merge task pane to create labels using the current blank document as the main document.

**b.** Select Avery standard 3612 – Business Card labels.

**c.** Create a new data source that includes the following fields: Title, First Name, Last Name, Phone, Fax, E-mail, and Hire Date. Add the following records to the data source:

| Title | First Name | Last Name | Phone | Fax | E-mail | Hire Date |
|-------|-----------|-----------|-------|-----|--------|-----------|
| Medical Director | Sandra | Bryson | (312) 555-3982 | (312) 555-6654 | sbryson@nwfh.com | 1/12/07 |
| Nurse Practitioner | Philip | Holm | (312) 555-2323 | (312) 555-4956 | pholm@nwfh.com | 3/22/05 |

**d.** Add four more records to the data source, including one with your name as the Administrative Assistant. Add other records for a Medical Assistant, Immunization Coordinator, and Pharmacy Technician.

**e.** Save the data source with the filename **Employee Data** to the drive and folder where your Data Files are located, then sort the data by Title.

**f.** In the first table cell, create the Northwest Family Health business card. Figure F-18 shows a sample Northwest Family Health business card, but you should create your own design. Include the clinic name, a street address, and the Web site address www.nwfh.com. Also include a First Name, Last Name, Title, Phone, Fax, and E-mail merge fields. (*Hint*: If your design includes a graphic, use a table to lay out the business card, and insert the graphic in a table cell. Use the Insert Merge Field dialog box to insert each merge field, adjusting the spacing between merge fields as necessary.)

FIGURE F-18

**g.** Format the business card with fonts, colors, and other formatting features. (*Note*: Use the Other Task Panes list arrow to reopen the Mail Merge task pane if necessary.)

**h.** Update all the labels, preview the data, make any necessary adjustments, then merge all the records to a new document.

**i.** Save the merge document with the filename **Business Cards Merge** to the drive and folder where your Data Files are located, print a copy, then close the file.

**j.** Save the main document with the filename **Business Cards Main** to the drive and folder where your Data Files are located, close the file, then exit Word.

# ▼ INDEPENDENT CHALLENGE 3

You need to create a class list for a fitness and nutrition class you teach for children who are overweight. You want the class list to include contact information for the children, as well as their age and Body Mass Index (BMI) at the time they registered for the class. You decide to use mail merge to create the class list. If you are completing the ACE steps, you will also use mail merge to create mailing labels.

**a.** Start Word, then use the Mail Merge task pane to create a directory using the current blank document.

**b.** Create a new data source that includes the following fields: First Name, Last Name, Age, BMI, Parent First Name, Parent Last Name, Address, City, State, Zip Code, and Home Phone.

**c.** Enter the following records in the data source:

| First Name | Last Name | Age | BMI | Parent First Name | Parent Last Name | Address | City | State | Zip Code | Home Phone |
|---|---|---|---|---|---|---|---|---|---|---|
| Sophie | Wright | 8 | 25.31 | Kerry | Wright | 58 Main St. | Camillus | NY | 13031 | 555-2345 |
| Will | Jacob | 7 | 20.02 | Bob | Jacob | 32 North Way | Camillus | NY | 13031 | 555-9827 |
| Brett | Eliot | 8 | 22.52 | Olivia | Eliot | 289 Sylvan Way | Marcellus | NY | 13032 | 555-9724 |
| Abby | Herman | 7 | 21.89 | Sarah | Thomas | 438 Lariat St. | Marcellus | NY | 13032 | 555-8347 |

**d.** Add five additional records to the data source using the following last names and BMIs:

O'Keefe, 24.03

George, 26.12

Goleman, 21.17

Siebert, 21.63

Choy, 23.45

Make up the remaining information for these five records.

**e.** Save the data source as **Kids Fitness Data** to the drive and folder where your Data Files are located.

**f.** Sort the records by last name, then click Next in the Mail Merge task pane.

**g.** Insert a table that includes six columns and one row in the main document.

**h.** In the first table cell, insert the First Name and Last Name merge fields, separated by a space.

**i.** In the second cell, insert the Age merge field.

**j.** In the third cell, insert the BMI merge field.

**k.** In the fourth cell, insert the Address and City merge fields, separated by a comma and a space.

**l.** In the fifth cell, insert the Home Phone merge field.

**m.** In the sixth cell, insert the Parent First Name and Parent Last Name merge fields, separated by a space.

**n.** Preview the merged data and make any necessary adjustments. (*Hint*: Only one record is displayed at a time when you preview the data.)

**o.** Merge all the records to a new document, then save the document with the filename **Kids Fitness Merge** to the drive and folder where your Data Files are located.

**p.** Press [Ctrl][Home], press [Enter], type **Fitness and Nutrition for Children** at the top of the document, press [Enter], type **Instructor:**, followed by your name, then press [Enter] twice.

**q.** Insert a new row at the top of the table, then type the following column headings in the new row: **Name**, **Age**, **BMI**, **Address**, **Phone**, **Parent Name**.

**r.** Format the class list to make it attractive and readable, save your changes, print a copy, then close the file.

**s.** Close the main document without saving changes.

### Advanced Challenge Exercise

- Open a new blank document, then use the Mail Merge task pane to create mailing labels using Avery standard 5162 – Address labels.

- Use the Kids Fitness Data data source you created, and sort the records in zip code order.

- In the first table cell, create your own address block using the Parent First Name, Parent Last Name, Address, City, State, and Zip Code merge fields. Be sure to include proper spacing and punctuation.

- Update all the labels, preview the merged data, merge all the records to a new document, then type your name centered in the document header.

- Save the document with the filename **Kids Fitness Labels Merge ACE** to the drive and folder where your Data Files are located, print a copy, close the file, then close the main document without saving changes.

**t.** Exit Word.

## ▼ INDEPENDENT CHALLENGE 4

Your boss has given you the task of purchasing mailing labels for a mass mailing of your hospital's annual report. The annual report will be sent to 55,000 people. Your hospital plans to use Avery standard 5160 white labels for a laser printer, or their equivalent, for the mailing. In this independent challenge, you will search for Web sites that sell Avery labels, compare the costs, and then write a memo to your boss detailing your purchasing recommendations.

**a.** Use your favorite search engine to search for Web sites that sell Avery labels or the equivalent. Use the keywords **Avery labels** to conduct your search.

**b.** Find at least three Web sites that sell Avery 5160 white labels for a laser printer, or their equivalent. Note the URL of the Web sites and the price and quantity of the labels. You need to purchase enough labels for a mailing of 55,000, plus enough extras in case you make mistakes.

**c.** Start Word, then use the Professional Memo template to create a memo to your boss. Save the memo as **5160 Labels Memo** to the drive and folder where your Data Files are located.

**d.** In the memo, make up information to replace the placeholder text in the memo header, be sure to include your name in the memo header, then type the body of your memo.

**e.** In the body, include a table that shows the URL of each Web site, the product name, the unit cost, the number of labels in each unit, the number of units you need to purchase, and the total cost of purchasing the labels. Also make a brief recommendation to your boss.

**f.** Format the memo so it is attractive and readable, save your changes, print a copy, close the file, then exit Word.

Using the Mail Merge task pane, create the post cards shown in Figure F-19. Use Avery standard 3611 – Post Card labels for the main document and create a data source that contains at least four records. Replace the doctor's name, Annabelle B. Lucas, with your name. Save the data source as **Eye Patient Data**, save the main document as **Appointment Card Main**, and save the merge document as **Appointment Card Merge**, all to the drive and folder where your Data Files are located. (*Hint:* Use a table to lay out the postcard; the clip art graphic uses the keywords "eye charts"; and the font is Comic Sans MS.) Print a copy of the postcards.

**FIGURE F-19**

## Annabelle B. Lucas, O.D.

387 East 72nd Street, New York, NY 10021
Telephone: 212-555-0890

Mr. Francisco Cortez
874 East 86th Street
Apt. 3B
New York, NY 10028

Our records indicate it is time for your eye exam. Please call our office now to schedule your appointment.

## Annabelle B. Lucas, O.D.

387 East 72nd Street, New York, NY 10021
Telephone: 212-555-0890

Ms. Mika Takeda
126 East 71st Street
Apt. 104
New York, NY 10022

Our records indicate it is time for your eye exam. Please call our office now to schedule your appointment.

# Working with Styles and Templates

## OBJECTIVES

| |
|---|
| Explore styles and templates |
| Create custom paragraph styles |
| Modify paragraph styles |
| Create and modify custom character styles |
| Create custom list and table styles |
| Rename, delete, and copy styles |
| Create a template |
| Revise and attach a template |

If you have a SAM user profile, you may have access to hands-on instruction, practice, and assessment of the skills covered in this unit. Log in to your SAM account and go to your assignments page to see what your instructor has assigned.

The sophisticated styles and templates available in Word allow you to format your documents quickly, efficiently, and professionally. In this unit, you learn how to apply existing styles to selected text in a document and how to create new custom styles. You also learn how to apply a template to a document and how to create a new template that contains styles. The Riverwalk Medical Clinic has hired you to produce profiles of clinic physicians for distribution to clinic patients. To save time, you decide to develop a template on which to base each physician profile. This template will include several custom styles, which you can periodically update. You use styles and templates to create and modify the physician profiles.

# Exploring Styles and Templates

You use styles and templates to automate document-formatting tasks and to ensure consistency among related documents. A **style** consists of various formats such as font style, font size, and alignment that are combined into one set that you can name. For example, a style called "Main Head" could be used to apply the Arial font, 14-point font size, bold, and a border style to selected text. A **template** is a file that contains the basic structure of a document, such as the page layout, headers and footers, styles, and graphic elements. ▓▓▓▓ You want to include styles in the template you plan to create for the physician profiles. You familiarize yourself with how you can use styles to automate formatting tasks and how you can use templates to create unified sets of documents.

## DETAILS

### Styles ▶

- Using styles helps you save time because you can update styles quickly and easily. For example, suppose you have applied a style named "Section Head" to each section head in a document. When you change the formatting in the Section Head style, Word automatically updates all the text formatted with that style. Imagine how much time you would save if your document contains 50 or 100 section headings that are all formatted with the Section Head style!

- Word includes four style categories: paragraph, character, list, and table. A **paragraph** style includes both character formats, such as font style, and paragraph formats, such as line spacing. You use a paragraph style when you want to format all the text in a paragraph at once. A **character** style includes character formats only. You use a character style to apply character format settings only to selected text within a paragraph. A **list** style allows you to format a series of lines with numbers or bullets and with selected font and paragraph formats. Finally, you create a **table** style to specify how you want both the table grid and the text in a table to appear. Figure G-1 shows a document formatted with the four kinds of styles.

- You work in the Styles and Formatting task pane to create, apply, and modify all four types of styles. In this task pane, you can use the list arrow next to each style name to select all text that has been formatted with a specific style, as shown in Figure G-2, to modify the style, to delete the style, or to create a new style.

- Text you type into a blank document is formatted with the paragraph style called **Normal style** until you specify otherwise. By default, text formatted with the Normal style uses 12-point Times New Roman as the font and the text is left-aligned and single-spaced.

### Templates ▶

- Every document you create in Word is based on a template. Most of the time, this template is the **Normal template** because the Normal template is loaded automatically when you start a new document. The styles assigned to the Normal template, such as Normal style, are available to all documents.

- You can create your own template or you can use one of the preset templates available in Word. When you create a new document based on a template, the styles included with the template are automatically assigned to the new document. You can also attach a template to an existing document and then apply the styles in the attached template to selected text in the document.

---

### Clues to Use

#### Exploring AutoFormats and the Style Gallery

AutoFormat and the Style Gallery are two Word features that allow you to apply styles quickly. When you use the AutoFormat feature, Word analyzes each paragraph in your completed document and then applies an appropriate style, depending on where the paragraph appears in the document. To access the AutoFormat feature, click Format on the menu bar, and then click AutoFormat. When you use the Style Gallery feature, you select a template and then all styles included in that template override the styles in the existing document. To access the Style Gallery, click Format on the menu bar, click Theme, then click Style Gallery in the Theme dialog box.

## FIGURE G-1: Document formatted with styles

**Paragraph** styles apply formatting to a paragraph, which might be one or more lines of text; this paragraph style includes italic and blue bottom border

A **List** style adds bullets or numbers to a series of paragraphs; this list style includes the book symbol

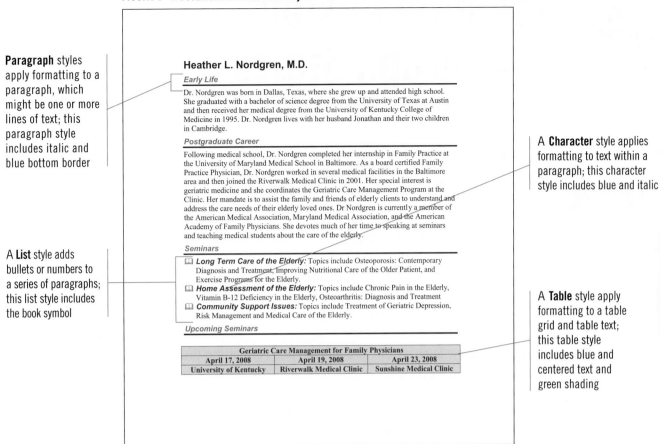

A **Character** style applies formatting to text within a paragraph; this character style includes blue and italic

A **Table** style apply formatting to a table grid and table text; this table style includes blue and centered text and green shading

## FIGURE G-2: Styles and Formatting task pane

Every heading formatted with the Profile Heading paragraph style is selected

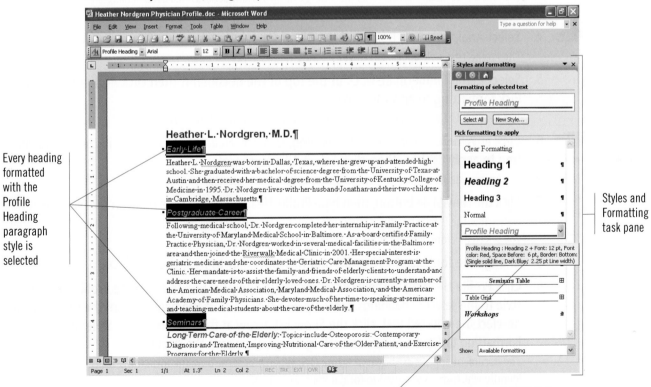

Styles and Formatting task pane

The formats associated with a style appear as a ScreenTip when you move your mouse over the style name in the Styles and Formatting task pane

# Creating Custom Paragraph Styles

A **paragraph style** is a combination of character and paragraph formats that you name and store as a set. You can create a paragraph style and then apply it to any paragraph. Remember that any line of text followed by a hard return is considered a paragraph—even if the line consists of only one or two words. 📖 You have written a profile of Clinic Director Carla Zimmerman. You decide to create your own custom paragraph styles for the headings and subheadings included in the profile.

## STEPS

1. **Start Word, open the file** WMP G-1.doc **from the drive and folder where your Data Files are located, save the file as** Carla Zimmerman Physician Profile, **then click the** Styles and Formatting button 🔠 **on the Formatting toolbar**

   The Styles and Formatting task pane opens. The Normal paragraph style is applied to the author's physician's name at the top of the document and to the paragraphs of text, and the Heading 2 style is applied to section heads such as Early Life.

2. **Click the** New Style button **in the Styles and Formatting task pane**

   The New Style dialog box opens, as shown in Figure G-3. In this dialog box, you enter a name for the new style, select a style type, and then select the formatting options you want applied to text formatted with the new style.

3. **Type** Profile Title **as the custom style name in the Name text box, press [Tab], then make sure that "Paragraph" appears in the Style type list box**

   The default style type is Paragraph. When you create a new paragraph style, you can base it on another style by selecting a style in the Style based on list box, or you can create a new style that is based on no preset style. When you base a style on an existing style, the settings for the existing style, as well as any changes you make to the settings, are included with the new style. By default, a new style is based on the Normal style.

4. **Select** Arial, 16 point, Bold, **and the** Blue **font color as shown in Figure G-4, then click** OK

   The Profile Title style appears in the Pick formatting to apply list box.

5. **Select** Carla Zimmerman, M.D. **at the top of the document, then click** Profile Title **in the Pick formatting to apply list box**

   The heading Carla Zimmerman, M.D. is formatted with the new Profile Title style.

6. **Click anywhere in the** Early Life **heading, click the** Heading 2 list arrow **in the Pick formatting to apply list box, then click** Select All 4 Instance(s)

   The four headings formatted with the Heading 2 style are selected.

7. **Click the** New Style button, **then type** Profile Heading **as the style name in the Name text box**

   Notice that the Profile Heading style is based on the Heading 2 style because this style was applied to the text you selected before opening the New Style dialog box.

8. **Change the font size to** 12 point **and the font color to** Red, **then click** OK

9. **Click** Profile Heading **in the Pick formatting to apply list box to apply the Profile Heading style to the selected headings, scroll up and click** Carla **at the beginning of the document to deselect the selected text, click the** Show list arrow **at the bottom of the Styles and Formatting task pane, click** Formatting in use, **then save the document**

   The document appears as shown in Figure G-5. When you show only the formatting in use, you can quickly identify which styles you used to format your document.

**FIGURE G-3:** New Style dialog box

By default, a new style is based on the Normal style

By default, after you format a paragraph with the new style, the new style is applied to the next paragraph when you press [Enter]

Enter a name for the new style in the Name text box

By default, the Paragraph style type is selected

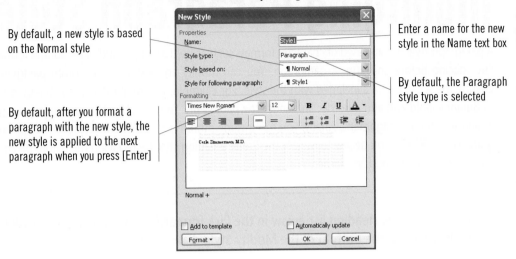

**FIGURE G-4:** Settings for Profile Title style

Arial font style selected

16-point font size selected

Appearance of text formatted with the Profile Title style

Bold selected

Blue font color selected

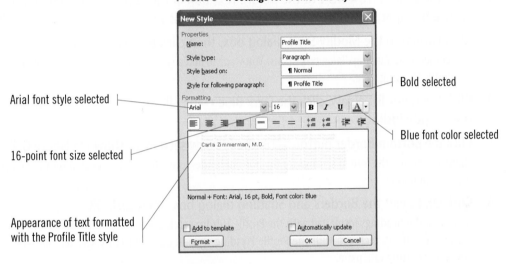

**FIGURE G-5:** Document formatted with custom styles

The style in the Style list box on the Formatting toolbar names the style applied to text at the location of the insertion point

Profile Title style applied

Profile Heading style applied

Only the styles currently in use are displayed in alphabetical order

Paragraph symbol indicates a paragraph style

Show list arrow

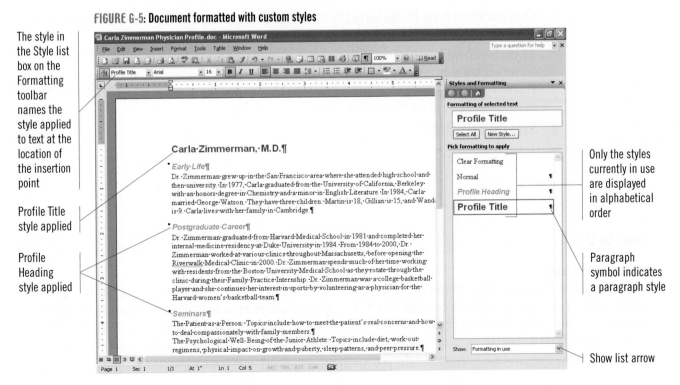

# Modifying Paragraph Styles

A paragraph style is composed of character formats such as bold and italic and of paragraph formats such as line spacing before and after a paragraph. You can modify an existing or a custom paragraph style to change the set of formats included with the style. For example, you might decide to change the font style to Britannic Bold and add a border line under the paragraph. You can also change paragraph formats such as line spacing and alignment. Finally, you can include numbers or bullets with text formatted with a paragraph style. ░░░░░ You decide to modify the Profile Heading style by reducing the Before paragraph spacing and by adding a bottom border.

## STEPS

1. **Click the Profile Heading list arrow in the Pick formatting to apply list box, click Modify, click Format at the bottom of the Modify Style dialog box, then click Paragraph**
   The Paragraph dialog box opens with the Indents and Spacing tab selected.

2. **Click the down arrow next to the Before text box in the Spacing section one time to reduce the Spacing Before a paragraph to 6 point as shown in Figure G-6, then click OK**

3. **Click Format in the Modify Style dialog box, then click Border**
   The Borders and Shading dialog box opens. You want to add a single line under each heading formatted with the Profile Heading style.

4. **Click the Color list arrow, click the Dark Blue color, click the Width list arrow, then click the 2 ¼ pt width**

**QUICK TIP**
You can also click the paragraph borders in the Preview section to select a border option.

5. **Click the Bottom Border button ▦ in the Preview section, as shown in Figure G-7**
   Figure G-7 shows the format settings for the bottom border line. The Preview section shows the placement of the bottom border.

6. **Click OK to exit the Borders and Shading dialog box, then click OK**
   All four of the headings formatted with the Profile Heading style are automatically updated. You can view all the format settings included with the Profile Heading style—or any currently selected text—by viewing the Reveal Formatting task pane.

7. **Click the word Early in the Early Life heading, click the Other Task Panes list arrow at the top of the Styles and Formatting task pane, then click Reveal Formatting**
   All the formatting associated with the text at the position of the insertion point appears in the Reveal Formatting task pane, as shown in Figure G-8. Information about text, paragraph, and section formatting is organized into categories in the Reveal Formatting task pane. Use the scroll bar as needed to view all of the formatting assigned to the selected text.

8. **Save the document**

### Clues to Use

#### Clearing formats

To quickly remove all the formatting from selected text, click Clear Formatting in the Pick formatting to apply list box in the Styles and Formatting task pane. All the styles and any other formats that have been applied to the selected text are instantly removed. This feature is most useful when you need to reformat text that has been formatted several times with various styles and options. To avoid unexpected results when working with styles, you may want to get into the habit of clearing the existing styles and then starting with a new style that you have created yourself and which includes only the formats you want.

**FIGURE G-6:** Before paragraph spacing reduced

Spacing section

Spacing before a paragraph reduced to 6 pt

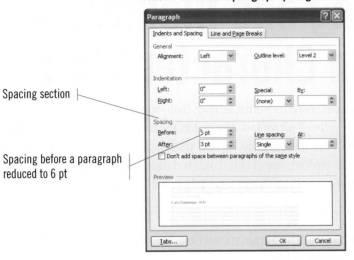

**FIGURE G-7:** Border options selected

Color list arrow

Bottom Border button

Preview of bottom border placement

Width list arrow

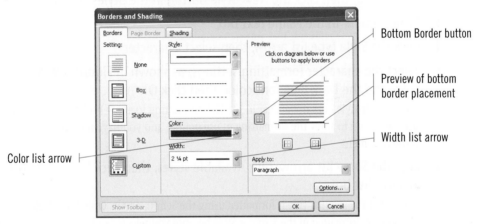

**FIGURE G-8:** Reveal Formatting pane with modified Profile Heading style applied

Profile Heading style after it has been modified

Other Task Panes list arrow

Text for which formatting is revealed

The formatting of selected text is described in the Reveal Formatting task pane

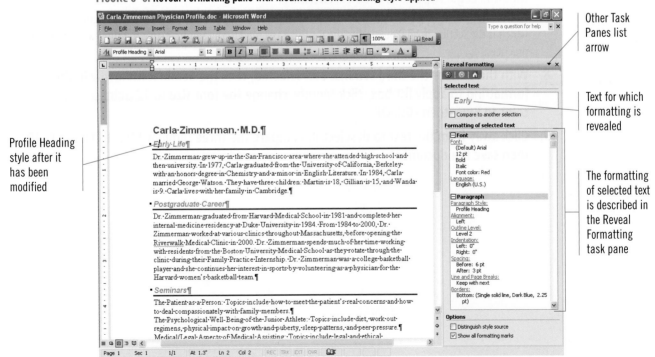

# Creating and Modifying Custom Character Styles

A **character style** includes character format settings that you name and store as a set. You apply a character style to selected text within a paragraph. Any text in the paragraph that is not formatted with the character style is formatted with the currently applied paragraph style. You use a character style to apply character formats such as the font, size of text, bold, and italic. You want to create a custom character style called Seminar to apply to each seminar title in the Seminars section of Carla's profile.

1. Scroll down the page to the Seminars section, then select the seminar title The Patient as a Person:, including the colon

2. Click the Other Task Panes list arrow in the Reveal Formatting task pane, click Styles and Formatting, then click the New Style button in the Styles and Formatting task pane

3. Type Seminar in the Name text box

4. Click the Style type list arrow, then select Character

5. Select the character formatting settings, as shown in Figure G-9: Arial, 14 point, Bold, Italic, and the Dark Blue font color, then click OK

   The Seminar style does not appear in the Pick formatting to apply list box because the Styles and Formatting task pane is set to show the Formatting in use option, and you have not yet applied the Seminar style to text in the document.

6. Click the Show list arrow, click Available styles, then click Seminar in the Pick formatting to apply list box

   Notice that the seminar title is formatted using the Seminar style. Only the selected characters The Patient as a Person: are formatted in the Seminar Style because you selected only them and not the entire paragraph.

7. Apply the Seminar style to The Psychological Well-Being of the Junior Athlete: and Medical/Legal Aspects of Medical Assisting:

   Notice that the font size assigned to the Seminar style is larger than the font size assigned to Seminars, which is the section head. You modify the font size assigned to the Seminar style to follow acceptable design practices.

8. With the text for the third seminar still selected, click the Seminar list arrow in the Pick formatting to apply list box, click Modify, change the font size to 12 point and the font color to Blue, then click OK

9. Click away from the text to deselect it, compare the three seminar titles to Figure G-10, then save the document

**FIGURE G-9:** Formatting options selected for the Seminar Character style

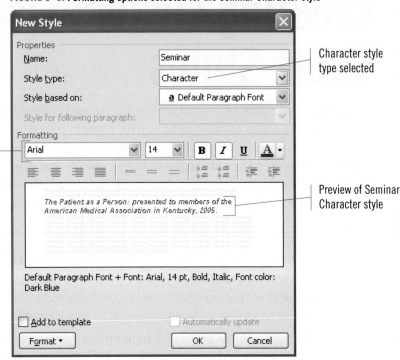

Character style type selected

Character formatting set as Arial font, 14-point font size, Bold, Italic, and Dark Blue font color

Preview of Seminar Character style

**FIGURE G-10:** Modified Seminar style applied

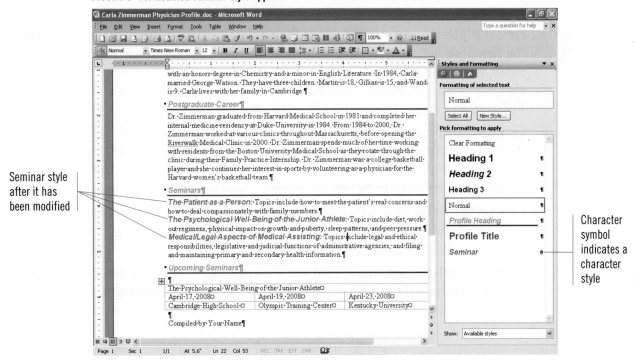

Seminar style after it has been modified

Character symbol indicates a character style

# Creating Custom List and Table Styles

A **list style** includes paragraph format settings that you use to format a series of paragraphs when you want the paragraphs to appear related in some way. For example, you can create a list style that adds bullet characters to a series of paragraphs or sequential numbers to a list of items. A **table style** includes formatting settings for both the table grid and the table text. ████████ You want to create a custom list style called Seminar to format the list of seminars with a special bullet character, and then you want to create a custom table style called Seminar Table to format the table at the end of the document.

## STEPS

1. **Click the** New Style button **in the Styles and Formatting task pane, type** Seminar List **in the Name text box, click the** Style type list arrow, **then select** List

   The New Style dialog box changes to show the formatting options for a list style, as shown in Figure G-11. You want to select a symbol as the bullet character for your bulleted list.

   > **TROUBLE**
   > You might need to scroll up to find the Book symbol.

2. **Click the** Insert Symbol button Ω **to open the Symbol dialog box, click the** Font list arrow, **scroll down and select** Wingdings **if it is not already selected, then click the** Book symbol **as shown in Figure G-12**

3. **Click** OK **to exit the Symbol dialog box, then click** OK **to exit the New Style dialog box**

4. **Click in the paragraph that describes** The Patient as a Person seminar, **click** Seminar List **in the Pick formatting to apply list box, then apply the** Seminar List style **to the paragraphs that describe the other two seminars**

   The three paragraphs in the Seminars section are formatted with the new Seminar List style.

   > **TROUBLE**
   > If you do not see the table gridlines, click Table, then click Show Gridlines.

5. **Press [Ctrl][End] to move to the end of the document, click anywhere in the** table, **click the** New Style button, **type** Seminar Table **in the Name text box, click the** Style type list arrow, **then select** Table

   The New Style dialog box changes to show formatting options for a table. You can base the style on one of the Word preset table styles or you can modify the default table style.

6. **Click the** Style based on list arrow, **scroll to select** Table Grid, **click the** Bold button, **click the** Font Color list arrow, **select the** Dark Blue color, **click the** Fill Color list arrow, **select the** Light Green color, **click the** Alignment button list arrow, **then click the** Align Center button

   The format settings required for the table are selected.

7. **Click** OK **to exit the New Style dialog box, then click** Seminar Table **in the Pick formatting to apply list box**

   The Seminar Table style is applied to the table.

8. **Verify that both the Seminars section and the table appear on the screen, compare the Seminars section and the table with Figure G-13, then save the document**

**FIGURE G-11:** Formatting options for a list in the New Style dialog box

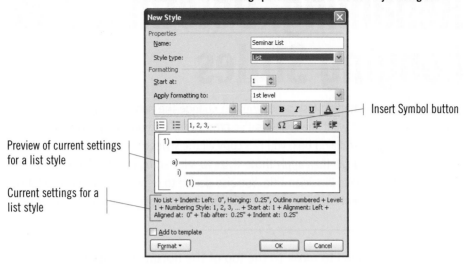

Insert Symbol button

Preview of current settings for a list style

Current settings for a list style

**FIGURE G-12:** Book symbol selected

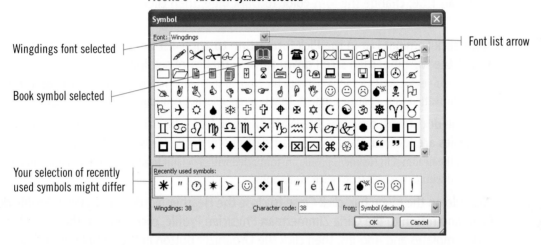

Wingdings font selected

Font list arrow

Book symbol selected

Your selection of recently used symbols might differ

**FIGURE G-13:** Custom List and Table styles applied

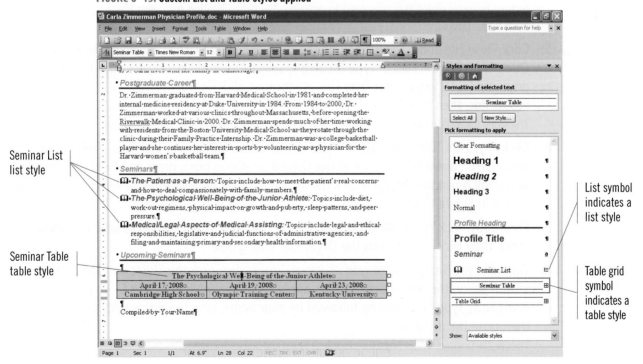

Seminar List list style

Seminar Table table style

List symbol indicates a list style

Table grid symbol indicates a table style

# Renaming, Deleting, and Copying Styles

In the Styles and Formatting task pane, you can change the name of a style and even delete it altogether. Sometimes you might want the styles you've created for one document to be available in another document. In the Organizer dialog box, you can copy all the styles you've saved with one document to another document, where you can then apply those styles to selected text. ▓▓▓▓▓ You decide to change the name of the Profile Title style to Physician Title. You also decide to remove the Seminar List style. Finally, you copy the styles to a document containing a physician profile that you've written for Dr. Heather Nordgren.

## STEPS

1. **Press [Ctrl][Home] to move to the top of the document, click the Profile Title list arrow in the Pick formatting to apply list box (you might need to scroll down), click Modify, type Physician Title, change the font color to Dark Blue, then click OK**

   The text "Carla Zimmerman" is formatted with the Physician Title style.

   > **TROUBLE**
   > Use the Pick formatting to apply scroll bar if necessary to view a style.

2. **Right-click Seminar List in the Pick formatting to apply list box, click Delete, click Yes to accept the warning, then scroll down to view the list of seminars**

   The seminar descriptions are formatted with the Normal style. After removing the Seminar List style, the text may be formatted with a hanging indent. That is acceptable; just continue with the next step.

3. **Save the document, open the file WMP G-2.doc from the drive and folder where your Data Files are located, then save it as Heather Nordgren Physician Profile**

   Some of the headings in Heather's profile are formatted with a default heading style and the seminar titles are formatted with a character style called Workshops.

4. **Click File on the menu bar, click Close to close the Heather Nordgren Physician Profile document and return to the Carla Zimmerman Physician Profile, click Tools on the menu bar, click Templates and Add-Ins, then click the Organizer button in the Templates and Add-ins dialog box**

   In the Organizer dialog box, you need to open the file called Heather Nordgren Physician Profile.doc and make it the Target file.

   > **QUICK TIP**
   > By default, only templates are listed.

5. **Click Close File under the list box on the right side in the Organizer dialog box, then click Open File, click the Files of type list arrow, select All Word Documents, navigate to the drive and folder where your Data Files are located, click Heather Nordgren Physician Profile.doc, then click Open**

   The styles assigned to the Heather Nordgren Physician Profile document appear in the list box on the right side.

6. **Click Physician Title in the list of styles in the Carla Zimmerman Physician Profile document (scroll down the left side of the Organizer dialog box), press and hold the [Shift] key, scroll down the list, then click the last style listed Table Normal to select the styles, as shown in Figure G-14**

7. **Click Copy, click Yes to All, click Close File on the right side, click Yes to save the document, then click Close to exit the Organizer dialog box**

8. **Open the file Heather Nordgren Physician Profile.doc, click the Styles and Formatting button ⬜ on the Formatting toolbar, apply styles as shown in Figure G-15, press [Ctrl][End], type Compiled by followed by your name, save the document, print a copy, then close the document**

   The file Carla Zimmerman Physician Profile is again the active document.

FIGURE G-14: Styles selected in the Organizer dialog box

Copy button

Style names selected

Source file

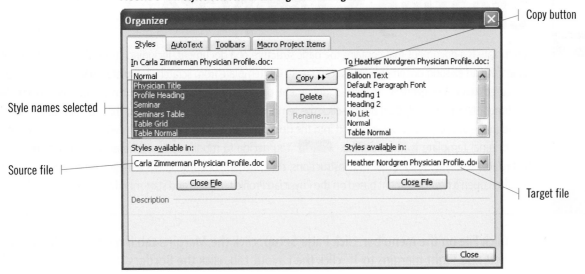

FIGURE G-15: Document after new styles applied

Physician Title style

Profile Heading style

Seminar style

Seminar Table style

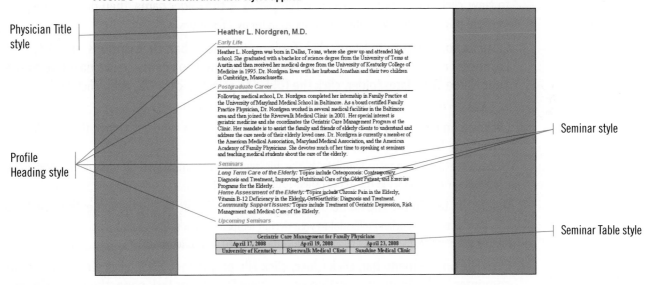

## Clues to Use

### Working in the Organizer dialog box

You copy styles from the document shown in the left side of the Organizer dialog box to a new document that you open in the right side of the Organizer dialog box. The document in the left side is the Source file because it contains the styles you want to copy. The document in the right side is the Target file because it receives the styles you copy. By default, the Target file is the Normal template.

# Creating a Template

A template is a document that contains the basic structure of a document, including styles. You can create a template from an existing document, or you can create the template from scratch. Templates that you create yourself are called **user templates**. To base a document on a template, you select On my computer in the New Document task pane, and then double-click the template to open a new document that contains all the formats stored in the template. You can enter text into the document and then save it, just as you would any document. The original template is not modified. ◄▬▬▬ You decide to modify some of the document settings, replace text related to Carla Zimmerman with instructions, then save the document as a template called Physician Profile. You then open a new document based on the Physician Profile template and start modifying it for a new physician.

## STEPS

1. Click File on the menu bar, click Page Setup, click the Margins tab if necessary, change the Left and Right margins to 1", click the Layout tab, click the Borders button, click Box, verify that the border color is Dark Blue and the border width is 2¼ point, then click OK

2. Press [Ctrl][Home], select Carla Zimmerman, M.D., type [Enter Physician Name Here], then enter the placeholder text, as shown in Figure G-16

   The Word document is ready to save as the Physician Profile template. You can save the template in the default location on your computer's hard drive or you can select a new location.

3. Minimize Word, right-click My Computer on your computer desktop, click Explore, navigate to the drive and folder where your Data Files are located, click File on the menu bar, point to New, click Folder, type Your Name Templates as the folder name, then press [Enter]

   You want this new folder to be the default location for user templates.

4. Close Explorer, return to Word, click Tools on the menu bar, click Options, click File Locations, click User templates, click Modify, click the Look in list arrow, navigate to the Your Name Templates folder, click the folder to select it, click OK, then click OK

   Now you can save the document on your screen as a template into the new folder.

5. Click File on the menu bar, click Save As, click the Save as type list arrow, then click Document Template (*.dot)

   When you select Document Template as the file type, Word switches to the default location for user templates—which you set as the folder called Your Name Templates.

6. Delete the text in the File name box, type Physician Profile as the filename, then click Save

   The file is saved as Physician Profile.dot to your default template location. The .dot filename extension identifies this file as a template file. You can create new documents based on this template.

7. Click File on the menu bar, click Close, click File on the menu bar, click New, click On my computer in the Templates section of the New Document task pane, then click General to make the General tab the active tab if necessary

   The default Templates dialog box opens and the template you saved to the Your Name Templates folder is available.

8. Click Physician Profile.dot, be sure the Document option button in the Create New section is selected, then click OK

   The template opens as a new document. Note that Document2 appears in the title bar. You can enter text into this document just as you would any document.

9. Replace the placeholder text with text, as shown in Figure G-17

10. Click File, click Save as, navigate to the drive and folder where your Data Files are located, type Forrest Quinn Physician Profile, then click Save

    The file Forrest Quinn Physician Profile is the active document.

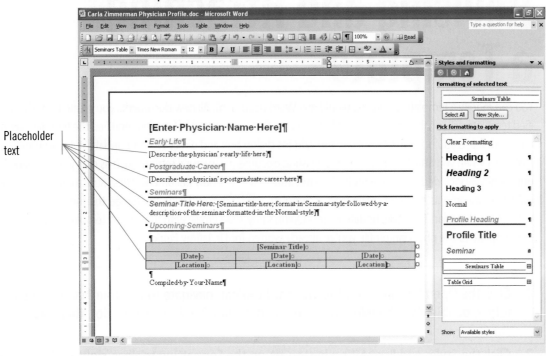

Placeholder text

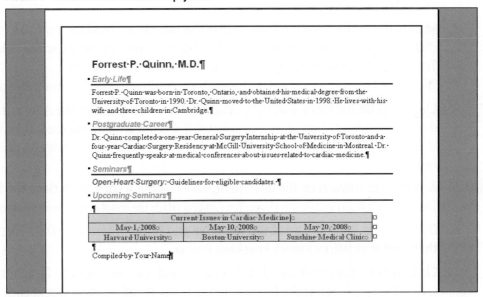

## Changing the default file location for user and workgroup templates

By default, user templates are stored in the Templates folder. The path for this folder is: C:/Documents and Settings/Administrator/Application Data/Microsoft/Templates. Note that a different folder might appear for Administrator, depending on how your computer system is set up. If the default location where user templates are saved has been changed, you can change back to the default location by selecting the Templates folder path in the File Locations tab of the Options dialog box.

You can also create templates to distribute to others. These templates are called **workgroup templates**. You select the location of a workgroup template in the File Locations tab of the Options dialog box, just as you select the location of a user template. To open the Options dialog box, click Tools on the Standard toolbar, then select Options.

Word 2003

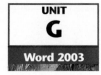

# Revising and Attaching a Template

You can modify a template just as you would any Word document. All new documents you create from the modified template will use the new settings. All documents that you created before you modified the template are not changed unless you open the Templates and Add-ins dialog box and direct Word to update styles automatically. Note that when you attach a template to an existing document, structural settings such as margins and page layouts originally included with the template are not attached to the new document. These structural settings affect only new documents that you create from a template. ███████ You decide to change the font style, size, and color of the Physician Title style, update Forrest Quinn's Physician Profile with the revised template, and then add the template to the physician profile you've already written for Dr. Jeffrey Patrick.

## STEPS

1. **Click the** Open button 📁 **on the Standard toolbar, navigate to the Your Name Templates folder, double-click the** folder name **to open it, click** Physician Profile.dot, **then click** Open
   The file opens.

2. **Click the** Styles and Formatting button 🔠 **on the Formatting toolbar, right-click** Physician Title **in the Pick formatting to apply list box, click** Modify, **change the font to** Bodoni MT Black **(or a similar font), change the font size to** 18 point, **change the font color to** Dark Teal, **then click** OK

3. **Modify the** Profile Heading style **so that the color is** Teal **and the font size is** 14 point, **click** File **on the menu bar, click** Save As, **click the Save as type list arrow, select** Document Template (*.dot) **if necessary, click** Save, **then close the template**
   The modified template is saved and the Forrest Quinn Physician Profile document is the active document.

4. **Click** Tools **on the menu bar, click** Templates and Add-Ins, **click the** Automatically update document styles option button **to select it if it is not already selected, then click** OK
   The Physician Title and Profile Heading styles in the Forrest Quinn Physician Profile are updated, as shown in Figure G-18.

   **TROUBLE**
   All of the page border might not print on some printers. Remove the page border if your printer cannot accommodate it.

5. **Be sure your name is on the document, save it, print a copy, then close the file**
   The document prints and the file closes. You can also attach the template to a new document.

6. **Open the file** WMP G-3.doc **from the drive and folder where your Data Files are located, then save it as** Jeffrey Patrick Physician Profile

7. **Click** Tools **on the menu bar, click** Templates and Add-Ins, **click the** Templates tab **if necessary, click** Attach, **select the** Physician Profile.dot **template, click** Open, **click the** Automatically update document styles check box, **then click** OK

8. **Open the Styles and Formatting task pane, then apply styles as shown in Figure G-19**
   The text is formatted with the styles, but the page border does not appear and the left and right margins are still set at 1.25". When you add the template to an existing document or update an existing document with a modified template, structural changes do not appear.

9. **Press** [Ctrl][End], **type** Compiled by **followed by your name, save the document, print a copy, close the file, then exit Word**

Physician Title
style updated

Profile Heading
style updated

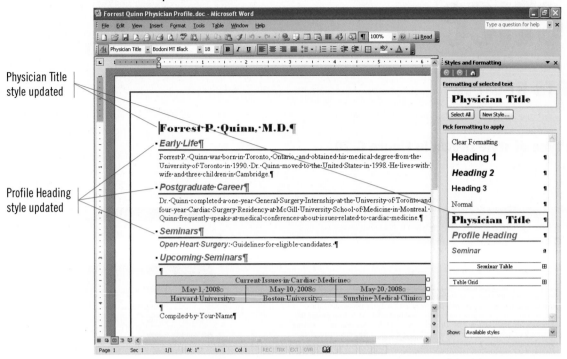

Physician Title style

Profile Heading style

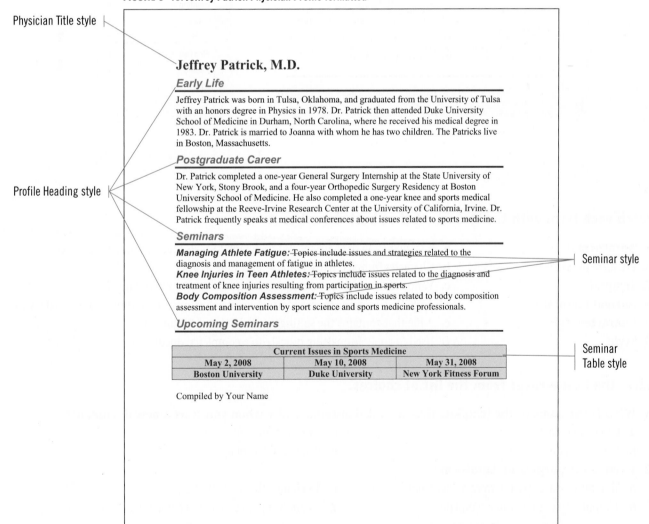

Seminar style

Seminar
Table style

# Practice

▼ CONCEPTS REVIEW

**Identify each type of style shown in Figure G-20.**

FIGURE G-20

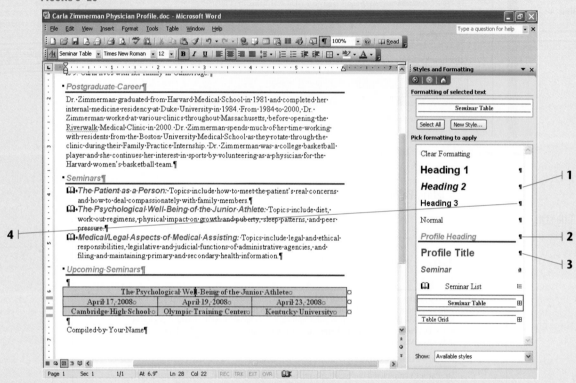

**Match each term with the statement that best describes it.**

5. **AutoFormat**
6. **Paragraph style**
7. **Template**
8. **Normal template**
9. **Character style**
10. **Style**

a. A combination of character and paragraph formats that are named and stored as a set
b. Character formats that you name and store as a set
c. Various formats that are combined into one set, which is named
d. A file that contains the basic structure of a document in addition to selected styles
e. A file that contains the settings available to all documents
f. Used to apply formatting quickly to a completed document

**Select the best answer from the list of choices.**

11. **What is the name of the template that is loaded automatically when you start a new document?**
   a. Global template
   b. User template
   c. Normal template
   d. Paragraph template

12. **What is the purpose of AutoFormat?**
   a. To remove extra spacing from a document
   b. To apply styles to text in a template
   c. To change the document type
   d. To apply a preset theme to a document

13. **Which of the following definitions best describes a paragraph style?**

   **a.** Format settings applied only to selected text within a paragraph

   **b.** Format settings applied to a table grid

   **c.** Format settings applied to the structure of a document

   **d.** Format settings applied to all the text in a paragraph

14. **How do you modify a style?**

   **a.** Double-click the style in the Styles and Formatting task pane.

   **b.** Right-click the style in the Styles and Formatting task pane, then click Modify.

   **c.** Right-click the style in the Styles and Formatting task pane, then click Revise.

   **d.** Click the style in the Styles and Formatting task pane, then click New Style.

15. **In which dialog box do you copy styles from one document to another?**

   **a.** Organizer dialog box

   **b.** New Document dialog box

   **c.** Styles dialog box

   **d.** Modify Styles dialog box

16. **Which selection from the Tools menu do you click to attach a template to a document?**

   **a.** Templates

   **b.** New templates

   **c.** General template

   **d.** Templates and Add-Ins

# ▼ SKILLS REVIEW

1. **Create custom paragraph styles.**

   **a.** Start Word, open the file WMP G-4.doc from the drive and location where your Data Files are stored, save it as **Skin Conditions**, then open the Styles and Formatting task pane.

   **b.** Create a new paragraph style called **Condition** with the Arial Black font, 16 point, and the Green font color.

   **c.** Apply the Condition style to Allergic Skin Conditions.

   **d.** Click the Contact Dermatitis heading, then select all the headings formatted with the Heading 3 style.

   **e.** Create a new style called **Condition Type** that is based on the Heading 3 style, but that changes the font size to 14 point, adds Underlining, and changes the font color to Brown.

   **f.** Apply the Condition Type style to the three selected headings, then deselect the text to view the change.

   **g.** Show only the formatting currently in use in the document, then save the document.

2. **Modify paragraph styles.**

   **a.** Click the Condition Type list arrow in the Pick formatting to apply list box, then click Modify.

   **b.** Click the Format button, open the Paragraph dialog box, change the After spacing to 4 point, then click OK.

   **c.** Click the Format button, open the Font dialog box, then select the Shadow font effect.

   **d.** Click OK in the Modify Style dialog box, then verify that the modified Condition Type style is applied to text formatted with the Condition Type style.

   **e.** Click any text formatted with the Condition Type style, open the Reveal Formatting task pane and view the formatting currently applied to the text, then save the document.

3. **Create and modify custom character styles.**

   **a.** Show the Styles and Formatting task pane, then create a new character style named **Description**.

   **b.** Select the Arial Black font, 12 point, Underlining, and the Brown font color, then click OK in the New Style dialog box.

   **c.** Show the Available styles, apply the Description style to the text Irritant contact dermatitis: and Allergic contact dermatitis:.

   **d.** Apply the Description style to the text Hives: and Angioedema: in the Hives and Angioedema section.

   **e.** Modify the Description style by changing the font size to 11 point and the color to Green, then save the document.

4. **Create custom list and table styles.**

   **a.** Create a List style called **Description List**.

   **b.** Select the right-pointing solid arrow symbol (➔) from the Wingdings character set. (*Hint*: Character code 232.)

   **c.** Accept the symbol, select the 14-point font size for the bullet character, then apply the style to each paragraph that describes a condition.

   **d.** Click the table at the bottom of the document, then create a Table style called **Treatment Table** based on the Table Grid style.

e. Select Dark Green for the font color, select Light Yellow for the fill color, change the font size to 14 point, select the Align Top Center alignment, then click OK in the New Style dialog box.
f. Apply the Treatment Table style to the table, then save the document.

**5. Rename, delete, and copy styles.**

a. Change the name of the Condition style to **Condition Category**, then change the font color to Dark Yellow, which is just above Lime. Check that the formatted text Allergic Skin Conditions at the beginning of the document is changed.
b. Delete the Description List style. (*Note*: After removing the Description List style, the text may be formatted with a hanging indent. That is acceptable; just continue with the next step.)
c. Save the document, then open the file WMP G-5.doc and save it as **Heart Conditions**.
d. Close the Heart Conditions file, make sure Skin Conditions is again the active document, click Tools on the menu bar, click Templates and Add-Ins, then click the Organizer button.
e. Close the file in the right of the Organizer dialog box, then open the Heart Conditions document. Remember to change the Files of type to Word documents.
f. Select all the styles in the Skin Conditions document, then copy them to the Heart Conditions document. Click Yes to All to overwrite existing style entries with the same name.
g. Close the Heart Conditions document in the Organizer dialog box, click Yes to save when prompted, then close the Organizer dialog box.
h. Open the file Heart Conditions.doc, then open the Styles and Formatting task pane. Apply the Condition Category style to the document title, apply the Condition Type style to all text formatted with the Heading 3 style, apply the Description style to the name of each individual condition (for example, Congenital abnormality:), then apply the Treatment Table style to the table.
i. Type **Prepared by your name** at the end of the document, save the document, print it, then close it.

**6. Create a template.**

a. Make sure that Skin Conditions is the active document.
b. Change the left and right margins to 1.5", and then add a 3-point Dark Yellow page border.
c. Select Allergic Skin Conditions at the top of the page, type **[Enter Condition Category Here]**, then delete text and enter directions so the document appears as shown in Figure G-21.
d. In Explorer, create a new folder called **Your Name Skills Review** in the drive and folder where your Data Files are located.
e. Change the file location for user templates to the new folder you named Your Name Skills Review.
f. Save the file as a template called **Condition Description** to the Your Name Skills Review folder, then close the template.
g. Create a new file based on the Condition Description template.
h. Replace the title of the document with the text **Respiratory Conditions**, then save the document as **Respiratory Conditions** to the location where your data files are stored.

FIGURE G-21

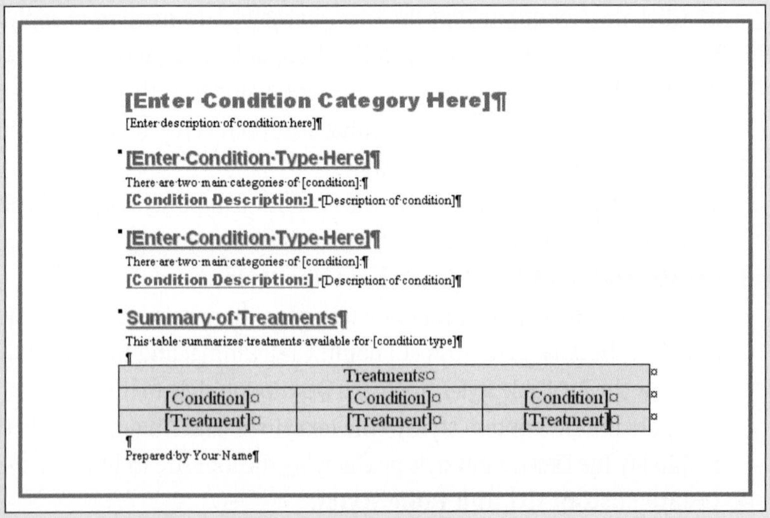
[Enter Condition Category Here]¶
[Enter description of condition here]¶
[Enter·Condition·Type·Here]¶
There·are·two·main·categories·of·[condition]:¶
[Condition Description:] ·[Description·of·condition]¶
[Enter·Condition·Type·Here]¶
There·are·two·main·categories·of·[condition]:¶
[Condition Description:] ·[Description·of·condition]¶
Summary·of·Treatments¶
This·table·summarizes·treatments·available·for·[condition·type]¶

| Treatments | | |
|---|---|---|
| [Condition] | [Condition] | [Condition] |
| [Treatment] | [Treatment] | [Treatment] |

Prepared·by·Your·Name¶

**7. Revise and attach a template.**

a. Open the Condition Description.dot template, change the font color in the Condition Category style to Dark Red, open the Save As dialog box and verify that the Save as type is Document Template, then save and close the template.
b. With the Respiratory Conditions document active, click Tools on the menu bar, click Templates and Add-ins, click the Automatically update document styles check box, then click OK.

c. Verify that the font color of text formatted with the Condition Category style has changed to Dark Red.

d. Save the document, then close it.

e. Open the file WMP G-6.doc, then save it as **Knee Conditions**.

f. Attach the Condition Description template to the document. Remember to click the Automatically update document styles check box in the Templates and Add-ins dialog box to select it.

g. Apply styles from the Condition Description template so that the Knee Conditions document resembles the other documents you have formatted for this Skills Review.

h. Type **Prepared by** followed by **your name** at the end of the document, save the document, print a copy, close all documents, then exit Word.

# ▼ INDEPENDENT CHALLENGE 1

You are the office manager of the Evergreen Medical Clinic in Seattle, Washington. The annual clinic softball game is coming soon and you need to inform the staff about the date and time of the game. To save time, you've decided to type the text of the memo without formatting and then to use the AutoFormat and Style Gallery features to format the memo attractively.

a. Start Word, open the file WMP G-7.doc from the drive and folder where your Data Files are located, then save it as **Clinic Softball Memo**.

b. Use the AutoFormat feature to apply styles to the document. (*Hint*: To apply an AutoFormat, click Format on the menu bar, click AutoFormat, click the AutoFormat now option button, then click OK.)

c. Open the Style Gallery and apply the Professional Memo template. (*Hint*: To open the Style Gallery, click Format on the menu bar, click Theme, then click the Style Gallery button. Select the Professional Memo template from the list of templates, click the Document option button even if it is already selected to see how the template appears when applied to the current document, then click OK.)

d. Open the Styles and Formatting task pane, then refer to Table G-1 to make the following changes to selected styles. If you do not have the fonts listed, select other fonts. (*Hint*: To identify the style assigned to specific text, click the text and then notice which style name is framed in the Pick formatting to apply list box.)

**TABLE G-1**

| style name | changes |
|---|---|
| Document Label | Arial Rounded MT Bold, 22-pt font size, Centered |
| Message Header | Arial font, 12-point font size, Before paragraph spacing to 6 point |
| Heading 1 | Arial Rounded MT Bold, 14-point font size, Bold |

e. Select Your Name in the message header, type **your name**, save the document, print it, close it, then exit Word.

# ▼ INDEPENDENT CHALLENGE 2

You are in charge of the hospital cafeteria at Valley View Hospital in Montreal. Staff and hospital guests can choose entrees from either a winter menu or a summer menu. You've already created an unformatted version of the winter menu. Now you need to format text in the winter menu with styles, open and save a new document for the summer menu, copy the styles from the winter menu document to the summer menu document, then use the styles to create a summer version of the menu. You will type your own entries for appetizers, entrees, salads, and desserts for the summer menu.

a. Start Word, open the file WMP G-8.doc from the drive and location where your Data Files are located, then save it as **Hospital Cafeteria Winter Menu**.

b. Create the styles as described in Table G-2.

c. Apply the Menu Title style to the two lines of the document title.

**TABLE G-2**

| style name and type | formats |
|---|---|
| Menu Title: paragraph | Arial, 18-point font size, Bold, Dark Teal, Center Alignment |
| Menu Categories: paragraph | Arial, 14-point font size, Bold Italic, Top and bottom border in 1 point and Dark Teal |
| Prices: paragraph | Right tab at 6" (*Hint*: Select Tabs from the Format menu in the New Style dialog box) |
| Menu Items: list | The Flower bullet character (✿) from Wingdings (*Hint*: The character code is 123) |

# ▼ INDEPENDENT CHALLENGE 2 (CONTINUED)

**d.** Apply the Menu Categories style to each menu category (for example, On the Lighter Side, Soups and Salads, and Entrees).

**e.** Select all the menu items in the On the Lighter Side category, apply the Prices style, then apply the Menu Items style. (*Note*: You must apply the styles in this order.)

**f.** Apply the Prices and the Menu Items styles to the remaining menu items in the document.

**g.** At the bottom of the document, press [Enter] twice, type **your name**, a **comma**, and **Manager**, apply the Normal style, save the document, then print it.

**h.** Create a new document, save it as **Hospital Cafeteria Summer Menu**, then close it.

**i.** Open the Organizer dialog box, copy the styles from the Hospital Cafeteria Winter Menu document to the Hospital Cafeteria Summer Menu document, then close the Organizer dialog box, saving files where prompted.

**j.** Open the Summer Menu document.

**k.** Create a menu similar to the winter menu, but with menu items more suitable for summer fare. For example, instead of Winter squash medley, you could include Mint-Raspberry Compote.

### Advanced Challenge Exercise

- Modify the Menu Title style so that it includes the Britannic Bold font, 20-point font size, and Brown.
- Modify the Menu Categories style so it includes Orange text and Brown top and bottom border lines.
- Modify the Menu Items list style so that the bullet is diamond shape and Orange. (*Hint*: To change the color of the bullet, click the Font Color button; the font is already orange from the previous step).
- Modify the Prices style so that the Right tab includes the 2 leader style (*Hint*: Select Tabs from the Format menu in the Modify Style dialog box).

**l.** Apply styles to appropriate text.

**m.** Two lines below the last entry in the menu, type **your name**, a **comma**, and **Manager**, apply the Normal style, save the document, print it, close the document, then exit Word.

# ▼ INDEPENDENT CHALLENGE 3

As the Office Administrator at Mountainview Medical Group, you are in charge of creating a design for a new staff newsletter that will be distributed to all clinic staff every three months. Another colleague has already developed text for the first newsletter. First, you create a template for the newsletter, then you apply the template to the document containing the newsletter text.

**FIGURE G-22**

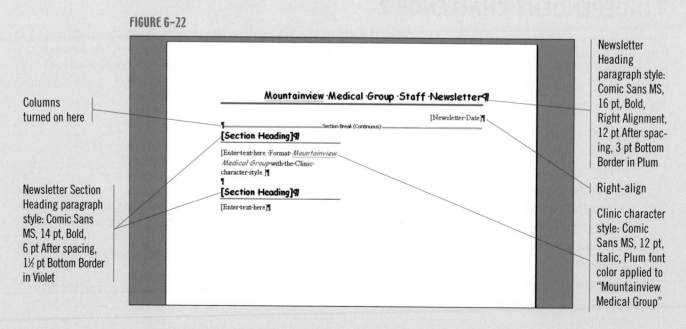

# ▼ INDEPENDENT CHALLENGE 3 (CONTINUED)

**a.** Start Word, then create the document shown in Figure G-22. Enter the content first, then create the styles shown in Figure G-22. (*Hint*: To create two columns, click to the left of the first occurrence of the text Section Heading, click Format on the menu bar, then click Columns. In the Columns dialog box, click two in the Presets section, click the Apply to list arrow, select This point forward, then click OK.)

**b.** Modify the default location for user templates so that they are saved in the folder you created previously named Your Name Templates. This folder should be in the drive and folder where your Data Files are located.

**c.** Save the document as a template named **Staff Newsletter.dot**, then close the template.

**d.** Open the file WMP G-9.doc from the drive and folder where your Data Files are stored, then save it as **October Staff Newsletter**.

**e** Attach the Staff Newsletter template to the document.

**f.** Change the left and right margins to 1.1", then apply the two-column format starting at the Verifying Patient Insurance Coverage heading. (*Note*: You need to apply the two-column format because options related to the structure of a document saved with a template are lost when you attach the template to an existing document.)

**g.** Apply styles to the appropriate text. (*Note*: The text Mountainview Medical Group appears three times in the newsletter.)

### Advanced Challenge Exercise

- Create a Table style called **Schedule**.
- Click the Apply formatting to list arrow, click Header row, then select Violet as the shading color, White as the font color, and Bold.
- Click the Apply formatting to list arrow, click Whole table, then select Lavender as the shading color and Dark Blue as the font color.
- Apply the Schedule style to the table in the Work Schedule section.

**h.** Type **Editor:** followed by your name so it is right-aligned at the end of the second column, save the document, print a copy, close the document, then exit Word.

# ▼ INDEPENDENT CHALLENGE 4

From the Microsoft Office Templates Web site, you can access a variety of templates. You can import any template from the Web site directly into Word and then modify it for your own purposes. You decide to find and then modify a template for a sales letter.

**a.** Open the New Document task pane, then click Templates on Office Online in the Templates section.

**b.** In a few seconds, the Microsoft Office Online Templates Home Web site opens in your browser.

**c.** Click Word under Microsoft Office Programs, click Business and Nonprofit under Letters and Letterhead, then click Letters for Nonprofit Organizations (scroll down, if necessary).

**d.** Scroll through the letters listed. You need to select one that you can adapt for a nonprofit health organization of your choice.

**e.** Select the letter you want to adapt, then click Download Now.

**f.** If necessary, read and accept the licensing agreement, click Yes to accept the Security warning, then click Continue. If another message box appears, click No. In a few moments, the letter appears in Word.

**g.** Modify the return address, recipient address, and content of the letter in Microsoft Word so it contains information relevant to a health organization of your choice.

**h.** Use AutoFormat to format the document as a letter.

**i.** From the Style Gallery, select a letter style to apply to the letter.

**j.** In the Styles and Formatting task pane, modify two styles to reflect settings you prefer.

**k.** Save the letter as **Nonprofit Letter from Microsoft Office Templates**, be sure your name appears in the signature block, print a copy, close the document, then exit Word.

Create a new document, then type the text and create the tables shown in Figure G-23. Do not include any formatting. Apply the Heading 1 style to the title, then modify it so that it appears as shown in Figure G-23. Apply the Heading 2 style to the names of the price lists, then modify the Heading 2 style so that it appears as shown in Figure G-23. Create a table style called **Price List** that formats each table as shown in Figure G-23. Save the document as **Massage Oils**, be sure your name appears at the end of the document, print a copy, then close the document.

FIGURE G-23

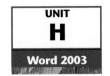

# Developing Multipage Documents

## OBJECTIVES

| |
|---|
| Build a document in Outline view |
| Work in Outline view |
| Add footnotes and endnotes |
| Navigate a document |
| Generate a table of contents |
| Generate an index |
| Modify pages in multiple sections |
| Work with master documents |

If you have a SAM user profile, you may have access to hands-on instruction, practice, and assessment of the skills covered in this unit. Log in to your SAM account and go to your assignments page to see what your instructor has assigned.

In Outline view, you use headings and subheadings to organize multipage documents, such as reports and manuals. These documents can include footnotes, cross-references, multiple sections, and even an index. You can also combine several documents—called subdocuments—into one master document. Tony Sanchez, RN, the Office Manager of Riverwalk Medical Clinic, asks you to help him develop guidelines related to office management, filing procedures, and receptionist duties. Tony plans to eventually use these documents as the basis of a Policy and Procedures Manual for the Clinic. You start by working in Outline view to revise the structure for the guidelines, and then you use several advanced Word features to format the document for publication.

**UNIT**
**H**

# Building a Document in Outline View

You work in Outline view to organize the headings and subheadings that identify topics and subtopics in multipage documents. In Outline view, each heading is assigned a level from 1 to 9, with Level 1 being the highest level and Level 9 being the lowest level. In addition, you can assign the Body text level to the paragraphs of text that enhance or clarify the document headings. Each level is formatted with one of the Word preset styles. For example, Level 1 is formatted with the Heading 1 style and the Body text level is formatted with the Normal style. ░░░░░ You work in Outline view to develop the structure of the guidelines on Medical Office Management.

## STEPS

> **QUICK TIP**
> Close the Getting Started task pane if it opens.

1. **Start Word, click the** Show/Hide ¶ button ¶ **on the Standard toolbar if necessary to show the paragraph marks, then click the** Outline View button ▤ **in the lower-left corner of the program window**

   The document appears in Outline view. Notice the Outlining toolbar below the Formatting toolbar at the top of the program window and the minus symbol in the document window. Table H-1 describes the buttons on the Outlining toolbar.

2. **Type** Management of the Medical Office

   Figure H-1 shows the text in Outline view. By default, the text appears at the left margin, is designated as Level 1, and is formatted with the Heading 1 style.

3. **Press** [Enter]**, click the** Demote button ⇥ **on the Outlining toolbar to move to Level 2, then type** Introduction

   The text is indented, designated as Level 2, and formatted with the Heading 2 style.

4. **Press** [Enter]**, then click the** Demote to body text button ⇥⇥ **on the Outlining toolbar**

5. **Type the following text:** This report discusses the management of the medical office in terms of three principal activities: designating staff positions, creating a policy and procedures manual, and maintaining medical and office supplies.**, then press** [Enter]

   The text is indented, designated as Body text level, and formatted with the Normal style. Notice that both the Level 1 and Level 2 text are preceded by a plus symbol ✚. This symbol indicates that the heading includes subtext, which could be a subheading or a paragraph of body text.

6. **Click the** Promote to Heading 1 button ⇤⇤ **on the Outlining toolbar**

   The insertion point returns to the left margin and the Level 1 position.

7. **Type** Designating Staff Positions**, press** [Enter]**, then save the document as** Medical Office Management **to the drive and folder where your Data Files are located**

   When you create a long document, you often enter all the headings and subheadings first to establish the overall structure of your document.

> **QUICK TIP**
> You can press [Tab] to move from a higher level to a lower level, and you can press [Shift][Tab] to move from a lower level to a higher level.

8. **Use the** Promote ⇤ **,** Demote ⇥ **, and** Promote to Heading 1 ⇤⇤ **buttons to complete the outline shown in Figure H-2**

9. **Place the insertion point after** Management of the Medical Office **at the top of the document, press** [Enter]**, click** ⇥⇥ **, type** Prepared by Your Name**, save the document, print a copy, then close it**

   The printed copy does not include the outline symbols.

**FIGURE H-1:** Level 1 text in Outline view

Level of current heading

Outlining toolbar

Minus symbol means that no other heading or text appears below the current heading

Outline View button

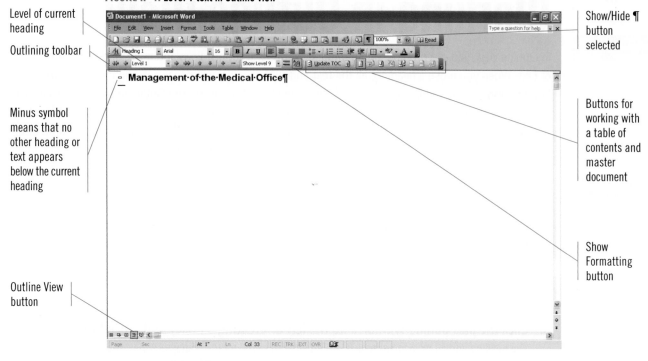

Show/Hide ¶ button selected

Buttons for working with a table of contents and master document

Show Formatting button

**FIGURE H-2:** Updated outline

Level 1 heading

Level 2 heading

Level 3 headings

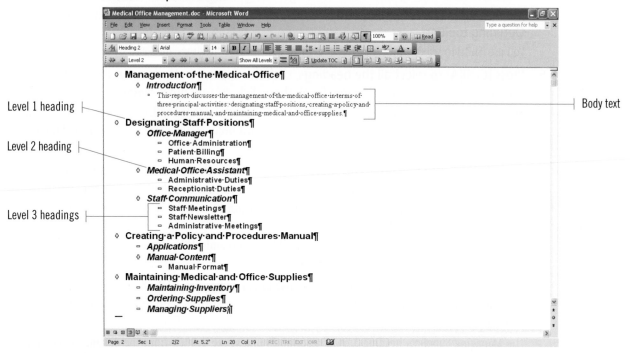

Body text

**TABLE H-1:** Outlining buttons on the Outlining toolbar

| button | use to | button | use to |
|---|---|---|---|
| | Promote text to level 1 | | Move a heading and its text down one line |
| | Promote text one level | | Expand text |
| Body text | Show outline level at insertion point placement | | Collapse text |
| | Demote text one level | Show All Levels | Show a specific level or levels |
| | Demote to body text | | Show only the first line of each paragraph |
| | Move a heading and its text up one line | | Show text formatting |

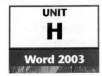
# Working in Outline View

In Outline view, you can promote and demote headings and subheadings and move or delete whole blocks of text. When you move a heading, all the text and subheadings under that heading move with the heading. You also can use the Collapse, Expand, and Show Level buttons on the Outlining toolbar to view all or just some of the headings and subheadings. For example, you can choose to view just the Level 1 headings so that you can quickly evaluate the main topics of your document. ✦✦✦✦ Tony has written a draft of the text he wants included in the guidelines for Medical Office Management. He asks you to work in Outline view to reorganize the structure of the document.

## STEPS

1. **Open the file** WMP H-1.doc **from the drive and folder where your Data Files are located, save it as** Medical Office Management Guidelines, **scroll through the document to get a sense of its content, then click the** Outline View button 🔲

2. **Click the** Show Level list arrow **on the Outlining toolbar, then click** Show Level 1
   Only the Level 1 headings appear, as shown in Figure H-3.

3. **Click the** plus outline symbol ✛ **to the left of** Creating a Policy and Procedures Manual
   The heading and all its subtext (which is hidden because the topic is collapsed) are selected.

4. **Press and hold** [Shift], **select the headings:** Designating Staff Positions, Maintaining Medical and Office Supplies, **and** Summary, **then click the** Demote button ➡ **on the Outlining toolbar**
   You use [Shift] to select multiple headings at once. The selected headings are demoted one level to Level 2.

5. **Press** [Ctrl][A] **to select all the headings, click the** Expand button ➕ **on the Outlining toolbar to expand the outline one level, then click** ➕ **two more times**
   The outline expands to show all the subheadings and body text associated with each of the selected headings. You can also expand a single heading by selecting only that heading, then clicking the Expand button until all the associated subheadings and body text appear.

QUICK TIP
You can also use your pointer to drag a heading up or down to a new location in the outline. A horizontal line indicates the placement.

6. **Click the** Collapse button ➖ **on the Outlining toolbar three times to collapse the outline, click** ✛ **next to** Creating a Policy and Procedures Manual **to select it, click the** Move Down button ⬇ **on the Outlining toolbar once, then double-click** ✛ **next to** Creating a Policy and Procedures Manual
   The outline for Creating a Policy and Procedures Manual expands. When you move a heading in Outline view, all subtext and text associated with the heading also move.

7. **Click the** Show Level list arrow, **select** Show Level 3, **double-click** ✛ **next to** Managing Suppliers **under the Maintaining Medical and Office Supplies heading, then press** [Delete]
   The Managing Suppliers heading and its associated subtext are deleted from the document. The revised outline is shown in Figure H-4.

8. **Click the** Show Level list arrow, **click** Show All Levels, **press** [Ctrl][End] **to move to the bottom of the document, press** [Enter] **twice, then type** Revised by **followed by your name**

9. **Save the document**

**FIGURE H-3:** Level 1 headings

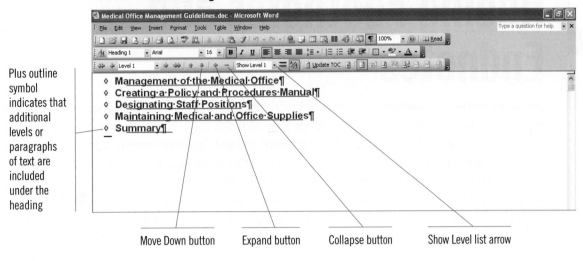

Plus outline symbol indicates that additional levels or paragraphs of text are included under the heading

Move Down button　　Expand button　　Collapse button　　Show Level list arrow

**FIGURE H-4:** Revised outline

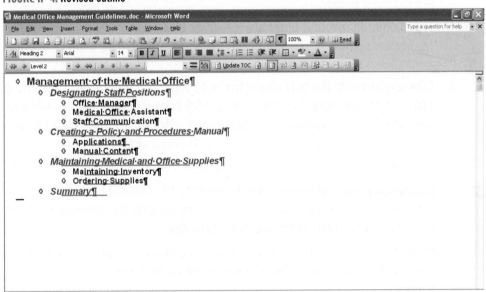

# Adding Footnotes and Endnotes

You use **footnotes** and **endnotes** to provide additional information or to acknowledge sources for text in a document. Footnotes appear at the bottom of the page on which the footnote reference appears; endnotes appear at the end of the document. You can use footnotes and endnotes in the same document. For example, a footnote can cite the source and an endnote can comment on information provided in the text. Every footnote and endnote consists of a **note reference mark** and the corresponding note text. When you add, delete, or move a note, any additional notes in the document are renumbered automatically.  You work in Print Layout view to add a footnote to the Medical Office Management Guidelines document and to edit footnotes you inserted earlier. You use the Find command to move quickly to the text you want to reference.

## STEPS

1. **Click the Print Layout View button ▣, press [Ctrl][Home] to move to the beginning of the document, click Edit on the menu bar, click Find, type regular basis in the Find what text box, click Find Next, click Cancel to close the Find dialog box, then press [→] once to position the insertion point following basis**

2. **Click Insert on the menu bar, point to Reference, then click Footnote**

   The Footnote and Endnote dialog box opens, as shown in Figure H-5.

3. **Click Insert**

   The insertion point moves to the footnote area at the bottom of the page, and the footnote that follows the new footnote is relabeled D.

4. **Type Common meeting times are weekly or bi-weekly.**

   The footnote reference marker appears after the word "basis," and the footnote text appears in the footnote area, as shown in Figure H-6.

5. **Click anywhere in the text above the note separator line to return to the document text, click Edit on the menu bar, click Go To, click Footnote in the Go to what list box, click in the Enter footnote number text box, type E, click Go To, then click Close**

   The insertion point moves to the footnote reference marker for E.

6. **Move the pointer over the footnote reference marker to view the footnote text**

7. **Double-click the footnote marker to move to the footnote at the bottom of the page, select the word details, type describes, scroll up until the document is visible, then click anywhere in the text above the note separator**

8. **Press [Ctrl][G], verify that E is selected in the Enter footnote number text box, type B, click Go To, click Close, select the superscript B that appears after patients, then press [Delete]**

   The footnote reference marker and its associated footnote are deleted. The footnote reference markers and the footnotes in the footnote area are relabeled.

9. **Click Insert on the menu bar, point to Reference, click Footnote, click the Number format list arrow, select the 1, 2, 3 number format, click Apply, scroll to view the footnotes on page 2, then save the document**

   The footnote reference markers and the footnotes are relabeled, as shown in Figure H-7.

**FIGURE H-5:** Footnote and Endnote dialog box

Footnotes selected by default

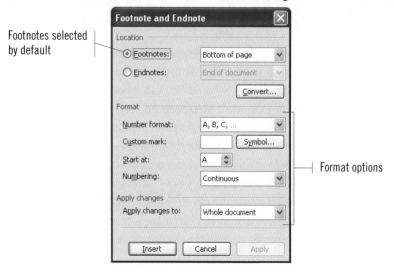

Format options

**FIGURE H-6:** Footnote text inserted in the footnote area

Footnote reference marker

New footnote text

Note separator

Footnotes automatically relettered sequentially

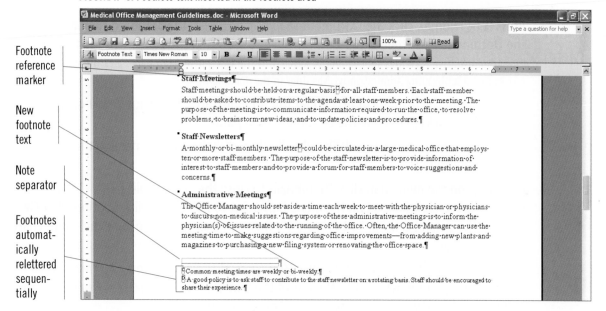

**FIGURE H-7:** Revised footnotes

New footnote format

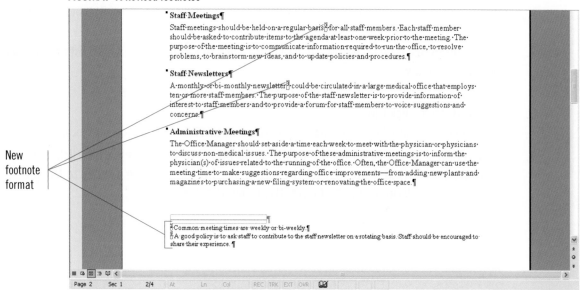

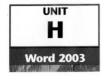
# Navigating a Document

You can use the document map, thumbnails, and cross-references to navigate through a multipage document. The **Document Map** pane shows all the headings and subheadings in the document and opens along the left side of the document window. You can quickly move through a document by clicking headings and subheadings in the Document Map pane. You can also view a thumbnail of each page in your document. A **thumbnail** is a smaller version of a page that appears in the Thumbnails pane to the left of the document window when you select thumbnails on the View menu. A **cross-reference** is text that electronically refers the reader to another part of the document, such as a numbered paragraph, a heading, or a figure. For example, if you make the text "below" an active hyperlink in "See Figure 1 below," then when "below" is clicked, the reader moves directly to Figure 1. ▒▒▒ You use the Document Map to navigate to a specific heading in the document so you can make a quick editing change. You use the Thumbnails feature to jump quickly to a specific page in the document, and, finally, you add a caption to the graphic of a pie chart and create a cross-reference to the pie chart.

## STEPS

1. **Press [Ctrl][Home], click the Document Map button ▣ on the Standard toolbar to open the Document Map, then click Administrative Meetings in the Document Map pane**

   The Administrative Meetings subheading is selected in the Document Map pane, and the insertion point moves to the subheading Administrative Meetings in the document.

2. **Select week in the first line of text under the Administrative Meetings heading, type month, then click ▣ to close the Document Map pane**

3. **Click View on the menu bar, click Thumbnails, then click the page containing the pie chart, as shown in Figure H-8**

4. **Click View on the menu bar, click Thumbnails to close the Thumbnails pane, click the pie chart to select it, click Insert on the menu bar, point to Reference, click Caption, click OK to enter the default caption text "Figure 1", then scroll as needed to view the entire chart**

   The caption "Figure 1" appears below the pie chart and is the element you want to cross-reference.

5. **Press [Ctrl][F], type principal areas, click Find Next, click Cancel, press [→] three times so the insertion point moves just to the left of the ¶ mark, type the text See Figure 1 as the beginning of a new sentence, then press [Spacebar] once**

6. **Click Insert on the menu bar, point to Reference, then click Cross-reference**

   In the Cross-reference dialog box, you select the Reference type, such as a Numbered item or Figure, and the cross-reference text, such as the words above or below.

7. **Click the Reference type list arrow, select Figure, click the Insert reference to list arrow, then select Above/below**

   Figure H-9 shows the options selected in the Cross-reference dialog box.

8. **Click Insert, then click Close**

   The word above is inserted because the figure appears before, that is, above the cross-reference.

9. **Type a period after above, move the pointer over above to show the [Ctrl] + click message, press and hold [Ctrl] to show ⭫, click the left mouse button to move directly to the pie chart caption, scroll up to see the figure, then save the document**

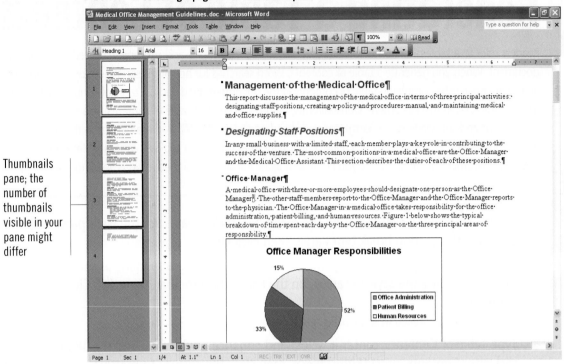

Thumbnails pane; the number of thumbnails visible in your pane might differ

FIGURE H-9: Cross-reference dialog box

Figure selected as the Reference type

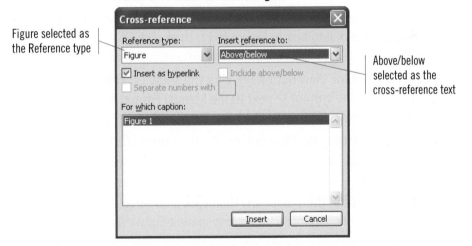

Above/below selected as the cross-reference text

Unit H  C5728  36011  Page 185  08/16/05  ALL

## Clues to Use

### Using bookmarks

A **bookmark** identifies a location or a selection of text in a document. To create a bookmark, you first move the insertion point to the location in the text that you want to reference. This location can be a word, the beginning of a paragraph, or a heading. Click Insert on the menu bar, then click Bookmark to open the Bookmark dialog box. In this dialog box, you type a name for the bookmark, then click Add. To find a bookmark, press [Ctrl][G] to open the Go To tab in the Find and Replace dialog box, click Bookmark in the Go to what list box, click the Enter bookmark name list arrow to see the list of bookmarks in the document, select the bookmark you require, click Go To, then close the Find and Replace dialog box.

# Generating a Table of Contents

Readers refer to a table of contents to obtain an overview of the topics and subtopics covered in a multipage document. When you generate a table of contents, Word searches for headings, sorts them by heading levels, and then displays the completed table of contents in the document. By default, a table of contents lists the top three heading levels in a document. Consequently, before you create a table of contents, you must ensure that all headings and subheadings are formatted with heading styles. ✎ You are pleased with the content of the document and are now ready to create a new page that includes a table of contents. Because you organized the document in Outline view, you know that all headings are assigned a Word heading style.

## STEPS

1. **Press [Ctrl][Home], click** Insert **on the menu bar, click** Break, **click the** Next page option button **in the Section break types area, then click** OK

2. **Press [Ctrl][Home], press [Enter] twice, select the** top paragraph mark, **as shown in Figure H-10, click the** Style list arrow **on the Formatting toolbar, then click** Clear Formatting

   The formatting associated with the paragraph is removed.

3. **Type** Table of Contents, **center it, select and enhance it with** Bold **and the** 18 pt **font size, click after** Contents, **press [Enter] twice, then clear the current formatting**

   The insertion point is positioned at the left margin where the table of contents will begin.

4. **Click** Insert **on the menu bar, point to** Reference, **click** Index and Tables, **then click the** Table of Contents tab

   The Table of Contents tab in the Index and Tables dialog box opens.

QUICK TIP

Depending on your computer settings, your Table of Contents (TOC) might appear with a gray background. The gray shading does not print.

5. **Click the** Formats list arrow, **click** Formal, **select** 3 **in the Show levels text box, type** 4, **compare the dialog box to Figure H-11, then click** OK

   A complete table of contents that includes all the Level 1, 2, 3, and 4 headings appears.

6. **Click the** Outline View button ⊞, **click the** Show Level list arrow, **click** Show Level 4, **click the** plus outline symbol ✛ **next to the Manual Format heading, then press [Delete]**

   The Manual Format heading and its related subtext are deleted from the document.

7. **Click the** Print Layout View button ▣, **then press [Ctrl][Home]**

   An error message appears in the table of contents next to the item you deleted.

TROUBLE

The first line of the TOC should appear black with white text when selected. If the background is gray with black text, repeat Step 8.

8. **Move the mouse to the left of** Management of the Medical Office **at the top of the table of contents until the** ⬧ **appears, then click** ⬧ **to select the entire table of contents at once**

   With the table of contents selected, you can update it to show the new page numbers.

9. **Right-click the** table of contents, **click** Update Field, **click the** Table of Contents title **to deselect the table of contents, then save the document**

   The completed table of contents appears, as shown in Figure H-12. Each entry in the table of contents is a hyperlink to the entry's corresponding heading in the document.

10. **Move the pointer over the heading** Staff Communication, **press [Ctrl], then click the** left mouse button

    The insertion point moves automatically to the Staff Communication heading in the document.

**FIGURE H-10:** Paragraph mark selected

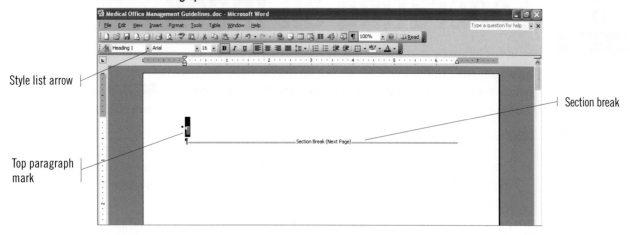

Style list arrow

Top paragraph mark

Section break

**FIGURE H-11:** Index and Tables dialog box

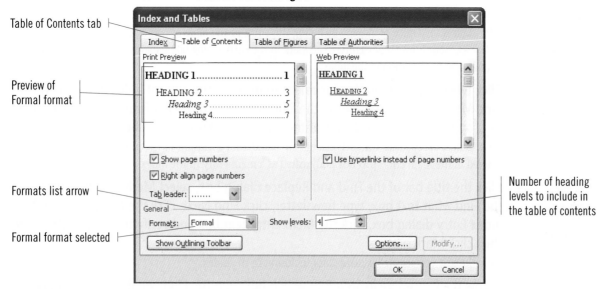

Table of Contents tab

Preview of Formal format

Formats list arrow

Formal format selected

Number of heading levels to include in the table of contents

**FIGURE H-12:** Updated table of contents

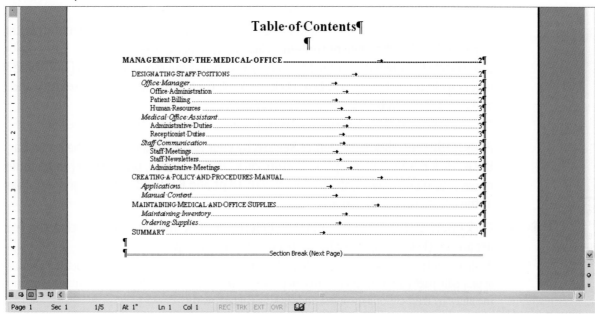

# Generating an Index

An **index** lists many of the terms and topics included in a document, along with the pages on which they appear. An index can include main entries, subentries, and cross-references. Once you have marked all the index entries, you select a design for the index, and then you generate it. ▰▰▰ You mark terms that you want to include in the index, create a new last page in the document, and then generate the index.

**STEPS**

1. **Press [Ctrl][Home], press [Ctrl] and click** Office Manager **in the table of contents, then select the text** Office Manager **in the paragraph following the Office Manager heading and just before the first footnote reference marker**

2. **Click** Insert **on the menu bar, point to** Reference, **click** Index and Tables, **click the** Index tab, **then click** Mark Entry

   The Mark Index Entry dialog box appears, as shown in Figure H-13.

3. **Click** Mark All

**QUICK TIP**

The XE field code appears when Show/ Hide ¶ is on. By default, the code does not print in your final document.

   All instances of "Office Manager," including the entry in the table of contents, are marked with the XE field code. "XE" stands for "Index Entry." The Mark Index Entry dialog box remains open so that you can continue to mark text for inclusion in the index.

4. **Click twice anywhere in the document to deselect the** current index entry, **press [Ctrl][F], type** Medical Office Assistant **in the Find what text box, click** Find Next, **click** Yes **if a message appears, click the** title bar **of the Mark Index Entry dialog box, then click** Mark All

   All instances of "Medical Office Assistant" are marked for inclusion in the index. By default, selected text is entered in the Main entry text box and treated as a main entry in the index.

**TROUBLE**

Click Yes if a message appears asking you to continue the search from the beginning of the document.

5. **Click the** title bar **of the Find and Replace dialog box, select** Medical Office Assistant **in the Find what text box, type** newsletter, **click** Find Next, **click the** title bar **of the Mark Index Entry dialog box, click the Main entry text box and verify that newsletter appears, then click** Mark

   Only the text you selected is marked for inclusion in the index.

6. **Follow the procedure in Step 5 to switch between the Find and Replace dialog box and the Mark Index Entry dialog box to find and mark the following main entries:** orientation, budget, medications, **and** biologics

   In addition to main entries, an index often has a subentry included under a main entry.

7. **Click the** title bar **of the Find and Replace dialog box, find the text** Staff Meetings **in the document, not in the table of contents, click the** title bar **of the Mark Index Entry dialog box, select** staff meetings **in the Main entry text box, type** Meetings, **press [Tab], type** staff meetings **in the Subentry text box, click** Mark All, **then close the Mark Index Entry and Find and Replace dialog boxes**

   The text "staff meetings" is marked as a subentry to appear following the Main entry, Meetings.

8. **Press [Ctrl][End], click to the left of** Revised by your name, **click** Insert **on the menu bar, click** Break, **click the** Next page option button, **click** OK, **type** Index, **press [Enter] three times to move your name down, enhance** Index **with** 18 pt **and** Bold **and** center alignment, **then click at the left margin above your name**

**QUICK TIP**

Depending on your computer settings, your index might appear with a gray background. The gray shading does not print.

9. **Click** Insert **on the menu bar, point to** Reference, **click** Index and Tables, **click the** Formats list arrow, **click** Fancy, **click** OK, **then save the document**

   As shown in Figure H-14, Word has collected all the index entries, sorted them alphabetically, included the appropriate page numbers, and removed duplicate entries. If you add or delete index entries, you can update the index by right-clicking the index and clicking Update Field.

**FIGURE H-13: Mark Index Entry dialog box**

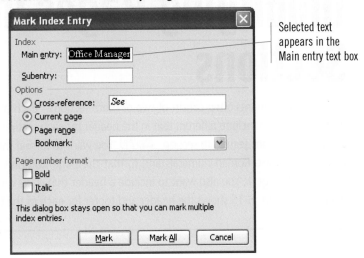

Selected text appears in the Main entry text box

**FIGURE H-14: Completed index**

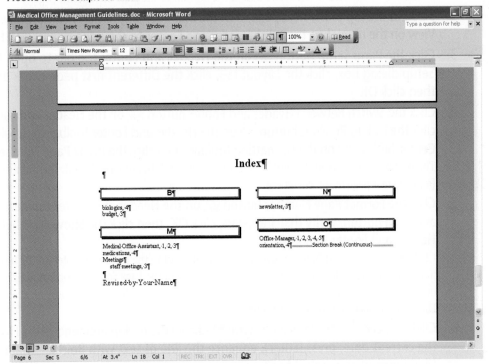

# Modifying Pages in Multiple Sections

Multipage documents often consist of two or more sections—each of which can be formatted differently. For example, you can include different text in the header for each section, or you can change how page numbers are formatted from section to section.  You want to format the page number on the table of contents page in lowercase Roman numerals and format the page numbers for the guidelines in regular numbers, starting with page 1. You also want to include a header that starts on the second page of the guidelines. The diagram in Figure H-15 shows the header and footer for each of the three document sections.

## STEPS

**QUICK TIP**
Two of the entries in the table of contents are marked for inclusion in the index. The index codes do not print in the completed document.

1. **Press [Ctrl][Home], click** Insert **on the menu bar, click** Page Numbers, **click the** Alignment **list arrow, select** Center, **click** Format, **click the** Number format list arrow, **click** i, ii, iii, **click** OK **to close the Page Number Format dialog box, click** OK **to close the Page Numbers dialog box, then scroll to the bottom of the page**
   Notice the "i" inserted in the footer area at the bottom of the table of contents page.

2. **Scroll to the top of the next page, click the** Management of the Medical Office **heading, click** View **on the menu bar, then click** Header and Footer **to show the Header and Footer toolbar**

**QUICK TIP**
When you want the first page in a section to be different from the other pages in the same section, you must be sure to select the Different first page option.

3. **Click the** Page Setup button 🔲 **on the Header and Footer toolbar to open the Page Setup dialog box, click the** Layout tab, **click the** Different first page check box **to select it, then click** OK

4. **Click the** Switch Between Header and Footer button 🔳 **on the Header and Footer toolbar, click the** Link to Previous button 🔳 **on the Header and Footer toolbar to deselect it, click the** Center button ≣ **on the Formatting toolbar, then click the** Insert Page Number button 🔲
   The number 2 appears in the First Page Footer - Section 2 because by default, the numbering is continuous from the first page in the document.

5. **Click the** Format Page Number button 🔳 **on the Header and Footer toolbar, click the** Start at option button, **verify that** 1 **appears, click** OK, **then click the** Show Next button 🔳 **on the Header and Footer toolbar**
   Clicking the Show Next button moves the insertion point to the header or footer on the next page of the document when the Different first page option is selected in the Page Setup dialog box. Clicking the Show Next button moves the insertion point to the header or footer of the next section of a document when the Different first page option is *not* selected.

6. **Click** 🔳, **click** 🔳 **to deselect it, type** Medical Office Management, **press [Tab] twice, type the** current date, **press [Enter], enhance the line of text with** Bold **and** Italic, **then click** Management **to deselect the text**
   The header appears as shown in Figure H-16. You deselected the Link to Previous button to make sure that only the header in this section contains the text you type into the header. You must deselect the Link to Previous button when you want the header in a section to be unique.

7. **Click** 🔳, **click** 🔳, **delete** Medical Office Management **and the** current date, **then click** Close **on the Header and Footer toolbar**
   When you click the Show Next button, the header for Section 3, which contains the index, appears. You delete the header text in section 3 so that it does not appear on the index page.

8. **Press [Ctrl][Home], right-click the** table of contents, **click** Update Field, **click the** Update entire table option button, **then click** OK

9. **Press [Ctrl][End], scroll as needed to view the Index, right-click the** index, **click** Update Field, **save the document, print a copy, then close it**
   The headers and footers appear in the printed document as indicated in Figure H-15.

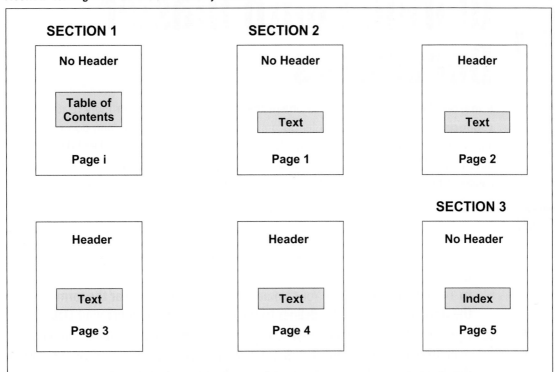

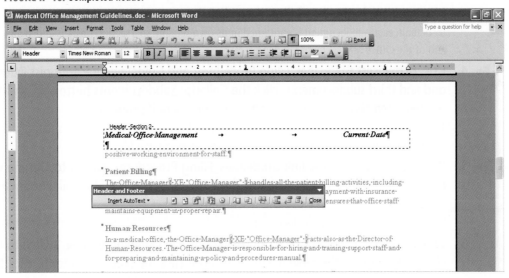

## Clues to Use

### Using text flow options

You adjust text flow options to control how text in a multipage document breaks across pages. To change text flow options, open the Paragraph dialog box on the Format menu, and then select the Line and Page Breaks tab. In the Pagination section of this tab, you can choose to select or deselect four text flow options. For example, you select the Widow/Orphan control option to prevent the last line of a paragraph from printing at the top of a page (a widow) or the first line of a paragraph from printing at the bottom of a page (an orphan). By default, Widow/Orphan is turned on. You can also select the Keep lines together check box to keep a paragraph from breaking across two pages.

Word 2003

# Working with Master Documents

A **master document** is a Word document that contains links to two or more related documents called **subdocuments**. You create a master document to organize and format long documents such as reports and books into manageable subdocuments, each of which you can open and edit directly from the master document. ▨▨▨ Tony has written guidelines for filing procedures and receptionist duties. He has also created a new version of the Medical Office Management Guidelines document. He asks you to create a master document that contains all three sets of guidelines.

## STEPS

1. Open a new blank Word document, type Medical Office Management Guidelines, center the text and enhance it with Bold and 26 pt, press [Enter] two times, change the font size to 14 pt, type Prepared by Your Name, press [Enter] twice, clear the formatting, then save the document as Office Guidelines to the drive and folder where your Data Files are located

**QUICK TIP**
The files should be in the drive and folder where your Data Files are located.

2. Open the file WMP H-2.doc, save it as Guidelines_Office Management, close the document, open the file WMP H-3.doc, save it as Guidelines_Filing Procedures, close the document, open the file WMP H-4.doc, save it as Guidelines_Receptionist Duties, then close the document
   The Office Guidelines document is again the active document.

3. Switch to Outline view, click the Show Formatting button ▨ if it is not selected, click the Insert Subdocument button ▨ on the Outlining toolbar, click Guidelines_Office Management in the list of files, then click Open
   By default, each subdocument is contained in its own section, so a section break is added automatically at the end of the Office Management Guidelines text.

**TROUBLE**
If you see a message about installing a converter, click No. If you see a message about saving in Word, click Yes.

4. Use ▨ to insert Guidelines_Filing Procedures and Guidelines_Receptionist Duties as the second and third subdocuments, click the Collapse Subdocuments button ▨ on the Outlining toolbar, then click OK to save the master document if prompted
   The three subdocuments appear, as shown in Figure H-17. To make changes to a subdocument, you open the subdocument in the master document or open the subdocument file.

**TROUBLE**
If the Web toolbar opens, close it.

5. Press [Ctrl] and click the link Guidelines_Filing Procedures, switch to Outline view when the document opens, show the top three levels, delete the Shelf Files subheading and its subtext, then save and close the document
   You are returned to the master document.

6. Click the Expand Subdocuments button ▨ on the Outlining toolbar, switch to Print Layout view, then scroll to the table of contents, right-click the table of contents, click Update Field, click the Update entire table option button, then click OK
   Now the table of contents includes the headings for the Filing Procedures Guidelines and the Receptionist Duties Guidelines.

7. Press [Ctrl] and click the Filing Procedures heading, double-click in the header, click the Link to Previous button ▨ to deselect it, change the header text to Filing Procedures, then click Close

8. Scroll down to the Receptionist Duties document on page 8, double-click in the header, click ▨ to deselect it, type Receptionist Duties, then click Close
   Each section of the guidelines now includes an appropriate header.

9. Save the document, print a copy of the title page, page 5, and page 8, close the document, then exit Word
   The title page and pages 5 and 8 are printed, as shown in Figure H-18.

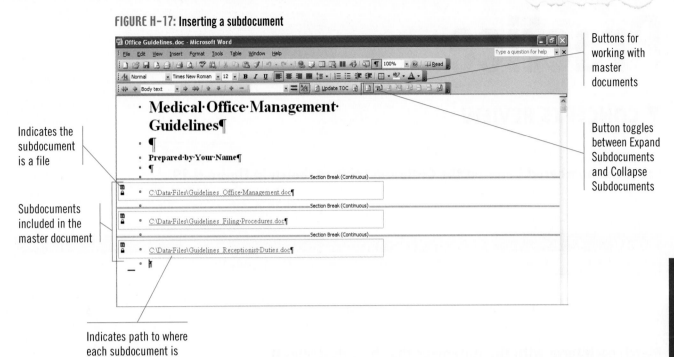

Buttons for working with master documents

Button toggles between Expand Subdocuments and Collapse Subdocuments

Indicates the subdocument is a file

Subdocuments included in the master document

Indicates path to where each subdocument is stored (yours will be different)

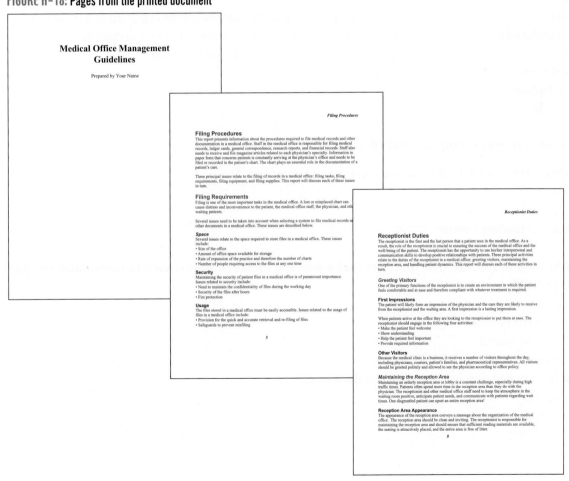

# Practice

## ▼ CONCEPTS REVIEW

**Label the numbered items on the Outlining toolbar shown in Figure H-19.**

FIGURE H-19

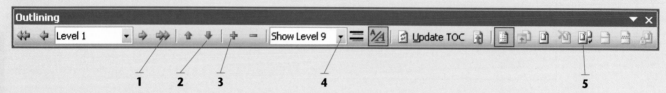

**Match each term with the statement that best describes it.**

6. **Table of contents**
7. **Demote button**
8. **Mark Index Entry dialog box**
9. **Footnote**
10. **Insert Subdocument button**
11. **Cross-reference**
12. **Demote to Body Text button**

a. Used to enter a lower-level heading in Outline view
b. Provides additional comments on information provided in the text
c. Included on the Master Document toolbar
d. Used to enter a paragraph of text in Outline view
e. List of topics and subtopics included at the beginning of a document
f. Text that refers the reader to another part of the document
g. Where you enter text for inclusion in an index

**Select the best answer from the list of choices.**

13. **In Outline view, which button do you click to move to Level 1?**
    a. Demote to Body Text button
    b. Promote to Level 1 button
    c. Promote to Heading 1 button
    d. Promote subtext button

14. **Which symbol in Outline view indicates that a heading includes subtext such as subheadings or paragraphs of text?**
    a. Plus outline symbol
    b. Minus outline symbol
    c. Slash outline symbol
    d. Level outline symbol

15. **Which feature can you use to navigate a document?**
    a. Thumbnails
    b. Cross-reference
    c. Document map
    d. All of the above

16. **On the Insert menu, which item do you select when you want to insert a table of contents?**
    a. Tools
    b. Index and Tables
    c. Reference
    d. Supplements

17. **Which button on the Header and Footer toolbar do you deselect to make sure that text you enter in a header or footer is unique from that section forward?**
    a. Same as Next button
    b. Same as Previous button
    c. Link to Previous button
    d. Show Formatting button

18. **What is a master document?**
    a. A document formatted in Outline view
    b. A short document included as part of a primary document
    c. A document containing two or more subdocuments
    d. A document containing two or more secondary documents

# ▼ SKILLS REVIEW

1. **Build a document in Outline view.**
   a. Start Word, switch to Outline view, type **Introduction by Your Name** as a Level 1 heading, press [Enter], type **Partnership Requirements** as another Level 1 heading, then press [Enter].
   b. Type **Background Information**, then use the Demote button to demote it to a Level 2 heading.
   c. Type the text shown in Figure H-20 as body text under Background Information.
   d. Use the Promote button to type the heading **Benefits** as a Level 2 heading, then complete the outline, as shown in Figure H-20.
   e. Save the document as **Partnership Agreement Outline** to the drive and folder where your Data Files are located, print a copy, then close the document.

   FIGURE H-20

   - **Introduction·by·Your·Name¶**
   ✧ **Partnership·Requirements¶**
       ✧ *Background·Information¶*
           □ This·section·provides·background·information·about·Presidio·Massage· Therapy·Clinic·and·discusses·how·the·partnership·could·benefit·both· Golden·Gate·Naturopathy·Clinic·and·Presidio·Massage·Therapy·Clinic.¶
       □ *Benefits¶*
       □ *Partnership·Need¶*
   ✧ **Products·and·Services¶**
       □ *Presidio·Massage·Therapy·Services¶*
       □ *Golden·Gate·Naturopathy·Services¶*
       □ *Package·Opportunities¶*
   ✧ **Financial·Considerations¶**
       □ *Projected·Revenues¶*
       □ *Financing·Required¶*
   □ **Conclusion¶**

2. **Work in Outline view.**
   a. Open the file WMP H-5.doc from the drive and folder where your Data Files are located, save it as **Partnership Agreement Proposal**, switch to Outline view, then show all Level 1 headings.
   b. Move the heading Financial Considerations below Products and Services.
   c. Select the Partnership Requirements heading, click the Expand button twice, collapse Benefits, collapse Partnership Need, then move Benefits and its subtext below Partnership Need and its subtext.
   d. Collapse the Partnership Requirements section to show only the Level 1 heading.
   e. Expand Products and Services, then delete Golden Gate Naturopathy Clinic Products and its subtext.
   f. Show all levels of the outline, press [Ctrl][End], press [Enter] once, type **Prepared by** followed by your name, then save the document.

# ▼ SKILLS REVIEW (CONTINUED)

3. **Add footnotes and endnotes.**
   a. In Print Layout view, find the words **Olympic Teams**, then position the insertion point after teams.
   b. Insert a footnote, which will be Footnote 2, with the default settings and the text: **Most Olympic athletes at the clinic are members of the Gymnastics or Diving teams**.
   c. In the document, go to Footnote 3, click in the footnote area, then change Appendix B to **Appendix C**.
   d. Click in the document, then find, read, and delete Footnote 1.
   e. Apply the a, b, c format to the footnotes, view the footnote area, then save the document.

4. **Navigate a document.**
   a. Open the Document Map and then navigate to Package Opportunities.
   b. Change Receptionist to **Medical Office Assistant** under the Package Opportunities heading, then close the Document Map.
   c. Open the Thumbnails pane, click the page containing the column chart graphic, close the Thumbnails pane, select the column chart in the document, then add **Figure 1** as a caption.
   d. Find the text **See Figure 1**, then insert a cross-reference to the figure using above/below as the reference text.
   e. Insert a period after the word **below**, test the cross-reference, scroll to see the figure, then save the document.

5. **Generate a table of contents.**
   a. Press [Ctrl][Home]. Use the Next page section break command to insert a new page above the first page.
   b. Press [Ctrl][Home], press [Enter] twice, select the top paragraph mark, clear the current formatting, enter **Table of Contents** at the top of the new first page, press [Enter] twice, enhance the text with 18 pt and Bold, then center it.
   c. Two lines below Table of Contents at the left margin, generate a table of contents using the Distinctive format and showing two levels.
   d. Use [Ctrl] + click to navigate to Partnership Need in the document, switch to Outline view, then delete Partnership Need and its subtext.
   e. Return to Print Layout view, update the table of contents, then save the document.

6. **Generate an index.**
   a. Find the words **sports medicine** and mark all occurrences for inclusion in the index.
   b. Find and mark the following main entries: **Embarcadero Center**, **Olympic teams**, and **gym**.
   c. Find **Personal Training Program**, click in the Mark Index Entry dialog box, select Personal Training Program in the Main entry text box, type **Physiotherapy Services**, press [Tab], type **Personal Training Program** in the Subentry text box, then click Mark All.
   d. Repeat the process to insert **Pilates classes** as a subentry of Physiotherapy Services.
   e. Insert a new page in a new section above the text Prepared by Your Name at the end of the document, press [Enter] twice at the top of the new page, then type **Index** at the top of the page and format it with Bold and 18 pt and center alignment.
   f. Click at the left margin above your name, press [Enter] twice, press the up arrow once, generate the index in the Bulleted format, then save the document.

7. **Modify pages in multiple sections.**
   a. Move to the beginning of the document, then open the Page Numbers dialog box and insert a right-aligned page number in the footer with the i, ii, iii format.
   b. Scroll down and click the title of the next page, then show the Header and Footer toolbar.
   c. Select Different first page in the Page Setup dialog box, then move to the header that will start on page 2 of Section 2, which is page 3 of the document.
   d. Deselect the Link to Previous button, type **Partnering Agreement: Embarcadero Physiotherapy Clinic**, center it, then format the text in Bold and Italic.
   e. Insert a right-aligned page number in the footer starting on the first page of Section 2. Use the 1, 2, 3 number format starting at 1. (*Hint*: Don't forget to deselect the Link to Previous button.)
   f. Remove the header from the index page.
   g. Update the table of contents and the index, save the document, print a copy, then close the document.

## ▼ SKILLS REVIEW (CONTINUED)

**8. Work with master documents.**

a. In a new blank document, type **Golden Gate Naturopathy Clinic Partnership Agreement** as a centered title formatted with Bold and 20 pt font size, press [Enter] twice, type **Prepared by** followed by your name in 14 pt, bold, and centered, press [Enter] twice, then clear the formatting.

b. Save the document as **Partnership Agreements**.

c. Open the files from the drive and folder where your Data Files are located, save them as follows, and close them: WMP H-6.doc as **Partnering_Embarcadero**; WMP H-7.doc as **Partnering_Bay Area**; and WMP H-8.doc as **Partnering_Presidio**.

d. In Outline view, insert the three files as subdocuments in the following order: Embarcadero, Bay Area, and Presidio.

e. Collapse and save the master document so just the filenames appear.

f. Use Ctrl + click to open the subdocument Partnering_Embarcadero. (*Note*: Click No if a message opens asking you to install a converter.)

g. Remove the subheading Partnership Need and its subtext and save and close the document. (*Note*: Click Yes if a message opens asking if it is OK to save in Word format.)

h. Expand the subdocuments, show all levels, switch to Print Layout view, then update the table of contents.

i. In Print Layout view, view the Header and Footer toolbar, change the header starting on the first page of the Partnering_ Bay Area subdocument to **Partnering Agreement: Bay Area Chinese Herbal Medicine Clinic**, then change the header starting on the first page of the Partnering_Presidio subdocument to **Partnering Agreement: Presidio Massage Therapy Clinic**.

j. Update the table of contents, print a copy of the table of contents page as the current page, then print the first page of the Bay Area subdocument (page 4), and the first page of the Presidio subdocument (page 7), save the document, close it, and exit Word.

## ▼ INDEPENDENT CHALLENGE 1

You work in the Finance Department of Super Strength, a successful fitness and spa facility in Orlando, Florida. Recently, Super Strength's owners began selling franchises. Your supervisor asks you to format a report that details the development of these franchise operations.

a. Start Word, open the file WMP H-9.doc from the drive and folder where your Data Files are located, then save it as **Super Strength Franchises**.

b. In Outline view, organize the document as shown in the table, start with Introduction, followed by Scope of the Report, and then move column by column. Note the headings are formatted with the green font color when the outline headings are applied because your supervisor modified the heading styles.

| Heading | Level | Heading | Level | Heading | Level |
|---|---|---|---|---|---|
| Introduction | 1 | Elinor Shore | 2 | Naples Clientele | 3 |
| Scope of the Report | 2 | Franchise Locations | 1 | Fort Lauderdale | 2 |
| Owner Information | 1 | Orlando | 2 | Fort Lauderdale Clientele | 3 |
| John Johnson | 2 | Orlando Clientele | 3 | Opening Schedules | 1 |
| Maria Sanchez | 2 | Naples | 2 | | |

c. Switch the order of Naples and its accompanying subtext so it follows Fort Lauderdale and its subtext.

**Advanced Challenge Exercise**

■ Switch to Print Layout view, use the Document Map to move directly to the Opening Schedules heading, then create a bookmark called **Dates** using the first of the three dates listed. (*Hint*: Select the heading Opening Schedules, click Insert on the menu bar, click Bookmark, type **Dates**, then click Add.)

■ Move to the beginning of the document and go to your bookmark. (*Hint*: Press [Ctrl][G], click Bookmark, click Go To, then click Close.)

■ Follow the same process to create a bookmark named **Location** that goes to the Franchise Locations heading, then close the Document Map.

# ▼ INDEPENDENT CHALLENGE 1 (CONTINUED)

**d.** Insert a footnote following the text **gourmet restaurants** that reads **One of these restaurants specializes in vegetarian and health-conscious cuisines.**

**e.** Create an index with appropriate Main entries and subentries. You could mark all locations and owners' names as Main entries and cross-reference owners with their specialties. For example, the owner Maria Sanchez could be listed as a cross-reference under the main entry **Massage Therapist** because Maria's specialty is massage therapy.

**f.** Create a new page in a new section at the end of the document, enter and format **Index** as the page title, then generate an index in the Modern format.

**g.** Create a footer with your name left-aligned and the page number right-aligned. The footer can print on every page.

**h.** Save the document, print a copy, close the document, then exit Word.

# ▼ INDEPENDENT CHALLENGE 2

You work as a Medical Office Assistant for several physicians at the Sunnydale Medical Clinic. One of the physicians, Dr. Logan, has asked you to create a master document containing an overview document and the History and Physical reports for three patients.

**a.** Start Word, open these files from the drive and folder where your Data Files are located, save them as follows, and close them: WMP H-10.doc as **History and Physical Reports_Overview**, WMP H-11.doc as **History and Physical Reports_Feldspur**, WMP H-12.doc as **History and Physical Reports_Manzini**, WMP H-13.doc as **History and Physical Reports_Hudson**.

**b.** Open History and Physical Reports_Overview, switch to Outline view, press [Ctrl][End], then add the other three files as subdocuments at the end of the document following the list of patient names. Use the order: Feldspur, Manzini, Hudson.

**c.** With the subdocuments expanded, switch to Print Layout view, then press [Ctrl][Home].

**Advanced Challenge Exercise**

- Scroll down to the Patients heading and the names of the three patients on page 1.
- Make Mark Hudson a cross-reference to the corresponding subdocument title. Select the text **Mark Hudson**, open the Cross-reference dialog box, select Heading as the reference type, then select the **HISTORY AND PHYSICAL: Mark Hudson** heading as the reference text. (*Note*: After pressing Insert, click after Mark Hudson, then press [Enter] so the names continue to appear as a list in the document.)
- Follow the same process to make the other two patients cross-references to their corresponding subdocuments.
- Test the Mark Hudson cross-reference. Move the pointer over the title, then use [Ctrl] + click to follow the link. Once your insertion point moves to the Mark Hudson subdocument, open the Document Map. Click the title Patients in the Document Map to navigate back to the list of titles.
- Repeat the previous step to test the other two cross-references.

**d.** Insert a new page with a section break at the beginning of the document, enter and format **Table of Contents** as the page title (*Hint*: Make sure Table of Contents is not formatted as Heading 1), then generate a table of contents with two levels in the Formal style.

**e.** On the Table of Contents page, add your name left-aligned in the footer, and the page number **i** right-aligned in the footer. On the History and Physical Reports page, add your name left-aligned in the footer, and the page number **1** right-aligned in the footer. Scroll through the document and modify the header text where required. You will need to include the correct hospital record number in the header for each patient. Also add your name and your initials where indicated at the end of each patient record.

**f.** Update the table of contents, save the document, print page 1, which prints a copy of the table of contents page and page 1 of the proposal, close the document, then exit Word.

# ▼ INDEPENDENT CHALLENGE 3

As the program assistant in the Applied Business Technology Department at Green Mountain College on Maui, you are responsible for creating and formatting reports about programs at the college. You work in Outline view to create a program report on the Medical Office Assistant program.

**a.** Create a new document and save it as **Medical Office Assistant Program Information Report**.

**b.** In Outline view, enter the headings and sub-headings for the report, as shown in the table starting with **Program Overview**, followed by **Career Opportunities**. You need to substitute appropriate course names for Course 1, Course 2, and so on. For example, courses in the first term of the Medical

| Heading | Level | Heading | Level |
|---|---|---|---|
| Program Overview | 1 | [Enter name for Course 1] | 3 |
| Career Opportunities | 2 | [Enter name for Course 2] | 3 |
| Admission Requirements | 2 | Second Term | 2 |
| Program Content | 1 | [Enter name for Course 1] | 3 |
| First Term | 2 | [Enter name for Course 2] | 3 |

Office Assistant program could be **Medical Office Procedures**, **Medical Systems and Transcription**, and so on.

**c.** Enter appropriate body text for each heading. For ideas, refer to college catalogs.

**d.** In Print Layout view, add a title page: include the name of the program, your name, and any other pertinent information. Format the title page text.

**e.** If necessary, insert a page break in the body of the report to spread it over two pages. Format the title page with no header and no page number. Format Page 1 of the report with no footer and a right-aligned page number in the header, starting with 1 using the 1, 2, 3 format. Format page 2 and the following pages of the report with the name of the program left-aligned in the footer, your name right-aligned in the footer, and a right-aligned page number in the header.

**f.** Save the document, print a copy, then close it.

# ▼ INDEPENDENT CHALLENGE 4

Many hospitals and other medical establishments post job opportunities on their Web sites. You can learn a great deal about opportunities in a wide range of medical fields just by checking out the job postings on these Web sites. You decide to create a document that describes a selection of jobs available on two Web sites of your choice.

**a.** Use your favorite search engine and the search phrase **healthcare jobs** to find two Web sites that post jobs in the healthcare industry.

**b.** On two Web sites, find a page that lists current job opportunities.

**c.** Identify two job categories (for example, Nursing jobs and Lab Technician jobs) on each Web site.

**d.** Create a new document in Word, then save it as **Online Job Opportunities**.

**e.** In Outline view, set up the document starting with the name of the Web site, and followed by Job Category 1, as shown in the table. (*Note*: You need to enter specific text for headings such as Nursing Jobs for Job Category 1 and Nursing-Acute Care for Job Posting 1.)

| Heading | Level | Heading | Level |
|---|---|---|---|
| Name of Web site 1 (for example, HospitalJobs.com) | 1 | Job Posting 2 | 3 |
| | | Job Category 2 | 2 |
| Job Category 1 | 2 | Job Posting 1 | 3 |
| Job Posting 1 | 3 | Job Posting 2 | 3 |

**f.** Repeat the outline for the other Web site.

**g.** Complete the Word document with information you find on the Web sites. Include a short description of each job you select.

**h.** Adjust the document spacing as needed so that the document prints over at least two pages.

**i.** Format the document so that a header starts on page 1 and includes the text **Online Job Opportunities for Your Name**. Include a page number on each page of the document in either the header or the footer.

**j.** Save the document, print a copy, close the document, then exit Word.

## ▼ VISUAL WORKSHOP

Open the file WMP H-14.doc, then save it as **Medical Ethics Term Paper**. Modify the outline so that it appears as shown in Figure H-21. You need to change the order of some sections. In Print Layout view, insert a new page in a new section at the beginning of the document, clear the formatting, enter and enhance the title **Table of Contents**, then generate a table of contents in the Distinctive style with three heading levels, as shown in Figure H-22. Be sure your name is on the document, then print one copy of the table of contents page and one copy of the first three levels of the document in Outline view, then save the document.

FIGURE H-21

- **Introduction**¶
  - *Medical·Ethics·Issues*¶
- **The·Moral·Climate·of·Health·Care**¶
  - *Role·of·the·Patient*¶
  - *Moral·Principals·in·Health·Care*¶
- **Ethics·and·Nursing**¶
  - *Nursing·as·Vocation*¶
  - *Ethical·Responsibilities*¶
- **Ethics·Traditions·**¶
  - *Moral·Development*¶
    - Stages·of·Moral·Development¶
  - *Ethical·Theories*¶
    - Morality¶
    - Teleological·Theories¶
    - Deontological·Theories¶
- **Conclusion**¶

FIGURE H-22

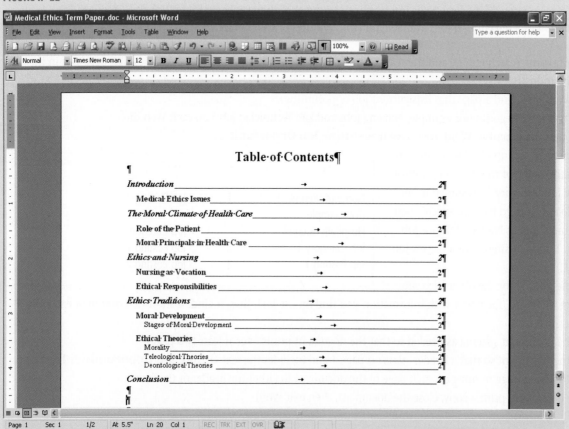

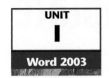

# UNIT I

# Building Forms

## OBJECTIVES

| |
|---|
| Construct a form template |
| Add and modify text form fields |
| Add drop-down and check box form fields |
| Use calculations in a form |
| Add Help to a form |
| Insert form controls |
| Format and protect forms |
| Fill in a form as a user |

If you have a SAM user profile, you may have access to hands-on instruction, practice, and assessment of the skills covered in this unit. Log in to your SAM account and go to your assignments page to see what your instructor has assigned.

Word provides the tools you need to build forms that users can complete within a Word document. A **form** is a structured document with spaces reserved for entering information. You create a form as a template that includes labeled spaces—called **form fields**—into which users type information. The form template can include check boxes, drop-down lists, formulas used to perform calculations, Help messages, and other form controls to make the form interactive. Finally, you can protect a form so that users can enter information into the form, but they cannot change the structure of the form itself. Tony Sanchez, RN, the Office Manager at the Riverwalk Medical Clinic, has decided to create a Patient Summary Sheet. He wants you to create a form to collect the data. You start by creating the form template.

# Constructing a Form Template

A Word form is created as a **form template**, which contains all the components of the form. As you learned in an earlier unit, a template is a file that contains the basic structure of a document, such as the page layout, headers and footers, and graphic elements. In the case of a form template, the structure usually consists of a table form that contains field labels and form fields. Figure I-1 shows a completed form template containing several different types of form fields. A **field label** is a word or phrase such as "Date" or "Location" that tells users the kind of information required for a given field. A **form field** is where the data associated with a field label is stored. Information that can be stored in a form field includes text, an X in a check box, a number, or a selection in a drop-down list. You need to create the basic structure of the form in Word, and then save the document as a template. You start by creating the form in Word, then saving it as a template to a new folder that you create in the drive and folder where your Data Files are located.

## STEPS

1. **Start Word, click** File **on the menu bar, then click** New **to open the New Document task pane**

2. **Click** On my computer **in the Templates section of the New Document task pane**
   The Templates dialog box opens.

3. **Verify** Blank Document **is selected, click the** Template option button **in the Create New section, then click** OK
   A new document appears in the document window and Template1 appears on the title bar.

4. **Type** Patient Summary Sheet, **center the text, enhance it with** Bold **and the** 18 pt **font size, press [Enter] twice, then clear the formatting**

5. **Click** Table **on the menu bar, point to** Insert, **click** Table, **enter** 2 **for the number of columns and** 13 **for the number of rows, then click** OK
   Figure 1-2 shows a table with gridlines and no borders.

6. **Type** Name:, **press [Tab], type** Date:, **press [Tab], then enter the remaining field labels and merge selected cells, as shown in Figure I-2**
   After you have created the structure for your form, you can save it as a template. First, you create a new folder to contain the template, and then you specify this folder as the location of user templates so that Word can find it.

7. **Minimize Word, right-click the** Start button <kbd>start</kbd> **on your computer desktop, click** Explore **to open Windows Explorer, navigate to the drive and folder where your Data Files are located, click** File, **point to** New, **click** Folder, **type** Your Name Form Templates **as the folder name, then press [Enter]**
   To have your templates stored in the same location, you set this new folder as the default location for user templates. A **user template** is any template that you create yourself.

8. **Close** Windows Explorer, **click** Template1 **on the taskbar, click** Tools **on the menu bar, click** Options, **click** File Locations, **click** User templates **in the list of File types, click** Modify, **click the** Look in list arrow, **select the** location **where you created the Your Name Form Templates folder, click the** folder **to select it, click** OK, **then click** OK

9. **Click the** Save button <kbd>💾</kbd> **on the Standard toolbar, verify that "Patient Summary Sheet.dot" appears in the File name text box, as shown in Figure I-3, then click** Save
   Word saves the template to the new folder you created.

> **TROUBLE**
> If your table shows borders, select the table, click the Outside Border list arrow on the Tables and Borders toolbar, then click No Border. If you do not see gridlines, click Table on the menu bar, then click Show Gridlines.

> **TROUBLE**
> To merge cells, click to the left of the row to select it, click Table on the menu bar, then click Merge Cells.

FIGURE I-1: Form construction

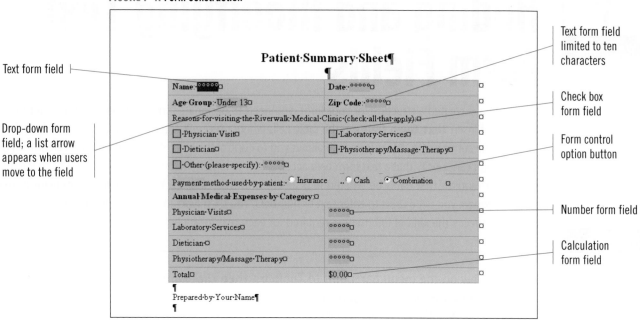

Text form field

Drop-down form field; a list arrow appears when users move to the field

Text form field limited to ten characters

Check box form field

Form control option button

Number form field

Calculation form field

FIGURE I-2: Table form

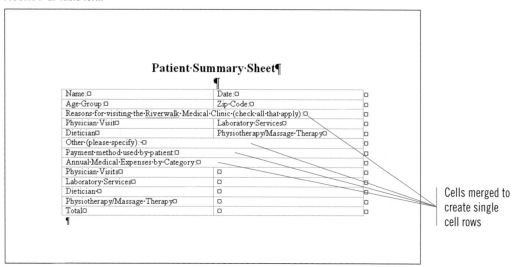

Cells merged to create single cell rows

FIGURE I-3: Saving a user template

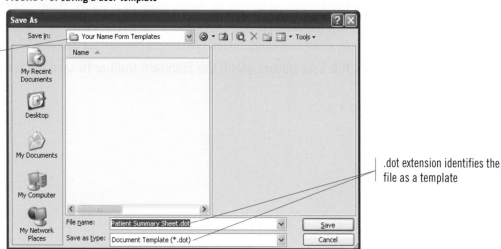

Save location is the folder you identified as the default location for template files

.dot extension identifies the file as a template

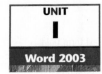

# Adding and Modifying Text Form Fields

After you have created a structure for your form, you need to designate form fields where users enter information. You insert **text form fields** in the table cells where users will enter text information, such as their names or the current date. A text form field allows you to control the kind of information users can enter. For example, you can specify that a text form field accepts only a numeric value, limits the number of characters entered, or requires that dates be entered in a specified format. You insert text form fields in the table cells where you need users to enter text or numbers. You then work in the Text Form Field Options dialog box to specify the kind of information required for each text form field.

STEPS

1. **Click View on the menu bar, point to Toolbars, then click Forms**

   The Forms toolbar contains the buttons used to create and modify the various elements of a form. Table I-1 describes each button on the Forms toolbar.

   > **TROUBLE**
   > If dots do not appear in the shaded rectangle, click the Show/Hide ¶ button on the Formatting toolbar.

2. **Click after Name:, press [Spacebar] one time, then click the Text Form Field button [ab] on the Forms toolbar**

   A gray shaded rectangle with five dots appears following Name. When completing the form, the user will be able to enter text into this form field.

3. **Press [Tab], click after Date:, press [Spacebar] one time, then click [ab]**

4. **Repeat Step 3 to insert a text form field after Zip Code: and after Other (please specify):**

   Figure I-4 shows the form with text form fields inserted in four table cells. You want each user who completes the form to enter a date in a specific format in the text form field following the Date label.

5. **Click the text form field next to Date:, then click the Form Field Options button [📋] on the Forms toolbar**

   The Text Form Field Options dialog box opens. In this dialog box, you specify options related to the format and content of the selected text form field.

   > **QUICK TIP**
   > If the user types 03/03/08, the date entered will appear as March 3, 2008.

6. **Click the Type list arrow, click Date, click the Date format list arrow, click MMMM d, yyyy, as shown in Figure I-5, then click OK**

   The text form field looks the same. In a later lesson, you will add a Help message to inform users how to enter the date.

7. **Click the text form field next to Zip Code, then click [📋]**

8. **Click the Maximum length up arrow until 10 appears, then click OK**

   You specify the number of characters a field can contain when you want to restrict the length of an entry. For example, a user completing this form can enter a five-digit zip code or a ZIP+4 code.

9. **Click the Save button [💾] on the Standard toolbar to save the template**

FIGURE I-4: Text form fields inserted

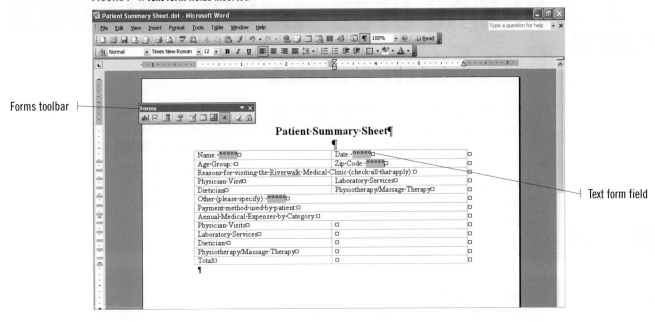

Forms toolbar

Text form field

FIGURE I-5: Text Form Field Options dialog box

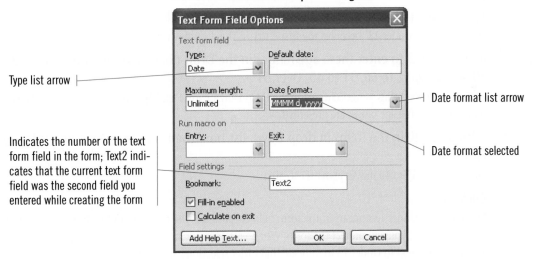

Type list arrow

Date format list arrow

Indicates the number of the text form field in the form; Text2 indicates that the current text form field was the second field you entered while creating the form

Date format selected

TABLE I-1: Buttons on the Forms toolbar

| button | use to | button | use to |
|--------|--------|--------|--------|
| abl | Insert a text form field | ⊞ | Insert a table/cell to contain form fields |
| ☑ | Insert a check box form field | ⮒ | Insert a frame to contain a form |
| 📋 | Insert a drop-down form field | a | Insert or remove shading from form fields |
| 🖳 | Open the Form Field Options dialog box, then modify the options of an inserted form field | ✐ | Reset form fields to their default settings |
| ✎ | Draw a table to contain form fields | 🔒 | Protect a form so that users can enter only data required for the form fields |

Word 2003

# Adding Drop-Down and Check Box Form Fields

In addition to text form fields, Word forms can include check box form fields and drop-down form fields. Users can use the pointer to make selections in check box or drop-down form fields. For example, users can click a check box to select it or they can select an item from a drop-down list. ▟▟▟▟ You want to be able to identify the age range of Riverwalk Medical Clinic patients. You decide to include a drop-down list of age ranges on your form. You also want to identify which medical services the patient received at Riverwalk Medical Clinic over the course of the year. You decide to provide check boxes next to the services so the person filling in the form can quickly identify them.

## STEPS

1. **Click after Age Group:, press [Spacebar] one time, then click the Drop-Down Form Field button ▦ on the Forms toolbar**

   A gray shaded rectangle without dots appears, indicating that the field is a drop-down form field and not a text form field.

2. **Click the Form Field Options button ▣ on the Forms toolbar**

   The Drop-Down Form Field Options dialog box opens. In this dialog box, you enter the selections you want to appear in the drop-down list.

3. **Type Under 13 in the Drop-down item text box, then click Add**

   The age group "Under 13" becomes the first entry in the drop-down list.

> **QUICK TIP**
> You can press [Enter] after typing each entry, or you can click Add.

4. **Repeat Step 3 to enter these age ranges in the Drop-down item text box: 13 to 19, 20 to 30, 41 to 50, 51 to 60, 31 to 40, Over 61**

   Figure I-6 shows the age ranges entered in the Drop-Down Form Field Options dialog box. You can change the order in which the age ranges are presented.

5. **Click 31 to 40 in the Items in drop-down list box, then click the Move up button ▴ two times**

   The age range 31 to 40 moves above 41 to 50.

6. **Click OK**

   The age range Under 13 appears in the form field because it is the first item in the drop-down form field list. In a later lesson, you will protect the form. When you open the protected form to complete it as a user, a list arrow appears next to Under 13 to indicate that other selections are available.

7. **Click to the left of Physician Visit in row 4, click the Check Box Form Field button ☑ on the Forms toolbar, then press [Spacebar] one time to insert a space between the check box and the text**

   A gray shaded box appears before the text "Physician Visit." After the form is protected, an X will appear in the box when a user selects it.

8. **Repeat Step 7 to insert check boxes, as shown in Figure 1-7, next to Laboratory Services, Dietician, Physiotherapy/Massage Therapy, and Other (please specify):**

   Figure I-7 shows the form with the text form fields, a drop-down form field, and check box form fields.

9. **Save the template**

**FIGURE I-6: Drop-Down Form Field Options dialog box**

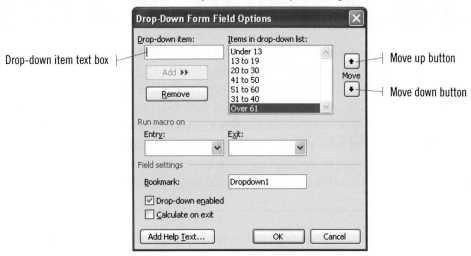

Drop-down item text box

Move up button

Move down button

**FIGURE I-7: Form fields inserted in a Word form**

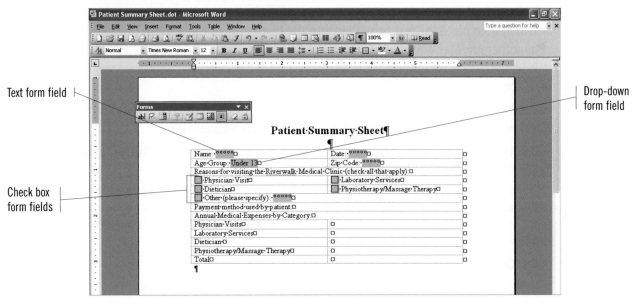

Text form field

Drop-down form field

Check box form fields

# Using Calculations in a Form

A Word form can be designed to perform calculations. For example, you can specify that a text form field should add a series of numbers. To perform calculations in a form, you must follow two steps. First, you specify each text form field that will be used to perform the calculation as Number type so that a user can only enter numbers. Second, you specify the text form field that contains the result of the calculation as Calculation type. You then type the mathematical formula that will perform the calculation in that text form field. **███████** You want to be able to enter the dollar amounts charged to the patient for selected medical services. The dollar amounts are based on billing information that the Finance Department provides. You want the form to calculate the total automatically as values are entered.

## STEPS

1.  **Click the blank cell to the right of Physician Visits in the table form, then click the Text Form Field button [abl] on the Forms toolbar**

2.  **Click the Form Field Options button [⚙] on the Forms toolbar, click the Type list arrow, then select Number**

    You change the text form field type to Number because you want users to be able to enter only a number.

3.  **Click the Number format list arrow, select the number format shown in Figure I-8, click the Calculate on exit check box, then click OK**

    You select the Calculate on exit check box because you want the number that users enter into the text form field to be included as part of a calculation. The three table cells under the current cell require the same text form field as the one you just created. You can save time by copying and pasting the text form field you just created.

4.  **With the form field selected, click the Copy button [📋] on the Standard toolbar, click the blank cell to the right of Laboratory Services, click the Paste button [📋] on the Standard toolbar, then paste the text form field into the blank cells to the right of Dietician and Physiotherapy/Massage Therapy**

    You want the cell to the right of Total to display the total of the values users enter in the four cells immediately above it.

5.  **Click the blank cell to the right of Total, click [📋], click [⚙] to open the Text Form Field Options dialog box, click the Type list arrow, then click Calculation**

6.  **Click in the Expression text box to the right of the = sign, type SUM(ABOVE), then compare the Text Form Field Options dialog box to Figure I-9**

    The formula =SUM(ABOVE) is a standard calculation expression that is recognized by programs such as Word and Excel. The =SUM(ABOVE) calculation expression calculates all the values entered in the designated text form fields. The designated text form fields must be above the text form field that contains the calculation expression, and the text form fields must use a Number format.

7.  **Click OK**

    The $0.00 entered next to Total indicates that the cell contains a calculation form field.

8.  **Compare your form to Figure I-10, then save the template**

FIGURE I-8: **Number format selected**

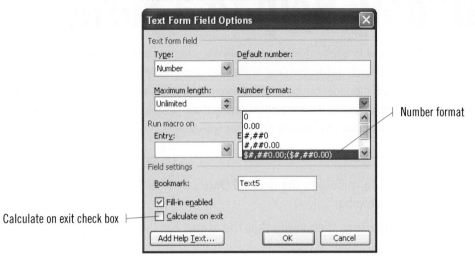

Number format

Calculate on exit check box

FIGURE I-9: **Calculation options selected**

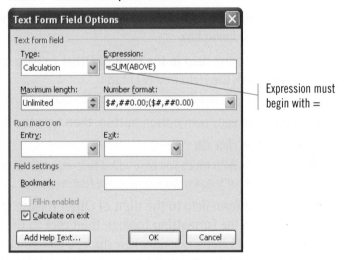

Expression must begin with =

FIGURE I-10: **Calculation form field inserted**

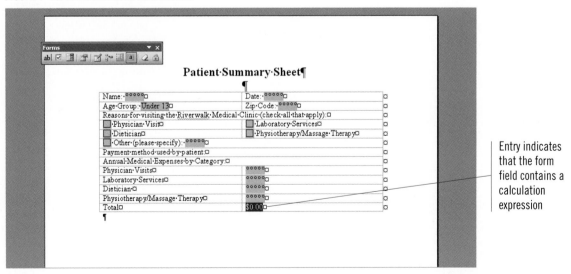

Entry indicates that the form field contains a calculation expression

Word 2003

# Adding Help to a Form

You can help users fill in a form quickly and easily by attaching Help messages to selected form fields. For example, you can include a Help message in the Date form field that advises users how to enter a correctly formatted date. Help messages can be set to appear on the status bar or when the user presses the [F1] function key. ▓▓▓▓ You want to include instructions that advise users how to enter the date. You also want to add instructions about how to complete the Other (please specify): form field.

1. **Click the** text form field **to the right of Date:, then click the** Form Field Options button 🖭 **on the Forms toolbar**

2. **Click** Add Help Text, **then verify that the** Status Bar tab **is selected**
   You can choose to include an AutoText entry such as a page number or the word "Confidential," or you can type your own Help message.

3. **Click the** Type your own option button, **then enter the Help text shown in Figure I-11**
   The text entered in the Status Bar text box will appear on the status bar when a user clicks the text form field next to Date.

4. **Click** OK **to exit the Form Field Help Text dialog box, then click** OK **to exit the Text Form Field Options dialog box**

5. **Click the** text form field **to the right of Other (please specify):, click** 🖭, **click** Add Help Text, **then click the** Help Key (F1) tab
   You can enter a Help message containing up to 225 characters in the Help Key (F1) text box.

6. **Click the** Type your own option button, **then type the Help text shown in Figure I-12**

7. **Click** OK, **then click** OK
   The text form fields to which you have added Help messages do not appear to change. You will see the Help messages in the last lesson when you fill in the form as a user.

8. **With the** text form field **to the right of Other (please specify): still selected, click the** Italic button 🇮 **on the Formatting toolbar, then click to the right of the text form field**
   The text form field does not appear to have changed. However, the Italic button on the Formatting toolbar is selected to indicate that any text entered in the text form field will appear in italic.

9. **Save the template**

FIGURE I-11: Status Bar Help

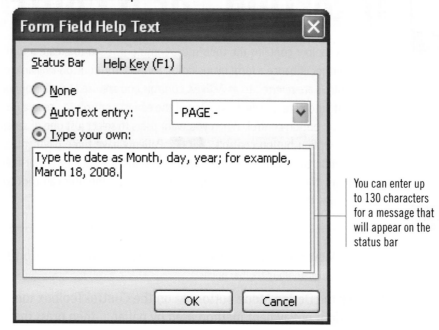

You can enter up to 130 characters for a message that will appear on the status bar

FIGURE I-12: Help Key (F1) text

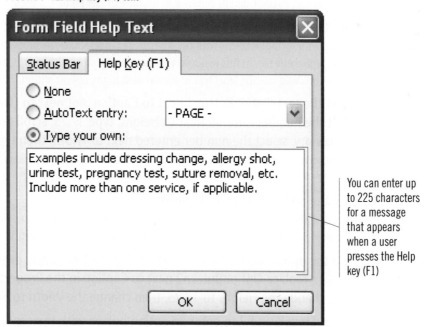

You can enter up to 225 characters for a message that appears when a user presses the Help key (F1)

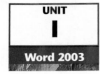

# Inserting Form Controls

The Forms toolbar contains the tools most commonly used to create a form that users complete in Word. You can further enhance a form by including some of the controls available on the Control Toolbox toolbar. These controls are referred to as ActiveX controls and are used to offer options to users or to run macros or scripts that automate specific tasks. One of the easiest controls to use in a form that users complete in Word is the Option button control. When you want users to select just one of several available options, you insert a series of Option button controls. Patients have three payment options: insurance, cash (which includes credit cards and a payment option through the Finance Department), or a combination of these two options. You decide to create Option buttons that the user can click to select which payment option describes how the patient pays for services.

## STEPS

QUICK TIP

Some controls in the Control Toolbox, such as the check box control, are also available on the Forms toolbar. To use most Control Toolbox controls, however, you need knowledge of Visual Basic.

1. **Click** View **on the menu bar, point to** Toolbars, **then click** Control Toolbox

   The Control Toolbox toolbar opens.

2. **Click the** Design Mode button **on the Control Toolbox toolbar, click the** blank area **to the right of Payment method used by patient:, then press the [Spacebar] one time**

   The Design Mode button becomes a floating toolbar, indicating that you are in Design Mode. You must be in Design Mode when you want to insert a control from the Control Toolbox toolbar to a selected cell.

3. **Click the** Option Button button **on the Control Toolbox toolbar to insert an option button control into the selected cell**

   Figure I-13 shows the option button with the button caption "OptionButton1" inserted in the selected cell. You need to change the properties of the control so that the label next to the option button shows the caption "Insurance". A **property** is a named attribute of a control that you set to define one of the control's attributes such as its size, its color, and its behavior in response to user input.

QUICK TIP

You can move and resize the Properties window. To move the window, click the title bar and drag the window to its new location. To resize the window, move ↖ over the lower-right corner of the Properties window, then click and drag ↖ to resize the Properties window.

4. **Click the** Properties button **on the Control Toolbox toolbar**

   The Properties window opens with the Alphabetic tab selected. The properties are listed in alphabetical order on the Alphabetic tab. In this window, you can identify properties such as the height and width of the option button and designate the label text to appear next to the option button.

5. **Select the text** OptionButton1 **next to Caption, not next to (Name), type** Insurance, **select** the number entered **next to Height, type** 17.25, **scroll down the Properties window if necessary, select** the number entered **next to Width, then type** 75

   The Properties window is shown in Figure I-14, and the caption "Insurance" appears next to the option button in the Word form. The measurements are in pixels.

6. **Click the** option button **in the form**

   The size of the option button changes to match the Properties that you entered in the Properties window. The measurements may vary slightly. For example, you might see 17.15 instead of 17.25.

7. **With the option button box still selected, press [→] once, press [Spacebar] two times, click** ⊙, **replace** OptionButton2 **next to Caption in the Properties window with the word** Cash, **change the Height to** 17.25, **then change the Width to** 50.25

8. **Repeat Steps 6 and 7 to enter an option button with the caption text** Combination, **a Height value of** 17.25, **and a Width value of** 90

   The three option buttons appear, as shown in Figure I-15.

9. **Close the Properties window, click the** Exit Design Mode button **on the Control Toolbox toolbar, close the Control Toolbox toolbar, then save the template**

   You must exit Design Mode after you insert a form control so that you can continue working with the form.

**FIGURE I-13: OptionButton1 inserted**

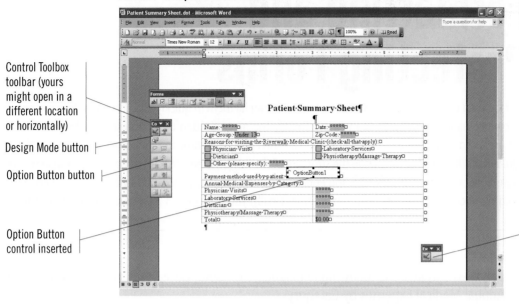

Control Toolbox toolbar (yours might open in a different location or horizontally)

Design Mode button

Option Button button

Option Button control inserted

Design Mode button can appear as a floating toolbar or anchored to the Status bar

**FIGURE I-14: Properties window**

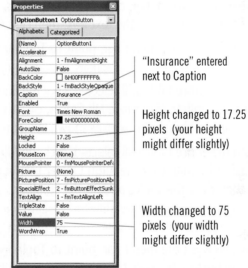

Alphabetic tab selected

"Insurance" entered next to Caption

Height changed to 17.25 pixels (your height might differ slightly)

Width changed to 75 pixels (your width might differ slightly)

**FIGURE I-15: Option buttons inserted**

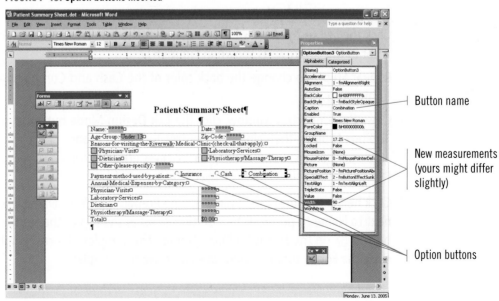

Drag toolbars and arrange as needed so you can see options while you work

Button name

New measurements (yours might differ slightly)

Option buttons

# Formatting and Protecting Forms

Forms should be easy to read onscreen so that users can fill them in quickly and accurately. You can enhance a table containing form fields and you can modify the magnification of a document containing a form so that users can easily see the form fields. You can then protect a form so that users can enter only the data required and *not* be able to change the structure of the form. When a form is protected, information can be entered only in form fields. ░░░░░ You enhance the field labels, add shading to the form, and change the background color of the option button controls. Finally, you protect and then save the form template.

## STEPS

1. Select Name in the first cell of the table, click the Bold button **B** on the Formatting toolbar, then enhance the following field labels with bold: Date, Age Group, Zip Code, and Annual Medical Expenses by Category

**TROUBLE**

If the table move handle is not visible, click Table on the menu bar, point to Select, then click Table.

2. Click the table move handle ⊞ at the upper-left corner of the table to select the table, click Table on the menu bar, click Table Properties, click the Row tab, click the Specify height check box, enter .3 in the text box, then click OK

3. Click View on the menu bar, point to Toolbars, then click Tables and Borders

   The Tables and Borders toolbar appears. You can use this toolbar to fill the entire table with shading.

4. With the entire table still selected, click the Shading Color list arrow 🔲 on the Tables and Borders toolbar, click More Fill Colors, click the Custom tab, enter settings in the Red, Green, and Blue text boxes, as shown in Figure I-16, then click OK

5. With the entire table still selected, click the Align Top Left list arrow 🔲 on the Tables and Borders toolbar, click the Align Center Left button 🔲, click away from the table to deselect it, then close the Tables and Borders toolbar

   The option buttons still have white backgrounds. You can change the background color of an ActiveX form control in the Properties window.

6. Click View on the menu bar, point to Toolbars, click Control Toolbox, click the Design Mode button 🔲, click the Insurance option button to select it, then click the Properties button 🔲 on the Control Toolbox toolbar to open the Properties window for the Insurance option button

**TROUBLE**

After changing a control property, click the option button, then press [→] to deselect the option button.

7. Click the cell to the right of BackColor, click the list arrow, then select the Light Green color in the top row, as shown in Figure I-17

8. Repeat Step 7 to change the back color of the Cash and Combination option buttons to light green

9. Close the Properties window, click the Exit Design Mode button 🔲 on the Control Toolbox toolbar, then close the Control Toolbox toolbar

   After you modify an ActiveX control, you need to exit Design Mode so that you can protect the form. When the Design Mode button is selected, you cannot protect a form.

10. Click below the form, press [Enter], type Prepared by Your Name, click the text form field next to Name to position the insertion point at the top of the form, click the Protect Form button 🔲 on the Forms toolbar, compare the completed form template to Figure I-18, close the Forms toolbar, then save and close the template

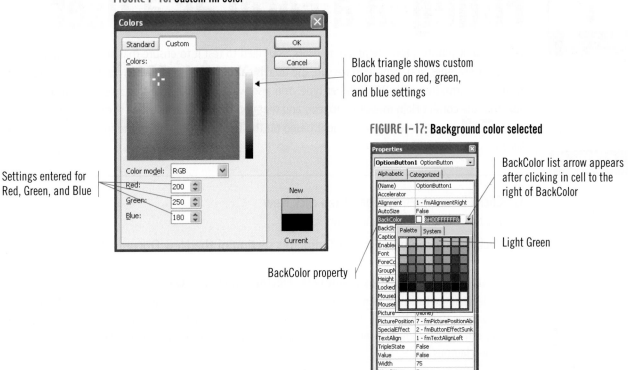

FIGURE I-16: Custom fill color

Black triangle shows custom color based on red, green, and blue settings

Settings entered for Red, Green, and Blue

BackColor property

FIGURE I-17: Background color selected

BackColor list arrow appears after clicking in cell to the right of BackColor

Light Green

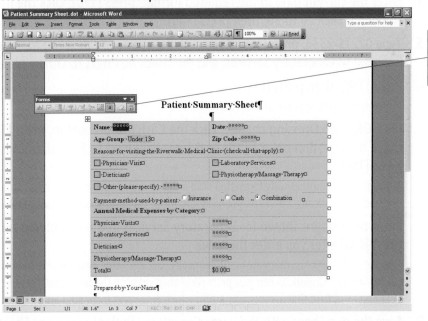

FIGURE I-18: Completed form template

Protect Form button selected, indicating that the form is protected

## Clues to Use

### Locking form fields

When you protect a form using the Protect Form button on the Forms toolbar, the form information, such as field labels, is protected or locked. A user can input information only in form fields and the input information must match the type specified by the person who originated the form. Sometimes, however, instead of protecting an entire form, you might want to lock certain form fields. For example, if you are entering numbers in a form for a budget and you want to be sure that the numbers do not inadvertently get changed, you can lock the form field after you enter the numbers. To lock a form field, and prevent changes to the current field results, click the field, then press [Ctrl][F11]. If you need to unlock a field to update the field results, click the field, then press [Ctrl][Shift][F11].

# Filling in a Form as a User

Before you distribute a form template to users, you need to test it to ensure that all the elements work correctly. For example, you want to make sure the total is calculated properly when numbers are entered in the form fields formatted with the Number type. You also want to make sure that selections appear in the list box, that the correct Help messages appear, and that you can easily select the check boxes and option buttons.  You open a new document based on the template, then fill in the form for a patient named Alice Wright, who is 23 years old.

## STEPS

1. **Click File on the menu bar, then click New**

   The New Document task pane opens.

2. **Click On my computer in the Templates section of the New Document task pane, click Patient Summary Sheet.dot, verify that the Document option button in the Create New section of the Templates window is selected, then click OK**

   Notice that the Patient Summary Sheet.dot file opens as a Word document, as indicated by the filename that appears on the title bar. The insertion point highlights the space following Name. The form is protected, so you can enter information only in spaces that contain text form fields, check boxes, drop-down lists, or option buttons.

3. **Type Alice Wright, then press [Tab]**

   The insertion point moves to the space following Date. Notice the Help message that appears in the status bar, telling you how to enter the date.

4. **Enter the current date in the required format, press [Tab], click the list arrow next to Under 13, click 20 to 30, then press [Tab]**

5. **Type 02215-2333, press [Tab], then click the check box next to Physician Visit, the check box next to Laboratory Services, and the check box next to Other (please specify):**

6. **Press [Tab], then press [F1]**

   The Help message appears, as shown in Figure I-19.

7. **Click OK, type Dressing change, click the Cash option button, press [Tab] two times to move the insertion point to the text form field next to Physician Visits, type 900, then press [Tab]**

   The amount is automatically formatted with a dollar sign, and the amount in the cell to the right of Total is updated automatically when you press [Tab] to move the insertion point out of the cell.

8. **Enter the amount shown for Laboratory Services in the completed form in Figure I-20; press [Tab] after you enter the value**

   The total—$1,200—is calculated automatically because this text field is a calculation type with the =SUM(ABOVE) formula. When you press [Tab] after entering the last value, the insertion point moves to the next text form field that accepts user input, which is the text form field after Name.

9. **Save the document with the name Completed Patient Summary Sheet to the drive and folder where your Data Files are located, print a copy, then close the document**

   After you use the Patient Summary Sheet template, it will be listed in the New from template section of the New Document task pane.

FIGURE I-19: **F1 Help message**

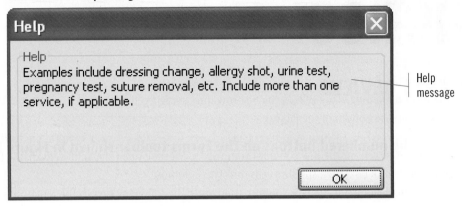

Help message

FIGURE I-20: **Expense amounts entered**

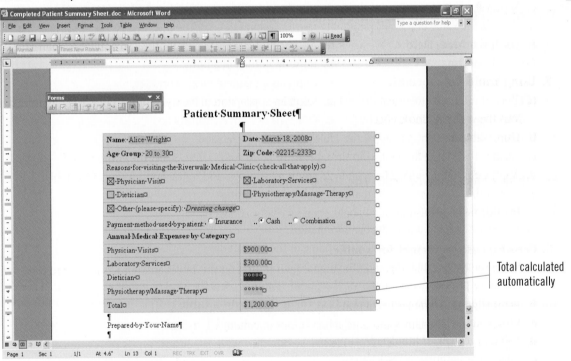

Total calculated automatically

## Clues to Use

### Editing a form template

To edit the structure of a form, you need to open the template, then click the Protect Form button on the Forms toolbar to deselect it. You can then make changes to the form by adding or removing form fields and modifying the appearance of the form. When you have finished modifying the form template, click the Protect Form button again, then save the template.

# Practice

**Identify each of the numbered buttons on the Forms toolbar shown in Figure I-21.**

FIGURE I-21

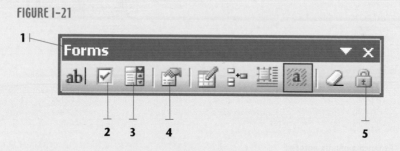

**Match each term with the statement that best describes it.**

6. **Drop-down form field**
7. **Control Toolbox**
8. **Text form field**
9. **[F1]**
10. **Calculation form field**
11. **Option button**

**a.** An area of a form into which users can enter information
**b.** A list of options in a form
**c.** Contains a mathematical expression
**d.** Contains a selection of ActiveX controls that can be inserted in a form
**e.** One type of ActiveX control
**f.** Help key

## Select the best answer from the list of choices

12. **What is a field label?**
    **a.** A space for users to enter variable information.
    **b.** A placeholder for text such as a user's name or the current date.
    **c.** A word or phrase, such as the user's current address, that is entered into a blank cell.
    **d.** A word or phrase such as "Date" or "Location" that tells users the kind of information required for a given field.

13. **What happens when you insert a text form field into a table cell?**
    **a.** A blank check box appears.
    **b.** A shaded rectangle with five dots appears.
    **c.** A blank bar outlined in black appears.
    **d.** A Help message appears to inform users what information to enter in the form field.

14. **How do you view the list of choices available in a drop-down form field?**
    **a.** Double-click the drop-down form field to insert a list arrow.
    **b.** Open the form as a user, click the drop-down form field, then click the list arrow.
    **c.** Right-click the drop-down form field, then click Activate.
    **d.** View the form in the Print Preview screen.

15. **How would you enter a Help message containing 200 characters?**
    **a.** Enter the Help message in the Type your own text box in the Status Bar tab of the Help Text dialog box.
    **b.** Enter the Help message in the form field.
    **c.** Edit the Help message so it contains only 130 characters, the accepted limit.
    **d.** Enter the Help message in the Type your own text box in the Help Key (F1) tab of the Help Text dialog box.

# ▼ SKILLS REVIEW

**1. Construct a form template.**

**a.** Start Word, open the New Document task pane if necessary, click the On my computer link, then create a new blank document as a template.

**b.** Check to ensure that Your Name Form Templates is designated as the folder to contain user templates. If necessary, refer to the lesson on Constructing a form template.

**c.** Type **Medical Office Assistant Program** and **Change of Grade Notification** on two lines, then center the text and enhance it with Bold and a 20-point font size.

**d.** Two lines below the title, clear the formatting, then create a table consisting of four columns and 13 rows.

**e.** Refer to Figure I-22. Type the text as shown. Merge cells in rows 2, 10, 11, 12, and 13 as shown. Apply bold to field labels as shown. (*Note*: You will align text later in the exercise.)

**f.** Save the template as **Change of Grade Notification** to the Your Name Form Templates folder.

**FIGURE I-22**

**Medical Office Assistant Program**
**Change of Grade Notification**

| | | | |
|---|---|---|---|
| **Student Number** | | **Date** | |
| **Student Name** | | | |
| **Course Title** | | **Course Number** | |
| **Original Letter Grade** | **Revised Letter Grade** | **Courses** | **Points** |
| A—4 | A—4 | Medical Transcription | |
| B—3 | B—3 | Clinical Procedures | |
| C—2 | C—2 | Computerized Medical Billing | |
| D—1 | D—1 | Anatomy and Related Physiology | |
| F—0 | F—0 | Pharmacology | |
| **Grade Point Average** | | | |
| **Reason for Grade Change (check one)** | | | |
| | | | |
| **Other (specify)** | | | |

**2. Add and modify text form fields.**

**a.** Show the Forms toolbar, if necessary.

**b.** Insert text form fields in the blank cells to the right of the following field labels: Student Number, Date, Student Name, Course Number, and Other (specify).

**c.** Modify the text form field next to Student Number so that users can enter up to six characters (numbers or a combination of number and letters).

**d.** Modify the text form field next to Date so that users must enter a date formatted as M/d/yyyy.

**e.** Save your changes to the template.

**3. Add drop-down and check box form fields.**

**a.** Insert a drop-down form field after Course Title.

**b.** In the Drop-Down Form Field Options dialog box, enter the following list of items: **Medical Transcription**, **Clinical Procedures**, **Computerized Medical Billing**, **Anatomy and Related Physiology**, and **Pharmacology**.

**c.** Move Anatomy and Related Physiology up to the top of the list and then move Medical Transcription above Pharmacology.

**d.** Insert a check box form field and a space to the left of each letter grade in the Original Letter Grade and Revised Letter Grade columns. Save the template.

**4. Use calculations in a form.**

**a.** Insert a text form field in the blank cell to the right of Medical Transcription with the Number type, the Number format set to 0, and the Calculate on exit check box selected.

**b.** Copy the text form field with number formatting to the next four cells (Clinical Procedures through Pharmacology).

**c.** Insert a text form field with the type set to Calculation in the blank cell to the right of Grade Point Average.

**d.** Type the expression **=SUM(ABOVE)/5**. This formula will add the numbers in the Points cells, then divide the total by 5 to determine the average.

**e.** Make sure the Number format is set to 0 and the Calculate on exit check box is selected before you exit the Text Form Field Options dialog box, then save the template.

**5. Add Help to a form.**

**a.** Add a status bar Help message in the Date form field that states: **Type the date in numerals as month, day, year; for example, 03/18/2008.**

**b.** Add a Help key (F1) Help message in the Other (specify): field that states: **Acceptable reasons include completion of work outstanding and acceptance of medical documentation.**

**c.** Save the template.

6. **Insert form controls.**

   a. Show the Control Toolbox toolbar. Make sure the Design Mode button is selected, then click the blank cell below the Reason for Grade Change field label.

   b. Insert an Option Button control with the following properties: Caption is **Calculation Error** and height is **18**.

   c. Insert an Option Button control in the next blank cell with the caption **Exam Retake** and a height of **18**.

   d. Close the Properties window, then exit Design Mode.

   e. Close the Control Toolbox toolbar, then save the template.

7. **Format and protect a form.**

   a. With the table selected, change the row height to **.35"**.

   b. Show the Tables and Borders toolbar, then change the text alignment for the entire table to Align Center Left.

   c. Align Top Center all four field labels in the row beginning with Original Letter Grade.

   d. Align Center all the form fields in the six cells under the cell with the Points label.

   e. Align Center Right the Grade Point Average field label.

   f. Select the table again, then change the colors in the Custom tab of the Colors dialog box to Red: **240**, Green: **220**, and Blue: **250**. (*Hint*: You should see a light lavender color.)

   g. View the Control Toolbox toolbar, then select Design Mode.

   h. With the Calculation Error option button selected, change the BackColor in the Properties window to light pink (last box in the top row of the color selections), which creates a two-tone effect—lavender for the form background and light pink for the option button.

   i. Repeat the preceding procedure to change the BackColor to light pink for the Exam Retake option button.

   j. Close the Properties window, then exit Design Mode. (*Note*: You must click the Design Mode button on the Control Toolbox toolbar to exit Design Mode.)

   k. Select the table, click Table on the menu bar, point to AutoFit, then click Distribute Columns Evenly.

   l. Protect the form, then close the Forms toolbar, the Tables and Borders toolbar, and the Control Toolbox toolbar.

   m. Save and close the template.

8. **Fill in a form as a user.**

   a. Open a new document based on the Change of Grade Notification template. (*Hint*: Make sure the Document option button in the Create New section of the Templates dialog box is selected.)

   b. Type **337888** as the Student Number, press [Tab], type the **current date**, press [Tab], type your name, select Pharmacology as the Course Title, enter **626** as the Course Number, select B as the Original Letter Grade, then select A as the Revised Letter Grade.

   c. Enter the points for each course as follows: Medical Transcription: **3**, Clinical Procedures: **2**; Computerized Medical Billing: **4**; Anatomy and Related Physiology: **2**; and Pharmacology: **4**.

   d. Press [Tab] and verify that the value in the Grade Point Average cell is 3.

   e. Select the Exam Retake option button. Check the F1 Help Message in the Other (specify): field.

   f. Save the document with the filename **Pharmacology Grade Change** to the drive and folder where your Data Files are located, print a copy, close the document, then exit Word.

## ▼ INDEPENDENT CHALLENGE 1

You work in the Administration Department at Fairview General Hospital in Bellingham, Washington. Several hospital administrators and senior medical staff have begun taking trips to hospitals around the world to investigate innovative programs in a variety of medical areas. Your supervisor asks you to help expedite the bookkeeping by creating an expense report form that can be completed online in Word.

   a. Start Word and open the file WMP I-1.doc from the drive and folder where your Data Files are located. Save it as a template called **Expense Report Form** to the Your Name Form Templates folder that you created to complete the lessons in this unit. (Refer to the first lesson in this unit, if necessary.)

   b. View the Forms toolbar.

c. Insert text form fields for the Name, Report Date, Extension, and Purpose of Travel field labels.

d. Specify the date format of your choice for the Report Date form field.

e. Change the type of the text form field next to Extension to Number and specify a maximum of four numbers.

f. Add a status bar Help message to the Purpose of Travel form field that states: **Specify the location(s) you visited and the hospital-related goals accomplished**.

g. Insert a drop-down form field in the blank cell to the right of Department that includes the following entries: **Board member**, **Hospital Administrator**, **Chief of Staff**, and **Researcher**. Put the list in alphabetical order.

h. Insert a text form field in the first blank cell in the Date column, select Date as the type, specify the M/d/yy date format, then copy the text form field and paste it to all the blank cells in the Date column.

i. Insert a drop-down form field in the first blank cell in the Category column. Include the following entries in the drop-down list: **Meals**, **Hotel**, **Air Fare**, and **Other**. Put the entries in alphabetical order.

j. Copy the drop-down form field and paste it to all the blank cells in the Category column.

k. Insert a text form field in the first blank cell in the Details column, then copy the text form field and paste it to all the blank cells in the Details column.

l. Insert a text form field in the blank cell below Amount, then change the text form field options so the type is Number, the format is 0.00, and the Calculate on exit check box is selected. Copy the text form field with Number formatting and paste it to all the blank cells in the Amount column, except the cell next to Total.

m. Insert a text form field in the blank cell to the right of Total, then change the form field options so the type is Calculation, the format is 0.00, the Expression is =SUM(ABOVE), and the Calculate on exit check box is selected.

n. Right-align the form fields in the Amount column and Total cell.

o. Protect the form, then save and close the template.

p. Open a new document based on the template.

q. Type **your name** and the **current date**, select the Researcher, type **5555** for the extension, then describe the Purpose for Travel as **Evaluating the Paradise Palms General Hospital**.

r. Use the information that follows to complete the form, be sure to fill in some information in each of the four columns for each expense.: **April 10: Round trip Air Fare from Seattle to Tahiti: $1800, April 11: Meals at Paradise Palms Resort: $200, April 12: Meals in various locations – receipts attached: $200, April 13: Meals including hosted dinner for Paradise Palms General Hospital administrators and key medical personnel, $550, April 13: Hotel accommodation for three nights at the Paradise Palms Resort: $1200, and April 13: Other described as Taxis and Miscellaneous Expenses: $300.**

s. Verify the total expenses are 4250.00, then save the document as **Completed Expense Report** to the drive and folder where your Data Files are located. Print a copy of the completed form, then close the document.

**Advanced Challenge Exercise**

FIGURE I-23

■ Open the Expense Report.dot as a template, then unprotect the form.

■ Click below the form, press [Enter], then clear the formatting.

■ Click the Insert Frame button on the Forms toolbar, draw a box approximately 5" wide

> **Trip Outcome**: Paradise Palms General Hospital sponsors an innovative treatment program for tropical diseases. I recommend we send two physicians from Fairview General Hospital to Paradise Palms General Hospital to learn about the program.¶
> ¶
> ☐ Agree   ☐ Disagree ¶

and 1.5" tall, then enter text and the two check box controls as shown in Figure I-23. Note that you need to select True for the AutoSize property for both controls and change the font of the caption to Arial and 18 point. (*Note*: Adjust the boxes manually as needed.)

■ Save the updated template as Expense Report Form_ACE.dot.

■ Exit design mode, protect the form, type your name in the form where indicated, click the Agree check box, print the form, then close the template.

# ▼ INDEPENDENT CHALLENGE 2

You are the Office Manager for the Atlantic Regional Health Authority, a medical center that has just instituted parking regulations for staff wanting to park in the new staff parking lot. Any staff member who wants to park in the lot must purchase a parking permit. You decide to create a Word form that staff members complete to purchase a parking permit. You will create the form as a Word template saved on the company's network. Staffers can open a new Word document based on the template, then complete the form in Word, or they can print the form and fill it in by hand.

**a.** Start Word, open the file WMP I-2.doc from the drive and folder where your Data Files are located, and save it as a template called **Parking Permit Requisition** to the Your Name Form Templates folder that you created to complete the lessons in this unit. (Refer to the first lesson in this unit, if necessary.)

**b.** View the Forms toolbar.

**c.** Insert a text form field in the blank cell to the right of Date. Format the text form field to accept dates entered in the format you prefer. Include a Help message that appears on the status bar and tells users how to enter the date.

**d.** Enter a text form field in the blank cell to the right of Name.

**e.** Insert a drop-down form field in the blank cell to the right of Department that includes the following entries: **Pediatrics**, **Emergency**, **ICU**, **Laboratory Services**, **General**.

**f.** Move entries so they appear in alphabetical order.

**g.** Insert a text form field in the blank cell to the right of Extension, then modify the text form field so that it accepts a maximum of four numbers. Include a status bar Help message that advises users to enter their four-digit telephone extension.

**h.** Insert check box form fields to the left of the selections in the fourth column (Full Time, Part Time, etc.). Leave a space between the check box and the first letter of each selection.

**i.** Insert an option button control in each of the blank cells in the last row of the form. The captions for the option buttons are as follows: **Check**, **Cash**, and **Pay Debit**.

**j.** Click the Exit Design Mode button on the Control Toolbox, then close the Control Toolbox.

**k.** Apply the Table Columns 5 Table AutoFormat to the table.

**l.** Show the Tables and Borders toolbar, then remove the shading from the cell that contains the Check option button. (*Hint*: You might find it easier to remove shading from the table cell if you show the Control Toolbox and enter Design Mode again.)

## Advanced Challenge Exercise

- Revise each of the three option buttons as follows:
- Change the foreground color (ForeColor) of each option button to Bright Blue. Note that the ForeColor is the text color.
- Change the Font to Impact and 16 point.
- Change the SpecialEffect to 0 – fmButtonEffectFlat.
- Change the TextAlign to 2 – fmTextAlignCenter.
- Set the width at 75 for the Check and Cash buttons and 100 for the Pay Debit button. Note that the width might change to 99.75 to fit the current table size. That is acceptable.
- Exit Design Mode.

**m.** Protect the form, then save and close the template.

**n.** Open a new document based on the template, then complete the form as a user. Type the **current date** and **your name**, select Full Time and Day Shift status, select the Pediatrics Department, enter any **four-digit extension**, then select Cash as the payment method.

**o.** Save the document as **Completed Parking Requisition** to the drive and folder where your Data Files are located, print a copy, close the document, then exit Word.

## ▼ INDEPENDENT CHALLENGE 3

You work as a Medical Office Assistant in the Reception area of Meadowbrook Hospital in Kansas City. Your supervisor has asked you to create a form that you can use to collect information from patients about their experience at the hospital.

a. Start Word, type **Meadowbrook Hospital** as the title and **Patient Feedback** as the subtitle, then enhance both titles attractively.

b. Save the document as a template named **Feedback Form** to the Your Name Form Templates folder you created to contain the form templates you created in this unit.

c. Plan a form similar to the one shown in Figure I-24 that contains the following field labels: **Name**, **Current Date**, **Room #**, and **Physician** and a section for ranking service components related to a hospital stay.

d. Enter text form fields in the cell to the right of Name, Current Date, and Room #, then enter a drop-down form field in the cell to the right of Physician that lists the names of five physicians of your choice. Be sure the names appear in alphabetical order in the drop-down list. Also be sure to assign the Date type to the Date form field, using a format of your choice. Finally, add a text form field next to the text Additional Comments. Be sure to leave a space between the text and the text form field.

**FIGURE I-24**

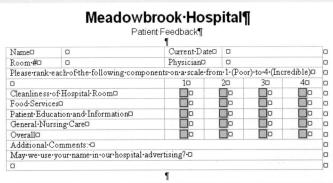

e. Insert check box form fields in the ranking section of your form.

f. In the last row of the table, insert two Option Button controls: one labeled **YES!** and one labeled **No thanks**. Format the option buttons so that they fit the table cell.

g. Format the form attractively, using one of the Table AutoFormats if you wish. (*Hint*: You might need to increase the row height so that the option buttons fit.)

h. Protect the form, save it, then close the template.

i. Open a new document based on the form template, then save it as **Completed Feedback Form** to the drive and folder where your Data Files are located.

j. Fill in the form as if you had stayed at Meadowbrook Hospital. Enter your name in the Name field.

k. Save the form, print a copy, close the form, then exit Word.

## ▼ INDEPENDENT CHALLENGE 4

Many hospitals and medical organizations maintain Web sites, which include online forms that patients can complete to participate in a survey, provide payment information, select products or services, and request information. You can learn a great deal about form design by studying some of the forms included on Web sites. You decide to search for hospitals or other medically related Web sites that include forms, identify the form controls used in the forms, and then describe two unusual or creative ways in which form controls are used to request information.

a. Open your Web browser and conduct a search for two hospitals and then follow links to find suitable forms. Find online forms rather than links to Word or PDF documents. Good areas to find forms are Research Management pages, Patient Services pages (for example "Find a Doctor"), and Donation pages.

b. Select a form from each of the two Hospital Web sites you explored.

c. Open the file WMP I-3.doc, then save it as **Form Evaluation** to the drive and folder where your Data Files are located.

d. Type **your name** and the **current date** in the spaces provided.

e. As directed in the Form Evaluation document, type the hospital names and copy the Web site addresses to the spaces provided, then follow the directions in the document to insert the required information.

f. Save the document, print a copy, then close it.

# ▼ VISUAL WORKSHOP

You work in Laboratory Services at Sunshine Medical Clinic in San Diego. You decide to make up a simple form that hospital workers can complete online and then e-mail to you when they want to request X-rays, CT scans, MRIs, and Ultrasounds. Create and enhance a form template, as shown in Figure I-25. Save the template as **Film Request Form** to the Your Name Form Templates folder containing all the form templates you've created for this unit. The items in the drop-down list for Job Title are **ER doctor**, **Pediatric nurse**, **Surgeon**, and **Triage nurse**. The items in the drop-down list for Films are **CT Scan**, **MRI**, **Ultrasound**, and **X-rays**. Set the MMMM d, yyyy format for the Current Date and Date Required fields, and set the HH:mm format for the Time Required field. (*Hint*: select Date as the Type and scroll the Date format list to find the time formats.) Protect the form, close the template, then open a new document based on the template. Complete the form with **your name**, the **current date**, Surgeon as the Job Title, Extension **4433**, an Ultrasound as the Films type, a **date** one week after the current date, a time of **2:00 p.m.**, Delivery checked, and special instructions of **Please deliver to Room 233**. Save the completed form as **My Film Request Form** to the drive and folder where your Data Files are located, print a copy, and close the document.

**FIGURE I-25**

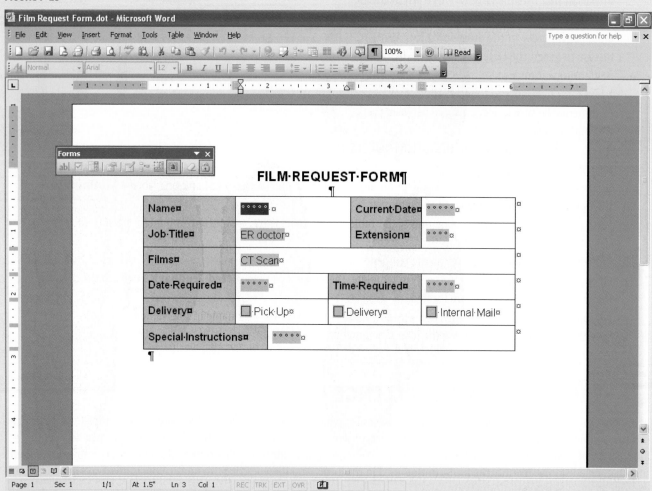

# Illustrating Documents with Graphics

## OBJECTIVES

Add graphics

Resize graphics

Position graphics

Create charts

If you have a SAM user profile, you may have access to hands-on instruction, practice, and assessment of the skills covered in this unit. Log in to your SAM account and go to your assignments page to see what your instructor has assigned.

Graphics can help illustrate the ideas in your documents, provide visual interest on a page, and give your documents punch and flair. In addition to clip art, you can add graphics created in other programs to a document, or you can use the drawing features of Word to create your own images. In this appendix, you learn how to insert, modify, and position graphics, and how to illustrate a document with charts. You are preparing materials for a staff meeting to discuss implementing a triage phone system at the clinic. You use the graphic features of Word to illustrate a telephone triage form and a handout that describes the distribution of incoming calls to the clinic by type.

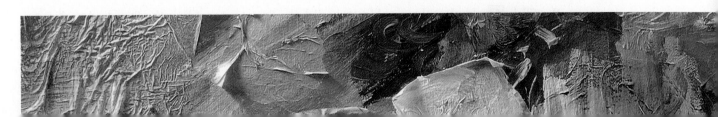

# Adding Graphics

Graphic images you can insert in a document include the clip art images that come with Word, photos taken with a digital camera, scanned art, and graphics created in other graphics programs. When you first insert a graphic it is an **inline graphic**—part of the line of text in which it is inserted. You move an inline graphic just as you would move text. To be able to move a graphic independently of text, you must apply a text-wrapping style to it to make it a **floating graphic**, which can be moved anywhere on a page. To insert clip art or another graphic file into a document, you use the Picture command on the Insert menu. You have formatted the text for a telephone triage form for potential urinary tract infections. You want to illustrate the form with the Riverwalk Medical Clinic logo, a graphic created in another graphics program. You use the Picture, From File command to insert the logo in the document, and then wrap the text around the logo.

## STEPS

1. **Start Word, open the file WMP 1-1.doc from the drive and folder where your Data Files are located, save it as UTI Triage, then read the document to get a feel for its contents**

   The document opens in Print Layout view.

   > **QUICK TIP**
   >
   > The Drawing button is a toggle button that you can use to display and hide the Drawing toolbar.

2. **Click the Show/Hide ¶ button ¶ on the Standard toolbar to display formatting marks, then click the Drawing button on the Standard toolbar to display the Drawing toolbar if it is not already displayed**

   The Drawing toolbar, located below the document window, includes buttons for inserting, creating, and modifying graphics. Table 1-1 describes the function of each button on the Drawing toolbar.

3. **Click before the heading Patient complains of... under the table, click Insert on the menu bar, point to Picture, then click From File**

   The Insert Picture dialog box opens. You use this dialog box to locate and insert graphic files. Most graphic files are **bitmap graphics**, which are composed of a series of small dots, called **pixels**, that define color and intensity. Bitmap graphics are often saved with a .bmp, .png, .jpg, .wmf, .tif, or .gif file extension. To view all the graphic files in a particular location, use the Files of type list arrow to select All Pictures. To view a particular type of graphic, use the Files of type list arrow to select the graphic type.

4. **Click the Files of type list arrow, click All Pictures if it is not already selected, use the Look in list arrow to navigate to the drive and folder where your Data Files are located, click the file RMC Logo.jpg, then click Insert**

   The logo is inserted as an inline graphic at the location of the insertion point. Unless you want a graphic to be part of a line of text, usually the first thing you do after inserting it is to wrap text around it so it becomes a floating graphic. To be able to position a graphic anywhere on a page, you must apply a text-wrapping style to it even if there is no text on the page.

   > **TROUBLE**
   >
   > If your Picture toolbar does not open, click View on the menu bar, point to Toolbars, then click Picture.

5. **Click the logo graphic to select it**

   Squares, called **sizing handles**, appear on the sides and corners of the graphic when it is selected, as shown in Figure 1-1. The Picture toolbar also opens. The Picture toolbar includes buttons for modifying graphics.

6. **Click the Text Wrapping button on the Picture toolbar**

   A menu of text-wrapping styles opens.

7. **Click Tight**

   The text wraps around the sides of the graphic, as shown in Figure 1-2. Notice that the sizing handles change to circles, indicating the graphic is a floating graphic, and an anchor and a green rotate handle appear. The anchor indicates the floating graphic is **anchored** to the nearest paragraph, so that the graphic moves with the paragraph if the paragraph is moved. The anchor symbol appears only when formatting marks are displayed.

8. **Click ¶, deselect the graphic, then click the Save button on the Standard toolbar to save your changes**

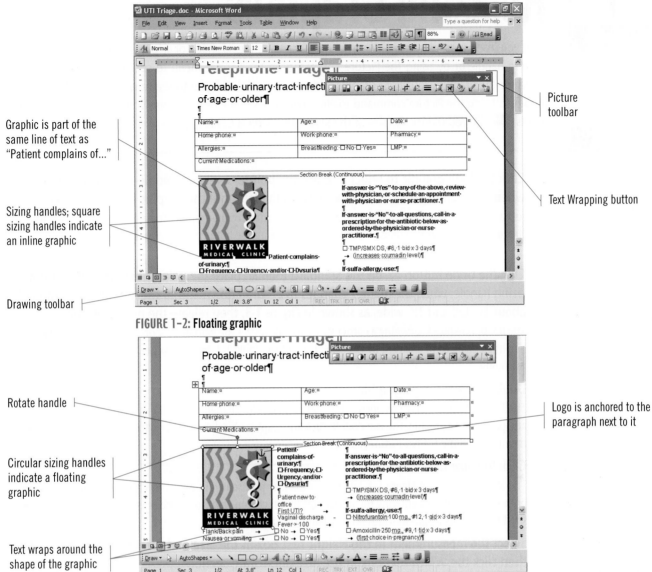

**FIGURE 1-1:** Inline graphic

Graphic is part of the same line of text as "Patient complains of..."

Sizing handles; square sizing handles indicate an inline graphic

Drawing toolbar

Picture toolbar

Text Wrapping button

**FIGURE 1-2:** Floating graphic

Rotate handle

Circular sizing handles indicate a floating graphic

Text wraps around the shape of the graphic

Logo is anchored to the paragraph next to it

**TABLE 1-1:** Buttons on the Drawing toolbar

| button | use to | button | use to |
|---|---|---|---|
| Draw ▾ | Open a menu of commands for grouping, positioning, rotating, and wrapping text around graphics, and for changing an AutoShape to a different shape | 🔳 | Insert a clip art graphic |
| | | 🔳 | Insert a picture from a file |
| ▨ | Select graphic objects | ♦▾ | Fill a shape with a color, a texture, a gradient, or a pattern |
| AutoShapes ▾ | Open a menu of drawing options for lines, shapes, and callouts | ✎▾ | Change the color of a line, an arrow, or a line around a shape |
| ╲ | Draw a straight line | A ▾ | Change the color of text |
| ↘ | Draw a straight line with an arrowhead | ═ | Change the style and weight of a line, an arrow, or a line around a shape |
| ▭ | Draw a rectangle or square | ┅ | Change the dash style of a line, an arrow, or a line around a shape |
| ○ | Draw an oval or circle | ⇄ | Change a line to an arrow; change the style of an arrow |
| 🅰 | Insert a text box | ▢ | Add a shadow to a graphic object |
| ◢ | Insert a WordArt graphic | ▥ | Make a graphic object three-dimensional |
| ✿ | Insert a diagram or an organization chart | | |

# Resizing Graphics

After you insert a graphic into a document, you can change its shape or size by using the mouse to drag a sizing handle or by using the Picture command on the Format menu to specify an exact height and width for the graphic. Resizing a graphic with the mouse allows you to see how the image looks as you modify it. Using the Picture command to alter a graphic's shape or size allows you to set precise measurements. ▓▓▓▓▓ You reduce the size of the Riverwalk Medical Clinic logo.

## STEPS

QUICK TIP
Click Ruler on the View menu to display the rulers.

1. **Click the logo graphic to select it, place the pointer over the middle-right sizing handle, when the pointer changes to ↔, drag to the left until the graphic is about 1½" wide**

   As you drag, the dotted outline indicates the size and shape of the graphic. You can refer to the ruler to gauge the measurements as you drag. When you release the mouse button, the image is narrower. Dragging a side, top, or bottom sizing handle changes only the width or height of a graphic.

QUICK TIP
If you enlarge a bitmap graphic too much, the dots that make up the picture become visible and the graphic is distorted.

2. **Click the Undo button ↺ on the Standard toolbar, place the pointer over the upper-right sizing handle, when the pointer changes to ↗ drag down and to the left until the graphic is about 1½" tall and 1⅛" wide, as shown in Figure 1-3, then release the mouse button**

   The image is reduced. Dragging a corner sizing handle resizes the graphic proportionally so that its width and height are reduced or enlarged by the same percentage. Table 1-2 describes other ways to resize objects using the mouse.

3. **Double-click the logo graphic**

   The Format Picture dialog box opens. It includes options for changing the coloring, size, scale, text wrapping, and position of a graphic. You can double-click any graphic object or use the Picture command on the Format menu to open the Format Picture dialog box.

4. **Click the Size tab**

   The Size tab, shown in Figure 1-4, allows you to enter precise height and width measurements for a graphic or to scale a graphic by entering the percentage by which you want to reduce or enlarge it. When a graphic is sized to **scale**, its height to width ratio remains the same.

TROUBLE
Your height measurement might differ slightly.

5. **Select the measurement in the Height text box in the Size and rotate section, type 1.15, then click the Width text box in the Size and rotate section**

   The width measurement automatically changes to 1.03". When the Lock aspect ratio check box is selected, you need to enter only a height or width measurement. Word calculates the other measurement so that the resized graphic is proportional.

6. **Click OK, then save your changes**

   The logo is resized to be precisely 1.15" tall and approximately 1.03" wide.

TABLE 1-2: Methods for resizing an object using the mouse

| do this | to |
| --- | --- |
| Drag a corner sizing handle | Resize a clip art or bitmap graphic proportionally from a corner |
| Press [Shift] and drag a corner sizing handle | Resize a drawing object, such as an AutoShape or a WordArt object, proportionally from a corner |
| Press [Ctrl] and drag a side, top, or bottom sizing handle | Resize any graphic object vertically or horizontally while keeping the center position fixed |
| Press [Ctrl] and drag a corner sizing handle | Resize any graphic object diagonally while keeping the center position fixed |
| Press [Shift][Ctrl] and drag a corner sizing handle | Resize any graphic object proportionally while keeping the center position fixed |

**FIGURE 1-3:** Dragging to resize an image

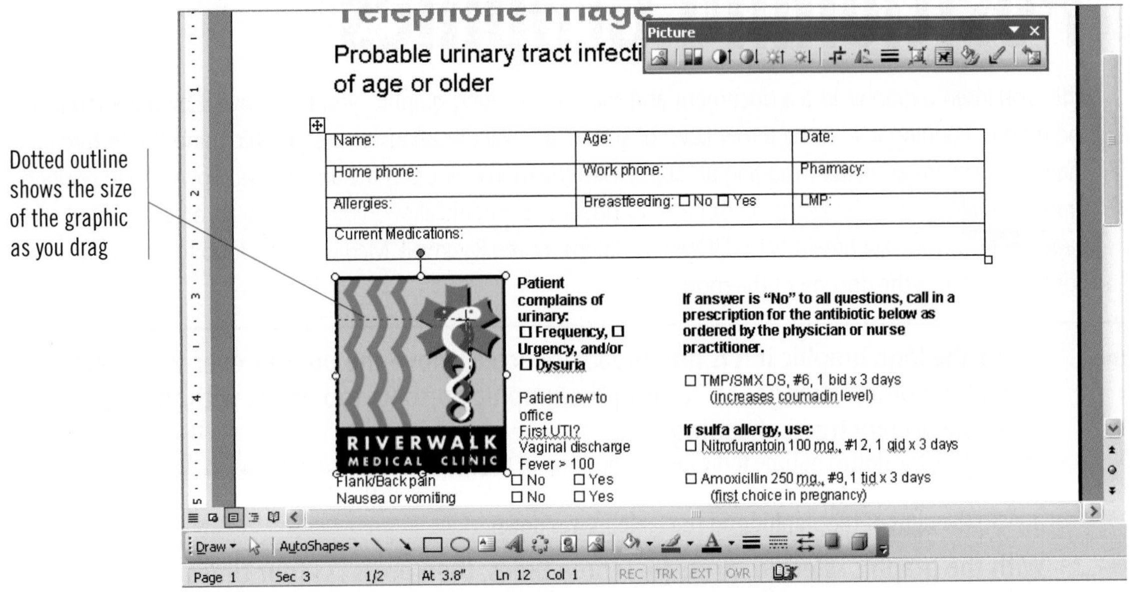

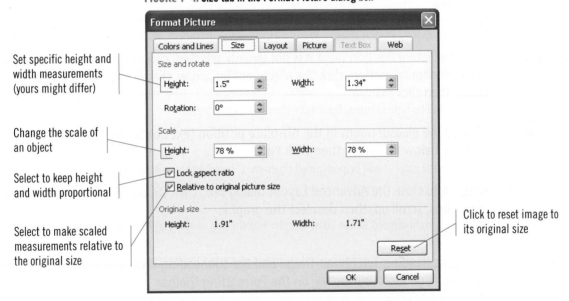

Dotted outline shows the size of the graphic as you drag

**FIGURE 1-4:** Size tab in the Format Picture dialog box

Set specific height and width measurements (yours might differ)

Change the scale of an object

Select to keep height and width proportional

Select to make scaled measurements relative to the original size

Click to reset image to its original size

## Clues to Use

### Cropping graphics

If you want to use only part of a picture in a document, you can crop the graphic to trim the parts you don't want to use. To crop a graphic, select it, then click the Crop button on the Picture toolbar. The pointer changes to the cropping pointer, and cropping handles (solid black lines) appear on all four corners and sides of the graphic. To crop one side of a graphic, drag a side cropping handle inward to where you want to trim the graphic. To crop two adjacent sides at once, drag a corner cropping handle inward to the point where you want the corner of the cropped image to be located. When you drag a cropping handle, the shape of the cropping pointer changes to correspond to the shape of the cropping handle you are dragging. When you finish adjusting the parameters of the graphic, click the Crop button again to turn off the crop feature. You can also crop a graphic by entering precise crop measurements on the Picture tab in the Format Picture dialog box.

# Positioning Graphics

After you insert a graphic into a document and make it a floating graphic, you can move it by dragging it with the mouse, nudging it with the arrow keys, or setting an exact location for the graphic using the Picture command on the Format menu. Dragging an object with the mouse or using the arrow keys allows you to position a graphic visually. Using the Picture command to position a graphic allows you to place an object precisely on a page. ▄▄▄▄▄ You experiment with different positions for the Riverwalk Medical Clinic logo to determine which position enhances the document the most.

## STEPS

QUICK TIP

To move an object only horizontally or vertically, press [Shift] as you drag.

1. **Select the** logo graphic **if it is not already selected, move the pointer over the graphic, when the pointer changes to** 🔾, **drag the** graphic **up so its top aligns with the top of the** Probable urinary tract... **heading**
   As you drag, the dotted outline indicates the position of the graphic. When you release the mouse button, the graphic is moved and the text wraps around the graphic. Notice that the Probable urinary tract... heading is now to the right of the graphic and the table moves down.

QUICK TIP

You can place a floating graphic anywhere on a page, including outside the margins.

2. **With the graphic selected, press [◄] three times, then press [▲] four times**
   Each time you press an arrow key the graphic is **nudged**—moved a small amount—in that direction. You can also press [Ctrl] and an arrow key to nudge an object in even smaller (one pixel) increments. Nudging the graphic did not position it exactly where you want it to be.

3. **Double-click the** graphic, **click the** Layout tab **in the Format Picture dialog box, then click** Advanced
   The Advanced Layout dialog box opens. The Picture Position tab, shown in Figure 1-5, allows you to specify an exact position for a graphic relative to some aspect of the document, such as a margin, column, or paragraph.

QUICK TIP

Use the Text Wrapping tab to change the text-wrapping style, to wrap text around only one side of a graphic, and to change the distance between the edge of the graphic and the edge of the wrapped text.

4. **Click the** Picture Position tab **if it is not already selected, click the** Alignment option button **in the Horizontal section, click the** Alignment list arrow, **click** Right, **click the** relative to list arrow, **then click** Margin
   The logo will be right-aligned, flush with the right page margin.

5. **Change the measurement in the Absolute position text box in the Vertical section to** 1, **click the** below list arrow, **then click** Page
   The top of the graphic will be positioned precisely 1" below the top of the page.

6. **Click** OK **to close the Advanced Layout dialog box, click** OK **to close the Format Picture dialog box, scroll up, then deselect the graphic**
   The logo is right-aligned at the right margin and the top of the graphic is positioned 1" below the top of the page.

TROUBLE

If the Picture toolbar remains open after you deselect the graphic, close it.

7. **Select the heading** Telephone Triage **and the subheading** Probable urinary tract..., **then click the** Align Right button **≣ on the Formatting toolbar**
   The text is right-aligned and wraps to the left of the logo, as shown in Figure 1-6.

8. **Press [Ctrl][End], type your name, save your changes, print, then close the file**

### Clues to Use

#### Narrowing a search for clip art

Searching for clip art with an active Internet connection gives you access to the thousands of clips available on the Microsoft Office Online Web site. With so many clips from which to choose, your search can be more productive if you set specific search criteria. To perform an initial search for a clip, type a word or words that describe the clip you want to find in the Search for text box in the Clip Art task pane, then click Go. If the clips returned in the Results box are too numerous or don't match the criteria you set, you can try using different keywords. You can also narrow your search by reducing the number of collections to search, or by limiting your search to a specific media type, such as photographs. To search specific collections, click the Search in list arrow in the task pane, then deselect the check box next to each collection you want to omit from the search. To search a specific media type, click the Results should be list arrow, then deselect the check box next to each type of clip you want to omit from the search. In both lists, you can click a plus sign next to a collection name or media type to expand the list of options. To read more hints on searching for clips, click the Tips for finding clips hyperlink in the Clip Art task pane.

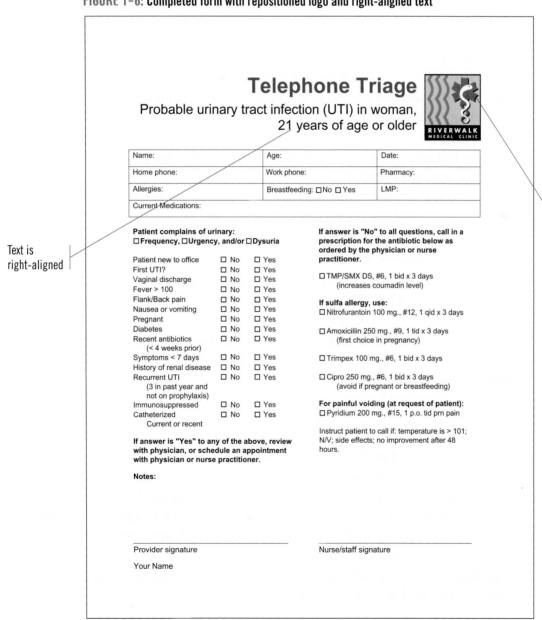

**FIGURE 1-5: Picture Position tab in the Advanced Layout dialog box**

Select to horizontally align a graphic relative to an aspect of the document

Select to position graphic a precise distance from an aspect of the document (your measurements might differ)

Select the aspect of the document you want to position the graphic relative to

**FIGURE 1-6: Completed form with repositioned logo and right-aligned text**

# Telephone Triage

Probable urinary tract infection (UTI) in woman, 21 years of age or older

**RIVERWALK**
MEDICAL CLINIC

| Name: | Age: | Date: |
|---|---|---|
| Home phone: | Work phone: | Pharmacy: |
| Allergies: | Breastfeeding: ☐No ☐Yes | LMP: |
| Current Medications: | | |

**Patient complains of urinary:**
☐Frequency, ☐Urgency, and/or ☐Dysuria

| | | |
|---|---|---|
| Patient new to office | ☐ No | ☐ Yes |
| First UTI? | ☐ No | ☐ Yes |
| Vaginal discharge | ☐ No | ☐ Yes |
| Fever > 100 | ☐ No | ☐ Yes |
| Flank/Back pain | ☐ No | ☐ Yes |
| Nausea or vomiting | ☐ No | ☐ Yes |
| Pregnant | ☐ No | ☐ Yes |
| Diabetes | ☐ No | ☐ Yes |
| Recent antibiotics | ☐ No | ☐ Yes |
| (< 4 weeks prior) | | |
| Symptoms < 7 days | ☐ No | ☐ Yes |
| History of renal disease | ☐ No | ☐ Yes |
| Recurrent UTI | ☐ No | ☐ Yes |
| (3 in past year and | | |
| not on prophylaxis) | | |
| Immunosuppressed | ☐ No | ☐ Yes |
| Catheterized | ☐ No | ☐ Yes |
| Current or recent | | |

**If answer is "Yes" to any of the above, review with physician, or schedule an appointment with physician or nurse practitioner.**

**Notes:**

**If answer is "No" to all questions, call in a prescription for the antibiotic below as ordered by the physician or nurse practitioner.**

☐ TMP/SMX DS, #6, 1 bid x 3 days
(increases coumadin level)

**If sulfa allergy, use:**
☐ Nitrofurantoin 100 mg., #12, 1 qid x 3 days

☐ Amoxicillin 250 mg., #9, 1 tid x 3 days
(first choice in pregnancy)

☐ Trimpex 100 mg., #6, 1 bid x 3 days

☐ Cipro 250 mg., #6, 1 bid x 3 days
(avoid if pregnant or breastfeeding)

**For painful voiding (at request of patient):**
☐ Pyridium 200 mg., #15, 1 p.o. tid prn pain

Instruct patient to call if: temperature is > 101; N/V; side effects; no improvement after 48 hours.

_____          _____
Provider signature                         Nurse/staff signature

Your Name

Text is right-aligned

Logo is aligned with the right margin and is 1" below the top of the page

# Creating Charts

Adding a chart can be an attractive way to illustrate a document that includes numerical information. A **chart** is a visual representation of numerical data and usually is used to illustrate trends, patterns, or relationships. The Word chart feature allows you to create many types of charts, including bar, column, pie, area, and line charts. You can add a chart to a document using the Picture, Chart command on the Insert menu. ██████ You create a handout that includes a chart showing the distribution of incoming phone calls, by type, to the clinic during the months of June and July. The staff will evaluate this information to help determine the necessity of a new triage phone system.

## STEPS

1. Open the file WMP 1-2.doc from the drive and folder where your Data Files are located, save it as Incoming Calls, then press [Ctrl][End]

   The insertion point is centered under the title.

**QUICK TIP**

To show the toolbars on two rows, click the Toolbar Options button at the end of the Formatting toolbar, then click Show Buttons on Two Rows.

2. Click Insert on the menu bar, point to Picture, then click Chart

   A table opens in a datasheet window and a column chart appears in the document. The datasheet and the chart contain placeholder data that you replace with your own data. The chart is based on the data in the datasheet. Any change you make to the data in the datasheet is made automatically to the chart. Notice that when a chart object is open, the Standard toolbar includes buttons for working with charts.

3. Click the datasheet title bar and drag it up so that the chart is visible, then move the pointer over the datasheet

   The pointer changes to ✛. You use this pointer to select the cells in the datasheet.

**QUICK TIP**

Click the Chart Type list arrow 📊 ▾ on the Standard toolbar to change the type of chart.

4. Click the East cell, type June, click the West cell, type July, click the gray 3 cell to select the third row, then press [Delete]

   When you click a cell and type, the data in the cell is replaced with the text you type. As you edit the datasheet, the changes you make are reflected in the chart.

5. Replace the remaining placeholder text with the data shown in Figure 1-7, then click outside the chart to deselect it

6. Click the chart to select the object, press [Ctrl], then drag the lower-right corner sizing handle down and to the right until the outline of the chart is approximately 7" wide

   The chart is enlarged and still centered.

**QUICK TIP**

Point to any part of a chart to see a ScreenTip that identifies the part. You can also use the Chart Objects list arrow on the Standard toolbar to select a part of a chart.

7. Double-click the chart to open it, click the View Datasheet button 📊 on the Standard toolbar to close the datasheet, click the legend to select it, then click the Format Legend button 📄 on the Standard toolbar

   The Format Legend dialog box opens. It includes options for modifying the legend. Select any part of a chart object and use 📄 to open a dialog box with options for formatting that part of the chart. In this case, the name of the button is Format Legend because the legend is selected.

8. Click the Placement tab, click the Bottom option button, then click OK

   The legend moves below the chart.

9. Click the June data series (any light blue bar), click 📄, click the Patterns tab in the Format Data Series dialog box if it is not already selected, click Light Orange (row 3, column 2) in the color palette in the Area section, click OK, then deselect the chart

   The color of the June data series changes to light orange. The completed handout is shown in Figure 1-8.

**QUICK TIP**

To edit a chart object, right-click it, point to Chart Object, then click Edit.

10. Type Prepared by followed by your name centered in the document footer, save your changes, print the handout, close the document, then exit Word

FIGURE 1-7: Datasheet and chart object

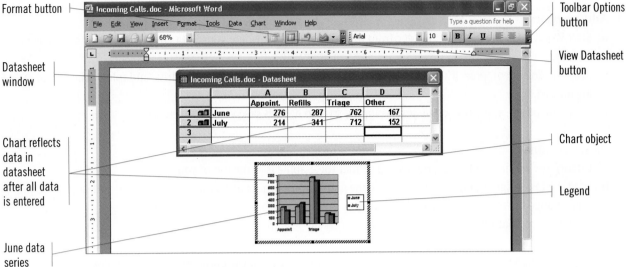

Format button

Datasheet window

Chart reflects data in datasheet after all data is entered

June data series

Toolbar Options button

View Datasheet button

Chart object

Legend

FIGURE 1-8: Completed handout with chart

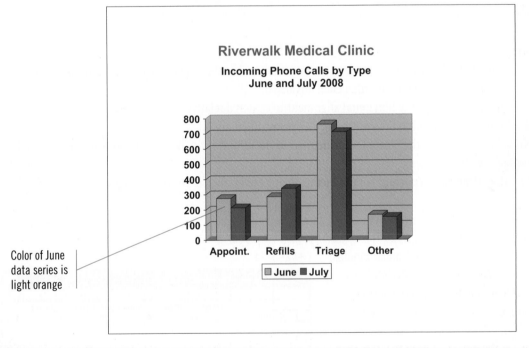

Color of June data series is light orange

## Clues to Use

### Creating diagrams and organization charts

Diagrams are another way to illustrate concepts in your documents. Word includes a diagram feature that allows you to quickly create and format several types of diagrams, including pyramid, Venn, target, radial, and cycle diagrams, as well as organization charts. To insert a diagram or an organization chart, click the Insert Diagram or Organization Chart button 🔅 on the Drawing toolbar or use the Diagram command on the Insert menu to open the Diagram Gallery, shown in Figure 1-9. Select a diagram type in the Diagram Gallery, then click OK. The diagram appears in a drawing canvas with placeholder text, and the Diagram toolbar opens. The Diagram toolbar contains buttons for customizing and formatting the diagram, and for sizing and positioning the drawing canvas. Use the AutoFormat button on the Diagram toolbar to apply colors and shading to your diagram.

FIGURE 1-9: Diagram Gallery

**Diagram Gallery**

Select a diagram type:

Organization Chart
Used to show hierarchical relationships

OK     Cancel

## ▼ SKILLS REVIEW

### 1. Add graphics.

**a.** Start Word, open the file WMP 1-3.doc from the drive and folder where your Data Files are located, then save it as **Sun Safety**.

**b.** Read the document, press [Ctrl][Home], then insert the file **Beach.jpg** from the drive and folder where your Data Files are located.

**c.** Select the photo, apply the Square text-wrapping style to it, then save your changes.

### 2. Resize graphics.

**a.** Change the zoom level to 50%, then scroll so that the graphic is at the top of your screen.

**b.** Drag the lower-right sizing handle to reduce the graphic proportionally so that it is about 3.5" wide and 2.75" high, then change the zoom level to Page Width.

**c.** Click the Crop button on the Picture toolbar.

**d.** Drag the bottom-middle cropping handle up approximately $1/2$", then click the Crop button again.

**e.** Double-click the photo, click the Size tab, then change the width of the photo to 4.25". (*Hint*: Make sure the Lock aspect ratio check box is selected.)

**f.** Save your changes.

### 3. Position graphics.

**a.** Drag the photo down and to the right to center it in the body text and so that the text wraps around the photo.

**b.** Double-click the photo, click the Layout tab, then click Advanced.

**c.** On the Picture Position tab, change the horizontal alignment to centered relative to the margins.

**d.** In the Vertical section, change the absolute position to 1.7" below the margin.

**e.** On the Text Wrapping tab, change the Bottom measurement to .18". (*Note:* If the Bottom text box is dimmed, click Square in the Wrapping Style section.)

**f.** Click OK to close the Advanced Layout and Format Picture dialog boxes, then save your changes.

### 4. Create charts.

**a.** Press [Ctrl][End], then insert a chart.

**b.** Click the Chart Type list arrow on the Standard toolbar, then click Pie Chart. (*Hint*: Use the Toolbar Options button as needed to locate the Chart Type button.)

**c.** Select the second and third rows in the datasheet, then press [Delete].

**d.** Replace the data in the datasheet with the data shown in Figure 1-10, then close the datasheet. (*Hint*: If the label in your datasheet is East, replace it with **Pie 1**. Use the scroll bars as needed to view columns A–E.)

FIGURE 1-10

| Sun Safety.doc - Datasheet | | A | B | C | D | E |
|---|---|---|---|---|---|---|
| | | Always | Often | Sometimes | Rarely | Never |
| 1 | Pie 1 | 41 | 34 | 15 | 6 | 4 |
| 2 | | | | | | |
| 3 | | | | | | |

**e.** Use the Chart Objects list arrow to select the Plot Area, open the Format Plot Area dialog box, then change the Border and Area patterns to None.

**f.** Select the Always 41% data point (the largest pie slice), open the Format Data Point dialog box, then change the Area color to Orange.

**g.** Select each remaining pie slice, open the Format Data Point dialog box, then change the color of each remaining slice to a different shade of orange or yellow.

**h.** Use the Chart Objects list arrow to select Series "Pie 1," open the Format Data Series dialog box, click the Data Labels tab, then make the data labels show the percentage.

**i.** Resize the chart object proportionally so it is about 6" wide and 4" tall.

**j.** Type **Prepared by** followed by your name centered in the document footer, save your changes, print the document, close the file, then exit Word.

# Collaborating on Documents

**OBJECTIVES**

| Track changes |
| Insert, view, and edit comments |
| Compare and merge documents |

If you have a SAM user profile, you may have access to hands-on instruction, practice, and assessment of the skills covered in this unit. Log in to your SAM account and go to your assignments page to see what your instructor has assigned.

Several Word features make it easier to create and edit documents in cooperation with other people. The Track Changes, Comment, and Compare and Merge features in Word facilitate collaboration when two or more people are working on the same document. In this appendix, you learn how to track and review changes to a document, how to insert and work with comments, and how to compare and merge two documents. ▓▓▓ You have circulated a copy of the Influenza Information Sheet to two of your colleagues for feedback. You use the Track Changes, Comment, and Compare and Merge features to review their suggestions for changes and to combine their feedback into a final document.

# Tracking Changes

A **tracked change** is a mark that shows where an insertion, deletion, or formatting change has been made in a document. When the Track Changes feature is turned on, each change that you or another reviewer makes to a document is tracked. In Print Layout view, text that is inserted in a document is displayed as colored, underlined text. Formatting changes and deleted text are shown in balloons in the right margin of the document. As you review the tracked changes in a document, you can choose to accept or reject each change. When you accept a change it becomes part of the document. When you reject a change, the text or formatting is restored to its original state. To turn tracked changes on and off, you use the Track Changes button on the Reviewing toolbar or the Track Changes command on the Tools menu. Your boss, Tony Sanchez, has used Track Changes to suggest revisions to your draft information sheet. You review Tony's tracked changes, accepting or rejecting them as you go, and then edit the document with your additional changes.

## STEPS

1. **Start Word, open the file WMP 2-1.doc from the drive and folder where your Data Files are located, then save it as Flu Draft 1**

   The document, which contains tracked changes, opens in Print Layout view, as shown in Figure 2-1. Notice that the Track Changes button on the Reviewing toolbar is enabled, indicating that tracked changes are turned on in the document. Any change you make to the document will be marked as a tracked change.

2. **Click the Next button** 🔁 **on the Reviewing toolbar**

   The insertion point moves to the first tracked change in the document, in this case, a sentence inserted in the introductory paragraph.

3. **Click the Accept Change button** 🔲 **on the Reviewing toolbar, then click** 🔁

   The sentence becomes part of the document and the insertion point moves to a balloon containing a comment. You will work with comments in the next lesson, so you skip over the comment for now.

4. **Click** 🔁

   The insertion point moves to the balloon containing the deleted text "virus."

5. **Click the Reject Change/Delete Comment button** 🔲 **on the Reviewing toolbar, click** 🔁**, then click** 🔲

   The deleted word "virus" is restored to the document, the insertion point moves to the inserted word "germ," then "germ" is removed from the document, returning the text to its original state, as shown in Figure 2-2.

6. **Click** 🔁 **to select the next tracked change, right-click the selected text, then click Accept Insertion on the shortcut menu**

   The sentence becomes part of the document text. You can accept or reject any tracked change by right-clicking it, then selecting the appropriate command on the shortcut menu.

7. **Scroll down until the heading When To Be Vaccinated on page 2 is at the top of your screen, select September in the first sentence under the heading, type October, place the insertion point before the period at the end of the paragraph, then type , usually April**

   Your tracked changes are added to the document using a different color, as shown in Figure 2-3.

8. **Click the Track Changes button** 🔲 **on the Reviewing toolbar to turn off the Track Changes feature, press [Ctrl][Home], replace Your Name with your name at the top of the document, then click the Save button** 🔲 **on the Standard toolbar to save your changes**

**FIGURE 2-1:** Reviewing toolbar and tracked changes

Reviewing toolbar

Vertical bars indicate the adjacent line includes a tracked change

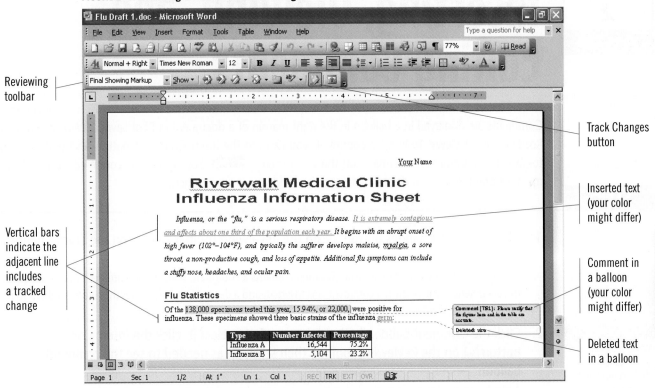

Track Changes button

Inserted text (your color might differ)

Comment in a balloon (your color might differ)

Deleted text in a balloon

**FIGURE 2-2:** Text restored to its original state

Tracked change text becomes part of the document

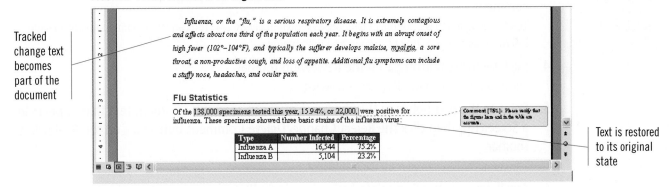

Text is restored to its original state

**FIGURE 2-3:** Tracked changes in the document

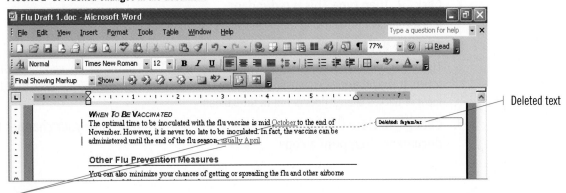

Deleted text

Your tracked changes appear in a color that is different from Tony's tracked changes (your color might differ)

# Inserting, Viewing, and Editing Comments

A **comment** is an embedded note or annotation that an author or reviewer adds to a document. Comments are displayed in a balloon in the right margin of a document in Print Layout, Web Layout, and Reading Layout views. To insert a comment, you can use the Insert Comment button on the Reviewing toolbar or the Comment command on the Insert menu. ▆▆▆ You review the comments in the document, respond to them or delete them, and then add your own comments.

**STEPS**

1. **Click the Track Changes button ▨ on the Reviewing toolbar to turn on the Track Changes feature, then scroll down until the heading Flu Statistics is at the top of your screen**

   The paragraph under the Flu Statistics heading contains a comment. Notice that comment marks appear in the document at the point the comment was inserted, and a dashed line leads from the right comment mark to the comment balloon in the margin.

2. **Click the comment balloon in the right margin to select it, click the Insert Comment button ▨ on the Reviewing toolbar, then scroll up as needed to see the comment balloon**

   A blank comment balloon is inserted in the document using a different color (the same color as your tracked changes). You respond to a comment by selecting the comment and then inserting your own comment.

3. **Type The numbers are correct., then click outside the comment balloon to deselect the comment**

   The text is added to the comment balloon, as shown in Figure 2-4. You can edit comment text by placing the insertion point in a comment balloon and then typing.

4. **Click the Next button ▨ on the Reviewing toolbar**

   The next comment in the document is selected.

5. **Point to the text between the comment markers, read the comment text that appears in a ScreenTip, then click the Reject Change/Delete Comment button ▨ on the Reviewing toolbar**

   The comment is removed from the manuscript.

6. **Scroll down, select Egg-related allergies. (including the paragraph mark) in the list at the top of page 2, then press [Delete]**

   "Egg-related allergies." is removed from the list and the list is renumbered.

7. **Click ▨, then type This is redundant.**

   A new comment is inserted in the document, as shown in Figure 2-5.

8. **Click the Reviewing Pane button ▨ on the Reviewing toolbar**

   The comments and tracked changes in the document are listed in the Reviewing Pane at the bottom of the screen. It's useful to view comments and tracked changes in the Reviewing Pane when the full text of a comment or tracked change does not fit in the balloon.

9. **Click ▨ to close the Reviewing Pane, press [Ctrl][Home], save your changes to the document, then print a copy**

**FIGURE 2-4:** Response comment in the document

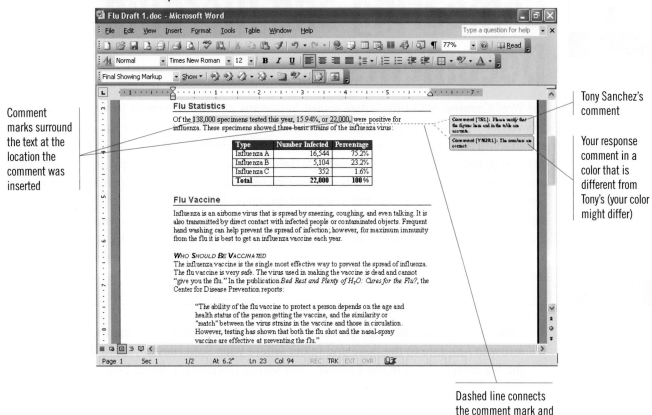

Comment marks surround the text at the location the comment was inserted

Tony Sanchez's comment

Your response comment in a color that is different from Tony's (your color might differ)

Dashed line connects the comment mark and the comment balloon

**FIGURE 2-5:** New comment in the document

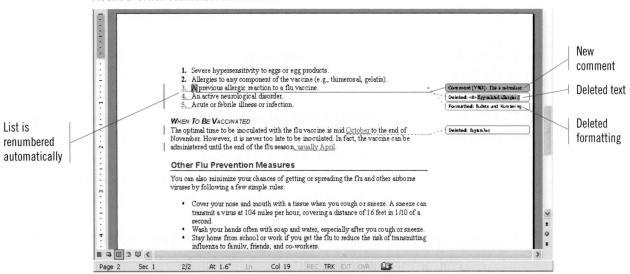

List is renumbered automatically

New comment

Deleted text

Deleted formatting

# Comparing and Merging Documents

The Word Compare and Merge feature is used to compare any two documents to show the differences between the two. Compare and Merge is often used to show the differences between an original document and an edited copy of the original. It is also used to merge the changes and comments of multiple reviewers into a single document when each reviewer edits the document using a separate copy of the original. When you compare and merge two documents, you have the option of merging the changes into one of the documents or of merging the changes into a new third document. The differences between the two documents are shown in the merged document as tracked changes. You can then examine the merged document, edit it, and save it with a new filename. ▓▓▓▓ A second colleague, Rebecca Haines, R.N., returns her revisions to you in a separate copy of the document. You use the Compare and Merge feature to merge your document with Rebecca's to create a new document that shows the differences between the two copies.

## STEPS

1. **Click** Tools **on the menu bar, click** Compare and Merge Documents, **use the** Look in list arrow **to navigate to the drive and folder where your Data Files are located, then select the file** WMP 2-2.doc **in the Compare and Merge Documents dialog box**

   The Compare and Merge Documents dialog box is shown in Figure 2-6. You use this dialog box to select the document that you want to merge with the current document. The file WMP 2-2.doc is the file that contains Rebecca's comments and tracked changes.

2. **Click the** Merge button list arrow **in the dialog box, click** Merge into new document, **make sure the** Your document option button **is selected in the dialog box that opens, then click** Continue with Merge

   Your document is merged with Rebecca's copy into a new document, as shown in Figure 2-7. Notice that each reviewer's comments and tracked changes are displayed in a different color in the merged document.

3. **Save the document as** Flu Draft 2 **to the drive and folder where your Data Files are stored**

   The document is saved with a new filename.

4. **Read the document to review the tracked changes, click the** Accept Change list arrow 🖉▾ **on the Reviewing toolbar, then click** Accept All Changes in Document

   All the tracked changes are accepted and become part of the document.

5. **Click the** first comment **to select it, click the** Insert Comment button 🖾 **on the Reviewing toolbar, type** Yes, **then click outside the comment balloon to deselect it**

   A new comment is added to the document, as shown in Figure 2-8.

6. **Scroll to page 2, right-click the** comment **on page 2, then click** Delete Comment

   The comment is deleted. After you have given your colleagues a copy of the file containing the remaining comments, you will delete the comments and finalize the document.

7. **Save your changes to the document, print a copy, close all open files, then exit Word**

FIGURE 2-6: Compare and Merge Documents dialog box

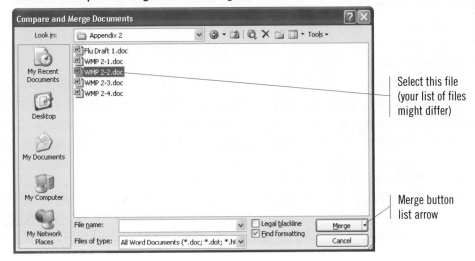

Select this file
(your list of files
might differ)

Merge button
list arrow

FIGURE 2-7: Merged document showing changes from each reviewer

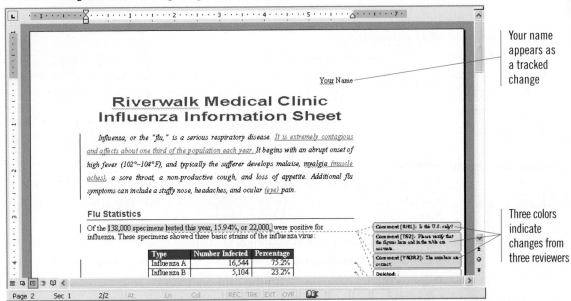

Your name
appears as
a tracked
change

Three colors
indicate
changes from
three reviewers

FIGURE 2-8: New comment

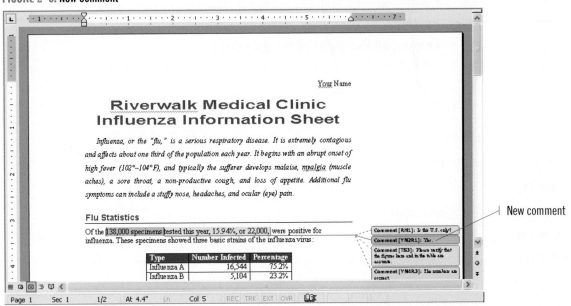

New comment

# ▼ SKILLS REVIEW

**1. Track changes.**

    **a.** Start Word, open the file WMP 2-3.doc from the drive and folder where your Data Files are located, then save it as **Scheduling Draft 1**.

    **b.** Change the zoom level to Page Width, then open the Reviewing toolbar if it is not already displayed.

    **c.** Using the Next button, review the tracked changes in the document, then press [Ctrl][Home] to return to the beginning of the document.

    **d.** Reject the first tracked change, then accept all remaining tracked changes in the document. Skip over the comments for now.

    **e.** Make sure the Track Changes feature is turned on.

    **f.** In the Five-step approach to scheduling appointments heading, change Five to **Six**.

    **g.** Add the following sentence as item number 4 in the numbered list: **Repeat the agreed-upon time to the patient.**

    **h.** Under the Processing new patients heading at the bottom of page 2, delete the sentence **All patient information is confidential.**

    **i.** Turn off the Track Changes feature, press [Ctrl][Home], replace Your Name with your name at the top of the document, then save your changes.

**2. Insert, view, and edit comments.**

    **a.** Scroll down, select the first comment, then delete the comment.

    **b.** Scroll down, select **The following table** in the last sentence of the first paragraph under the Determining the Time... heading, insert a new comment, then type **Should we create a table for each physician?**

    **c.** Scroll down, select the next comment, insert a new comment, then type **Yes.**

    **d.** Press [Ctrl][Home], save your changes to the document, then print a copy.

**3. Compare and merge documents.**

    **a.** Open the Compare and Merge Documents dialog box.

    **b.** Navigate to the drive and folder where your Data Files are located, select the file WMP 2-4.doc, click the Merge button list arrow, then click Merge into new document.

    **c.** Choose to keep the formatting changes from your document, then continue with the merge.

    **d.** Save the merged document as **Scheduling Draft 2** to the drive and folder where your Data Files are located.

    **e.** Review the tracked changes in the document, reject the changes under the Our policy heading, then accept all the remaining tracked changes.

    **f.** Delete all the comments.

    **g.** Save your changes to the document, print a copy, close all open files, then exit Word.

# Glossary

**Alignment** The position of text in a document relative to the margins.

**Anchored** The state of a floating graphic that moves with a paragraph or other item if the item is moved; an anchor symbol appears with the floating graphic when formatting marks are displayed.

**Application** *See* Program.

**Ascending order** Lists data alphabetically or sequentially (from A to Z, 0 to 9, or earliest to latest).

**AutoComplete** A feature that automatically suggests text to insert.

**AutoCorrect** A feature that automatically detects and corrects typing errors, minor spelling errors, and capitalization, or inserts certain typographical symbols as you type.

**Automatic page break** A page break that is inserted automatically at the bottom of a page.

**AutoText** A feature that stores frequently used text and graphics so they can be easily inserted into a document.

**Bitmap graphic** A graphic that is composed of a series of small dots called "pixels."

**Boilerplate text** Text that appears in every version of a merged document.

**Bold** Formatting applied to text to make it thicker and darker.

**Bookmark** Text that identifies a location or a selection of text in a document.

**Border** A line that can be added above, below, or to the sides of a paragraph, text, or a table cell; a line that divides the columns and rows of a table.

**Bullet** A small graphic symbol used to identify items in a list.

**Cell** The box formed by the intersection of a table row and table column.

**Cell reference** A code that identifies a cell's position in a table; each cell reference contains a letter (A, B, C, and so on) to identify its column and a number (1, 2, 3, and so on) to identify its row.

**Center** Alignment in which an item is centered between the margins.

**Character spacing** Formatting that changes the width or scale of characters, expands or condenses the amount of space between characters, raises or lowers characters relative to the line of text, and adjusts kerning (the space between standard combinations of letters).

**Character style** A named set of character format settings that can be applied to text to format it all at once.

**Chart** A visual representation of numerical data, usually used to illustrate trends, patterns, or relationships.

**Click and Type** A feature that allows you to automatically apply the necessary paragraph formatting to a table, graphic, or text when you insert the item in a blank area of a document in Print Layout or Web Layout view.

**Click and Type pointer** A pointer used to move the insertion point and automatically apply the paragraph formatting necessary to insert text at that location in the document.

**Clip** A media file, such as a graphic, photograph, sound, movie, or animation, that can be inserted into a document.

**Clip art** A collection of graphic images that can be inserted into documents, presentations, Web pages, spreadsheets, and other Office files.

**Clip Organizer** A library of the clips that come with Word.

**Clipboard** A temporary storage area for items that are cut or copied from any Office file and are available for pasting. *See also* Office Clipboard and System Clipboard.

**Column break** A break that forces text following the break to begin at the top of the next column.

**Comment** An embedded note or annotation that an author or a reviewer adds to a document; appears in a comment balloon when working in Page Layout view.

**Copy** To place a copy of an item on the Clipboard without removing it from a document.

**Crop** To trim away part of a graphic.

**Cross-reference** Text that electronically refers the reader to another part of the document.

**Cut** To remove an item from a document and place it on the Clipboard.

**Cut and paste** To move text or graphics using the Cut and Paste commands.

**D**ata field A category of information, such as last name, first name, street address, city, or postal code.

**Data record** A complete set of related information for a person or an item, such as a person's name and address.

**Data source** In a mail merge, the file with the unique data for individual people or items; the data merged with a main document to produce multiple versions.

**Datasheet** A table grid that opens when a chart is inserted in Word.

**Delete** To permanently remove an item from a document.

**Descending order** Lists data in reverse alphabetical or sequential order (Z to A, 9 to 0, or latest to earliest).

**Document** The electronic file you create using Word.

**Document map** A pane that shows all the headings and subheadings in a document.

**Document properties** Details about a file, such as author name or the date the file was created, that are used to organize and search for files.

**Document window** The workspace in the program window that displays the current document.

**Drag and drop** To move text or a graphic by dragging it to a new location using the mouse.

**Drop cap** A large dropped initial capital letter that is often used to set off the first paragraph of an article.

**E**ndnote Text that provides additional information or acknowledges sources for text in a document and that appears at the end of a document.

**F**ield A code that serves as a placeholder for data that changes in a document, such as a page number.

**Field name** The name of a data field.

**File** An electronic collection of information that has a unique name, distinguishing it from other files.

**Filename** The name given to a document when it is saved.

**Filename extension** Three letters that follow the period in a filename; for example, .doc for a Word file and .xls for Excel files.

**Filter** In a mail merge, to pull out records that meet specific criteria and include only those records in the merge.

**First line indent** A type of indent in which the first line of a paragraph is indented more than the subsequent lines.

**Floating graphic** A graphic to which a text wrapping style has been applied, making the graphic independent of text and able to be moved anywhere on a page.

**Font** The typeface or design of a set of characters (letters, numbers, symbols, and punctuation marks).

**Font effect** Font formatting that applies a special effect to text, such as a shadow, an outline, small caps, or superscript.

**Font size** The size of characters, measured in points (pts).

**Footer** Information, such as text, a page number, or a graphic, that appears at the bottom of every page in a document or a section.

**Footnote** Text that provides additional information or acknowledges sources for text in a document and that appears at the bottom of the page on which the footnote reference appears.

**Form field** The location where the data associated with a field label is stored.

**Form template** A file that contains the structure of a form. Users create new forms from a form template; data entered into new forms based on a form template do not affect the structure of the template file.

**Format Painter** A feature used to copy the format settings applied to the selected text to other text you want to format the same way.

**Formatting marks** Nonprinting characters that appear on screen to indicate the ends of paragraphs, tabs, and other formatting elements.

**Formatting toolbar** A toolbar that contains buttons for frequently used formatting commands.

**Full screen view** A view that shows only the document window on screen.

**G**etting Started task pane A task pane that contains shortcuts for opening documents, for creating new documents, and for accessing information on the Microsoft Web site.

**Gridlines** Nonprinting lines that show the boundaries of table cells.

**Gutter** Extra space left for a binding at the top, left, or inside margin of a document.

**H**anging indent A type of indent in which the second and subsequent lines of a paragraph are indented more than the first.

**Hard page break** *See* Manual page break.

**Header** Information, such as text, a page number, or a graphic, that appears at the top of every page in a document or a section.

**Header row** The first row of a table that contains the column headings.

**Highlighting** Transparent color that can be applied to text to call attention to it.

**Horizontal ruler** A ruler that appears at the top of the document window in Print Layout, Normal, and Web Layout view.

**Hyperlink** Text or a graphic that opens a file, Web page, or other item when clicked. Also known as a link.

**I-beam pointer** The pointer used to move the insertion point and select text.

**Indent** The space between the edge of a line of text or a paragraph and the margin.

**Indent marker** A marker on the horizontal ruler that shows the indent settings for the active paragraph.

**Index** Text that lists many of the terms and topics in a document, along with the pages on which they appear.

**Inline graphic** A graphic that is part of a line of text in which it was inserted.

**Insertion point** The blinking vertical line that shows where text will appear when you type in a document.

**Italic** Formatting applied to text to make the characters slant to the right.

**Justify** Alignment in which an item is flush with both the left and right margins.

**Keyboard shortcut** A combination of keys or a function key that can be pressed to perform a command.

**Landscape orientation** Page orientation in which the page is wider than it is tall.

**Left indent** A type of indent in which the left edge of a paragraph is moved in from the left margin.

**Left-align** Alignment in which the item is flush with the left margin.

**Line spacing** The amount of space between lines of text.

**List style** A named set of format settings, such as indents and outline numbering, that can be applied to a list to format it all at once.

**Mail Merge** Combines a standard document, such as a form letter, with customized data, such as a set of names and addresses, to create a set of personalized documents.

**Main document** In a mail merge, the document with the standard text.

**Manual page break** A page break inserted to force the text following the break to begin at the top of the next page.

**Margin** The blank area between the edge of the text and the edge of a page.

**Master document** A Word document that contains links to two or more related documents called subdocuments.

**Menu bar** The bar beneath the title bar that contains the names of menus; clicking a menu name opens a menu of program commands.

**Merge** To combine adjacent cells into a single larger cell.

**Merge field** A placeholder that you insert in the main document to indicate where the data from each record should be inserted when you perform a mail merge.

**Mirror margins** Margins used in documents with facing pages, where the inside and outside margins are mirror images of each other.

**Negative indent** A type of indent in which the left edge of a paragraph is moved to the left of the left margin.

**Nested table** A table inserted in a cell of another table.

**Normal style** The paragraph style that is used by default to format text typed into a blank document.

**Normal template** The template that is loaded automatically when a new document is inserted in Word.

**Normal view** A view that shows a document without margins, headers and footers, or graphics.

**Note reference mark** A number or character that indicates additional information is contained in a footnote or endnote.

**Nudge** To move a graphic a small amount in one direction using the arrow keys.

**Office Assistant** An animated character that offers tips and provides access to the program's Help system.

**Office Clipboard** A temporary storage area shared by all Office programs that can be used to cut, copy, and paste multiple items within and between Office programs. The Office Clipboard can hold up to 24 items collected from any Office program. *See* Clipboard and System Clipboard.

**Open** To use one of the methods for opening a document to retrieve it and display it in the document window.

**Outdent** *See* Negative indent.

**Outline view** A view that shows the headings of a document organized as an outline.

**Overtype mode** A feature that allows you to overwrite existing text as you type.

**Page border** A graphical line that encloses one or more pages of a document.

**Paragraph spacing** The amount of space between paragraphs.

**Paragraph style** A named set of paragraph and character format settings that can be applied to a paragraph to format it all at once.

**Paste** To insert items stored on the Clipboard into a document.

**Pixels** Small dots that define color and intensity in a graphic.

**Point**  The unit of measurement for text characters and the space between paragraphs and characters; 1/72 of an inch.

**Portrait orientation**  Page orientation in which the page is taller than it is wide.

**Print Layout view**  A view that shows a document as it will look on a printed page.

**Print Preview**  A view of a file as it will appear when printed.

**Program**  Task-oriented software (such as Excel or Word) that enables you to perform a certain type of task such as data calculation or word processing.

**Property**  A named attribute of a control set to define one of the control's attributes such as its size, its color, and its behavior in response to user input.

# Reading Layout view  A view that shows a document so that it is easy to read and annotate.

**Right indent**  A type of indent in which the right edge of a paragraph is moved in from the right margin.

**Right-align**  Alignment in which an item is flush with the right margin.

# Sans serif font  A font, such as Arial, whose characters do not include serifs, which are small strokes at the ends of letters.

**Save**  To store a file permanently on a disk or to overwrite the copy of a file that is stored on a disk with the changes made to the file.

**Save As**  Command used to save a file for the first time or to create a new file with a different filename, leaving the original file intact.

**Scale**  To resize a graphic so that its height to width ratio remains the same.

**ScreenTip**  A label that appears on the screen to identify a button or to provide information about a feature.

**Scroll**  To use the scroll bars or the arrow keys to display different parts of a document in the document window.

**Scroll arrows**  The arrows at the ends of the scroll bars that are clicked to scroll a document one line at a time.

**Scroll bars**  The bars on the right edge (vertical scroll bar) and bottom edge (horizontal scroll bar) of the document window that are used to display different parts of the document in the document window.

**Scroll box**  The box in a scroll bar that can be dragged to scroll a document.

**Section**  A portion of a document that is separated from the rest of the document by section breaks.

**Section break**  A formatting mark inserted to divide a document into sections.

**Select**  To click or highlight an item in order to perform some action on it.

**Serif font**  A font, such as Times New Roman, whose characters include serifs, which are small strokes at the ends of letters.

**Shading**  A background color or pattern that can be applied to text, tables, or graphics.

**Shortcut key**  *See* Keyboard shortcut.

**Sizing handles**  The black squares or white circles that appear around a graphic when it is selected; used to change the size or shape of a graphic.

**Smart tag**  A purple dotted line that appears under text that Word identifies as a date, name, address, or place.

**Smart Tag Actions button**  The button that appears when you point to a smart tag.

**Soft page break**  *See* Automatic page break.

**Sort**  To organize data, such as table rows, items in a list, or records in a mail merge, in ascending or descending order.

**Split**  To divide a cell into two or more cells.

**Standard toolbar**  A toolbar that contains buttons for frequently used operating and editing commands.

**Status bar**  The bar at the bottom of the Word program window that shows the vertical position, section, and page number of the insertion point, the total number of pages in a document, and the on/off status of several Word features.

**Style**  A named collection of character and/or paragraph formats that are stored together and can be applied to text to format it quickly.

**Subdocument**  A document contained within a master document.

**Subscript**  A font effect in which text is formatted in a smaller font size and placed below the line of text.

**Superscript**  A font effect in which text is formatted in a smaller font size and placed above the line of text.

**Symbols**  Special characters that can be inserted into a document using the Symbol command.

**System Clipboard**  A clipboard that stores only the last item cut or copied from a document. *See* Clipboard and Office Clipboard.

# Tab  *See* Tab stop.

**Tab leader**  A line that appears in front of tabbed text.

**Tab stop**  A location on the horizontal ruler that indicates where to align text.

**Table**  A grid made up of rows and columns of cells that you can fill with text and graphics.

**Table style**  A named set of table format settings that can be applied to a table to format it all at once.

**Task pane**  An area of the Word program window that contains shortcuts to Word formatting, editing, research, Help, clip art, mail merge, and other features.

**Template**  A formatted document that contains placeholder text you can replace with your own text; a file that contains the basic structure of a document.

**Text form field**  A location in a form where users enter text.

**Title bar** The bar at the top of the program window that indicates the program name and the name of the current file.

**Toggle button** A button that turns a feature on and off.

**Toolbar** A bar that contains buttons that you can click to perform commands.

**Tracked change** A mark that shows where an insertion, deletion, or formatting change has been made in a document.

**Type a question for help box** The list box at the right end of the menu bar that is used to query the Help system.

**U**ndo To reverse a change by using the Undo button or command.

**URL (Uniform Resource Locator)** A Web address.

**User template** Any template created by the user.

**V**ertical alignment The position of text in a document relative to the top and bottom margins.

**Vertical ruler** A ruler that appears on the left side of the document window in Print Layout view.

**View** A way of displaying a document in the document window; each view provides features useful for editing and formatting different types of documents.

**View buttons** Buttons to the left of the horizontal scroll bar that are used to change views.

**W**eb Layout view A view that shows a document as it will look when viewed with a Web browser.

**Wizard** An interactive set of dialog boxes that guides you through a task.

**Word processing program** A software program that includes tools for entering, editing, and formatting text and graphics.

**Word program window** The window that contains the Word program elements, including the document window, toolbars, menu bar, and status bar.

**Word-wrap** A feature that automatically moves the insertion point to the next line as you type.

**WordArt** A drawing object that contains text formatted with special shapes, patterns, and orientations.

**Workgroup Templates** Templates created for distribution to others.

# Index